CIM STUDY TEXT

Professional Certificate in Marketing

Marketing in Practice

In this May 2004 edition

- Fully updated for exams in December 2004 and June 2005
- Comprehensive review of past new-syllabus papers
- Material supporting integrative assessment
- Updated exam tips and case study examples

BPP Professional Education
May 2004

Third edition May 2004
First edition August 2002

ISBN 0 7517 1588 3 (previous edition 0 7517 1219 1)

British Library Cataloguing-in-Publication Data
A catalogue record for this book
is available from the British Library

Published by

BPP Professional Education
Aldine House, Aldine Place
London W12 8AW

www.bpp.com

Printed in Great Britain by W M Print
45-47 Frederick Street
Walsall, West Midlands
WS2 9NE

We are grateful to the Chartered Institute of Marketing for permission to reproduce in this text the syllabus and past examination questions. We are also grateful to Karen Beamish of Stone Consulting for preparing the integrative assessment material. We would also like to thank Mike Hyde, Senior Examiner, for updating this text.

How to use this Study Text

Aims of this Study Text

To provide you with the knowledge and understanding, skills and applied techniques required for passing the exam

The Study Text has been written around the CIM Professional Certificate in Marketing Syllabus (reproduced below, and cross-referenced to where in the text each topic is covered).

- It is **comprehensive**. We do not omit sections of the syllabus as the examiner is liable to examine any angle of any part of the syllabus - and you do not want to be left high and dry.
- It is **on-target** - we do not include any material which is not examinable. You can therefore rely on the BPP Study Text as the stand-alone source of all your information for the exam.

To allow you to study in the way that best suits your learning style and the time you have available, by following your personal Study Plan (see below)

You may be studying at home on your own until the date of the exam, or you may be attending a full-time course. You may like to (and have time to) read every word, or you may prefer to (or only have time to) skim-read and devote the remainder of your time to question practice. Wherever you fall in the spectrum, you will find the BPP Study Text meets your needs in designing and following your personal Study Plan.

To tie in with the other components of the BPP Effective Study Package to ensure you have the best possible chance of passing the exam

Recommended period of use	Elements of BPP Effective Study Package
3 - 12 months before exam	**Study Text** Acquisition of knowledge, understanding, skills and applied techniques
1 - 6 months before exam	**Practice & Revision Kit (9/2004)** There are numerous examination questions to try, graded by topic area, along with realistic suggested solutions prepared by marketing professionals in the light of the Examiner's Reports. The Stage 1 syllabus kits include a bank of short-form interactive questions.
1 - 6 months before exam	**Success Tapes** Audio cassettes covering the vital elements of your syllabus in less than 90 minutes per subject. Each tape also contains exam hints to help you fine tune your strategy.
1 - 6 months before exam	**Passcards** Handy, pocketsized revision notes you can take anywhere and use to refresh the essential knowledge you need.

Settling down to study

By this stage in your career you may be a very experienced learner and taker of exams. But have you ever thought about *how* you learn? Let's have a quick look at the key elements required for effective learning. You can then identify your learning style and go on to design your own approach to how you are going to study this text - your personal Study Plan.

Key element of learning	Using the BPP Study Text
Motivation	You can rely on the comprehensiveness and technical quality of BPP. You've chosen the right Study Text - so you're in pole position to pass your exam!
Clear objectives and standards	Do you want to be a prizewinner or simply achieve a moderate pass? Decide.
Feedback	Follow through the examples in this text and do the Action Programme and the Quick Quizzes. Evaluate your efforts critically - how are you doing?
Study Plan	You need to be honest about your progress to yourself - do not be over-confident, but don't be negative either. Make your Study Plan (see below) and try to stick to it. Focus on the short-term objectives – completing two chapters a night, say - but beware of losing sight of your study objectives.
Practice	Use the Quick Quizzes and Chapter Roundups to refresh your memory regularly after you have completed your initial study of each chapter.

These introductory pages let you see exactly what you are up against. However you study, you should:

- **read through the syllabus and teaching guide** - this will help you to identify areas you have already covered, perhaps at a lower level of detail, and areas that are totally new to you
- **study the examination paper section**, where we show you the format of the exam (how many and what kind of questions etc).

Key study steps

The following steps are, in our experience, the ideal way to study for professional exams. You can of course adapt it for your particular learning style (see below).

Tackle the chapters in the order you find them in the Study Text. Taking into account your individual learning style, follow these key study steps for each chapter.

Key study steps	Activity
Step 1 *Chapter Topic List*	Study the list. Each numbered topic denotes a **numbered section** in the chapter.
Step 2 *Setting the Scene*	Read it through. It is designed to show you **why the topics in the chapter need to be studied** - how they lead on from previous topics, and how they lead into subsequent ones.
Step 3 *Explanations*	Proceed **methodically** through the chapter, reading each section thoroughly and making sure you understand.
Step 4 *Key Concepts*	**Key concepts** can often earn you **easy marks** if you state them clearly and correctly in an appropriate exam.
Step 5 *Exam Tips*	These give you a good idea of how the examiner tends to examine certain topics – pinpointing **easy marks** and highlighting **pitfalls**.
Step 6 *Note Taking*	Take **brief notes** if you wish, avoiding the temptation to copy out too much.
Step 7 *Marketing at Work*	Study each one, and try if you can to add flesh to them from your **own experience** - they are designed to show how the topics you are studying come alive (and often come unstuck) in the **real world**.
Step 8 *Action Programme*	Make a very good attempt at each one in each chapter. These are designed to put your **knowledge into practice** in much the same way as you will be required to do in the exam. Check the answer at the end of the chapter in the **Action Programme review**, and make sure you understand the reasons why yours may be different.
Step 9 *Chapter Roundup*	Check through it very carefully, to make sure you have grasped the **major points** it is highlighting
Step 10 *Quick Quiz*	When you are happy that you have covered the chapter, use the **Quick Quiz** to check your recall of the topics covered. The answers are in the paragraphs in the chapter that we refer you to.

Developing your personal Study Plan

Preparing a Study Plan (and sticking closely to it) is one of the key elements in learning success.

First you need to be aware of your style of learning. There are four typical learning styles. Consider yourself in the light of the following descriptions. and work out which you fit most closely. You can then plan to follow the key study steps in the sequence suggested.

Learning styles	Characteristics	Sequence of key study steps in the BPP Study Text
Theorist	Seeks to understand principles before applying them in practice	1, 2, 3, 7, 4, 5, 8, 9, 10 (6 continuous)
Reflector	Seeks to observe phenomena, thinks about them and then chooses to act	
Activist	Prefers to deal with practical, active problems; does not have much patience with theory	1, 2, 8 (read through), 7, 4, 5, 9, 3, 8 (full attempt), 10 (6 continuous)
Pragmatist	Prefers to study only if a direct link to practical problems can be seen; not interested in theory for its own sake	8 (read through), 2, 4, 5, 7, 9, 1, 3, 8 (full attempt), 10 (6 continuous)

Next you should complete the following checklist.

Am I motivated? (a) [ ]

Do I have an objective and a standard that I want to achieve? (b) [ ]

Am I a theorist, a reflector, an activist or a pragmatist? (c) [ ]

How much time do I have available per week, given: (d) [ ]

- the standard I have set myself
- the time I need to set aside later for work on the Practice and Revision Kit
- the other exam(s) I am sitting, and (of course)
- practical matters such as work, travel, exercise, sleep and social life?

Now:

- take the time you have available per week for this Study Text (d), and multiply it by the number of weeks available to give (e). (e) [ ]
- divide (e) by the number of chapters to give (f) (f) [ ]
- set about studying each chapter in the time represented by (f), following the key study steps in the order suggested by your particular learning style.

This is your personal **Study Plan**.

Short of time?

Whatever your objectives, standards or style, you may find you simply do not have the time available to follow all the key study steps for each chapter, however you adapt them for your particular learning style. If this is the case, follow the Skim Study technique below (the icons in the Study Text will help you to do this).

Skim Study technique

Study the chapters in the order you find them in the Study Text. For each chapter, follow the key study steps 1-2, and then skim-read through step 3. Jump to step 9, and then go back to steps 4-5. Follow through step 7, and prepare outline Answers to the Action Programme (step 8). Try the Quick Quiz (step 10), following up any items you can't answer. You should probably still follow step 6 (note-taking).

Moving on...

However you study, when you are ready to embark on the practice and revision phase of the BPP Effective Study Package, you should still refer back to this Study Text:

- as a source of **reference** (you should find the list of Key Concepts and the index particularly helpful for this)
- as a **refresher** (the Chapter Roundups and Quick Quizzes help you here).

Important note: The *Marketing in Practice* Study Text

The *Marketing in Practice* syllabus is designed to be highly practical, drawing together and applying the key skills and background knowledge obtained from the other Stage 1 modules. It has a strong syllabus content of its own, which adds to the knowledge gained so far, particularly with subject areas such as

- conference/exhibition/show organisation
- financial/numeric tasks

in addition to which students should, by now, be able to:

- draw on information from a variety of sources, and learning from all Stage 1 areas
- apply that information and learning in an integrated fashion, to workplace and/or simulated (case study) marketing projects

So, for example, when 'Market Research' appears in this Syllabus, it is assumed that you will have covered market research theory and techniques as part of your other studies. Here, you might be required to design a market research questionnaire as part of a co-ordinated programme of customer database management and usage in the context of an intended product launch, incorporating information across the marketing mix (*Marketing Fundamentals*) in the light of competitor activity (*Marketing Environment*). And the whole thing will have to be both correctly and persuasively written (*Customer Communications*). The following diagram demonstrates some of the links between the modules.

This BPP Study Text for *Marketing in Practice* therefore relates to the syllabus in a practical, integrative way. It is designed specifically to help you apply your learning from the other modules, whether to workplace tasks and assessments or to an examination Case Study.

Key Concepts

In order to help you transfer your learning to the real world, we use this feature to introduce you to some of the technical terms, abbreviations and 'buzzwords' used by marketing professionals. (These also appear in list form at the back of the Text.)

Marketing at Work

The syllabus specifically requires students to develop an awareness of what marketers are actually doing 'out there': what new initiatives are being attempted; what is working and what is not; how different organisations tackle the same tasks. We encourage you to collect cuttings of ads, examples of promotions, articles on marketing campaigns (for example in *Campaign, PR Week, Marketing Week* and other relevant journals and newspaper Media sections). We also encourage you whenever possible (and when professional discretion allows) to swap stories of successes, failures and house styles with other students and practitioners. Our 'Marketing at Work' section will help - but it should only be a prompter to the kind of insatiable curiosity about other people's efforts that makes a good marketing professional.

Action Programme

Marketing in Practice may be assessed through workplace tasks, skills audits and/or an integrated Case Study approach. You must get used to attempting a wide variety of marketing tasks and analysing your performance according to relevant criteria. Our Action Programme exercises take you step by step through this active learning process.

We have devised an **on-going Case Study ('The Needle Works')** which forms the basis for some of the Action Programmes in each chapter. The Needle Works is a small but expanding retail business in a niche market, so that your role as Marketing Assistant requires both hands-on organisation and co-ordination (as it might in a larger organisation) and input to the decision-making process (so that you can apply your tactical knowledge and skills).

Background to 'The Needle Works' Case Study

This includes a range of information which you will require to tackle Action Programmes throughout this Study Text and is found on page (xiv). You may like to detach or photocopy this page for easier reference.

A note on pronouns

On occasions in this Study Text, 'he' is used for 'he or she', 'him' for 'him or her' and so forth. Whilst we try to avoid this practice it is sometimes necessary for reasons of style. No prejudice or stereotyping according to sex is intended or assumed.

Syllabus and guidance notes

Aim

The *Marketing in Practice* module is the application of marketing in context at this Stage and also forms the summative assessment for this Stage. It aims to assist participants to integrate and apply knowledge from all the modules at this Stage.

Participants will not be expected to have any prior qualifications or experience in a marketing role. They will be expected to be conversant with the content of the other three modules at this Stage before undertaking this module.

Related statements of practice

This syllabus has been based on the statements of marketing practice, a set of practical statements defining what tasks marketers perform at various stages of the marketing career.

Hb.1 Contribute to project planning and budget preparation

Hb.2 Monitor and report on project activities

Hb.3 Complete and close down project activities on time and within budget

Jb.1 Collect, synthesise, analyse and report measurement data

Jb.2 Participate in reviews of marketing activities using measurement data

Kb.1 Exchange information to solve problems and make decisions

Kb.2 Review and develop one's skills and competencies

Kb.3 Embrace change and modify behaviours and attitudes

Learning outcomes

Participants will be able to:

- Collect relevant data from a variety of secondary information sources.
- Analyse and interpret written, visual and graphical data.
- Devise appropriate visual and graphical means to present marketing data.
- Make recommendations based on information obtained from multiple sources.
- Evaluate and select media and promotional activities appropriate to the organisation's objectives and status and to its marketing context.
- Calculate and justify budgets for marketing mix decisions.
- Develop relationships inside and outside the organisation.
- Apply planning techniques to a range of marketing tasks and activities.
- Undertake basic marketing activities within an agreed plan and monitor and report on progress.
- Gather information for, and evaluate marketing results against, financial and other criteria.

Knowledge and skill requirements

Element 1: Gathering, analysing and presenting information (20%) (Marketing Environment)		
		Covered in chapter(s)
1.1	Identify sources of information internally and externally to the organisation, including ICT-based sources such as intranet and Internet.	1
1.2	Maintain a marketing database, information collection and usage.	2
1.3	Investigate customers via the database and develop bases for segmentation.	2
1.4	Explain information gathering techniques available.	3
1.5	Source and present information on competitor activities across the marketing mix.	4
1.6	Investigate marketing and promotional opportunities using appropriate information gathering techniques.	4
1.7	Gather information across borders.	1, 3

Element 2: Building and developing relationships (20%) (Customer Communications)		
2.1	Describe the structure and roles of the marketing function within the organisation.	5
2.2	Build and develop relationships within the marketing department, working effectively with others.	5
2.3	Explain the 'front line' role: receiving and assisting visitors, internal and external enquiries.	6
2.4	Represent the organisation using practical PR skills, including preparing effective news releases.	8
2.5	Explain the supplier interface: negotiating, collaborating, operational and contractual aspects.	7
2.6	Explain how the organisation fits into a supply chain and works with distribution channels.	7
2.7	Use networking skills in the business world.	8
2.8	Explain the concept and application of e-relationships.	6, 7
2.9	Describe techniques available to assist in managing your manager.	5

Element 3: Organising and undertaking marketing activities (20%) (Marketing Fundamentals)		
		Covered in chapter(s)
3.1	Describe the scope of individuals' roles in marketing: meetings, conferences, exhibitions, outdoor shows, outlet launches, press conferences.	10
3.2	Identify alternative and innovative approaches to a variety of marketing arenas and explain criteria for meeting business objectives.	9, 10
3.3	Demonstrate an awareness of successful applications of marketing across a variety of sectors and sizes of business.	10
3.4	Explain how marketing makes use of planning techniques: objective setting; and co-ordinating, measuring and evaluating results to support the organisation.	9
3.5	Appraise and select a venue based on given criteria and make appropriate recommendations.	11
3.6	Explain how an organisation should host visitors from other cultures and organising across national boundaries.	10

Element 4: Co-ordinating the marketing mix (20%) (Marketing Fundamentals)		
4.1	Select media to be used based on appropriate criteria for assessing media opportunities, and recommend a media schedule.	12
4.2	Evaluate promotional activities and opportunities including sales promotion, PR and collaborative programmes.	13
4.3	Explain the process for designing, developing and producing printed matter, including leaflets, brochures and catalogues.	14
4.4	Analyse the impact of pricing decisions and role of price within the marketing mix.	15
4.5	Describe the current distribution channels for an organisation and evaluate new opportunities.	15
4.6	Describe how organisations monitor product trends.	15
4.7	Explain the importance of the extended marketing mix: how process, physical aspects and people affect customer choice.	15
4.8	Explain the importance of ICT in the new mix.	15

Element 5: Administering the marketing budget (and evaluating results) (20%)

		Covered in chapter(s)
5.1	Demonstrate an ability to manipulate numbers in a marketing context.	16-18
5.2	Explain the process used for setting a budget and apportioning fixed and overhead costs.	16
5.3	Explain how organisations assess the viability of opportunities, marketing initiatives and projects.	4, 17
5.4	Prepare, present and justify a budget as the basis for a decision on a marketing promotion.	17
5.5	Make recommendations on alternative courses of action.	17
5.6	Examine the correlation between marketing mix decisions and results.	18
5.7	Evaluate the cost effectiveness of a marketing budget, including a review of suppliers and activities.	18

Related key skills for marketers

There is only so much that a syllabus can include. The syllabus itself is designed to cover the knowledge and skills highlighted by research as core to professional marketers in organisations. However, marketing is performed in an organisational context so there are other broader business and organisational skills that marketing professionals should also posses. The 'key skills for marketers' are therefore an essential part of armoury of the 'complete marketer' in today's organisations. They have been identified from research carried out in organisations where marketers are working.

'Key skills for marketers' are areas of knowledge and competency common to business professionals. They fall outside the CIM's syllabus, providing underpinning knowledge and skills. As such they will be treated as systemic to all marketing activities, rather than subjects treated independently in their turn. While it is not intended that the key skills are formally taught as part of programmes, it is expected that tutors will encourage participants to demonstrate the application of relevant key skills through activities, assignments and discussions during learning.

Using ICT and the Internet

- Planning and using different sources to search for and select information; explore, develop and exchange information and derive new information; and present information including text, numbers and images.

Using financial information and metrics

- Planning and interpreting information from different sources; carrying out calculations; and presenting and justifying findings.

Presenting information

- Contributing to discussions; making a presentation; reading and synthesising information and writing different types of document.

Improving own learning and performance

- Agreeing targets and planning how these will be met; using plans to meet targets; and reviewing progress.

Working with others

- Planning work and agreeing objectives, responsibilities and working arrangements; seeking to establish and maintain cooperative working relationships; and reviewing work and agreeing ways of future collaborative work.

Problem solving

- Exploring problems, comparing different ways of solving them and selecting options; planning and implementing options; and applying agreed methods for checking problems have been solved.

Applying business law

- Identifying, applying and checking compliance with relevant law when undertaking marketing activities.

Assessment

CIM will normally offer two forms of assessment for this module from which centres or participants may choose: written examination and an integrative assessment. Guidance on the integrative assessment can be found on page (xxvii).

Overview and rationale

Approach

The *Marketing in Practice* syllabus, first launched in September 1999, requires a broad and practical demonstration of marketing, rather than any depth of understanding at a strategic level. The module will test participants' ability to draw on a wide range of subject matter and put forward practical, well-argued recommendations.

Marketing in Practice is the province of the well-rounded and versatile marketer, and aims to replicate the challenges, diversity and pace of a typical first marketing role. From an educational standpoint, it seeks to integrate the full Stage 1 syllabus, and as such is best suited towards the latter phases of Stage 1 course delivery, or, alternatively, it can be run throughout the year alongside the other three modules.

This module offers the opportunity to put into practice the entire Stage 1 syllabus, integrate key skills, and draw on participants' experience. It should be lively and fun for all involved. It rounds off Stage 1 and so provides a springboard for Stage 2, which builds on the knowledge and skills at Stage 1 and goes on to develop participants for a role in operational marketing management.

Syllabus content

As stated above, this syllabus aims to integrate fully the other three modules at this level, and assist the participant to put new learning into practice. Its integrative nature is broken down further in the next section.

Element 1: Gathering, analysing and presenting information

Points to stress here are the need for business decisions to be based on information, sources of information that can be accessed, and the need to evaluate the information. There is a strong practical element, and information-gathering techniques are examined. Segmentation is also touched upon – not in any great depth but as a practical tool to use in marketing situations.

This should be used to reinforce learning from the *Marketing Environment* module (Stage 1) and participants should be encouraged to share practice from their own organisations.

A typical exam task here might be: identify sources of information for an organisation, and how to use that information in making decisions.

Element 2: Building and developing relationships

This section is concerned with the people aspect of marketing. Commencing inside the marketing department, it then looks across the organisation, before examining relationships outside – whether with suppliers or further down the supply chain.

This integrates well with *Customer Communications* (Stage 1). Studies should combine the human aspects with the procedural and contractual to give a realistic view of the real world. This section very much lends itself to a highly interactive approach. This area also supports the new *Marketing Management* module at Stage 2.

A typical exam task here might be: identify important relationships in an organisation, and list practical ways to improve them.

Element 3: Organising and undertaking marketing activities

Research has shown that many marketing assistants have responsibility for organising a variety of events, from sales meetings to full-blown conferences, and from exhibitions to corporate hospitality. Participants should be encouraged to share experiences to compare and contrast different approaches. Again, there is a strong practical element, and it is essential that participants have a grasp of costing and can evaluate the success of activities undertaken.

This builds on knowledge from both *Marketing Fundamentals* and *Customer Communications.*

A typical exam task here might be: produce a plan using a Gantt chart for a conference in 3 months time.

Element 4: Co-ordinating the marketing mix

'Co-ordinating' is a key word – this is not strategic management of the mix. For example, participants at this level would not decide pricing strategy, but may be asked to report on the effects of a pricing decision. They may not deal with strategic advertising, but may control local advertising.

Similar demarcations apply across the mix. In line with research findings, there is a heavy emphasis on promotional activity, but all 7Ps and their application should be explored, building on the input in *Marketing Fundamentals*. Budgeting and dealing with information are also important features in this section. This topic is developed further in *Marketing Planning* (Stage 2).

A typical exam task here might be: produce an advertising schedule, and draft a press release.

Element 5: Administering the marketing budget (and evaluating results)

This need not strike fear into tutors or participants; practical and tactical are again watchwords for this section. Company accounts, discounted cash flows etc are not needed at this level. There is however a need for an appreciation of costs, how they are apportioned, and how cost effective are marketing activities. As such, basic manipulation of figures is essential. The acid test of a participant's ability is whether or not the following questions can be answered:

'How much does it cost, how do we split the costs, what will the result be, and is it worth doing?'

This section intends to provide a basic understanding of finance in business to underpin progress to *Marketing Planning* (Stage 2), and the critical element of 'control' at Stage 3.

A typical exam task here might be: calculate likely results from two alternative courses of action.

Websites

The Chartered Institute of Marketing	
www.cim.co.uk www.cim.virtualinstitute.com www.cimtutors.com (Tutors only) www.marketingportal.cim.co.uk	The CIM site with information and access to learning support for participants. Full details of all that's new in CIM's Educational offer including their newsletter – Education Express.

Publications on line	
www.ft.com	Extensive research resources across all industry sectors, with links to more specialist reports.
www.timesonline.co.uk	One of the best online versions of a quality newspaper.
www.economist.com	Useful links, and easily-searched archives of articles from back issues of the magazine.
www.mad.co.uk	Marketing Week magazine online.
www.marketing.haynet.com	Marketing magazine online.
www.stir.ac.uk/marketing/academy	Journal of Marketing Management online, the official Journal of the Academy of Marketing
http://mitsloan.mit.edu/smr/index.html	Free abstracts from Sloan Management Review articles
www.hbsp.harvard.edu	Free abstracts from Harvard Business Review articles
www.ebusiness.uk.com	Allows subscription to a new monthly paper-based magazine containing up to date case studies and updates on ebusiness trends
www.ecommercetimes.com	Daily enews on the latest ebusiness developments

Sources of useful information	
www.1to1.com	The Peppers and Rogers One-to-One Marketing site which contains useful information about the tools and techniques of relationship marketing
www.balancetime.com	The Productivity Institute provides free articles, a time management email newsletter, and other resources to improve personal productivity
www.bbc.co.uk/edu	The Learning Zone at BBC Education contains extensive educational resources, including the video, CD Rom, ability to watch TV programmes such as the News online, at your convenience, after they have been screened
www.busreslab.com	Useful specimen online questionnaires to measure customer satisfaction levels and tips on effective Internet marketing research
www.lifelonglearning.co.uk	Encourages and promotes Lifelong Learning through press releases, free articles, useful links and progress reports on the development of the University for Industry (UFI)
www.marketresearch.org.uk	The Market Research Society. Contains useful material on the nature of research, choosing an agency, ethical standards and codes of conduct for research practice
www.nielson-netratings.com	Details the current levels of banner advertising activity, including the creative content of the ten most popular banners each week
www.open.ac.uk	Some good Open University videos available for a broad range of subjects
www.open.gov.uk	Gateway to a wide range of UK government information
www.srg.co.uk	The Self Renewal Group – provides useful tips on managing your time, leading others, managing human resources, motivating others etc

www.statistics.gov.uk	Detailed information on a variety of consumer demographics from the Government Statistics Office
www.durlacher.com	The latest research on business use of the Internet, often with extensive free reports
www.cyberatlas.com	Regular updates on the latest Internet developments from a business perspective
www.nua.ie	Regular updates on the latest Internet developments from a business perspective
http://ecommerce.vanderbilt.edu	eLab is a corporate sponsored research centre at the Owen Graduate School of Management, Vanderbilt University
www.kpmg.co.uk www.eyuk.com www.pwcglobal.com	The major consultancy company websites contain useful research reports, often free of charge
http://web.mit.edu	Massachusetts Institute of Technology site has extensive research resources
www.adassoc.org.uk	Advertising Association
www.dma.org.uk	The Direct Marketing Association
www.theidm.co,uk	Institute of Direct Marketing
www.export.org.uk	Institute of Export
www.bl.uk	The British Library, with one of the most extensive book collections in the world
www.inst-mgt.org.uk	Institute of Management
www.ipd.co.uk	Institute of Personnel and Development
www.emerald-library.com	Full text journal articles on a range of business topics
www.whatis.com	Directory of Internet terminology
www.isi.gov.uk	The Information Society site with details of government projects, white papers and pending legislation
www.w3.org	An organisation responsible for defining worldwide standards for the Internet

Case studies

www.1800flowers.com	Flower and gift delivery service that allows customers to specify key dates when they request the firm to send them a reminder, together with an invitation to send a gift
www.amazon.co.uk	Classic example of how Internet technology can be harnessed to provide innovative customer service
www.broadvision.com	Broadvision specialises in customer 'personalisation' software. The site contains many useful case studies showing how communicating through the Internet allow you to find out more about your customers
www.doubleclick.net	DoubleClick offers advertisers the ability to target their advertisements on the web through sourcing of specific interest groups, ad display only at certain times of the day, or at particular geographic locations, or on certain types of hardware
www.facetime.com	Good example of a site that overcomes the impersonal nature of the Internet by allowing the establishment of real-time links with a customer service representative
www.streamwave.co.uk	Online demonstrations of the latest technological developments which will form the basis of the next generation of Internet Marketing communication applications
ww.hotcoupons.com	Site visitors can key in their postcode to receive local promotions, and advertisers can post their offers on the site using a specially designed software package

The exam paper

'Case study' format

Part A

	Marks
Compulsory question relating to the case study	40

Part B

Three questions from a choice of six relating to the case study (20 marks each)	60
	100

The new syllabus Pilot Paper and BPP's suggested answers are reproduced at the back of the Study Text.

December 2003

Part A (compulsory question worth 40 marks)

1 Small marina and boat club, managed by a volunteer committee, membership has been dropping and income is insufficient to cover costs: proposals for change are now on the table.

(a) Calculate the current annual income (from data given)
(b) Calculate projected annual income of changes implemented (from data given)
(c) Letter to club members, seeking support for changes

Part B (three questions, 20 marks each)

2 Relationship building, given part-time/volunteer working
3 Suitability of marina as a conference venue; points looked for
4 Information needed for, and use of, member database
5 Media plan (within set budget) for advertising the marina
6 Use of the extended marketing mix to promote a new venture
7 Role of ICT in marketing the marina

June 2003

Part A (compulsory question worth 40 marks)

1 Independent local radio station. There are plans to raise the station's role in the community and raise listener figures. The station stages live concerts annually and is planning next year's event.

(a) Calculate the profit made by this year's concert (from data given)
(b) Calculate projected revenue and profit for next year's concert (from data given)
(c) Use of the full extended marketing mix by a radio station

Part B (three questions, 20 marks each)

2 Briefing notes: advantages and disadvantages of radio as an advertising medium
3 Use of ICT to build listener loyalty
4 Information needed to profile audience, and how obtained
5 Letter to local newspaper suggesting collaborative promotion
6 Key contacts and relationship building for marketing/promotions executive
7 Use of promotional mix to ensure success of next year's concert

December 2002

Part A (compulsory question worth 40 marks)

1 Ghana-based importer of cars for supply through appointed retailers Africa-wide. Marketing plans include: database marketing, improved advertising, a special anniversary event, and a new retailer.

(a) Assess advantages and disadvantages of co-operative advertising by retailer and importer

(b) Calculate monetary value of advertising under two options (from data given)

(c) Calculate costs of both options (from data given)

(d) Recommend one of the options

Part B (three questions, 20 marks each)

2 Venue selection criteria and planning Gantt chart for anniversary event
3 Draft response, and further information needs, for new retailer proposal
4 Guidelines for retailers on selecting advertising media
5 Use of full marketing mix to ensure success of new retailer relationship
6 Information needs for new database, and how obtained
7 Use of Internet in relationships with retailers and manufacturers

Pilot Paper

Part A (compulsory question worth 40 marks)

1 Company providing an Internet portal for a range of business services and information for the foreign investors in Hungary. Expansion is planned into other countries, and the relationship with the current advertising agency is being reviewed.

(a) Calculate cost savings by changing agency (from data supplied)
(b) Sample briefing document to show info required in an agency brief
(c) Problems of dealing with a new agency/supplier

Part B (three questions, 20 marks each)

2 Competitor audit: how to identify them; information needed, how to obtain/verify the information

3 Steps and Gantt chart for planning a launch event in Turkey

4 Using all elements of promotional submix to promote a 'virtual' company

5 Calculate the company's most profitable business and the effect of changes (from data given)

6 Letter to potential web advertisers; other possible approaches

7 Information needed about website visitors, and how it can be used.

Review of past examination papers

This examination paper is unique in that it is all centred around a single organisation, rather than having a spread of questions focusing on different sectors. This need not be a cause of fear, and there would be no use in trying to 'spot' the context of the next exam as it is really unpredictable. What you do need to do is imagine you work at the organisation in the case, and to consider what is different or special about those circumstances. This means drawing on your absorbed marketing knowledge plus common sense.

The 'Needle Works' case study which is featured throughout the book is good practice, and allows the reader to 'get into role' in the manner needed to pass this examination: see the background information on page (xiv) when you are ready to begin.

There is a clear pattern to the questions featured in each exam paper to date. Section 1 (compulsory) always includes some calculations. These do not involve complex formulae or financial and accounting techniques, but require addition, subtraction, multiplication and division, together with percentages and what may best be described as 'manipulation'. This means seeing how figures relate to each other and how they impact on each other.

All the data you need is given in the question. Sometimes (as the examiner noted in a recent report) numerical data is given in *words* ('a hundred members', 'two thousand dollars'): you need to read carefully in order not to miss the relevance of such phrases to your calculations.

Certain key themes have tended to feature in Part B questions: use of the promotional mix (in the given scenario); use of the extended marketing mix (in the given scenario); use of Information and Communication Technology (in the given scenario); what information is needed, and how it can be obtained, for specific database and other applications; likely problems in establishing and building working relationships within a firm or supply chain; planning an event (in the given scenario); using a particular promotional tool, such as advertising (in the given scenario).

We have repeated the phrase 'in the given scenario' because – while key themes and syllabus areas are a useful guide to study and revision – this exam requires you to apply broad frameworks of knowledge to particular contexts: a virtual organisation, an international market, a media organisations, a not-for-profit organisations and so on.

What the examiner says

In The December 2003 Examiner's Report, the examiner noted that *Marketing in Practice* papers generally 'attempt to replicate the feel of a busy morning or afternoon's work for a marketing assistant'.

Part A questions are a source of high (sometimes full) marks, for candidates who get to grips with basic calculations. The examiner noted that it is very important to state (as requested in the paper) any assumptions made when making calculations and recommendations. There are marks available for the assumptions themselves – and they also help the examiner to reward calculations which might otherwise appear incorrect.

Candidates frequently throw away marks by not reading questions carefully enough: fulfilling one objective instead of two, discussing the promotional mix instead of the extended marketing mix (7Ps) and so on.

Proposals made need to fit the scenario given *and* be realistic and cost-effective. As an example, candidates advocated a small marina as a major event venue – even though there was little vehicular access: this just wouldn't work! You need to absorb yourself in the detail of the scenario as far as possible.

'General' questions (about the use of ICT or the extended marketing mix, say) are not merely general questions! Marks are available for how tools can be *applied* to the specific context and task mentioned. 'Detailed comments and ideas around what could be done were well rewarded.'

Under the heading of *Future Themes*, the examiner set out the following.

> 'Anytime, any place, anywhere is the only clue to future subject matter in cases! ... There are, however, recurrent themes. The first question will always include calculations, but a look through previous papers will show that these need be no more than addition, subtraction, multiplication, division and percentages. Working through a few papers is the best thing any candidate could do. Other likely tasks include 'write a letter/press release', 'prepare a media schedule,' 'advise on suitability of venue', and 'how can ICT be used ...'.
>
> Likewise, application of some or all of the seven 'Ps' is highly likely to feature in future MIP examinations.'

Preparing for the examination

The first and most important thing to say is: don't enter for this examination until you are ready.

Marketing in Practice is a summative paper for the entire Certificate level. This means it should be at the end, summarising all that has been learnt during the year's study. So anyone trying to do this paper before they have studied the other subjects does not stand a high chance of passing.

The syllabus of this module draws heavily on the other three papers, but needs a very different approach. It is no use knowing a theory or list of facts in this paper.

Convenient frameworks, mnemonics and lists, such as criteria for selecting a conference venue, will not in themselves gain many marks: most marks are available for applying the framework to the case study context. (What are the good and bad points of the proposed venue? What sort of venue will be appropriate and affordable for *this* event?)

As you study the content of this and other Certificate level syllabuses, begin to ask yourself:

- How would this apply to a bigger/smaller organisation?
- How would this work in an international/multinational context?
- How would this apply to a not-for-profit or voluntary sector organisation?
- How would I go about this with a much bigger/smaller budget?
- What organisations might this tool/technique/tactic be more/less suitable for?
- What alternative methods might I use, and in what circumstances?

This Study Text includes a sample case study to help you get used to *applying* information and frameworks. However, asking yourself questions such as the above will help to increase your *flexibility* in applying them to a range of organisation types, markets and specific terms.

Towards the end of your studies, attempt *at least* one complete exam paper, to make sure that you have grasped the case study approach.

Working with numbers

In every paper so far there has been a numerically based question in the compulsory section, so expect this again.

A good tip here is to underline all the numeric information which may be needed. Remember that numeric information may also be given in words.

> The company sells £4,000,000 worth of products each month, half of them being in product group A. A quarter are in product group B, while the rest are divided equally between product groups C and D. A price rise of 10% is proposed for 2004 for groups A and D. Double this increase is planned for the other groups. What will next year's revenue be?

Most readers would have underlined £4,000,000 and 10%, but the words quarter and double are also key. 'Divided equally' also gives numeric information.

However, the words 'month' and 'year' also give numeric information. In an exam, many candidates would calculate accurate figures and then throw away marks by not multiplying by twelve!

Other exam tips

Pace yourself. You have 180 minutes and 100 marks are available. Work out for yourself how long you should be spending on questions or parts of questions.

Plan your answers systematically, according to the precise requirements of the question set. If there are 10 marks available for stating why the organisation should do something, aim to give five good reasons with enough justifying argument to earn two marks each. Add as much plausible, scenario-appropriate detail as possible.

Guide to Assignment Routes: Marketing in Practice

- Aims and objectives of this guide
- Introduction
- Assignment Route structure and process
- Preparing for assignments: general guide
- Presentation
- Time management
- Tips for writing assignments
- Writing reports
- Resources to support assignment route

Aims and objectives of this *Guide to Assignment Route*

- To understand the scope and structure of the Assignment Route process
- To consider the benefits of learning through Assignment Route
- To assist students in preparation of their assignments
- To consider the range of communication options available to students
- To look at the range of potential assessment areas that assignments may challenge
- To examine the purpose and benefits of reflective practice
- To assist with time-management within the assessment process

Introduction

At time of writing, there are over 80 CIM Approved Study Centres that offer the Assignment Route option as an alternative to examinations. This change in direction and flexibility in assessment was externally driven by industry, students and tutors alike, all of whom wanted a test of practical skills as well as a knowledge-based approach to learning.

At Stage 1, all modules are available via this Assignment Route route. Assignment Route is however optional, and examinations are still available. This will of course depend upon the nature of delivery within your chosen Study Centre.

Clearly, all of the Stage 1 subject areas lend themselves to assignment-based learning, due to their practical nature. The assignments that you will undertake provide you with an opportunity to be creative in approach and in presentation. They enable you to give a true demonstration of your marketing ability in a way that perhaps might be inhibited in a traditional examination situation.

Assignment Route offers you considerable scope to produce work that provides existing and future employers with evidence of your ability. It offers you a portfolio of evidence which demonstrates your abilities and your willingness to develop continually your knowledge and skills. It will also, ultimately, help you frame your continuing professional development in the future.

It does not matter what type of organisation you are from, large or small, as you will find substantial benefit in this approach to learning. In some cases, students have made their own organisation central to their assessment and produced work to support their organisation's activities, resulting in subsequent recognition and promotion: a success story for this approach.

So, using your own organisation can be beneficial (especially if your employer sponsors you). However, it is equally valid to use a different organisation, as long as you are familiar enough with it to base your assignments on it. This is particularly useful if you are between jobs, taking time out, returning to employment or studying at university or college.

To take the Assignment Route option, you are required to register with a CIM Accredited Study Centre (ie a college, university, or distance learning provider). Currently you would be unable to take the Assignment Route option as an independent learner. If in doubt you should contact the Awarding Body who will provide you with a list of local Accredited Centres offering Assignment Route.

Structure and process

The assignments that you will undertake during your studies are normally set by CIM centrally, and not by the study centre. All assignments are validated to ensure a standard approach. This standardised approach to assessment enables external organisations to interpret the results on a consistent basis.

The *Marketing in Practice* assignment is slightly different to the other assignments at Stage 1 and is formally known as the Integrative Project.

You will probably realise from your studies in other Stage 1 subjects that *Marketing in Practice* provides you with the basis for putting your knowledge-based learning into practice. Therefore the assessment aims to integrate the knowledge that you have gained from *Marketing Fundamentals, Marketing Environment* and *Customer Communications.*

The purpose of each element of the Integrative Project is to enable you to demonstrate your ability to research, analyse and problem solve in a range of different situations. You will be expected to approach your assignment work from a marketing perspective, addressing the assignment brief directly, and undertaking the tasks required. Each element will relate directly to your module and will be applied against the content of the syllabus.

The project brief provides an aim. The brief will ask you to undertake a range of tasks and activities related to your learning, but applied to your own organisation (or one that you know well).

- You will be required to undertake a number of tasks, spread throughout your learning programme. Each task will involve investigation by you within your chosen organisation, and you will write up your findings and make recommendations.
- Each task will earn you marks for the Marketing in Practice module (see the table below), and links to theory you will have covered in the other three subject areas. These links are shown with each task.
- There will be five tasks in total. Four are directly related to the Stage 1 syllabus, and the final one is a Reflective Statement very similar to those introduced in the other three Stage 1 modules.
- Further marks will also be awarded for the various presentation and communication requirements of the assignment brief. The rationale for this award will be provided with the assignment.
- The length of your assessment should be approximately 4,000 to 5,000 words. The word limit for each task will be provided by CIM within the assignment brief and should be adhered to.

All of the Assignments clearly indicate the links with the syllabus and the assignment weighting (ie the contribution each assignment makes to your overall marks).

The marking process for the Integrative Project differs from the other Stage 1 subjects in that once your Assignments have been completed and submitted to your Study Centre, they will be forwarded to the CIM and marked by CIM markers. There is then a rigorous moderation process implemented by the

CIM, which feeds into the CIM Examination Board. After this, all marks are forwarded to you by CIM (not your centre) in the form of an examination result. Your centre will be able to you provide you with some written feedback on overall performance, but will not provide you with any detailed mark breakdown.

Preparing for Assignments: a guide

The whole purpose of this guide is to assist you in presenting your assessment professionally, both in terms of presentation skills and overall content. In many of the assignments, marks are awarded for presentation and coherence. It might therefore be helpful to consider how best to present your assignment. Here you should consider issues of detail, protocol and the range of communications that could be called upon within the assignment.

Presentation of the Assignment

You should always ensure that you prepare two copies of your Assignment, keeping a soft copy on disc. On occasions assignments go missing, or second copies are required by CIM.

- Each Assignment should be clearly marked up with your name, your study centre, your CIM Student registration number and ultimately at the end of the assignment a word count. The assignment should also be word-processed.
- The assignment presentation format should directly meet the requirements of the assignment brief, (ie reports and presentations are the most called for communication formats). You **must** ensure that you assignment does not appear to be an extended essay. If it does, you will lose marks.
- The word limit will be included in the assignment brief. These are specified by CIM and must be adhered to.
- Appendices should clearly link to the assignment and can be attached as supporting documentation at the end of the report. However failure to reference them by number (eg Appendix 1) within the report and also marked up on the Appendix itself will lose you marks. Only use an Appendix if it is essential and clearly adds value to the overall Assignment. The Appendix is not a waste bin for all the materials you have come across in your research, or a way of making your assignment seem somewhat heavier and more impressive than it is.

Time management for Assignments

One of the biggest challenges we all seem to face day-to-day is that of managing time. When studying, that challenge seems to grow increasingly difficult, requiring a balance between work, home, family, social life and study life. It is therefore of pivotal importance to your own success for you to plan wisely the limited amount of time you have available.

Step 1: Find out how much time you have

Ensure that you are fully aware of how long your module lasts, and the final deadline (eg 10 weeks, 12 weeks, 14 weeks etc). If you are studying a module from September to December, it is likely that you will have only 10-12 weeks in which to complete your assignments. This means that you will be preparing assignment work continuously throughout the course.

Step 2: Plan your time

Essentially you need to work backwards from the final deadline, submission date, and schedule your work around the possible time lines. Clearly if you have only 10-12 weeks available to complete three assignments, you will need to allocate a block of hours in the final stages of the module to ensure that all of your assignments are in on time. This will be critical, as all assignments will be sent to CIM by a set day. Late submissions will not be accepted, and no extensions will be allowed. Students who do not submit will be treated as a 'no show', and will have to re-enter for the next assessment period and undertake an alternative assignment.

Step 3: Set priorities

You should set priorities on a daily and weekly basis (not just for study, but for your life). There is no doubt that this mode of study needs commitment (and some sacrifices in the short term). When your achievements are recognised by colleagues, peers, friends and family, it will all feel worthwhile.

Step 4: Analyse activities and allocate time to them

Consider the range of activities that you will need to undertake in order to complete the assignment and the time each might take. Remember, too, there will be a delay in asking for information and receiving it.

- Preparing terms of reference for the assignment, to include the following.

1	A short title
2	A brief outline of the assignment purpose and outcome
3	Methodology – what methods you intend to use to carry out the required tasks
4	Indication of any difficulties that have arisen in the duration of the assignment
5	Time schedule
6	Confidentiality – if the assignment includes confidential information ensure that this is clearly marked up and indicated on the assignment
7	Literature and desk research undertaken

This should be achieved in one side of A4

- A literature search in order to undertake the necessary background reading and underpinning information that might support your assignment
- Writing letters and memos asking for information either internally or externally
- Designing questionnaires
- Undertaking surveys
- Analysis of data from questionnaires
- Secondary data search
- Preparation of first draft report

Always build in time to spare, to deal with the unexpected. This may reduce the pressure that you are faced in meeting significant deadlines.

Warning!

The same principles apply to a student with 30 weeks to do the work. However, a word of warning is needed. Do not fall into the trap of leaving all of your work to the last minute. If you miss out important information or fail to reflect upon your work adequately or successfully you will be penalised for both. Therefore, time management is important whatever the duration of the course.

Tips for writing Assignments

Everybody has a personal style, flair and tone when it comes to writing. However, no matter what your approach, you must ensure your assignment meets the requirements of the brief and so is comprehensible, coherent and cohesive in approach.

Think of preparing an assignment as preparing for an examination. Ultimately, the work you are undertaking results in an examination grade. Successful achievement of all four modules in a level results in a qualification.

There are a number of positive steps that you can undertake in order to ensure that you make the best of your assignment presentation in order to maximise the marks available.

Step 1 – Work to the Brief

Ensure that you identify exactly what the assignment asks you to do.

- If it asks you to be a marketing manager, then immediately assume that role.
- If it asks you to prepare a report, then present a report, not an essay or a letter.
- Furthermore, if it asks for 2,500 words, then do not present 1,000 or 4,000 unless in both instances it is clearly justified, agreed with your tutor and a valid piece of work.

Identify if the report should be formal or informal, who it should be addressed to, its overall purpose and its potential use and outcome. Understanding this will ensure that your assignment meets fully the requirements of the brief and addresses the key issues included within it.

Step 2 – Addressing the Tasks

It is of pivotal importance that you address each of the tasks within the assignment. Many students fail to do this and often overlook one of the tasks or indeed part of the tasks.

Many of the assignments will have two or three tasks, some will have even more. You should establish quite early on, which of the tasks:

- Requires you to collect information
- Provides you with the framework of the assignment, ie the communication method.

Possible tasks will include the following.

- Compare *and contrast.* Take two different organisations and compare them side by side and consider the differences ie the contrasts between the two.
- *Carry out primary or secondary research.* Collect information to support your assignment and your subsequent decisions
- Prepare a plan. Some assignments will ask you to prepare a plan for an event or for a marketing activity – if so provide a step by step approach, a rationale, a time-line, make sure it

is measurable and achievable. Make sure your actions are very specific and clearly explained. (Make sure your plan is SMART.)

- Analyse a situation. This will require you to collect information, consider its content and present an overall understanding of the actual situation that exists. This might include looking at internal and external factors and how the current situation evolved.
- Make recommendations. The more advanced your get in your studies, the more likely it is that you will be required to make recommendations. Firstly considering and evaluating your options and then making justifiable recommendations, based on them.
- Justify decisions. You may be required to justify your decision or recommendations. This will require you to explain fully how you have arrived at this decision and to show why, supported by relevant information, this is the right way forward. In other words, you should not make decisions in a vacuum; as a marketer your decisions should always be informed by context.
- Prepare a presentation. This speaks for itself. If you are required to prepare a presentation, ensure that you do so, preparing clearly defined PowerPoint or overhead slides that are not too crowded and that clearly express the points you are required to make.
- Evaluate performance. It is very likely that you will be asked to evaluate a campaign, a plan or even an event. You will therefore need to consider its strengths and weaknesses, why it succeeded or failed, the issues that have affected it, what can you learn from it and, importantly, how can you improve performance or sustain it in the future.

All of these points are likely requests included within a task. Ensure that you identify them clearly and address them as required.

Step 3 – Information Search

Many students fail to realise the importance of collecting information to support and underpin their assignment work. However, it is vital that you demonstrate to your centre and to the CIM your ability to establish information needs, obtain relevant information and utilise it sensibly in order to arrive at appropriate decisions.

You should establish the nature of the information required, follow up possible sources, time involved in obtaining the information, gaps in information and the need for information.

Consider these factors very carefully. CIM are very keen that students are seen to collect information, expand their mind and consider the breadth and depth of the situation. In your Personal Development Portfolio, you have the opportunity to complete a Resource Log, to illustrate how you have expanded your knowledge to aid your personal development. You can record your additional reading and research in that log, and show how it has helped you with your portfolio and assignment work.

Step 4 – Develop an Assignment Plan

Your assignment needs to be structured and coherent, addressing the brief and presenting the facts as required by the tasks. The only way you can successfully achieve this is by planning the structuro your Assignment in advance.

Earlier on in this unit, we looked at identifying your tasks and, working backwards from the release date, in order to manage time successfully. The structure and coherence of your assignment needs to be planned with similar signs.

In planning out the Assignment, you should plan to include all the relevant information as requested and also you should plan for the use of models, diagrams and appendices where necessary.

Your plan should cover your:

- Introduction
- Content
- Main body of the assignment
- Summary
- Conclusions and recommendations where appropriate

Step 5 – Prepare Draft Assignment

It is good practice to always produce a first draft of a report. You should use it to ensure that you have met the aims and objectives, assignment brief and tasks related to the actual assignment. A draft document provides you with scope for improvements, and enables you to check for accuracy, spelling, punctuation and use of English.

Step 6 – Prepare Final Document

In the section headed 'Presentation of the Assignment' in this unit, there are a number of components that should always be in place at the beginning of the assignment documentation, including labelling of the assignment, word counts, appendices numbering and presentation method. Ensure that you adhere to the guidelines presented, or alternatively those suggested by your study centre.

Writing reports

Students often ask 'what do they mean by a report?' or 'what should the report format include?'.

There are a number of approaches to reports, formal or informal: some report formats are company specific and designed for internal use, rather than external reporting.

For Assignment Route process, you should stay with traditional formats.

Below is a suggested layout of a Management Report Document that might assist you when presenting your assignments.

- A Title Page – includes the title of the report, the author of the report and the receiver of the report
- Acknowledgements – this should highlight any help, support, or external information received and any extraordinary co-operation of individuals or organisations
- Contents Page – providing a clearly structured pathway of the contents of the report – page by page
- Executive Summary – a brief insight into purpose, nature and outcome of the report, in order that the outcome of the report can be quickly established
- Main body of the report divided into sections, which are clearly labelled. Suggested labelling would be on a numbered basis eg:
    - 1.0 Introduction
    - 1.1 Situation Analysis
    - 1.1.1 External Analysis
    - 1.1.2 Internal Analysis

- Conclusions – draw the report to a conclusion, highlighting key points of importance, that will impact upon any recommendations that might be made
- Recommendations – clearly outline potential options and then recommendations. Where appropriate justify recommendations in order to substantiate your decision
- Appendices – ensure that you only use appendices that add value to the report. Ensure that they are numbered and referenced on a numbered basis within the text. If you are not going to reference it within the text, then it should not be there
- Bibliography – whilst in a business environment a bibliography might not be necessary, for an assignment-based report it is vital. It provides an indication of the level of research, reading and collecting of relevant information that has taken place in order to fulfil the requirements of the assignment task. Where possible, and where relevant, you could provide academic references within the text, which should of course then provide the basis of your bibliography. References should realistically be listed alphabetically and in the following sequence
  - Author's name and edition of the text
  - Date of publication
  - Title and sub-title (where relevant)
  - Edition 1st, 2nd etc
  - Place of publication
  - Publisher
  - Series and individual volume number where appropriate.

Resources to support Assignment Route

The aim of this guidance is to present you with a range of questions and issues that you should consider, based upon the assignment themes. The detail to support the questions can be found within your BPP Study Text and the 'Core Reading' recommended by CIM.

Refer back to the list of websites on page (xix). You will find useful support information within the CIM Student website www.cim.co.uk -: www.cimvirtualinstitute.com, where you can access a wide range of marketing information and case studies. You can also build your own workspace within the website so that you can quickly and easily access information specific to your professional study requirements. Other websites you might find useful for some of your assignment work include www.wnim.com - (What's New in Marketing) and also www.connectedinmarketing.com - another CIM website.

Integrative Project

We are not at liberty to give you specific guidance on the *Marketing in Practice* Integrative Project. However, it will be useful to consider possible assignment themes, and how you might approach the subject areas in terms of research, a questioning approach and meeting the requirements of the brief. The format is usually predetermined by CIM, and generally takes the form of a report or presentation.

Please note that like the examination papers, CIM issue a new Integrative Project for each exam board session. You will find your learning from *Marketing Fundamentals*, *Marketing Environment* and *Customer Communications* useful within this module, so perhaps you might want to look back at key areas, particularly when completing the actual assignment task. You will find your previous learning a good source of reference.

You should also note that as with other modules you will be encouraged to use your own organisation as the source for your assignment, and therefore all assignments will involve you in undertaking tasks directly related to it.

It might be useful to focus your mind on the learning outcomes of the *Marketing in Practice* module, as well as the related skills for marketers. Look back at page (xii) to see these again.

(i) By considering what the learning outcomes are for the module, you will understand the scope of the task ahead of you in terms of completing the Assignment Route process.

(ii) Key skills are undoubtedly something that most students will have come across by now. They demonstrate the importance of not just acquiring knowledge, but being able to apply it through the use of a range of related key skills for marketers. In undertaking Assignment Route project work, you will find that the key skills are not only used, but also continually stretched and developed.

Discussion of this year's themes will be available on the CIM area of the BPP website later in 2004.

Reflective Statement

The final part of your assignment will ask you to prepare a reflective statement, where you will be required to reflect upon your activities and your personal development in the selected areas for the duration of your course. This is a very underestimated part of the assignment, and one many students fail to address effectively. It is this part of the assignment that actually brings all of your work together.

There are a number of key components that you should always include

- Where did you start off at the very beginning of this course? What were your particular strengths, weaknesses and knowledge gaps within Marketing in Practice and the link subjects?
- What activities have you been involved in to achieve completion of your assignments?
- What did you do well?
- What could you have done better, and why?
- Do you feel that you have improved throughout the module?
- What value has this learning process added to your overall learning experience?
- Do you feel that the work undertaken will benefit you in your future personal development and organisational development?
- How will you continue to develop this area in the future? How do you anticipate you might use it?

One of the key considerations must be the 'future'. Many people see reflection as 'thinking about something that has happened in the past'. Whilst this is true, we must also reflect upon 'how this will help us in the future'.

You may find that as a result of this learning process your career aspirations have completely changed. You may find that you have become more confident and ambitious, and that through consolidating your learning in this way you have considerably more to offer. If this is the case do not be afraid to say so, and demonstrate how the whole learning process has influenced you and how it will drive you forward.

Earlier in this guide you were provided with a range of skills in relation to approaches to assignments, research and report formation. With the above information and the approaches describe you should be able to produce a professional assignment. Refer back to the earlier part of the unit on how to present assignments and research if necessary.

Where appropriate provide relevant examples so that you can show your tutor and CIM what your organisation does. This will help to back you up in your evaluation and justifications.

Summary: Marketing in Practice

You may have come to the end of the unit feeling that this is going to be hard work. Well you would be right in thinking this. But, as we suggested in the early part of this unit, it is likely to be one of the most beneficial learning processes you will embark upon, as you take your CIM qualifications.

The process of development prepares you to be a marketing professional in the future. It provides you with practical experience and an opportunity to apply the theory in a practical situation. You will demonstrate to your existing or future employer that you have the ability to learn, develop, grow, progress and contribute significantly to the marketing activity within the organisation.

You have been provided with a range of hints and tips in presentation of assignments, development and approaches to your assignments.

Assignment Route, like examinations, is a serious business, and you should consider the level of ongoing commitment that this process requires. The more you put in the more you are likely to get out. It will not be enough to leave all of your work to the end of the course as it destroys the ethos and benefit of the assignment. Use it as a continuous development tool for the duration of the course. A structured approach to the learning process will maximise its benefits to you.

We have tried to give you some insight into how to approach the tasks that you will embark upon within the Integrative Project. However, please ensure that you read the assignment carefully when it arrives, and address it directly. We have aimed to show you the level of detail you should enter into in order to produce an effective and professional piece of work.

The CIM qualifications are professional qualifications and therefore, to be successful you must take a professional approach to your work.

Background to case study: 'The Needle Works'

Background information

The Needle Works Ltd is a company retailing and distributing a wide range of products and services related to needlecraft. It currently has one large high street store and a small factory.

The Needle Works' products initially consisted of various kits, patterns and supplies (threads and yarns, needles, hoops) for common forms of needlecraft, sourced from designers and manufacturers in the UK and USA. These suppliers range from major corporations to small providers, especially in the emerging arena of hand-spun and naturally dyed materials.

In recent years, The Needle Works has diversified into

(a) more specialised craft niches, with materials, patterns and related products for particular forms such as silk embroidery, goldwork, beadwork and teddy-bear making;

(b) related retail areas such as instructional and coffee-table books and magazines, accessories (such as collectible thimbles, technical aids like magnifying lights and scissor-holders);

(c) related services, including finishing and framing of craft works (and pictures and posters), the design and manufacture of adjustable tapestry frames (on which work-in-progress is mounted and stretched), the valuation (for insurance purposes) of finished works, and the charting of designs.

The craft market is specialised, but surprisingly diverse. The customers at The Needle Works' London store include many women aged 50+, but also a small proportion of men, and an increasing number of young people of both sexes, due to a renaissance of interest in hand-made and decorated textiles in design and fashion colleges. Several ethnic communities (notably Middle-Eastern and central European) are regular customers, and tourists, particularly from the Far East, are major one-off customers. There are also some 'institutional' clients, such as old age homes and therapy units since traditional crafts are seen as a way of improving motor skills, increasing self-esteem and controlling stress.

The Needle Works is a family-founded and owned business, which has grown by word-of-mouth and specialist response to the market's needs over the years. It is relatively unstructured, since the management team is quite small.

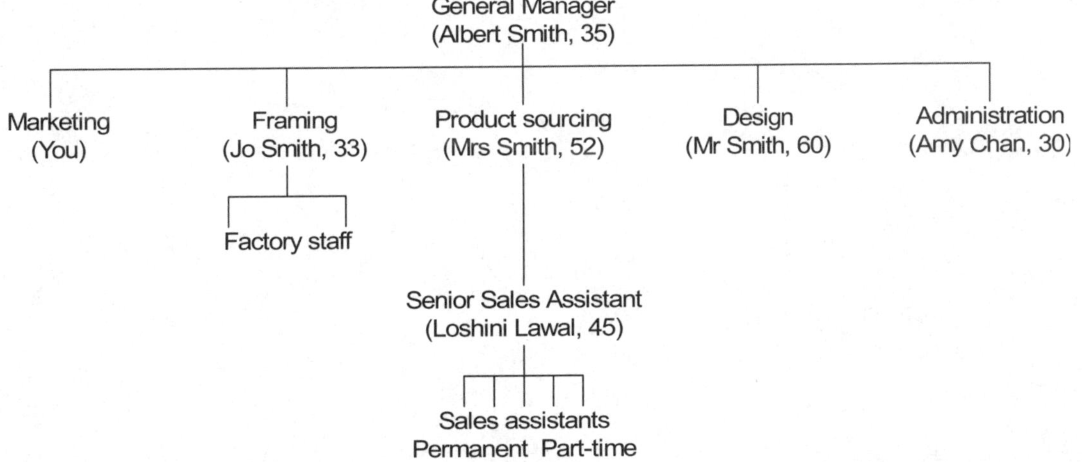

Mr and Mrs Smith founded the business. Their eldest son, Albert, has recently been appointed General Manager in order to modernise the business. He has now appointed you, with the title of Marketing Co-ordinator, to 'take in hand' the marketing of the store and its services.

Marketing has so far been rudimentary, and there is no 'marketing budget' as such: each task is tackled separately on the basis of need and cost-effectiveness. Some advertising used to be placed in specialised magazines in the craft sector, but a high-street presence, word-of-mouth and the boast of having 'the UK's largest range of needlecraft designs and supplies' has seen a steady level of business, without further promotion. This has been aided by:

(a) the gradual disappearance of small competitors, giving The Needle Works increasing status as a needlecraft 'Super Store', and increasing market share; and

(b) attractive in-store displays, promotions and seasonal sales.

Turnover is in the region of £2.6 million per year. (An average purchase is £20. Prices range from 60p for thread to £600 for a large kit.) There is a customer database, generated by a Visitor's Book in the store, in which all visiting customers are asked to enter their name, address and comments. (These are mostly of a 'love your store!' variety.) These names and addresses are periodically typed into a basic Microsoft Access database, together with order details entered into the store's point of sale computer. There are currently 10,000 names and addresses on this database.

Any promotional items (discount vouchers, mailing letters and so on) are produced in-house. The office computer has some basic DTP software. Susan Jones 'can design a bit', and Mr Smith is an accomplished calligrapher and illustrator.

Albert Smith has recently acquired the lease of additional floor space in the block of which The Needle Works showroom has the street-level frontage. This presents a significant opportunity to expand the business. Current ideas include a knitting supplies shop (a logical extension to a related craft area) and a craft education centre, running classes in the various crafts for which the business sells supplies (both a direct revenue-earner and a promotional, market-expanding tool).

This is the context in which you have been employed as Marketing Co-ordinator. Good luck!

The Needle Works
6-10 High Street
Old Town
London NW

Part A

Gathering, analysing and presenting information

1 Information for Marketing

Chapter Topic List	
1	Setting the scene
2	The importance of information
3	Marketing research
4	Sources of information
5	Evaluating, presenting and using information

Learning Outcomes

- ☑ Collect relevant data from a variety of secondary information sources
- ☑ Analyse and interpret written, visual and graphic data
- ☑ Devise appropriate visual and graphical means to present marketing data

Syllabus References

- ☑ Identify sources of information internally and externally to the organisation, including ICT based sources such as intranet and Internet
- ☑ Gather information across borders

Key Concepts Introduced

- Marketing research
- Primary and secondary data
- Internet
- Information and Communications Technology (ICT)
- Quantitative research
- Qualitative research

1 Setting the scene

1.1 Part A of this Study Text deals with the gathering, analysing and presenting of information for marketing. This chapter introduces the idea that information is vital for decision making, and gives an overview of the types of information that can be obtained through marketing research. It also discusses the various sources of information. You can draw upon your studies of *Marketing Environment* here.

1.2 On completion of this chapter you should be able to:

- Recognise the importance of information in marketing, planning and decision making
- Outline the uses of marketing research
- Appreciate the variety of information sources available inside and outside the organisation
- Evaluate the quality and cost-effectiveness of information obtained
- Appreciate the variety of ways in which information can be presented for business use

1.3 Chapters 2, 3 and 4 explore further aspects of information gathering. Chapter 2 focuses on the customer database as a source of information for marketing. Chapter 3 gives you some practical research skills for tapping into primary sources. Chapter 4 expands on the need and methodologies for gathering information about the marketing environment, competitor activity and marketing opportunities.

1.4 This chapter should be regarded as an introduction to concepts and skills which underpin the whole *Marketing in Practice* syllabus and assessment.

(a) **Building and developing relationships** (as we will discover in Part B of this Text) requires the exchange of information and tapping into information sources.

(b) **Organising and undertaking marketing activities** (Part C) requires the gathering of information on options, costs, schedules, availability and a host of other strategic and operational matters.

(c) **Co-ordinating the marketing mix** (Part D) likewise requires the monitoring of the marketing environment and competitor activity, the strengths and weaknesses of the organisation's marketing plans, and the effects of pricing decisions, product developments and promotional messages on performance.

(d) **Administering the marketing budget and evaluating results** (Part E) requires detailed costing and performance feedback information.

1.5 Not least, the assessment of *Marketing in Practice* by case study requires you to assimilate a body of information and to use that information in decision-making and in carrying out marketing tasks. You are also required to appreciate what further information might be needed in order to make decisions, and where it might be obtained.

Exam Tip

The essential point to remember is the role that information plays in all marketing activity and decision-making. You may be tempted to take this for granted, but it is the core underlying theme of this syllabus.

2 The importance of information

2.1 It would be impossible to list all the possible uses of information in a business organisation. In a sense, an organisation is a **system of information flows**: Figure 1.1

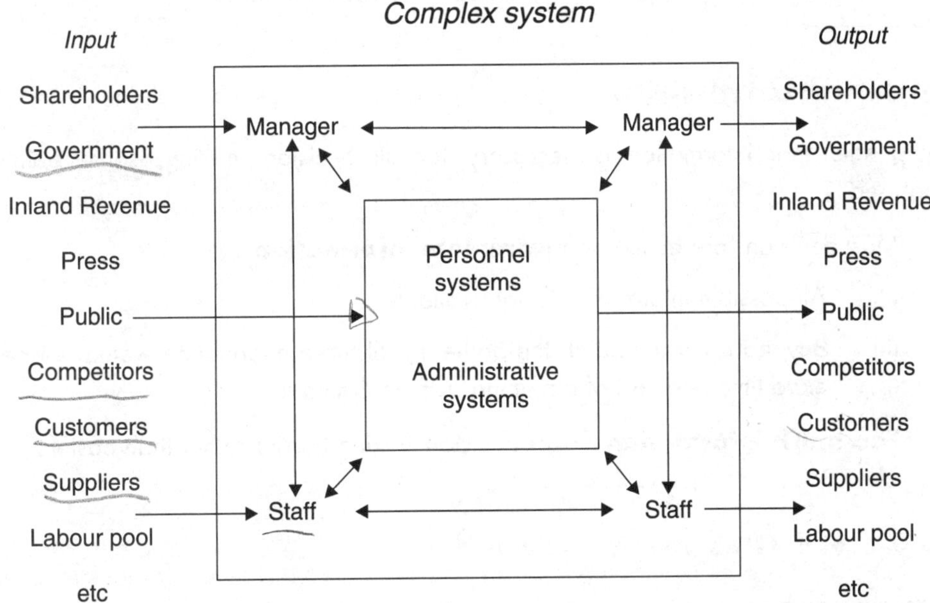

Figure 1.1: The organisation as an information system

2.2 All human **action and decision-making** is based, consciously or unconsciously, on information: about the environment, the needs or wants of the individual, the likely outcomes of the action or decision (based on past experience or the advice of others) and so on.

2.3 Since an organisation is defined as a 'social arrangement for **the controlled performance of collective goals**' (Huczynski and Buchanan, 2001) it is even more important that decisions should be rational and based on appropriate information about all the variables involved, about the goals to be reached, and about the performance process and results.

Marketing at Work

Procter & Gamble have devised a Statement of Business Principles, setting out 10 guiding principles for all their activity. The top three are as follows:

1 *Plan all action in advance.* Always forecast business in relation to expenditure, always check that the business is reaching according to forecast, and always be ready to adjust plans as necessary.

2 *Base all actions on facts.* One fact is worth many judgements. Strive always to find the factual truth as a subject before acting. This applies to all fields of business: product, packaging, advertising, promotions and expenditure.

3 *Always know the objective of your actions.* Know what advertising, individual promotions and sales plans are intended to do and judge their success by whether they achieve objectives.

2.4 Drucker (1955) wrote that: 'Marketing is the whole business seen from the point of view of its final result, that is from the **customer's** point of view'. A marketing orientation to business suggests that the purpose of business activity is to find out what people want, and to give it to them: to **make what you can sell**, not sell what you can make.

How much information?

2.5 Having said that information is necessary for all decision making, some points must be recognised.

(a) Most decisions are based on **incomplete information**.

(i) All possible information is not available

(ii) Beyond a certain point, the gathering of more information would not be worth the extra time and cost of obtaining and analysing it

(b) **Too much information** makes decision-making harder rather than easier.

Where do we find information?

2.6 Information can be sourced:

(a) **Inside the organisation**. This is information we already have, such as sales figures, reports, price lists, literature, customer information etc. It may be stored electronically in a central database or in forms and files scattered throughout the organisation.

(b) **Outside the organisation**. Information we don't have, but can get access to, often at a cost.

The marketing information system

2.7 As you will appreciate from your *Marketing Environment* studies, the marketing information system is 'the framework for the day-to-day management and structuring of information gathered regularly from sources both inside and outside an organisation' (Dibb *et al.*, 2001). Such information may include the following.

- Prices
- Advertising expenditure
- Sales
- Competitor activity
- Distribution costs
- Stock levels

Action Programme 1

Make a poster of the three Procter & Gamble business principles listed earlier.

Exam Tip

Sources and uses of information are frequent areas of exam questioning. Make sure you can distinguish clearly between aspects such as:

(i) *What sort of information is needed*
(ii) *Where the information can be obtained*
(iii) *How the information will be obtained*
(iv) *What it will be used for*

3 Marketing research

Key Concept

Marketing research is 'the process of gathering, interpreting and reporting information to help marketers solve specific marketing problems or take advantage of marketing opportunities'.

Dibb *et al.*

3.1 Marketing decisions are made under conditions of uncertainty and risk. Marketing research aims to **reduce the risk** by providing information about the variables involved in the decision, and the possible outcomes of particular decisions and actions.

3.2 A wide variety of information may be relevant to marketing decisions.

(a) **Market research** involves the gathering of information about the market for a particular produce or service : consumer attitudes, environmental influences on supply and demand, competition, product usage and so on.

- Analysis of the market potential for existing products
- Forecasting likely demand for new products
- Sales forecasting for all products
- Study of market trends
- Study of the characteristics of the market
- Analysis of market shares

(b) **Product research** is concerned with the product - whether in development, new, improved or already on the market - and how customers respond (or are likely to respond) to it.

- Customer acceptance of proposed new products
- Comparative studies between competitive products
- Studies into packaging and design
- Forecasting new uses for existing products
- Test marketing
- Research into the development of a product line (range)

(c) **Price research**

- Analysis of elasticities of demand
- Analysis of costs and contribution or profit margins
- The effect of changes in credit policy on demand
- Customer perceptions of price (and quality)

(d) **Sales promotion research**

- Motivation research for advertising and sales promotion effectiveness
- Analysing the effectiveness of advertising on sales demand
- Analysing the effectiveness of individual aspects of advertising such as copy and media used
- Establishing sales territories
- Analysing the effectiveness of salesmen
- Analysing the effectiveness of other sales promotion methods

(e) **Distribution research**

- The location and design of distribution centres
- The analysis of packaging for transportation and shelving
- Dealer supply requirements
- Dealer advertising requirements
- The cost of different methods of transportation and warehousing

As you can see, information can be gathered across the 'four Ps' of the marketing mix (and indeed the 'seven Ps' of the extended marketing mix, as we will discuss in Chapter 15), and the marketing environment.

Exam Tip

A key theme of questions under the new syllabus has been 'What information do you need for ...?'. In June 2003, it was for profiling the customer (audience) base of a local radio station. In December 2003, it was for a proposed database of current and future members of a small boat club. Questions also tend to ask 'How could this information be obtained?' (as in June 2003) and/or 'How could this information be used?' (as in December 2003). Get used to asking these three questions in relation to decisions you make – or read about in your studies.

Primary and secondary research

3.3 One way of classifying research approaches is by the nature of the sources of data they use.

Key Concepts

Primary data are data collected especially for a particular purpose, directly from the relevant source.

Secondary data are data which have already been gathered and assembled for other purposes or general reference.

Primary sources of consumer information, for example, would be the consumers themselves. Primary research is usually **'field research'**, involving surveys, interviews, questionnaires, observation or experiments. These techniques will be discussed in Chapter 3.

Secondary sources of consumer information would include published statistics and reports on consumer behaviour, books, Internet sites and so on. They are accessed by **'desk research'** which can often be carried out literally from the researcher's desk (given access to appropriate reference sources). We discuss these sources of information below.

Quantitative and qualitative research

3.4 Another way of classifying research approaches is according to the type of data gathered.

Key Concepts

Quantitative research gathers statistically valid, numerically measurable data.

Qualitative research focuses on information that is difficult to quantify, such as values, attitudes, opinions, beliefs and motivations.

Quantitative research answers questions such as: How many? What percentage? How often? How many times? How much? Where? This is essentially *demographic*, statistical information, telling the marketer who buys what, and where, in what quantities and at what price.

While quantitative data may show that 75% of men aged 18-35 drive a car, *qualitative* data might reveal how they go about choosing a car, how they feel about their car, what would make them change cars and so on. This is essentially *psychographic* information.

As we will see in Chapter 3, quantitative data is usually gathered by survey, and qualitative data by personal interviews and discussion groups. Both types of data may be gathered from primary and/or secondary sources.

Action Programme 2

Give examples of qualitative and/or quantitative data that might be gathered in the following circumstances.

(a) The sales of a product appeared to be declining in a particular region
(b) You wanted to know whether customers would support night-time opening
(c) You were about to schedule TV advertising

4 Sources of information

4.1 As we saw above, **primary** sources of information are basically 'the horse's mouth' whomever that may be: customers, consumers, supply chain partners or other businesses. We will look at techniques for gathering primary data in Chapters 2 and 3 of this Text.

4.2 Here, we will look at **secondary** sources of information.

- **Existing data** generated and held by the organisation
- **Published information**, both general and industry specific
- Bought-in **market research reports**
- The **Internet**
- General '**environmental scanning**'

Internal data records

4.3 The following information gathered in the course of operations and transactions may be relevant to marketing planning and control.

- **Production data** about quantities produced, materials and labour used etc
- Data about **inventory**
- Data about **sales** volumes
- Data about **marketing**, promotion and brand data
- All **cost and management accounting** data
- **Financial management data**

4.4 Such information often goes back several years, so that comparisons can be made and trends extrapolated.

Published information

4.5 The **government** is a major source of economic, industrial and demographic information. Examples of government publications are as follows.

(a) *The Annual Abstract of Statistics* and its monthly equivalent, the *Monthly Digest of Statistics*. These contain data about manufacturing output, housing, population etc.

(b) *Economic Trends* (monthly) and *Social Trends* (annually) and *Labour Market Trends* (monthly).

(c) *Census of Population.* The Office for National Statistics publishes continuous datasets including the National Food Survey, the Household Survey and the Family Expenditure Survey.

(d) *Census of Production* (annual). This has been described as 'one of the most important sources of desk research for industrial marketers'. It provides data about production by firms in each industry in the UK.

(e) *British Business*, published weekly by the Department of Trade and Industry, gives data on industrial and commercial trends at home and overseas.

(f) *Business Monitor* (published by the Office for National Statistics), gives detailed information about various industries.

4.6 **Official statistics** are also published by other government bodies such as the European Union, the United Nations and local authorities.

4.7 **Non-government sources** of information include the following.

(a) Companies and other organisations specialising in the provision of economic and financial data (eg Reuters and the Thomson Extel Survey).

(b) Directories and yearbooks, such as Kompass or Kelly's Directory.

(c) Professional institutions (eg Chartered Institute of Marketing, Chartered Management Institute, Institute of Practitioners in Advertising).

(d) Specialist libraries, such as the City Business Library in London, collect published information from a wide variety of sources.

(e) Trade associations, trade unions and Chambers of Commerce.

(f) Trade and professional journals, newspapers and commentaries (and their websites).

(g) Commercial organisations such as banks and TV networks.

(h) Surveys produced by research agencies (Gallup, MORI, Mintel, Euromonitor).

Marketing at Work

Euromonitor's website makes available (at cost) detailed profiles of countries and markets. Summaries can be viewed free. Links to relevant information sources are also provided. For example:

Country factfile: Malaysia

Socio-economic indicators

	Unit	*1999*	*2000*	*2001*
Population aged 0-14	'000	7,473.3	7,587.0	7,645.8
Population aged 65+	'000	896.49	922.47	953.07
Consumer expenditure on food	USD million	7,207.6	8,384.5	8,613.6
New registrations of passenger cars	'000	255.88	296.56	302.02
Possession of colour TV set	per 100 households	90.30	90.26	90.25

'In our reports you will find:

- latest market size data, market share data and forecasts
- company profiles, brand shares and rankings
- distribution trends and in-depth strategic analysis.'

Business information sources

Bank Negara Malaysia www.bnm.gov.my

Jabatan Perangkaan Malaysia (Department of Statistics Malaysia) www.statistics.gov.my'

www.euromonitor.com

4.8 While some of the above sources are general and others trade-, market- or profession-specific, bear in mind that general information may be applicable to your target market: keep an open mind and active 'antennae' for relevant data. Department of Transport budgets, for example, may be on the need-to-know list for car manufacturers.

Action Programme 3

Does your organisation, or individual department, have a library or libraries of published materials such as books, reference works, trade journals or newspapers? What titles are regularly stocked? How often is the information updated? How is the information categorised or indexed?

Bought-in reports

4.9 Much of the above published material is in the public domain. It is accessible and inexpensive to gather, but may need considerable analysis and processing in order to produce sufficiently targeted information for a specific organisation's needs. On the other hand, tailor-made information is only available by commissioning or undertaking primary research, which is a costly exercise.

4.10 A middle course may be to buy in reports prepared externally, whether as primary research for another organisation which is then syndicated, or as a commercial service to industry data users.

Audits

4.11 Various audits generate published reports which can be bought by marketers.

Consumer panels or home audit panels

4.12 **Consumer panels** consist of a representative sample of consumers who have agreed to have their attitudes and buying habits monitored over a period of time. There are established panels for the purchase of groceries, consumer durables, cars, baby products and many others.

4.13 Audits of Great Britain (AGB) ran the Television Consumer Audit for 25 years which estimated the purchase of groceries and frozen foods for home consumption in a sample of 6,300 households in the UK. It has recently been replaced by the high-tech Superpanel, which allows the households to scan data directly from purchases into the database by means of barcodes after every shopping trip.

4.14 **Consumer panels** generate a vast amount of data which need to be sorted if they are to be digestible.

(a) Standard trend analysis shows how the market and its major brands have fared since the last analysis, grossed up to reflect the population.

(b) Special analyses depend on industrial preferences.

- Source of purchase analysis
- Frequency of purchase analysis
- Demographic analysis
- Tracking of individuals, to show their degree of brand loyalty

Trade and retail audits

4.15 **Trade audits** are carried out among panels of wholesalers and retailers, and the term 'retail audits' refers to panels of retailers only. A research firm sends 'auditors' to selected outlets at regular intervals to count stock and deliveries, thus enabling an estimate of throughput to be made. Sometimes it is possible to do a universal audit of all retail outlets. EPOS makes the process both easier and more universal.

4.16 The audits provide details of the following.

(a) **Retail sales** for selected products and brands, sales by different type of retail outlet, market shares and brand shares.

(b) **Retail stocks** of products and brands (enabling a firm subscribing to the audit to compare stocks of its own goods with those of competitors).

(c) **Selling prices** in retail outlets, including information about discounts.

The Internet – 'cyber research'

4.17 According to Gabay (2002), companies venturing towards marketing via the Internet need to ask three questions.

- Who wants our product/service?
- Why would they go on the Internet to find it?
- How can we stop them going for competitor sites instead?

4.18 Reports are available to answer questions on the who, why and how often of Internet usage, but the most common method of research is via search engines (entering key words into the 'Search' box).

Key Concept

The **Internet** (or 'information superhighway', or 'World Wide Web') is a collection of computers and computer networks, via which users can access and share database information, and send and receive electronic messages world-wide at speed.

Key Concept

Information and Communication Technology (ICT) is a collective term for computer and telecommunication based technologies, used extensively in modern communication and data processing applications. ICT includes: the Internet, websites and email; mobile phone applications; digital TV and radio; database management and customer relationship management (CRM) software; and so on.

4.19 The Internet can be a fast, efficient way to search for and access secondary data world-wide.

(a) Governments, educational institutions, libraries, commercial organisations and agencies have '**home pages**' on the **World Wide Web** which contain information and include links to other sites where information can be found. Well-designed sites typically have their own indexes and menus, as well as marked hypertext links that allow the browser to 'jump' to related areas and topics.

(b) **Search engines** (such as Yahoo!, Lycos, and Excite) maintain large databases of web pages, and can be used to locate relevant sites by word search.

Marketing at Work

For a comprehensive list of search engines (aka. information sites) on the web, Gabay (2002) suggests that 'the best source of online research is to ask for views from your existing circle of customers and associates as well as employees and suppliers'. You could also look at www.cyberatlas.com for research reports which summarise current and forecast usage of the Internet.

(c) **Internet indexes** are another way of locating information on a particular subject: Yahoo! is currently the biggest and most popular index available.

(d) '**Newsgroups**' and mailing lists act as a kind of bulletin board service, where people post messages and articles on various topics.

4.20 It can be difficult conducting an efficient data search unless you know what you are doing. However, the Internet is friendly enough for you to be able to **browse** in areas of interest and follow links. As you discover relevant sources information, you can 'bookmark' them, or add them to your 'Favourites' list to create a shortcut for regular reference.

Exam Tip

When an exam question asks you to enumerate the 'uses of ICT' in marketing, you may immediately think of promotional uses (such as web- or email-based marketing) and/or customer relationship management uses (such as computer-telephony integration and databases). Don't forget the information-gathering applications of ICT: accessing databases and reports for market information, inviting customers to fill in online feedback forms, gathering e-mail contacts and so on.

Intranet

4.21 Intranets are mini versions of the Internet connecting computers within an organisation. Each employee or terminal has a browser which gives access to corporate information.

4.22 Intranets can be used to disseminate corporate information on a wide variety of topics, as well as to facilitate file-sharing and database access. Potential applications may be illustrated by the following examples.

(a) Silicon Graphics' intranet has 150,000 pages and is used daily by about 4,000 of the company's 8,000 staff. Besides being used as the company's daily newspaper the intranet has been found to be a particularly effective method of induction for new staff.

(b) One of the most successful intranet uses is the personal Web page, which allows anyone in the firm to see what their colleagues are doing and how they are progressing.

(c) Extensive internal databases can be built, so that an employee can enter search words and bring up relevant files and data (eg on customers or suppliers, product availability, market research and so on).

(d) Intranets offer a new way of putting together '**groupware**' – software to support group working.

General 'environmental scanning'

4.23 Environmental scanning is simply the process of keeping your 'radar' switched on to what is going on in your market place. **Market intelligence** can be gleaned in many ways.

- Any newspaper, magazine, trade or academic journal
- Conferences, exhibitions, trade shows
- Personal contacts in the trade
- Personal experience and observation of the market

Action Programme 4

Here is a small selection of headlines from *The Daily Telegraph.*

(a) Two tube strikes a week being planned by unions
(b) Inquiries pour in for jobs at Siemens
(c) Protesters halt royal tree felling
(d) Film comeback for Mickey Mouse at 67

In each case what sort of organisations should take note of the articles as part of their environmental scanning for marketing threats and opportunities?

Gathering information across borders

4.24 Most of the secondary sources surveyed so far in section 4 have their counterparts in other countries.

(a) Foreign **governments and international bodies** (such as the United Nations) publish reports and statistics.

(b) Foreign **trade associations** and industry bodies publish surveys. Many also have international links.

(c) **International news** and information agencies (such as Reuters) publish world-wide reports.

(d) **Resource guides** (such as the British Overseas Trade Board's *Market-Search*) provide links to recommended international sources of information.

(e) International **newspapers and journals** are available (in print, and frequently also on the Internet).

(f) **Internet sites** give access to foreign educational and governmental institutions and their databases, and to the websites of commercial organisations around the world. Access is not restricted to working hours (which helps when there are time differences) and information can be downloaded for later translation.

Marketing at Work

Check out some of the following sites. How helpful are they likely to be for (a) businesses in the local market and (b) researchers from overseas?

China

National Bureau of Statistics	www.stats.gov.cn
Ministry of Foreign Trade & Economic Co-operation	www.moftec.gov.cn
Department of International Co-operation, State Information Center, CEInet Data Co Ltd	www.ce.cei.gov.cn

Poland

Glowny Urzad Statystyczny (GUS) (Central Statistical Office)	www.stat.gov.pl
Narodowy Bank Polandi (National Bank of Poland)	www.nbp.pl

5 Evaluating, presenting and using information

Evaluating data

5.1 All data collected should be **evaluated** using the following criteria.

(a) Is the data **relevant** to the purpose for which it was collected?

(b) Is it **up-to-date**?

(c) Is it **reliable and accurate**?

(d) Is the source of the data **credible** and objective, or unbiased? Look for the following.

(i) The source's **reputation**, and your own past experience of its accuracy and reliability.

(ii) **Internal evidence** that the information is accurate, consistent, balanced and supported by evidence.

(iii) The source's **interests, motives, values and purpose** in compiling the information. Is the source trying to persuade you of something, market something or disguise something?

(e) Is the data subject to **confirmation**, or comparison with data from other sources? Are you prepared to risk basing decisions on uncorroborated data?

(f) Is the data based on a large and representative statistical sample of the relevant population?

(g) Has the data been gathered in a way that makes it **meaningful and reliable**? Has the same question been put to all respondents? Were all terms consistently defined? Did researchers lead or suggest 'right' answers? Were the respondents influenced by the researcher, or each other, or the desire to be 'nice'?

(h) Has the data collection and analysis been worthwhile? Has it fulfilled its purposes at a **reasonable cost** in money, time and effort?

Analysis and presentation of research findings

5.2 Quantitative research quite often presents 'raw data': lists or tables of numbers, or ticks in boxes. This data must be analysed in order to identify key features, trends, probabilities and averages.

5.3 Qualitative research also presents 'raw data' in the form of records of words in narrative form. This data must be analysed in order to summarise, interpret, categorise and measure the frequency of responses, for presentation in quantitative or statistical form.

5.4 **Management information**, or **decision-support** information, resulting from data analysis must be formatted for **presentation** to the target user.

- Printed tables
- Charts
- Graphs
- Narrative reports
- Oral presentation with visual aids
- Interpretation and recommendations

All these formats are covered in the *Customer Communications* module. Particular applications (such as using a Gantt chart to schedule advertising media or event planning) are covered in relevant chapters of this Text.

Marketing at Work

Ten largest Internet markets in Europe, 2003 (in millions of Internet users)

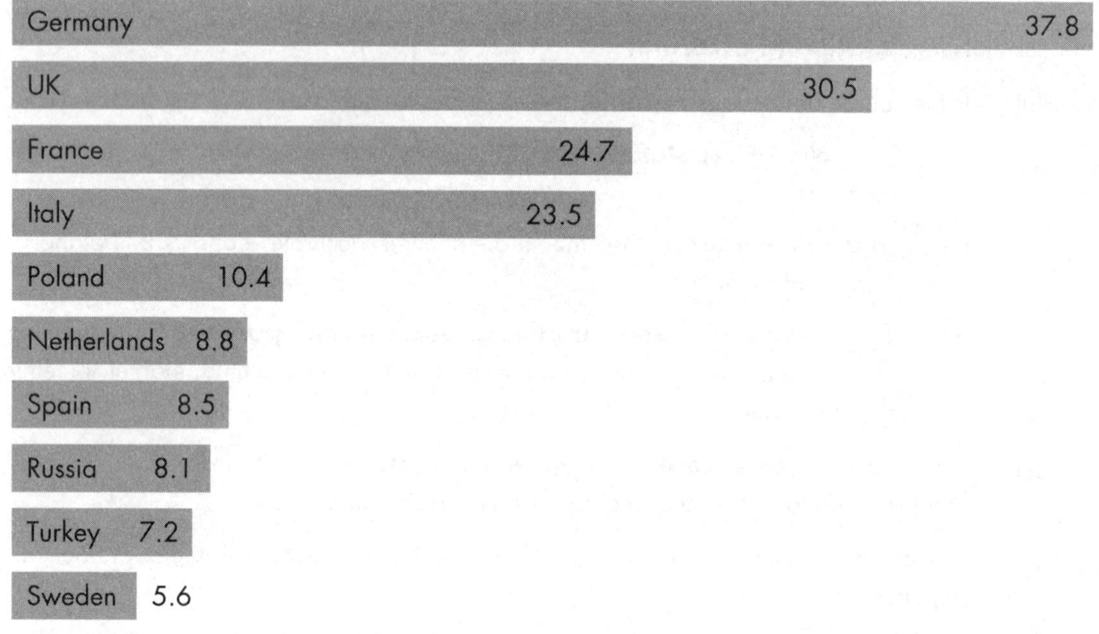

Note: Total of ten largest countries is 165.1 million Internet users comprising 79% of all European Internet users.

Source: eMarketer, February 2004

5.5 The way in which information will be processed and presented, as discussed in detail in *Customer Communications*, depends on:

- **Its intended audience**. Who will be required to use and understand the information? What types of data and formats will help them get the best use out of the information? What level of detail and/or sophistication will they be able to absorb and use?
- **Its intended purpose**. What will the information be used for? What does it need to demonstrate or prove most clearly? (A trend? A correlation between one variable and another? A frequency distribution, indicating the concentration of buyers in one market segment or another? Key differences in buyer behaviour that might suggest a basis for market segmentation?) How (and how frequently) will it need to be accessed, in order to fulfil its purposes? (Eg Will it be used every time a customer calls, as part of a customer relationship management system?)

Key uses of marketing information

5.6 We will be looking at this in more detail throughout this Text, but you should be aware from the outset of the range of uses to which information about markets, customers and the business environment can be put.

(a) **Segmenting markets**, so that 'groups' of customers and potential customers with similar characteristics can be *targeted* with effective marketing strategies and so that the organisation's offering can be appropriately *positioned* to appeal to appropriate segments, to maximise return on marketing investment.

(b) **Marketing planning**: planning, organising and undertaking marketing activities which will be relevant to the needs, wants and preferences of the target market; taking into account environmental constraints, including competitor activity, legal regulation and consumer trends; supplying relevant information to employees.

(c) **Relationship marketing**: building databased records of customer buying activity and preferences, so that further contacts and follow-up offers can be tailored and even personalised accordingly (eg individually addressed letters/emails, special offers and loyalty incentives based on past transaction history).

(d) **Supply chain relationship management**: building similar records of contacts, transaction history and performance of suppliers, distributors and other partners in the value chain, so that their performance can be managed in future.

(e) **Managing the organisation's communications and profile**: using environmental data to drive change in the organisation's culture and image (eg responding to increasing consumer pressure towards corporate social responsibility in regard to the environment, fair employment practices and so on).

(f) **Evaluating marketing activity**, using feedback from customers and other stakeholders to assess the effectiveness of marketing plans and adjust them where required.

Action Programme 5

The Needle Works

As the new Marketing Co-ordinator of The Needle Works, you decide you quickly need to get a handle on the commercial craft supply trade, and needlecraft in particular. You also need to get some sense of how The Needle Works' sales break down by product group.

(a) Make a list of some of the information sources you will tap into most easily and with least cost, in order to gain some general market intelligence.

(b) The only immediately available sales information comes from the EPOS print-out used by Loshini Lawal to motivate the sales assistants.

Week Commencing:

Sales by assistant by product

	Thread (units)	Kits (units)	Frames (units)	Patterns (units)	Accessories (units)	TOTAL
Loshini	40	20	5	25	30	**120**
Jane	15	10	-	-	5	**30**
Sarah	10	5	-	10	15	**40**
Tom	20	7	3	-	-	**30**
Sarina	5	10	-	10	10	**35**
Rafi	10	10	-	5	20	**45**
TOTAL	**100**	**62**	**8**	**50**	**80**	**300**

(i) If the profits generated by each product are as follows, which sales assistant has generated the least profit?

Thread	£2
Kits	£1
Frames	£3
Pattern	£2
Accessories	£1

(ii) You would like to know which products are doing better than others. Present this information in diagram form, so you can show the rest of the management team.

(iii) What does your analysis so far not take into account?

(iv) Suggest ways of improving overall team performance.

Chapter Roundup

- **Information** (measurement, facts and data, analysis) is required for **rational decision making**, particularly for marketing, which requires a detailed, realistic understanding of the customer's needs and wants, the marketing mix and the marketing environment.
- Decisions must be made with **partial information**, to avoid analysis paralysis, and must sometimes allow for **non-rational influences**, particularly when **innovation** is required.
- **Marketing research** can operate across the extended marketing mix and the marketing environment.
- Data may be **qualitative** (psychographic) and/or quantitative (statistical, demographic) and derived from primary and/or secondary sources.
- **Secondary sources** of information include:
  - internal data records
  - published information
  - bought-in reports
  - the Internet and intranet
  - general environmental scanning

  All these sources are available **internationally**.
- Data must be **evaluated** for:
  - relevance
  - up-to-dateness
  - accuracy
  - the credibility and objectivity of the source
  - corroboration/confirmation
  - correct methodology in sampling and data collection
  - cost-effectiveness
- Data must be **analysed** and **presented** as information, accessible and relevant to the needs of the intended user.

Quick Quiz

1. How much information is required to make a decision?
2. What is product research?
3. Give five examples of internal data that could be used for marketing research.
4. Give three examples of industry/trade specific publications.
5. What information is generated by a consumer panel?
6. Give three examples of sources of information on the Internet.
7. Give five examples of sources of overseas market intelligence.
8. How can you evaluate the credibility and objectivity of a data source?
9. How is raw quantitative and qualitative data converted into management information?
10. List three uses of customer data.

Now try Question 1 in the Question Bank

Action Programme Review

1 If you think this is a frivolous exercise, consider that:

- these three principles are the key to all the marketing activities discussed in this Study Text, and a useful checklist for effective action
- the presentation of information is an important marketing skill in itself

2 (a) Quantitative data on sales volume comparing region-on-region and year-on-year to establish amount (units, value, %) and rate of decline. Qualitative data on why consumers are less happy with the product.

(b) Quantitative data on volume of sales in comparable times/markets during night hours, percentage support among sample groups. Qualitative data about people's attitudes to night shopping, possible fears (related to area?).

(c) Quantitative data on audience figures at scheduled times, demographics of audience, cost of advertising. Qualitative data on audience response to the ad.

3 This is important information for any workplace research you may have to do - not least, for assessment of your skills in this area of the syllabus!

4 Here are some suggestions. You may have other ideas.

(a) Coach firms, car park owners, environmental groups, regional competitors of organisations likely to be adversely affected in London.

(b) Competitors at Siemens, recruitment consultants.

(c) Land developers, environmental groups.

(d) Makers of teeshirts, watches, toys, nostalgia-related goods.

It is a good idea to get into the habit of playing this game whenever you read a newspaper. One day you may spot a golden opportunity for your organisation that all competitors miss.

5 (a) Some sources you may have identified include: women's magazines and specialist craft/needlecraft magazines; craft suppliers' and guilds' Internet sites; and personal contacts (including colleagues and customers).

(b) (i)

	Thread	**Kits**	**Frames**	**Patterns**	**Accessories**	**Profit**
Loshini	40 × 2	20	5 × 3	25 × 2	30	**195**
Jane	15 × 2	10			5	**45**
Sarah	10 × 2	5		10 × 2	15	**60**
Tom	20 × 2	7	3 × 3			**56**
Sarina	5 × 2	10		10 × 2	10	**50**
Rafi	10 × 2	10		5 × 2	20	**60**

Jane generated the least profit £45

(ii) We have chosen a pie chart.

PRODUCT SALES (w/c: [date])

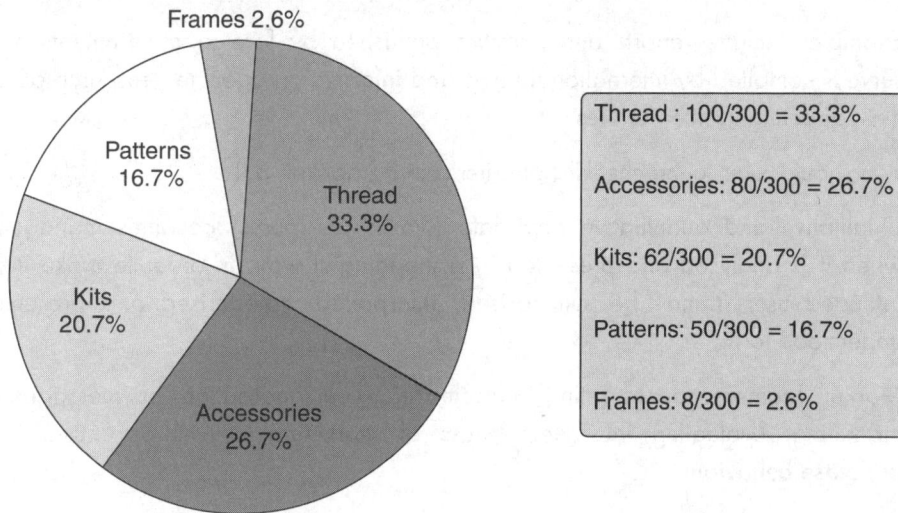

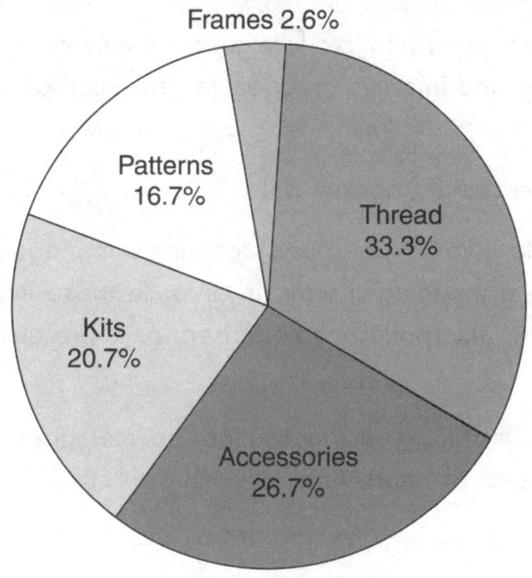

Thread : 100/300 = 33.3%

Accessories: 80/300 = 26.7%

Kits: 62/300 = 20.7%

Patterns: 50/300 = 16.7%

Frames: 8/300 = 2.6%

(iii) The staff sales chart does not take into account that Loshini is the only full-time staff member (given in the background information): the others are only part-time. Neither the staff sales chart nor the product sales chart take into account the relevant values of the products. The frames are expensive items, whereas the high-performing threads are very cheap. Overall, for example, kits may have brought in most revenue, and Tom may have performed better in terms of sales value than sales units.

(iv) Ways of improving overall team performance may include:

(1) Giving incentives on certain products.

(2) Organising product training (some staff do not sell any of certain products).

(3) Organising staff rotas to give the best coverage of product expertise at all times.

(4) Training on sales technique.

Answers to Quick Quiz

1 The right amount! Most decisions are based on incomplete information in conditions of uncertainty. Data reduces risk of the unknown, but the future is unpredictable. Gathering and analysing data costs money.

2 How customers respond (or might respond) to a given product.

3 Production data, sales volumes, management accounting statistics, financial and management reports and information on marketing, promotion and brand.

4 There are examples from every industry. Our examples include *Marketing Week* for marketers (make sure you have a copy!), *The Bookseller* for booksellers and publishers and the *Building Services Journal* for those who serve the construction industry.

5 Consumer panels give information about consumer attitudes and buying habits over a period of time.

6 You could have suggested: the homepages of government institutions, educational establishments, libraries or agencies, newsgroups or Internet search engines.

7 Examples include reports and statistics published by foreign governments and agencies, the surveys compiled by international news and information agencies, resource guides, international newspapers and Internet sites.

8 You should refer to the checklist of criteria in Paragraph 5.1.

9 Qualitative and quantitative raw data (words or figures) becomes management information when it is analysed and presented in a meaningful way. In order to make it accessible to the intended user it may be summarised, interpreted, categorised and presented in an easily understood form.

10 Market segmentation/targeting; customisation/personalisation of messages for relationship marketing; evaluating the effectiveness of marketing activity via customer feedback and purchase behaviour.

2 The Customer Database

Chapter Topic List	
1	Setting the scene
2	Data
3	Building a database
4	Maintaining the database
5	Investigating customers via the database
6	Customer relationship management
7	Segmentation
8	Using database information

Learning Outcomes

☑ Collect relevant data from a variety of secondary sources

☑ Analyse and interpret written, visual and graphic data

Syllabus References

☑ Maintain a marketing database, information collection and usage

☑ Investigate customers via the database and develop bases for segmentation

Key Concepts Introduced

- Database
- Internet
- Website
- E-commerce
- Segmentation
- Demography
- Psychography

1 Setting the scene

1.1 In Chapter 1 we outlined some of the many sources of information that can be used to support marketing decisions. In this chapter, we look at how that information can be stored and accessed, in the form of a database. It will help you to:

- Understand the structure and use of database systems
- Collect information on customers and leads for input to the database
- Appreciate how the customer database can be used for market analysis
- Use basic segmentation as a practical marketing tool
- Appreciate the scope and limitations of database usage

Key Concept

A **database** is a comprehensive, structured collection or file of data which can be accessed by different users for different applications.

1.2 In theory, a database is simply a coherent structure for the storage and use of data. It involves the centralised storage of information.

- **Common data** for all users to share
- Avoidance of **data duplication** in files kept by different users
- **Consistency** in the organisation's use of data
- **Flexibility** in the way in which shared data can be queried, analysed and formatted

1.3 Such a structure could be fulfilled by a centralised file registry or library, or a self-contained data record like a master index card file. In practice, however, large scale databases are created and stored on **computer** systems, using **database application packages**, such as Microsoft Access.

2 Data

Data storage

2.1 Computer database packages allow data to be stored in a coherent structure, in one place.

(a) **Data** are the raw components of information: names, dates, item descriptions, prices, colours, addresses.

(b) **Fields** are the labels given to types of data. Kaufeld (1996) refers to them as 'places for your data to live'. A customer database, for example, might include fields such as: title (data = Mr), first name (data = Joseph), last name (data = Bloggs), Company (data = Anon Ltd), Address, Phone Number, Fax Number, Contact Type (data = customer), interests (data = widgets).

(c) **Records** are the collections of fields relevant to one entry. (Kaufeld suggests 'all the homes on one block') So all the above data fields for a particular customer (Mr Bloggs) make up one customer record.

(d) **Tables** (or database files) are collections of records that describe similar data ('all the blocks in one neighbourhood'). All the customer records for a particular region or product may be stored in such a file.

(e) **Databases** (or catalogues) are collections of all the tables (and other formats which can be created from them) relating to a particular set of information ('a community of neighbourhoods'). So your customer database may include tables for various regions' customers, product customers and customer contacts, plus various reports and queries that you use to access different types of information.

2.2 There are two basic kinds of database.

(a) A **flat file system** lumps all the data into single table databases, like a phone directory where names, addresses, phone numbers and fax numbers are stored in the same file.

(b) A **relational database** system allows greater flexibility and storage efficiency by splitting the data up into a number of tables, which can nevertheless be linked and integrated together. For example, one table may contain customer names and addresses/contact details, while others track sales transactions by outlet or product and another, customers' payment histories. A linking field such as a customer number would allow you to interrogate all three tables, generate an integrated report on a particular customer's purchases and payments, or a list of customers who had made multiple purchases with a poor payment record.

2.3 **Flat systems** are easy to build and maintain, and are quite adequate for applications such as mailing lists, or membership databases. **Relational systems** integrate a wider range of business functions, for invoicing, accounting, inventory and marketing analysis. If your organisation already operates a relational system, learn how to use it. If you are required to set up or build a relational system, get help: use a 'wizard' or template (in the database package) or ask an expert - at least the first time.

Data manipulation

2.4 Basic features of database packages allow you to do many things.

(a) **Find particular records**, using any data item you know.

(b) **Sort records alphabetically**, numerically or by date, in ascending or descending order.

(c) **Filter records**, so that you 'pull out' and view a selection of records based on specified criteria (all addresses in a certain postcode, for example, or all purchasers of a particular product).

(d) **Interrogate records**, generating the selection of records based on a complex set of criteria, from one or more linked tables. For example, you might specify that you want all customer records where the field 'City' equals 'London' or Birmingham' AND where the field 'Product' equals 'Widget' AND where the field 'Purchase Date' is between 'Jan 2001' and 'Jan 2002'. The query would generate a table consisting of customers in London and Birmingham who purchased Widgets in 2001.

(e) **Calculate and count** data entries. For example, if you wanted to find out how many customers had purchased each product, you could run a query that asked the database to group the data by the field 'product' and then count by field 'Customer ID' or 'Last

Name'. It would count the number of customer ID numbers or names linked to each product. You could also ask to 'sum' or add up all the values in a field: total number of purchases, or total purchase value.

(f) **Format** selected data for a variety of uses such as reports, forms, mailing labels, charts and diagrams.

2.5 You will probably be working with a database that has already been created for you, using a particular software package. It is up to you to get to know how to use it and how your organisation wants its data structured and formatted.

2.6 As we proceed to talk about 'building a database' we will mainly focus on the gathering of the data, rather than database design: if you want to know more about the latter, talk to IT experts in your organisation, or borrow the handbook to one of the popular database packages.

Action Programme 1

Find out what type(s) of database your organisation (or college) uses, and for what applications. If possible, get access to the database and browse through the index, directory or switchboard to see what databases/catalogues contain what database files or tables, queries, reports and forms, with what fields.

3 Building a database

Feasibility study: is it worth having a database?

3.1 The survey *Impact of Computerised Sales And Marketing Systems In The UK* (by the Hewson Consulting Group, cited in Jay, 1998) found significant agreement that effective marketing databases will be the key to successful marketing in future. However, it also found that ineffective databases are a drain on resources and morale. There are several barriers to the effective use of database systems in sales and marketing.

- **Lack of motivation** by key players
- **The high costs** of the system (discussed further below)
- The **limitations** of software/hardware capability
- **Resistance to change**, coupled with lack of confidence in the perceived benefits
- Problems with **internal communications** and complex implementation issues
- The **lack of business experience** among IT specialists

3.2 The **direct** costs of setting up a sales and marketing system (the cost of hardware and software) only amount to about 45% of the total cost. **Indirect** and often hidden costs include consultancy, the time spent training staff, loss of selling time while training plus on-going costs of maintenance.

3.3 However, there are potential benefits of the system.

(a) Increased **sales and/or market share** (due to enhanced lead follow-up, cross-selling, customer contact and so on)

(b) Increased **customer retention** (though better targeting and contact)

(c) Better **use of resources** and cost reduction (through targeting, less duplication of information-handling)

(d) Better **decision-making** (through quality management information)

(e) **Competitive advantage**

Benefits of a central customer database

3.4 These can be represented diagrammatically as follows: Figure 2.1.

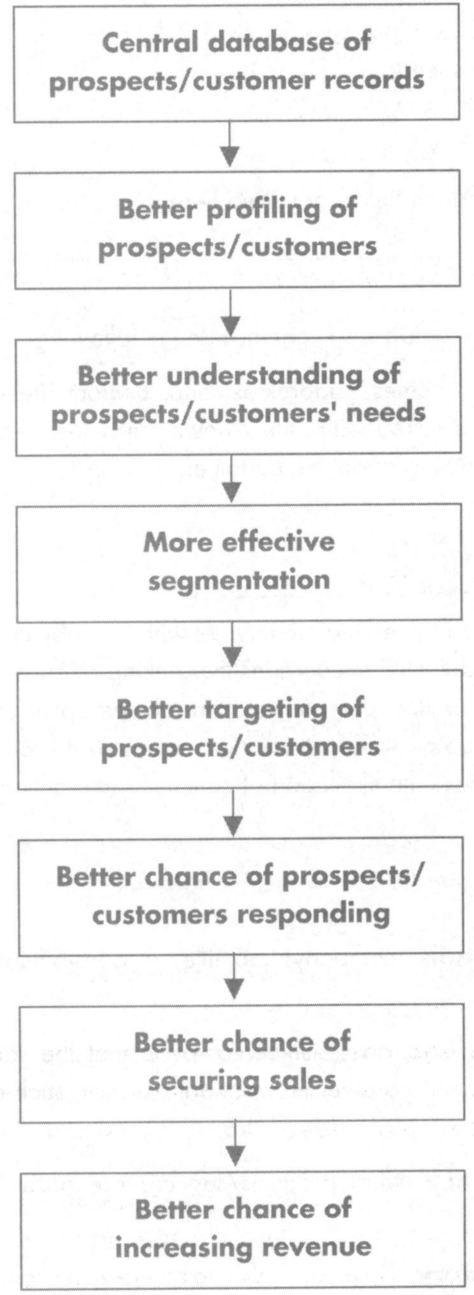

Figure 2.1: Benefits of a central customer database

A customer database

Action Programme 2

Can your organisation's database answer the following questions?

- Who are our customers?
- What do they want?
- Where do they come from?
- Why do they come to us?
- What do they buy?
- How much do they spend?
- When do they buy?
- How often do they buy

Maybe it has other information fields, not listed here.

3.5 A comprehensive customer database might include the following.

(a) **Customer titles**, names, addresses and contact (telephone, fax, e-mail). E-mail addresses should be linked with other known attributes, because an email address on its own usually says nothing about the customer.

Marketing at Work

It is important to use data obtained via the Internet with the subject's full knowledge and permission. 'Permission marketing' encourages the seeking of an individual's consent before he or she is marketed to. In practice, companies often provide opt-in or opt-out boxes for the customer to tick. Backing up personal information requests with some kind of incentive (eg entry in a prize draw) will increase the likelihood of continued interaction and permission from the customer.

(b) **Professional details** (company; job title; responsibilities), especially for business-to-business marketing

(c) **Personal details** (sex, age, number of people at the same address, spouse's name, children, interests, and any other relevant data known, such as newspapers read, journals subscribed to)

(d) **Transaction history** (what products/services are ordered, how often, how much is spent)

(e) **Call/contact history** (sales or after-sales service calls made, complaints/queries received, meetings at shows/exhibitions)

(f) **Credit/payment history** (credit rating, amounts outstanding, aged debts)

(g) **Current transaction/details** (items currently on order, dates, prices, delivery arrangements)

(h) **Special account details** (membership number, loyalty or incentive points earned, discount awarded), where customer loyalty or incentive schemes or valued customer cards are used.

3.6 Each of these items will be in a separate field (and, in a relational database, perhaps separate tables) in your database. When designing new tables, the following procedure is recommended.

(a) List and briefly describe the reports, lists, mailing labels and whatever else you want to come out of the system. **What will you want to use the data for** and in what form will it be most useful? What combinations of information will you want to pull together? How will you want them sorted?

(b) **Sketch out samples** of the above reports, lists, mailing labels and so on. This will give you an idea of the format and content of the fields you will require in your table(s).

(c) **List and name all the fields you will require**. If you are designing the table from scratch, you will also need to specify the type of field (date, numbers, text and so on) and other technical details. Include a 'primary key', a field in which the data will be unique for each record (such as a customer ID number or product code) for indexing purposes.

(d) **Organise the fields** into one or more tables. For a flat system, pick a logical order that will make data input easy. For a relational database, group together data that naturally goes together (for example, name, address, telephone, fax, (e-mail for a contacts or mailing list table) and link together tables that are related (as most of the tables suggested in paragraph 3.5 might be).

Where does customer information come from?

3.7 Customer information may come from the following sources.

(a) **EPOS** (Electronic Point of Sale) recorded data on all sales transactions and orders. Transaction details may be input manually, or by bar code reader or 'swiping' of magnetic-stripped customer cards.

(b) **Transaction documents**, such as order forms, invoices, credit applications and customer account records.

(c) **Details gathered by telemarketers** (incoming and outgoing calls) and salespersons on every contact with customers.

(d) Details provided by customers on customer care, feedback and market research **forms/questionnaires**.

(e) Details provided by customers on on-pack coupons, entry forms or phone lines for **promotional competitions**, prize draws or incentives.

(f) Details provided by customers when applying for credit accounts, discount schemes, valued customer cards and other **loyalty and incentive schemes**.

(g) Details provided by customers who visit **shows and exhibitions**.

Websites as sources of data

3.8 A very important source of customer information is the company website on the Internet. Few major brands do not have their own web pages. Most advertisements in other media (press, TV or radio) direct consumers to web addresses for further information or online ordering.

Key Concepts

Internet A network of computer networks stretching across the world, linking computers of different types.

Website A coherent document readable by a web browser, containing simple text or complex hypermedia presentations.

E-commerce The use of the Internet for commercial transactions.

Dibb *et al.* (2001)

Exam Tip

A question on the Pilot Paper asks about the information that a company might need about its website visitors, and how such information may be used to build the business. Here is a brief answer.

Questions to ask web visitors	Possible uses
1. Why did you visit our site?	Understanding reasons for visits will help in improving services/generating traffic
2. What information did you look for?	Are we providing the information that we should?
3. Did you find it?	Customer satisfaction – is the site user friendly and comprehensive?
4. Which pages did you visit?	Demonstrating 'hit' rates to potential advertisers
5. Did you find the information relevant?	Customer satisfaction/likelihood of repeat visits
6. Was the site easy to use?	As above
7. What did you particularly like or dislike?	Suggestions for future development of the site
8. What is your area of business?	Market research into customer profiles
9. Where are you based?	Potential for expansion may be indicated
10. Would you be interested in receiving regular updates?	Promotion of new services and events

3.9 'Offline' mail order companies have been selling lists of customer data for years, and online companies should be able to collect the same types of information. People have become used to giving various geographical and lifestyle details on websites as they browse around, but these same people may never have completed a more traditional paper-based questionnaire. A trail of the **'clicks'** performed by a visitor to a site will show what pages they are most interested in.

3.10 The growing popularity of **e-mail marketing** is creating a demand for lists of e-mail addresses.

Marketing at Work

AutoTrader has a second-hand car-search website which asks users to enter their name, postal and e-mail addresses before it will look for a car to match their specifications. This enables geographic profiling, not possible on e-mail addresses alone.

3.11 As we have already indicated, **online data collection** is no different to offline data collection. The same rules of data protection apply. Users of websites must be given the chance to opt out.

Marketing at Work

'Give an individual something of real value in exchange for their data, be upfront about what you intend to do with it and they will let you into all sorts of personal secrets . . . The VirginConnect WebPlayer allows users to surf the Net and use e-mail. To receive the device customers must log onto a website and complete a questionnaire covering topics such as shopping preferences, music and entertainment interests and web usage . . . And in accepting the machine, customers are also agreeing to receive targeted banner ads and emails from Virgin and other marketers.'

Marketing Business, June 2000

3.12 What follows is specimen **questionnaire for online data collection** by a retail company.

'Shopping Experience' Evaluation

1. How often do you visit one of our stores?
   - ❍ Every day
   - ❍ Several times a week
   - ❍ About once a week
   - ❍ Several times a month
   - ❍ About once a month
   - ❍ Less than once a month

2. How would you rate our stores in the following areas?

	Excellent	Very Good	Good	Fair	Poor
Ease of access	❍	❍	❍	❍	❍
Quality of merchandise	❍	❍	❍	❍	❍
Availability and helpfulness of staff	❍	❍	❍	❍	❍
General attractiveness	❍	❍	❍	❍	❍

3. How likely are you to:

	Very Likely	Somewhat Likely	Somewhat Unlikely	Not at all Likely
Return to our stores?	❍	❍	❍	❍
Recommend our stores?	❍	❍	❍	❍

4. What do you like most about our stores?

5. What do you like least about our stores?

6. What features would you like added or changes you would like made to our stores?

Thank you for taking the time to give us your feedback.

Contacts databases

3.13 As well as a database of existing customers, the organisation may wish to build a database of sales leads, prospects and other contacts as a **mailing list**.

- **Contact titles**, names, addresses and contact (telephone, fax, (e-mail) details
- **Professional details** (company name, address, contact details, job title) in a business-to-business context
- **Contact 'type'** - exhibition visitor, referral, engineer, 'cold' contact, bought-in list
- **Contact's interests** in a particular product/service area
- **Contact history** (whether called/mailed, whether responded, whether followed up, whether purchased)

Where does contact information come from?

3.14 Contact or mailing list information may come from various sources.

(a) **Recommendation** and referrals from customers (whether spontaneous or through 'introduce a friend' schemes or referral requests)

(b) **Enquiries** for further information, in response to advertising, promotion and PR (via telephone, mail, 'hits' on website)

(c) Enquiries compiled at **exhibitions** and fairs

(d) **Leads** brought back by salespeople, not yet converted into sales

(e) Details provided in response to **promotional competitions**, prize draws and incentives. Every 'send in for your chance to win' or 'send in to claim your discount' coupon should be a vehicle of capture of mailing list data: this will often be their primary purpose

(f) Relevant **secondary sources**

(g) Specialist **mailing list suppliers**. Lists can be hired or bought from commercial list owners: they can often be appropriately segmented (we discuss this further below)

(h) The **in-house database** of non-competing organisations in the same market, who may be willing to swap or rent lists. If you buy anything by post, you end up on a mailing database, and are often given the opportunity to receive, or decline to receive, information on related products.

Action Programme 3

What secondary sources might provide relevant names, addresses, company and contact details?

3.15 It may not be worthwhile building an in-house contact list, or relying on it to reach a wide range of potential customers. Most direct marketing is based on lists rented from **list brokers**, who generate mailing labels or conduct mailings themselves. There is a large catalogue of lists varying from specific magazine subscribers, to consumer and business lists across all market sectors. The cost of renting a list ranges from £40 per thousand to hundreds of pounds per thousand, with an additional charge for any selection criteria you require when they generate the list (geographical area, age) and any handling they undertake on your behalf.

3.16 List brokers can be found in the Direct Marketing Press or via the Direct Marketing Association.

4 Maintaining the database

4.1 If the customer database is linked to **online transaction processing** (for example, via EPOS), purchase data will automatically be updated with each new transaction. However, a typical contacts database will have to be regularly and systematically **maintained**.

(a) Contacts who become customers should be transferred to the customer database.

(b) Any up-dated or altered information should be entered in the database such as change of address.

(c) Additional information obtained from contacts should be added to the relevant records.

(d) New names and records should periodically be added to the database, and names which have received no response should be deleted.

(e) Requests from customers or members of the public to have their details erased from the database should be honoured.

(f) New fields can be added to the database design as new types of information become available.

(g) Remember that in **business-to-business** markets, contacts often move to different companies. This represents a **networking opportunity**.

5 Investigating customers via the database

5.1 There are a number of ways in which a database can be interrogated to derive information for marketing planning.

Identifying the most profitable customers

5.2 The Italian economist Vilfredo Pareto was the first to observe that in human affairs, 20% of the events result in 80% of the outcomes. This has become known as Pareto's law, or the 80/20 principle. It shows up quite often in marketing. In general a small number of existing customers are 'heavy users' of a product or service and generate a high proportion of sales revenue.

5.3 A customer database which allows purchase frequency and value per customer to be calculated indicates to the marketer who the potential heavy users are, and therefore where the promotional budget can most profitably be spent.

Action Programme 4

Suggest three strategies for getting revenue from frequent or loyal users of your products.

Identifying buying trends

5.4 By tracking purchases per customer (or customer group, as we will discuss below), you may be able to identify certain customer types.

(a) **Loyal repeat customers** who cost less to retain than new customers cost to find and attract.

(b) '**Backsliding**' or lost customers, who have reduced or ceased the frequency or volume of their purchases.

(c) **Seasonal** or local purchase patterns may be identified.

(d) Purchase patterns are often in response to **promotional campaigns**. Increased sales volume or frequency following promotions is an important measurement of their effectiveness.

Identifying marketing opportunities

5.5 More detailed information (where available) on customer likes and dislikes, complaints, feedback and lifestyle values may offer useful information and guidance.

- **Product** improvement
- **Customer care** and quality programmes
- New **product development**
- **Decision-making** across the marketing mix

5.6 Simple data fields such as 'contact type' will help to evaluate how contact is made with customers, of what types and in what numbers. Business leads may be generated most often by trade conferences and exhibitions. Light or one-off users will be attracted by promotional competitions and incentives, and loyal customers by personal contact through representatives.

5.7 Customers can be investigated using any data field included in the database. How many are on e-mail or the Internet? How many have spouses or children? These parameters allow the marketer to **segment** the customer base for marketing purposes.

6 Customer relationship management

6.1 Customer Relationship Management (CRM) is big business, driven by Internet and database developments. It is covered in detail in the *Customer Communications* module. The following summary (Figure 2.2) should refresh your memory:

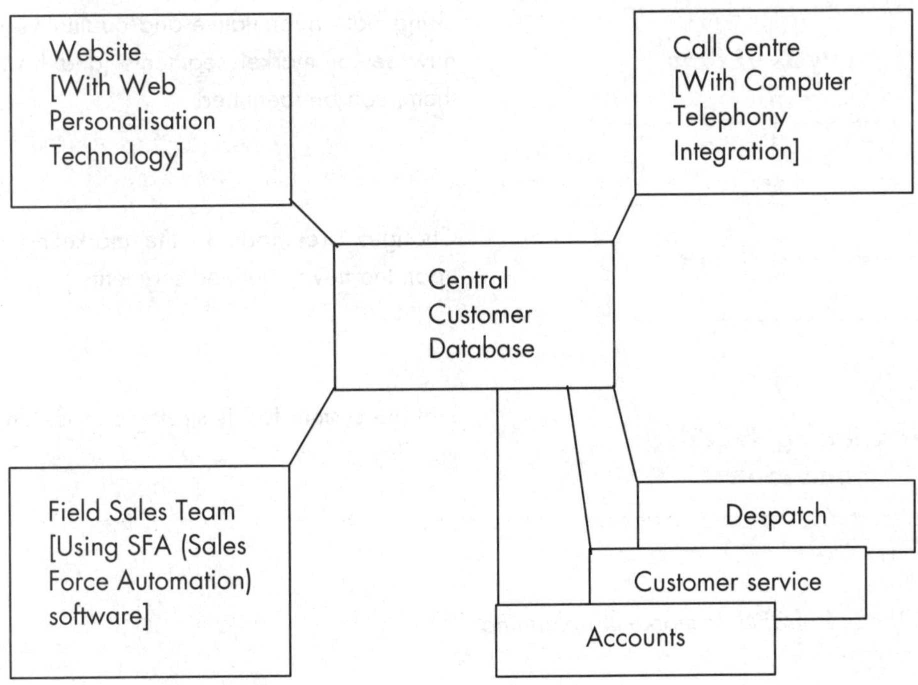

Figure 2.2: CRM systems

6.2 CRM should be regarded first and foremost as an **integrated business process** which integrates individual customer data from multiple sources.

Exam Tip

This exam always contains an ICT-themed question, often in the form: 'What role could ICT play in ...?' or 'How can the firm make best use of ICT to ...?'. There are a couple of things to note with such questions.

(a) ICT includes IT (computers, databases) and CT (networks, phones): ICT applications therefore embrace a wide range of applications – not just the Internet. In the context of CRM, ICT includes sales force automation, computer-telephony integration, databases and so on.

(b) Consider carefully what ICT is being asked to do. If it is to 'build the business' or 'market the business', the scope is wide: you'll need to think about communications, promotions, advertising (e-mail, SMS, web) and so on. In June 2003, you were asked to discuss how ICT could be used 'to build the loyalty' of radio listeners: this is more of a relationship marketing/CRM question.

A CRM system contains four distinct sub-processes: Figure 2.3.

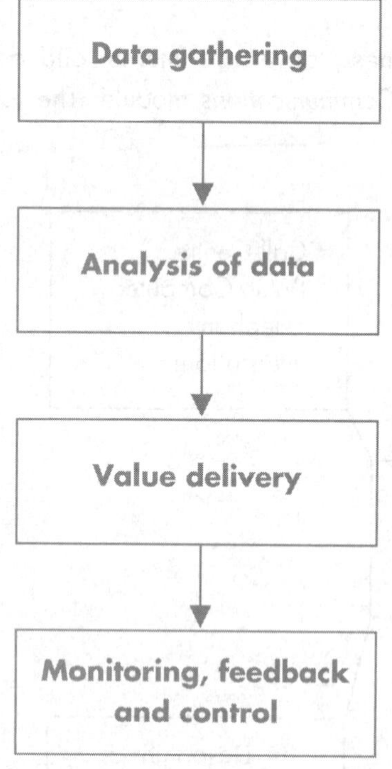

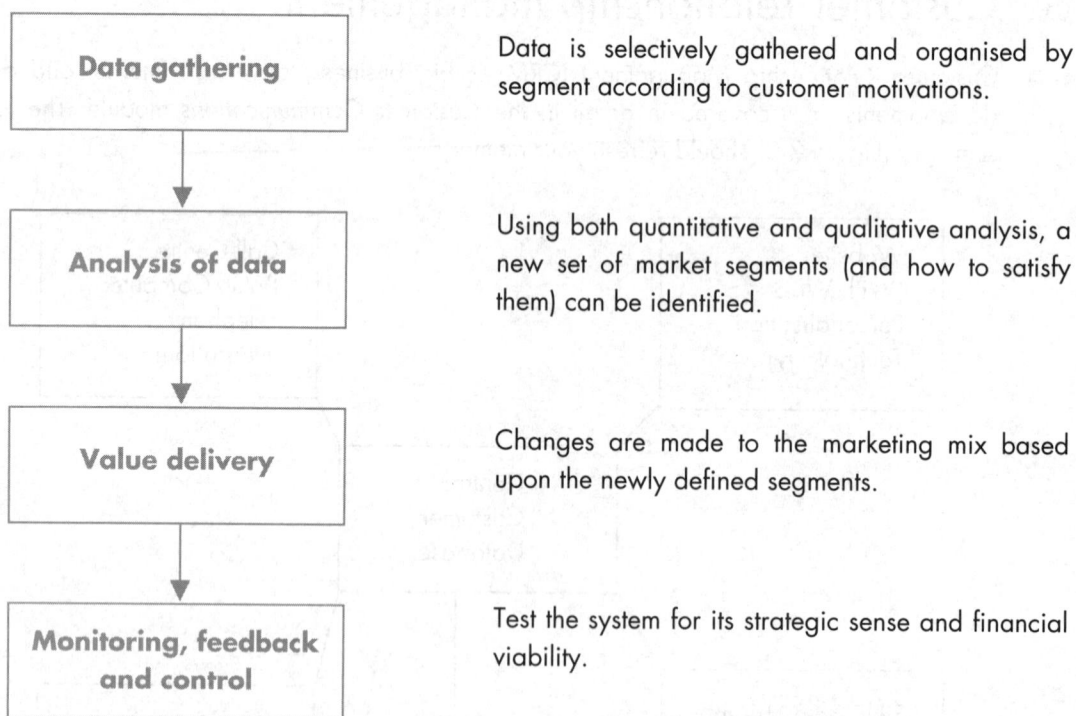

Stage	Description
Data gathering	Data is selectively gathered and organised by segment according to customer motivations.
Analysis of data	Using both quantitative and qualitative analysis, a new set of market segments (and how to satisfy them) can be identified.
Value delivery	Changes are made to the marketing mix based upon the newly defined segments.
Monitoring, feedback and control	Test the system for its strategic sense and financial viability.

Figure 2.3: The use of CRM in marketing planning

Marketing at Work

Niewierski (2004) offers the following advice on how to make best use of a customer database (through postcard marketing).

'It's a fact that your customers are your best leads – the people most likely to purchase your products and services are the ones who have paid for them before and been happy with the results. Profit is not just about acquiring new customers, it is about fostering the relationships you already have. And it is also a fact that it costs far less money to retain customers by building loyalty than it does to go out and acquire new ones. ... There are a few rules to bear in mind when marketing to contacts in your company database.

'Rule#1 Collect all of your customers' information

It sounds like a no-brainer but you would be surprised. The more information that you can gather on your customers, the more you will be able to select and target individual customers with relevant specials. ...

'Rule#2 Don't treat your customers like prospects

When you collect the information in your database, make sure that you differentiate between people who have placed an order in the past and people who have not. Customers want to feel like you are paying attention to them and so when they have placed a few orders with you they will not appreciate a '10% discount for first-time buyers' postcard.

'Rule#3 Don't let your designs get stagnant

'When you are mailing to databases of people that you have never spoken to before it is acceptable to send them the same postcard multiple times. This strategy can help to increase recognition and eventually increase your response rate. However, when dealing with existing customers, you need to mix things up a bit. Your mailings should be attention grabbing and informative to stand out in their mail.'

Niewierski (2004)

6.3 The key point about CRM is that it enables the use of customer data:

(a) **To enhance customers' experience of doing business with the firm**. Sales force automation, linked to central databases, for example, enables sales people to give customers accurate up-to-date product/price/availability/delivery information. Computer-telephony integration (CTI) allows telephone operators to address customers by name and to have account details to hand.

(b) **To enhance relationship with the customer**, fostering customer loyalty. Customisation and (increasingly) personalisation of marketing messages and offers makes the customer feel known and valued – as well as increasing the likelihood of purchase (because of effective targeting).

(c) **To target the organisation's offerings** on the basis of actual buying patterns and preferences of individual consumers – not just segment characteristics (Peppers and Rodgers, 1993; Postma, 1999).

(d) **To capture increasingly detailed and up-to-date customer information**, for more sophisticated uses. Starting with name and address details (allowing direct marketing), the organisation may through subsequent contacts elicit information about buying or media preferences (allowing targeted offers) to more personal details (such as birthdays, for 'special' relationship-building messages).

(e) **To enable all of the above as efficiently and cost-effectively as possible**, by integrating data storage and interrogation.

6.4 Marketers need to evaluate results to examine what went right (and wrong), so that the information can be used for future activities. Often customer feedback is gathered, but not acted upon.

Action Programme 5

It has been suggested that CRM fails to meet customer expectations 55-70% of the time. Why might this be?

6.5 We also look at customer relationship management in the context of **'e-relationships'** in Chapter 6.

7 Segmentation

Key Concept

Segmentation is the process by which consumers are grouped together according to identifiable characteristics that are relevant to their buying behaviour, thereby allowing marketers more effectively to target one or more segments of the market with the marketing mix.

Bases for segmentation

7.1 Clearly, there are very many possible characteristics of buyers which could be used to segment markets, because people and groups are complex entities. Whatever characteristic or criteria is selected as a basis for segmentation, the resulting market segment needs to have certain attributes.

(a) **Measurable**. Information must exist or be obtainable (cost effectively) about the defining characteristic. The location and age of customers, for example, is more readily identified than their personality traits.

(b) **Accessible**. The organisation must be able to reach the defined segment by marketing methods. No mailing list or telesales strategy would be available, for example, for blue-eyed people, but wearers of tinted contact lenses could effectively be reached via opticians and chemists.

(c) **Substantial**. The defined segment should be large enough to be worth separate consideration and targeting of marketing effort, not just in size, but in potential profitability. Old people in the lowest socio-economic bracket may not be as profitable as the group of 18 year olds in the same bracket, who are likely to have a larger spending span and potential upward mobility.

(d) **Homogeneity**. The defined group should act broadly as a group for marketing purposes! A segment is not really a segment if individuals and groups within it react very differently to price changes or promotional messages. Segmentation by age or gender alone might cover a wide range of buying patterns, depending on spending points, lifestyle, education and ethnic origin.

(MASH might be a useful acronym to use as a checklist).

7.2 Effective segmentation offers a number of benefits for consumer and marketer alike.

- The organisation is in a better position to **spot and service customer needs** and wants
- The **marketing mix can be adjusted** to the particular requirements of each segment
- Consumers should benefit from **increased choice**, and more closely tailored products
- Targeted marketing should lead to **lower cost of sales**

7.3 Some of the main variables on which market segmentation is carried out at the strategic level include the following.

(a) **Demographics**. Statistics on the age, gender, marital status, family and household size, income, occupation and education of a population. These data are quantifiable, accessible and relatively cost-effective, and can readily identify potential markets and trends such as shifts in age and income distributions. In practice, demographic segmentation is carried out on the basis of age, gender and income/occupation, or combinations, such as 'the affluent elderly', 'young adult males' or 'yuppies'.

Key Concept

Demography is the study of measurable statistics of a population, such as age, gender, family structure, income, occupation and education.

(b) **Social status and social class**. In the UK, there is a popular stratification into 'working class', 'middle class' and 'upper class', but objective measures of social class consist mainly of socio-economic variables such as income, education and occupation and residential area. There are various classifications, of which the JICNAR Social Grades (A, B, C1, C2, D, E) are most commonly used for marketing purposes.

(c) **Family life cycle (FLC)**, which reflects the structure, membership and pre-occupations of the family over time, which correlates to changes in income, expenditure and consumption priorities. Developmental stages include batchelorhood, newly-married couple, parenthood ('full nest'), post-parenthood ('empty nest') and solitary survivor. In addition, there are now models to take account of later marriages, childless couples, single parents and non-family households.

(d) **Psychographics**. Lifestyle or AIO (Activities, Interests and Opinions) analysis. Psychographic segmentation classifies people according to their values, attitudes and motivations. 'Lifestyle' refers to distinctive choices about how to live that are made by communities. 'Upwardly mobile' and 'security and status seeking' are two examples of lifestyle categories.

Key Concept

Psychography is a form of consumer research which builds up psychological or psycho-social profiles of consumers or consumer groups.

Databases for segmentation

7.4 A customer database may be sophisticated enough, and sufficiently subject to detailed analysis, to contain socio-economic, geo-demographic or other classifications.

(a) Residential post-codes, for example, can be cross-referenced to ACORN targeting classifications of residential areas by affluence or demographic composition.

(b) Occupational or job title details may be cross-referenced to JICNAR social groupings, such as ABC1.

(c) Age, spouse and children details may be cross-referenced to family life cycle stages.

7.5 However, more basic segmentation is available through the simplest database, and may be equally valuable as an everyday marketing tool. Common bases for segmentation which can be built into database fields include the following.

(a) **Gender**. Products generally targeted by gender include cosmetics, clothing, cars and even financial services.

(b) **Age**. The 'youth market' has emerged strongly as a distinct target group for clothes, media, music and even banks. Other products are targeted at the 'grey' spending power of older people such as special health insurance.

(c) **Geographic location**. Despite sophisticated classifications of geo-demographics, the simple location of customers can be of great practical use to the database marketers such as when advertising the launch of a retail outlet in a particular area, or selecting cinemas, outdoor party sites and local radio stations.

(d) **Socio-economic group**. The JICNAR grade is useful information because it is used throughout the marketing industry by market researchers and the media.

Social Grade	*Description of occupation*	*Example*
A	Higher managerial and professional	Company director
B	Lower managerial and supervisory	Middle manager
C1	Non-manual	Clerk
C2	Skilled manual	Electrician
D	Semi- and un-skilled manual	Labourer
E	Those receiving no income from employment and casual workers	Unemployed

(e) **Interests and previous purchases**. This is one of the most obvious bases for segmentation, and one of the most practical uses of the database. If enquirers have asked about particular products or services, or customers have purchased one or more products in a related group, then they can be segmented by product, for the purposes of information on promotions, new products in the same line or product improvements.

(f) **Contact type and source**. If the database includes a field corresponding to 'where did you hear about us/our product?', customers can also be segmented as consumers of particular media (for the purposes of advertising planning) or frequenters of particular retail outlets (for the purpose of in-store sales promotions).

(g) **Purchase volume, frequency and loyalty**, eg heavy and light users.

Action Programme 6

The Needle Works

From the background information you have been able to glean as the new Marketing Co-ordinator of the Needle Works answer the following questions.

(a) How might the company usefully segment its customer database, and for what purposes?
(b) How might you improve the data-gathering process in order to achieve this?

Segmenting business databases

7.6 While industrial markets are usually smaller, more easily identified and more easily reached than consumer markets (via trade media, conferences, shows and directories) they can still usefully be segmented.

(a) **By location**

(b) **By size**, giving a broad indication of the need for products and services such as management training or human resource consultancy

(c) **Usage rates**: supply planning will be carried out on the basis of heavy, medium or light consumption of raw materials and parts

(d) **Trade/industry classification**: manufacturing, media, finance and publishing which may use different products and services, or use them in different ways, and will be targeted through different media

(e) **By product use**: the needs of an organisation for cars for use by its sales force may be different to those of an organisation hiring cars out to the public

8 Using database information

8.1 We have already mentioned many of the ways in which database information can be used. The following is a summary of the main ones.

(a) Uses of **direct mail**

- To maintain customer contact between (or instead of) sales calls
- To generate leads and 'warmed' prospects for sales calls

- To promote and/or sell products and services direct to customers
- To distribute product or service information

(b) **Transaction processing**. Databases can be linked to programmes which generate order confirmations, despatch notes, invoices, statements and receipts.

(c) **Marketing research and planning**. The database can be used to send out market surveys, and may itself be investigated to show purchasing patterns and trends.

(d) **Contacts planning**. The database can indicate what customers need to be contacted or given incentives to maintain their level of purchase and commitment. A separate database may similarly be used to track contacts at conferences and trade shows and invitation lists to marketing events.

(e) **Product development and improvement**. Product purchases can be tracked through the product life cycle, and weaknesses and opportunities identified from records of customer feedback, complaints or warranty/guarantee claims.

Data security and controls

8.2 Most customers, and consumers in general, are by now aware that when they supply their names and addresses they will be used in various ways. Most would accept that the details will be kept on file or in a mailing list, and many would expect to be sent information about goods and services by the same company. They may, however, be irritated to find that their details have been passed on to other companies, or that they are on a list for frequent or wide-ranging promotional information.

8.3 Many direct marketers now state clearly, when inviting customers or respondents to provide name and address details, the use to which the details will be put. It is also common to offer an opt-out from details being re-used or passed on.

8.4 **Legislation** and regulation exists to protect consumers from misuse of personal details held on computer, unsolicited mail and invasion of privacy.

(a) There are now stringent trading practices and regulations in the direct mail industry, administered by the Direct Mail Services Standards Board (DMSSB) and Mail Order Protection Scheme (for display advertisements in national newspapers that ask for money in advance).

(b) **The Mailing Preference Service** allows customers to state whether they would - and more often, would not - be willing to receive direct mail on a range of specific areas.

(c) **The Data Protection Acts 1984 and 1998** provide that data users (organisations or individuals who control the contents of files of personal data and the use of personal data) must register with the Data Protection Registrar. They must limit their use of personal data (defined as any information about an identifiable living individual) to the uses registered.

Data Protection Principles

Personal data held by data users

(1) The information to be contained in personal data shall be obtained, and personal data shall be processed, **fairly and lawfully**. Processing means amending, adding to, deleting or rearranging the data, or extracting the information that forms the data (eg printing out).

(2) Personal data shall be held only for one or more **specified** (registered) and lawful purposes.

(3) Personal data held for any purpose or purposes shall not be used or disclosed in any manner **incompatible** with that purpose or those purposes.

(4) Personal data held for any purpose or purposes shall be **adequate, relevant and not excessive** in relation to that purpose or those purposes.

(5) Personal data shall be **accurate** and, where necessary, kept up-to-date. 'Accurate' means correct and not misleading as to any matter of fact.

(6) Personal data held for any purpose or purposes shall not be kept for longer than is necessary for that purpose or those purposes. Data users should therefore review their personal data regularly, and delete any data which no longer serve a purpose.

(7) An individual shall be entitled at reasonable intervals, and without undue delay or expense:

- (i) to be **informed** by any data user whether he/she holds personal data of which that individual is the subject
- (ii) to **access** to any such data held by a data user
- (iii) where appropriate, to have such data **corrected or erased**

Action Programme 7

Write to the Mailing Preference Service and ask to be put on the mailing list for business services, whatever product or industry sector you work in, or anything else that interests you. See how many direct marketers there are out there - and how accurate their mailing list labels and general targeting are!

Chapter Roundup

- A **database** is a comprehensive structured collection of data (usually computerised) which can be accessed by different users for different applications.
- Databases allow for the **collection and storage of data**, and also for **interaction** with data through various forms of interrogation, calculation and report formatting.
- The **feasibility** and **cost-effectiveness** of building an in-house database should be studied. For direct marketing purposes, alternatives include rented or bought-in mailing lists.
- **Customer and contact details** can be sourced from a wide range of transactions, feedback mechanisms, promotional mechanisms and secondary sources. All data must be periodically reviewed for **accuracy** and **up-to-dateness**.
- Customer databases can be **interrogated** to identify profitable customers, buying patterns and trends, marketing opportunities and market segments.
- **Segmentation** can be done on any basis that is measurable, accessible, substantial and homogenous. The four main **strategic bases for segmentation** are demographics, psychographics, social class and family life cycle, but simpler bases such as gender, age, location, purchases, contact source and purchase volume/frequency/loyalty may be used through database queries.
- **Database information** can be used for a variety of sales support, direct marketing, promotion management and marketing analysis applications. However, certain **constraints on data use** exist to protect the individual, including the Data Protection Acts and Mailing Preference Service.

Quick Quiz

1 What are (a) fields, (b) records and (c) tables in database terminology?

2 How might (a) customer and (b) contact information be gathered?

3 What factors make a good external mailing list?

4 What should be done with 'undeliverable' mailshot items?

5 How does the '80/20 rule' apply to marketing; and how can the database be used to capitalise on it?

6 What are (a) demographics and (b) psychographics?

7 List the JICNAR scale of social grades.

8 What are the main purposes of direct mail?

Now try Question 2 in the Question Bank

Action Programme Review

1 If you can't get access to a database at work, try the local library, where you may find that the 'index card' system has been computerised as a database. Or use an Internet search engine or browser to interrogate some online databases. This is not really something you can learn from books - have a go!

2 Your own research.

3 Some suggestions: The Yellow Pages, Business Pages, membership lists of clubs and trade/professional organisations, catalogues of attendees at conferences, exhibitions and trade shows, subscription lists for relevant journals, directories of directories and other industry 'who's who' lists, advertiser contact details in various media.

4 (a) Encouraging them to buy more on each purchase occasion, (for example, by offering a suite of related products and services)

(b) Encouraging them to buy more frequently (for example, by offering incentive discounts)

(c) Encouraging them to stay with you longer, or customer retention (for example, by offering loyalty incentives like frequent flyer programmes)

5 There may be poor understanding of customers, such as a failure to realise that customer needs have changed. CRM programmes need to ensure that the right customers are targeted with the right information and promotions.

6 (a) The customer base could usefully be segmented along the lines of the market as a whole, targeting groups such as women 50+, middle-eastern and central European customers (heavy users, loyal), 18-25 year olds in fashion and design courses (a new market to be developed), and age care therapy institutions (long-term customers). These should also be segmented according to whether they are local to the store and are therefore potential regular *retail* customers, and those more distant and even international (eg tourists) as future mail order prospects. Unless some homogeneity can be found in the male customers, they may not be a useful or accessible segment to target. The EPOS system should be investigated to see whether there are distinct segments or buying patterns for particular styles of needlework, and for various product lines: yarns, patterns, accessories, frames or services. The regular customer groups could be targeted with additional purchase incentives or loyalty/reward schemes (perhaps a Needle Works Club Card?). The new youth market should be accessible via colleges, and targeted with a more youthful design-focused message. This information will also help to select advertising media for new products, such as the proposed knitting supply shop and education centre.

(b) No current database information directly taps into the above segments, especially interest in knitting or classes. Launch information on these areas can be segmented only by locality, since they will require personal presence at the showroom.

The EPOS system gives good quality information about sales per product per week and where customers place orders, (eg for frames or framing services) per customer. Most customer data is captured via the Visitors' Book. It would be impractical for sales staff to input customer data for every non-account, over the counter transaction, so it is recommended that the Visitors' Book system be kept - but upgraded to collect better quality information.

Instead of an open 'comments' section, it should have columns that customers can tick to express interest and request more information on particular crafts, products and most importantly on knitting supplies and educational activities/classes. These interests could be added as a field to the customer database ('interests') to trigger selective mailings to interested customers. Gender information could also be derived from the titles and names supplied, and added to the database. (Age and ethnic origin are more personal to ask about, and may have to be part of a more general 'targeting' of promotions and advertising, based on staff's general 'feel' for the market.)

7 You can always get your name taken off again later if your mailbox won't stand the strain!

Answers to Quick Quiz

1 (a) Fields: labels given to different types of data
  (b) Records: collections of fields relevant to one entry
  (c) Tables: collections of records that describe similar data

2 (a) Electronic point of sale, transaction documents, telemarketers and salespeople, customer care feedback and market research.

  (b) Enquiries through a website, mailshot, exhibitions or tradefairs, recommendations from other customers, relevant secondary data or swapped, rented or bought-in lists.

3 A good external mailing list comprises targeted leads with full personal information – name, contact details, position (for business-to-business customers) and their history of contact with your company : everything in other words to help you demonstrate their (potential) custom is valued and that that you are efficient and pleasant to deal with.

4 This is valuable information in keeping your customer database up-to-date.

5 The 18/20 Principle (or Pareto's Law) is that 20% of events result in 80% of outcomes. In marketing terms, a high proportion of revenue is received through a relatively small base of customers.

6 (a) The study of measurable statistics of a population.

  (b) A form of customer research which builds up a psychological or psycho-social profile of consumer groups.

7 JICNAR scale: A – higher managerial and professional; B – Lower managerial and supervisory; C1 – Non-manual; C2 – Skilled manual; D – Semi-skilled and unskilled manual; E – Those receiving no income from employment/casual workers.

8 There are four main functions for direct mail.

- To maintain customer contact between (or instead of) sales calls
- To generate leads and warm prospects for sales calls
- To promote and/or sell products and services direct to customers
- To distribute product or service information

Basic Research Techniques

3

Chapter Topic List	
1	Setting the scene
2	Research planning
3	Sampling
4	Questionnaires
5	Qualitative research
6	Other research techniques
7	Gathering information across borders

Learning Outcome

☑ Collect relevant data from a variety of information sources

Syllabus References

☑ Explain information gathering techniques available

☑ Gather information across borders

Key Concept Introduced

- Population

1 Setting the scene

1.1 In Chapter 1, we discussed the various sources of information available to organisations when researching customers, market opportunities, competitor activity, the marketing environment and consumer behaviour. We looked in detail at **secondary sources** of information, used in **desk research**. In Chapter 2, we went on to focus on customer research via the database.

1.2 In this chapter, we look at how **primary sources** of information can be tapped via **field research**.

1.3 Remember that **marketing research** aims to collect, analyse, interpret and use data on the marketing organisation and its environment, while **market research** is a narrower activity focusing on specific markets.

1.4 On completion of this chapter, you should be able to:

- Plan a basic marketing research project
- Demonstrate a working knowledge of marketing research techniques
- Carry out basic sampling
- Design a questionnaire

2 Research planning

2.1 Research involves the following basic steps.

- Defining the question or problem
- Defining the range of options available
- Designing the research project
- Collecting the data
- Analysing and interpreting the data
- Presentation of findings and recommendations

The first three steps form the **planning stage** of the research. We will look at them in a bit more detail.

Defining the problem and available options

2.2 Marketing and market research will only be worthwhile and cost effective if it is designed to address real and relevant marketing and sales issues: opportunities, threats, strengths or weaknesses, or real problems.

2.3 Some clarification of possible answers or options may be helpful in designing the research. If there is a decline in sales, for example, the research may focus on the likely effects of **pricing** decisions, the choice of **distribution** channels, alterations to the product, or an increase in **promotional activity**. Questions can then focus on relevant areas.

- Who buys what, in what quantity and where from?
- Who doesn't buy, and why?
- What are the shopping habits/buying power of those buying or not buying?
- What products are selling best?
- How aware are people of the promotional message?

Designing the research

2.4 Once the researchers know what question is to be answered, or problem resolved, they can determine other issues.

(a) The specific **objectives** of the research: for example, to interview customers in a region with declining sales to determine the reasons for the decline.

(b) What **data is already available** previously collected by research, available from existing records or feedback from existing marketing activities, or from secondary sources.

(c) What **type of data** is needed: secondary or primary, quantitative or qualitative or a blend of both.

(d) What **sources of data** (secondary or primary) will be most appropriate. What sample of what population will be interviewed, for example should the question be asked of customers, or potential customers who don't buy the product, or those who consume the product and/or influence the purchase decision, but are not actually buyers? (This is discussed in Section 3 below).

(e) What **mechanism** will most effectively and efficiently collect the data: postal survey, personal interview, focus group?

(f) **Who** will carry out the data collection: in-house or external services? (This is discussed further below.)

(g) Precisely what **format**, questions and incentives the research mechanism (questionnaire, interview, discussion guide) will have. A badly worded or designed questionnaire, for example, may fail to gather the answers required. (This is discussed in Sections 4 and 5 below.)

Who will do the research?

2.5 The decision of whether to plan and carry out research in-house or use management consultants or a specialist research agency, depends on several factors.

(a) External agencies offer several benefits.

- **Trained and experienced** staff, who can design appropriate vehicles
- **Objectivity**, which may produce a clearer view of the questions to be asked
- **Security** and confidentiality: screened questioners, and respondent anonymity
- **Cost-effectiveness**, where the above are critical to the research's effectiveness

Marketing at Work

Marketing research moves online

Some websites, aimed at particular user profiles, are offering partner companies access to target demographic groups. Given the low cost and speed of response of online surveys, plus the ability to reach hard-to-find groups, such methods are likely to become increasingly popular.

'The teenage girls' website Mykindaplace.com has been using online surveys for the past 12 months to help its sponsorship partners to find answers to questions quickly. In 2001, it ran a beauty survey for Maybelline . . . the survey drew around 4,000 responses over a weekend, and, with the incentive amounting to no more than the chance to win one of 100 Maybelline Lipliners, the total cost of running the survey came in at around £35 . . . Furthermore, responses to each of the questions were broken down by age and region, giving the client a clearer picture of age-related and regional differences in the perception of the brand.'

Marketing Business, April 2002

(b) **Do-it-yourself research** often makes sense.

- Where **data is readily available** to in-house staff
- Where in-house staff understand the **nature of the problem** and target audience
- Where the **budget is very limited**
- Where the **confidentiality** of the research is crucial

2.6 In the rest of this chapter we take a practical approach: guiding you in designing and doing research yourself. If you do use a consultancy, you will need to provide them with a detailed **written brief.**

- The **research problem** to which an answer is required
- The **intended use** of the data collected
- The **budgetary** constraints
- Any **background information** which will put the problem in context

The importance of research planning

2.7 Wasted research can be attributed to poor planning.

- Inadequate briefing of researchers
- Poor problem/question/decision definition
- Neglect of available sources, or poor selection of sources
- Poor research design, using an inappropriate vehicle or using it ineffectively
- Lack of ownership of the project

3 Sampling

Key Concept

Population, for research purposes, is all the items or individuals who fall into the specified target group into which the research will be carried out.

In order to ensure that the sample is genuinely random, it is necessary to start with a **sampling frame**. Items can then be selected by random number tables or computer-generated random number selection, so that no conscious or unconscious selection is involved.

4 Questionnaires

4.1 A **questionnaire** is essentially a **data capture instrument**, as are diaries and recording devices discussed later in this chapter. It lists all the questions to which the researcher wants the respondent to answer, and it records the response of the interviewee.

(a) A **structured questionnaire** lists all questions to be asked in a logical sequence, specifying the precise wording to be used in the response (eg through multiple choice), and providing categories for recording the replies (eg using tick boxes or rating scales).

(b) An **unstructured questionnaire**, by contrast, may simply be a set of open-ended questions to which the respondent can write replies in his or her own words.

Types of question

4.2 There are two main ways in which questions can be asked: **open-ended** (unstructured) and **closed/set-choice** (structured).

(a) Does the question allow the respondent to finish his own answer, in his own words? Open questions introduce variety and allow the full range of possible responses and new information (rather than the respondent merely selecting from your assumptions). An open question may be worded like this:

'How did you travel to work today?'

Alternatively, the questionnaire could offer a range of possible responses, making the data easier to process by both respondent and research analyst.

(b) Does the question make it as easy as possible for the respondent to answer, in terms of time and effort required? Avoid questions that require respondents to perform calculations or write long responses. Try to offer lists of options, tick boxes or scales.

Action Programme 1

What types of problem can you envisage arising from the use of multiple choice questions? How can such problems be overcome?

How are questionnaires administered?

4.3 Questionnaires can be administered by any of the following means.

(a) **Telephone surveys**. Where the questionnaire is conducted as an interview over the phone, and results recorded by the interviewer, this offers speedy, interactive responses over a wide geographical area. Questions will have to be even shorter and simpler to allow for the absence of visual support.

(i) Have a list of at least twice as many interviewees as you require respondents (because of no-answers and do-not-wish-to-be-interviewed responses).

(ii) Allow sufficient time per call. Getting hold of the right person takes time, and respondents typically reply at greater length than required in order to explain choices.

(b) **Postal surveys**. The questionnaire is sent to the respondent to complete and return: this may be done by conventional post, or fax, or e-mail. This is a cheap method of reading a large sample, and avoids the bias inherent in personal contact, but attention will need to be given to some areas.

- The ease of completion by the respondent
- The unambiguous nature of questions in order to produce quality answers
- Incentives to complete and return the survey

(c) **Personal interviews** in homes, on the streets, or at retail outlets. Interviewer bias and leading becomes a factor, but so does the personal interaction, which can motivate quality responses. Being labour intensive, personal interviews are costly for large samples, but secure a high response rate compared to other survey vehicles.

4.4 Survey response rates vary widely. Anything from 12-70% is 'normal' for consumer surveys. Your customer database will elicit higher responses than a 'cold' mailing. In addition, the Institute of Direct Marketing has suggested the following techniques to boost the response to a postal survey.

Technique	Percentage response increase
A clean customer file for sample selection	+150
A first reminder (letter)	+26
A second reminder (phone)	+25
Introductory questions of high interest to respondent	+19
Incentive	+18
Second reminder (letter and questionnaire plus reply envelope)	+12
Second class post	+8
First class post	+5
Questionnaire on yellow paper	+4

Source: *The Practitioner's Guide to Direct Marketing*

5 Qualitative research

5.1 Qualitative research is the process which aims to collect qualitative primary data, although qualitative data are also collected in the process of quantitative research, primarily questionnaires.

(a) Its main **methods** are the open-ended interview, whether this be a depth interview (one-to-one) or a group discussion (focus group), and projective techniques.

(b) The **form** of the data collected is narrative rather than isolated statements reduceable to numbers.

(c) Its main **purpose** is to **understand consumer behaviour** and perceptions.

5.2 The key to qualitative research is to allow the respondents to say what they feel and think in response to flexible, 'prompting' questioning, rather than to give their responses to set questions and often set answers in a questionnaire.

Depth interviews

5.3 In a depth interview the key line of communication is between the interviewer and the respondent. They have an open-ended conversation, not constrained by a formal questionnaire, and the qualitative data are captured as narrative by means of an audio or video tape.

(a) **What type of interview?** Although depth interviews are usually one-to-one, there may be more than one respondent and there may also be an informant, there to give information about tangible things (eg how big the organisation's purchase budget is) but not about his own attitudes.

(b) **How long should it be?** Genuine depth interviews interpret the meanings and implications of what is said and can therefore take some time. By contrast, a mini-depth interview may take only 15 minutes, because it can focus on one, predefined topic like a pack design.

(c) **How structured should it be?** It can be totally open-ended, ranging over whatever topics come up, or it can be semi-structured with an interview guide and perhaps the use of show material.

(d) **Should show material be used?** The type of material that is commonly used includes mock-ups or prototypes, storyboards or concept boards, narrative tapes and animatics, a form of cartoon.

(e) **Where should the interview take place?** Usually at home or in the workplace.

Focus groups

5.4 When planning qualitative research using group discussions, a number of factors need to be considered.

(a) **Type of group**. A standard group is of 7-9 respondents, but other types may also be used.

(b) **Membership**. Who takes part in the discussion depends on who the researcher wants to talk to (users or non-users, for instance) and whether they all need to be similar (homogenous). A focus group is typically demographically balanced, in line with the target population.

(c) **Number of groups**. Having more than 12 groups in a research project would be very unusual.

(d) **Recruitment**. Usually on the basis of a quota sample: respondents are screened by a short questionnaire to see whether they are suitable. In order to persuade them to join in, the members are usually given an incentive plus expenses.

(e) **Discussion topics**. These will be decided by the researcher with regard to the purpose of the group discussion, and the data required.

(f) **Easing the respondents into the process**. There should be an introductory section (10 minutes).

- The purpose of focus groups
- Instructions
- The discussion is being taped/observed
- Round robin introductions by the group

The advantages and disadvantages of group discussions and depth interviews are as follows.

Group discussions	
Advantages	Disadvantages
■ Less intimidating ■ Easily observed ■ Range of attitudes can be measured ■ Social aspect reflects real world ■ Dynamic and creative ■ Cheaper	■ Participants may not express what they really think - they may be inhibited or they may be showing off ■ Views may be unrealistic - meaningful in a group context but not for the individual
Depth interviews	
Advantages	Disadvantages
■ Decision making processes can be analysed ■ Majority and minority opinion can be captured ■ Sensitive topics more easily discussed ■ Unusual behaviour can be discussed	■ Time consuming ■ Less creative ■ More expensive ■ Gives depth, but not breadth (compared to surveys, questionnaires)

5.5 'Focus groups are used ... especially in the areas of brand image monitoring or development, brand positioning, with products and services that are more complex or emotive in nature, and where qualitative data is more important than quantitative data. The strength of the focus group methodology is in depth. It can never replace professionally designed structured surveys, by questionnaire, phone, or interview for breadth. A moderator can probe when information provided is shallow or superficial, which is an inherent problem with structured surveys or mail questionnaires. The *real* reasons for consumer decision making can often be elicited that traditional surveys cannot hope to uncover. For brand-image generation, the data elicited by a professionally conducted focus group is generally far more useful than the less personal survey method' (Davies, 2002).

Marketing at Work

'Focus groups are particularly useful in in Asia, where:

- The exchange of information by word of mouth is central to not only to our cultures, but also the way business is done. Business means building up a relationship, and only when you have met and talked to people over an extended time do relationships move to the level of more open exchange of views that are central to good business. And the same applies for consumers.
- Many countries like China, Taiwan, Indonesia, Thailand, Malaysia and the Philippines are multi-cultural. Many consumers in Asia are at least bilingual and more often than not people can talk and converse in certain dialects, while to read or write in those dialects is far more difficult. Translating questionnaires often results in changes in the 'meaning' of questions, resulting in misunderstanding and invalid results. The focus group setting can reduce a lot of these difficulties.

'On the other hand, difficulties include:

- A casual way of life – and urban traffic jams – making it difficult to get focus groups together! (Invite extra people).
- Conditioning to keep one's opinion to oneself in order not to cause others to 'lose face'. (Requires a longer warm-up period.)
- Different languages and dialects. (Allow more time for discussion, transcription and analysis.)
- Gender/age values, which may inhibit younger people or women from giving feedback. (Consider segregated groups.)'

Davies (2002)

If you are interested, the full text of Davies' excellent article can be viewed at www.orientpacific.com/focusgroups

---

Projective techniques

5.6 **Projective techniques** provide stimuli to which interviewees respond, in such a way as to reflect their unconscious beliefs and motivations.

5.7 A number of techniques might be employed.

(a) **Third person**, or 'friendly martian' as it is sometimes called, is designed to get the respondent talking about issues. The researcher asks the respondent to describe what someone else might do. For example; 'If someone wanted to buy a house, what would they need to do?'

(b) **Word association** is based on an assumption that if a question is answered quickly, it is spontaneous and sub-conscious thoughts are therefore revealed. The person's conscious mind does not have time to think up an alternative response. ('What immediately comes into your mind when you hear the following' etc).

(c) **Sentence completion** is a useful way to get people to respond quickly so that underlying attitudes and opinions are revealed.

Men who watch football are ....?

Women wear red to ....?

(d) In **thematic apperception tests** (TAT tests), people are shown a picture and asked to describe what is happening in the picture. They may be asked what happened just before or just after the picture. It is hoped that the descriptions reveal information about deeply held attitudes, beliefs, motives and opinions stored in the sub-conscious mind.

5.8 The major drawback with projective techniques is that the answers require skilled analysis and interpretation. The techniques are most valuable in providing **insights** rather than answers to specific research questions.

6 Other research techniques

6.1 Other research techniques that you should be aware of, although you are less likely to carry them out yourself, include the following.

(a) **Experiments**

Laboratory experiments set up an artificial environment in which factors can be manipulated and compared to a 'control' so as to isolate the effects of particular factors. This is most often used for measuring response to advertisements and packaging, before (pre-testing) and after (post-testing) release.

Field experiments test out products and promotions in realistic surroundings, to give an idea of how they will perform. Examples include **in-house placement tests** (where a sample or panel of consumers tries out and evaluates the product at home), store tests (where sample stores trial products or point-of-sale material) and **test marketing** (where the marketing plan is carried out in a limited area).

(b) **Observation**

Interviews give information on what people say they will do and even what they think they will do: they cannot tell the researcher what people will actually do. Observation involves watching and recording behaviour.

Direct observation has a watcher observing (or even interacting with) the target population, as it reacts to product displays in store, for example.

Behaviour can also be **recorded** by mechanical devices which measure eye movement or emotional reactions (in response to ads) or track movement through retail space (in response to displays).

(c) **Recorded data**

Questionnaires are a way of recording data. Other examples may be found.

(i) **Diaries** completed by the sample of respondents are used to record consumer behaviour or media behaviour (how TV, radio and other media are used). This is time-consuming for the subject, so should be confined to short periods.

(ii) **Electronic recording systems** such as EPOS (Electronic Point of Sale systems) or video recording in stores.

The use of the Internet

6.2 Company websites can be used to assess the effectiveness of marketing on the Internet. Any such research should adhere to the usual principles:

- Define objectives
- Collect the data
- Analyse the data
- Report the results
- Take the necessary action

6.3 **Log files** are present on web servers that enable companies to see which pages and items each visitor selects. This provides a wealth of market research information. Analysing these files will show which contact leads to a successful outcome, such as a sale. Different customer profiles can be set up, using **online registration** and questionnaires.

Marketing at Work

Dell Computers (www.dell.com) records online sales, as well as telephone orders generated by site visits. They can do this because they have a unique telephone number advertised on the website to use when placing orders.

6.4 Traditional market research techniques can also be used on the Internet:

- Questionnaires (such as the example in Chapter 2)
- Troubleshooting
- Online focus groups

7 Gathering information across borders

7.1 As with secondary research (discussed in Chapter 1), there are certain added complexities to gathering primary data from **international** sources.

(a) **Language barriers**. Questionnaires may have to be translated. Particular care should be given to the implications of trigger words in rating scales, such as **semantic differential scales**, in translation. (The differentials between poor-fair-good-excellent may be altered in direct translation to another language).

(b) **Cultural differences**. Assumptions about people, for example, in sampling and question design, should be challenged. Qualitative research in particular will be subject to interpretation, and cultural assumptions (even with regard to simple matters such as body language and facial expression) may distort the results.

(c) **Demographics**. Demographic information (used in sampling, for example, to ensure proportional representation) will have to be obtained and analysed for each country in which research will be carried out. In some countries, this information may be less sophisticated or less readily available.

(d) **Distance and time**. If you are using personal methods of data gathering, travel distances and even telephone costs and time-differences may make the delays and costs of running the research from the home office prohibitive. Researchers will have to be selected and briefed in the overseas region.

(e) **Secondary sources**, available through international agencies, the Internet or international branches of your organisation, may be more attractive than commissioning overseas research.

(f) **Overseas partners**. Information sources should include overseas agents and distributors, foreign branches of the organisation's bank, consultancies or ad agencies, UK embassies and trade delegations and foreign sections of professional bodies. International trade shows and exhibitions in which the organisation is taking part may be a good opportunity to gather information.

Chapter Roundup

- **Research planning** involves:
  - defining the need for information
  - specifying research objectives
  - evaluating data available
  - defining relevant types and sources of data
  - deciding on the data collection vehicle
  - planning and briefing
- Data can be collected from the whole **population** via a census. More commonly, the population is reflected in a representative **sample**, which may be selected using random, quasi-random (systematic, stratified or multi-stage) or non-random (quota or cluster) sampling.
- **Questionnaires** for use in surveys may be structured or unstructured, and questions correspondingly closed or open.
- **Qualitative research** elicits narrative, subjective data, via depth interviews, group discussion (focus) groups and/or projective techniques.
- **Other research techniques** include observation, experimentation and data recording.

Quick Quiz

1 Why should an organisation not merely collect all the data it can?

2 What are the advantages of doing research 'in-house'?

3 What are the effects of poor research planning?

4 What is a sampling frame, and how is it used in (a) random sampling, (b) systematic sampling and (c) stratified sampling?

5 What are the three types of question in terms of what they seek to find out?

6 List three ways in which a respondent can be motivated to return a questionnaire.

7 What are the advantages and disadvantages of qualitative research groups?

8 How might language and cultural differences affect the gathering and interpretation of research data?

Now try Question 3 in the Question Bank

Action Programme Review

1 Here are some ideas. You may have thought of others.

(a) Capturing a full range of possible responses to a question such as 'In which store do you buy the majority of your clothes?' can be impractical. This problem can be overcome by listing the most popular stores and using an 'other (please specify)' option.

(b) The position of the alternative responses may introduce bias. This problem can be overcome (but not entirely) by producing different versions of the questionnaire.

(c) An unbalanced set of alternative responses could be provided such as the following.

Q: What do you think of TV programme 'XXX'?

A:	1	2	3
	Too boring	Very dull	Indifferent

Obviously such response sets should not be used.

Answers to Quick Quiz

1 Targeting the data most relevant information for decision making and processing it effectively ensures good value for the time and money resources committed to its collection.

2 Where the data is available, the advantages are: staff knowledge, cost and confidentiality.

3 Paragraph 2.7 lists the five key problems.

4 (a) A sampling frame is a numbered list of all the items or individuals in a target population.

(b) Systematic sampling works by selecting a random starting point in the sampling frame and then every n^{th} item thereafter.

(c) Stratified sampling divides the sampling frame into relevant sectors or categories and then subdivides these as many times as necessary to drill down to detailed information.

5 The three main types of question are behavioural, attitudinal and classification.

6 Three from: clean customer file for sample selection, reminders by letter and telephone, high interest introductory questions, incentives, eye catching presentation.

7 Refer to the table in Paragraph 5.4.

8 Great attention has to be paid to avoid different connotations accidentally introduced through translation or by different cultural outlooks.

Investigating Marketing Opportunities 4

Chapter Topic List	
1	Setting the scene
2	Internal marketing audit
3	External appraisal
4	The competitor intelligence system
5	Investigating marketing and promotional opportunities

Learning Outcomes

- ☑ Collect relevant data from a variety of secondary information sources
- ☑ Make recommendations based on information obtained from multiple sources
- ☑ Evaluate and select media and promotional activities appropriate to the organisation's objectives and status and to its marketing context
- ☑ Gather information for, and evaluate marketing results against, financial and other criteria

Syllabus References

- ☑ Source and present information on competitor activities across the marketing mix
- ☑ Investigate marketing and promotional opportunities using appropriate information gathering techniques

Key Concepts Introduced

- Marketing audit
- Capability profile
- Competitor analysis

1 Setting the scene

1.1 The Chartered Institute of Marketing identifies **marketing strategy** and its components as a key business process.

- Reviewing the company's **competitive position**
- The systematic collection and use of **market information**
- Involvement of **all levels of staff** in collecting market information

1.2 In this chapter, we deal with the gathering of some of the information required for strategic marketing planning.

(a) Information on competitors' activities

(b) Information about the company's own strengths and weaknesses

(c) Information about the marketing environment, and factors that pose threats or opportunities to marketing activity

(d) Information about specific opportunities to launch or competitively position products

1.3 So, on completion of this chapter, you should be able to:

- source and present information on competitor activity across the marketing mix (including competitor pricing comparison)
- undertake a basic swot analysis of the marketing organisation and its environment
- gather and evaluate information on marketing and promotional opportunities

1.4 We do not cover the purposes, theory and processes of strategic planning here: it is dealt with in detail in the *Marketing Environment* and *Marketing Fundamentals* syllabuses (and corresponding BPP Study Texts).

1.5 Nor do we discuss, in this chapter, the kinds of **policy decisions and actions** that might be taken **in response to the information gathered** on competitors, on the company's current marketing performance and on emerging opportunities and threats. This is the subject of Part D of this Text, and particularly Chapter 15, which discusses the use of such information across the extended marketing mix. Again, that material builds on *Marketing Fundamentals.*

1.6 What this chapter does is apply the information-gathering strategies discussed in Chapters 1-3 to internal, environmental and competitor analysis. As such, it relates closely to your *Marketing Environment* studies.

2 Internal marketing audit

Key Concept

A **marketing audit** is 'a comprehensive, systematic, independent and periodic examination of a company's - or business unit's - marketing environment, objectives, strategies and activities, with a view of determining problem areas and opportunities and recommending a plan of action to improve the company's marketing performance.' (Kotler *et al.*, 1999)

2.1 At the level of planning and co-ordinating marketing activities, the internal part of a marketing audit will pay attention to several issues.

(a) **Marketing capabilities**: what resources, strengths and weaknesses does the marketing organisation have to build on?

(b) **Marketing performance**: how effective is marketing activity across the marketing mix, compared to objectives?

(c) **Competitive effectiveness**: what are the actual and potential sources of the organisation's competitive advantage?

Key Concept

A **capability profile** is a description of the potential ability of an organisation to operate in its markets: the assets on which it can build, in terms of skills, knowledge, reputation, organisation and management, infrastructures and attitudes.

2.2 A number of sources of **internal data** are available for gathering the above information, including past internal and market research reports, forecasts, budgets and performance data (sales, revenue and profit figures, customer feedback records, cost analysis, personnel performance appraisals). By looking at trends (worsening or improving over time) or by comparing measures or ratios with other firms in the same sector, it may be possible to identify key strengths and weaknesses.

2.3 However, a systematic audit should be undertaken as a quantitative and qualitative research exercise. Data can be gathered by questionnaire, canvassing a wide variety of opinions (at all levels of the organisation), plus selected supply chain partners and customers.

2.4 A checklist of some of the areas for evaluation is as follows. If you added a rating scale for each (1-10, say, or poor-fair-good-excellent) you would have the basis of a questionnaire or discussion guide.

1 *Capabilities*

(a) To what extent does the organisation as a whole have a marketing orientation? Is the customer genuinely the focus of our plans and objectives?

(b) What is our public image/reputation?

(c) How effectively are the customer's needs understood and conveyed throughout the firm by the marketing function?

(d) How flexible/responsible/efficient is the organisation of the marketing department?

(e) Are there clear, realistic, measurable marketing objectives?

(f) Are sufficient resources being committed to marketing to enable the objectives to be achieved? Is the division of costs between different products and activities sensible and supportive?

(g) Are our procedures for gathering data, formulating marketing plans and evaluating performance efficient and effective? Have planning and control been successfully carried out?

(h) Is our management information system adequate and effective?

(i) Are we in a strong or weak bargaining position in relation to sources of supply, quality, delivery and price of materials and services?

(j) What is the size, skill base, and efficiency of our marketing function and sales force? Do we motivate, train and develop marketing personnel?

(k) Do we encourage communication, innovation and feedback at all levels of the organisation?

(l) Is our management style strong or weak, and in what ways? Is it suited to the business culture?

(m) What is the strength of our key brands?

(n) What is the strength of customers' brand loyalty?

(o) How widely do we develop networks and build trade and customer relationships?

2 *Performance* (4 Ps or 7 Ps)

(a) Are sales revenue and profit contribution meeting forecasts?

(b) Is the product mix 'healthy'? Is product demand growing, stable or likely to decline? Are we well placed in growth markets? Are products being developed or improved in line with customer needs and product trends?

(c) How successful are our new product launches? How effective is our research and development?

(d) How does our product and process quality measure up to standard?

(e) Is the product reaching consumers effectively and efficiently? Are delivery lead times and standards as planned?

(f) Are the sales teams and/or direct marketing campaigns successful in winning orders?

(g) Are our price levels appropriate (for supply and demand, customer attitudes, competitor pricing)?

(h) Is the marketing message reaching the target audience? How effective are our advertising and promotional campaigns?

(i) Are we retaining and focusing marketing effort on profitable customers? As sales revenue rises, is contribution, or profit, also increasing?

(j) Have we reached target levels of customer/client service? Are we still improving?

(k) Do all marketing activities show returns on investment?

3 *Competitive effectiveness*

(a) What markets are competitors targeting?

(b) What competitor products are in direct competition with ours?

(c) What market segments or niches do we serve uniquely or strongly?

(d) How are our products differentiated from those of competitors? How are they unique in areas which are highly regarded by consumers?

(e) How do our product/service/delivery quality standards compare with our competitors?

(f) How effective are our R & D schedules? Do we beat competitors to new product launches?

(g) Are we gaining/retaining or losing market share in contested markets?

(h) How effectively and efficiently do we gather data about our competitors?

2.5 You should be able to sense that while sections 2 and 3 lend themselves to quantitative analysis, section 1 is quite subjective.

2.6 The purpose of the analyses is to express, qualitatively and quantitatively, which areas of marketing activity have strengths to be exploited and which have weaknesses to be minimised or eliminated. Key areas which significantly affect the department or organisation's objectives should be highlighted for attention.

Action Programme 1

Use the above checklist as an interview discussion guide for an impromptu marketing audit. Use it on yourself, to appraise your own organisation (set up a suitable rating scale) or ask a fellow student or colleague to work through some or all of the questions with you.

3 External appraisal

3.1 We mentioned **environmental scanning** in Chapter 1. Information on the external environment can be gathered from a wide variety of sources.

- Primary sources at the interface between the organisation and the environment (ie customers, suppliers and distributors).
- Secondary sources (outlined in detail in Chapter 1).

Action Programme 2

Just to test your background knowledge, what are 'SLEPT' factors, and what *other* areas would a marketing organisation want to be aware of?

3.2 It is easy to be overwhelmed by the volume of relevant environmental information on offer. However, the following may be helpful, as a process for creating usable intelligence: Figure 4.1.

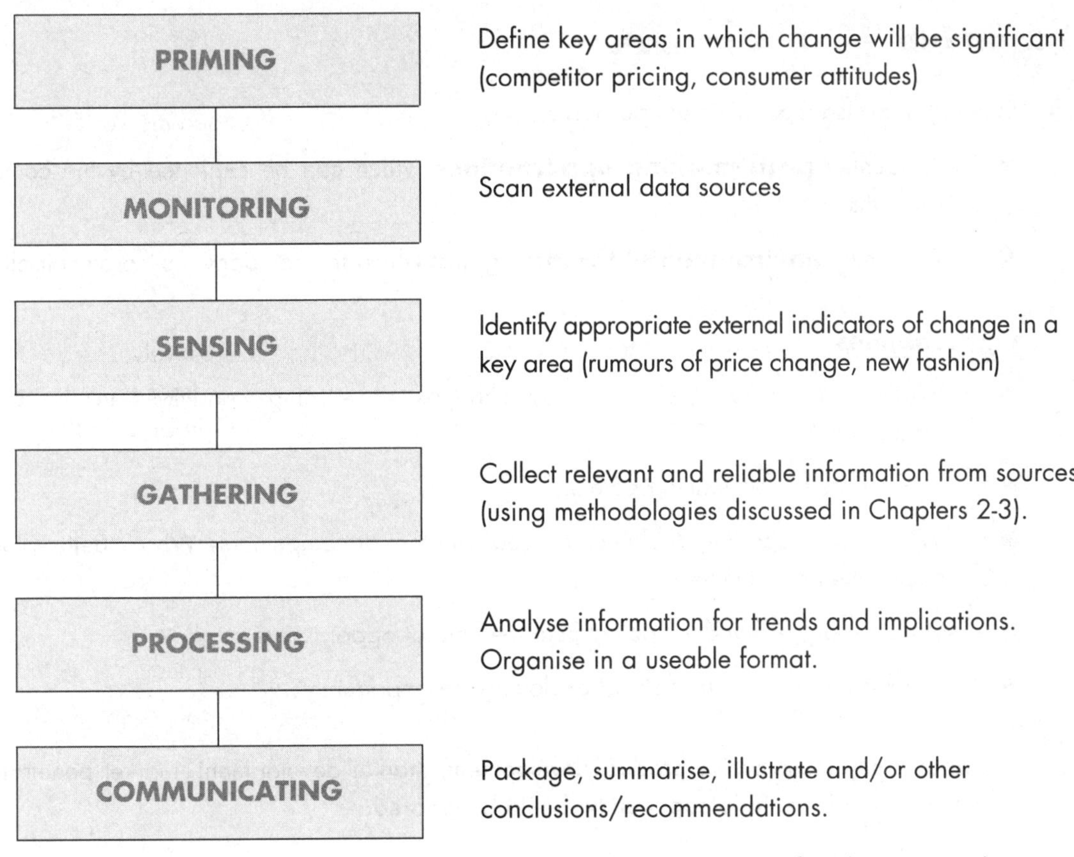
PRIMING
Define key areas in which change will be significant (competitor pricing, consumer attitudes)
MONITORING
Scan external data sources
SENSING
Identify appropriate external indicators of change in a key area (rumours of price change, new fashion)
GATHERING
Collect relevant and reliable information from sources (using methodologies discussed in Chapters 2-3).
PROCESSING
Analyse information for trends and implications. Organise in a useable format.
COMMUNICATING
Package, summarise, illustrate and/or other conclusions/recommendations.

Figure 4.1: A process for environmental scanning

3.3 The first stage is particularly important. Even in environmental scanning, with the best will in the world you cannot find what you don't know you're looking for! The research equivalent is doing a keyword search in an index, or database, or on the **Internet**.

Action Programme 3

Square Wheels plc is a UK firm producing pedal bicycles. It has a major factory in the UK, and has also acquired a plant in Tijuana (Mexico) near the US border, and another in Romania, formerly a state-run concern, and still managed by the same team. Square Wheels sells all over Europe and the Americas and also in India and China, where it has a licensing agreement with local manufacturers, enabling it to have a presence in the market. Bikes are perceived as leisure goods in Europe and North America, whereas they are essential means of transport in India and China. The R & D department has recently come up with a new product idea: a battery-powered motor which can be affixed to the bike for extra power going up hill! It is thought that this might encourage a wider audience in hilly areas and among older users.

From the mini-scenario given:

(a) How complex is Square Wheels' environment?

(b) Identify the political/legal risks to which it is vulnerable.

(c) What might be some implications of (i) population growth in China and India and (ii) the changing age structure of the populations of Europe (fewer young people)?

(d) What ecological or environmental concerns should Square Wheels monitor?

Opportunities and threats

3.4 External appraisal has two main purposes.

- To identify **profit-making opportunities** which can be exploited by the company's strengths
- To identify **environmental threats** against which the company must protect itself

Opportunities

- What opportunities are posed by changes or existing conditions in the business environment?
- What is their profit-making potential?
- What is our capability profile compared with that of competitors? Who is better placed to exploit the opportunities?
- What is our performance potential in the field of opportunity?
- What are the costs and risks of exploiting the opportunity?

The opportunity may involve product development, market development, market penetration or diversification. No realistic opportunity should be ignored.

Threats

- What threats might arise to us or our business environment?
- How will competitors be affected?
- How will we be affected?
- Do we have strengths to deal with the threat, or do weaknesses need to be corrected in order for us to survive the threat?
- What contingency plans are required?

Marketing at Work

The following is an example (in executive summary form) of the kind of market data available from research and database organisations, in this case Euromonitor.

The cosmetics and toiletries market in Poland

2002 saw only moderate growth for sales of Polish cosmetics and toiletries. However, the advance in sales for cosmetics and toiletries was higher than in the majority of other fast-moving consumer goods. Due to a decrease in the disposable income of the average consumer, there was an increasing demand for cheaper cosmetics and toiletries in the latter part of the review period. This trend was pronounced in baby care, depilatories and sun care, which historically were dominated by more expensive products.

Polish manufacturers strike in

Recent years saw the expansion of domestic manufacturers, which substantially increased their value share. This advance not only happened in skin care, where local players have always had an influence, but also in sun care, baby care and hair care, which were traditionally led by multinationals. The domination of multinationals was very strong at the beginning of the review period. Their positions weakened through the review period, this was visible across cosmetics and toiletries. Good quality and reasonable price stood behind local manufacturers' success.

Hair care the biggest but depilatories most dynamic

Depilatories represented the fastest growing product group in cosmetics and toiletries between 2001-2002 as well as all through the review period. Sales of depilatories were negligible at the beginning of the 1990s. The introduction of female-specific depilatory products, combined with changes in lifestyle, helped this fast development. All through the review period, hair care accounted for the largest growth in cosmetics and toiletries, with shampoo dominating. However colorants substantially increased its share between 1997-2002.

Future prospects good

The per capita consumption of cosmetics and toiletries is still at a very low level in comparison with European countries. This suggests further sales development in the near future. Poland is expected to join the EU in May 2004. It is very likely that this will not only stimulate sales but also will attract more investors.

www.euromonitor.com/cosmetics_and_toiletries_in_Poland 10 March 2004

4 The competitor intelligence system

Key Concept

Competitor analysis is the identification and qualification of the relative strengths and weaknesses (compared with competitors or potential competitors), which could be of significance in the development of a successful competitive strategy.

4.1 The **competitor intelligence system** is a formal term for the procedures used to obtain data for competitor analysis. We will look at three aspects of competitor intelligence-gathering.

- **Who** are your competitors?
- **What** should you know about them?
- **Where** do you get the information?

Who are your competitors?

4.2 Organisations need to be aware of the following.

(a) **Who are their existing and potential competitors?**

Competitors need not be producers of similar products or directly competing brands, nor similar types of organisation operating in the same market or market segment. The competitors of book publishers, for example, include not only other book publishers, but producers of alternative products (CD-Rom publishers, video producers, audio books, computer packages) and producers of other products which absorb people's discretionary spending on leisure and gifts.

Look at the following diagram:

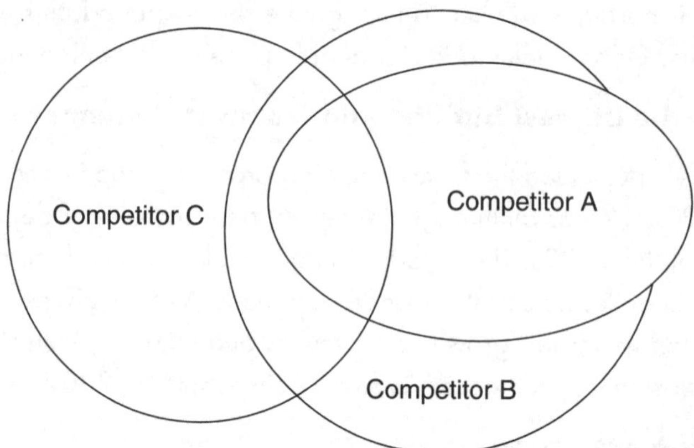

Competitor B is clearly a key 'head-to-head' competitor of A, because their markets overlap. However, competitor C - despite its serving a different market in general - has a product or promotional angle that brings it into competition with A and B.

(b) **Who are their key competitors?**

In a market where there is one or more competitors, marketing decisions may be influenced by what a competitor does or is about to do. (A price war, in which competitors successively undercut each other until one of them withdraws, is the simplest example.) Some competitors will have more power in the market than others, and it will be important to know who they are. Key competitors will be those with a **large or growing market share**, those with highly **differentiated or focused** products or services and those with a **capability profile** that would allow them to capitalise on opportunities.

Marketing at Work

Coca Cola defines its competitors as:

- Pepsi, in the cola market
- All other soft drinks
- Tea and coffee
- Tap water

Coca Cola's chief executive has declared that 'the main competitor' is tap water: any other share definition is too narrow.

Action Programme 4

Whom would you list as the competitors of

(a) a bank?
(b) a petrol station?

What do you need to know about competitors?

4.3 You need to know how they compare with you in terms of goals, capabilities, performance and competitive effectiveness. Anything you do, ask yourself whether they do it differently, and if so, how?

Marketing at Work

One of the best ways of gathering information about a competitor is to undertake a **mystery shopper** exercise. This is where you pretend to be an actual prospective customer of an organisation, but are actually collecting information about

- the organisation
- its products/services
- its prices
- the way it treats customers

Some organisations, particularly retail chains employ 'mystery shoppers' to find out information about their own company and use this as a source of measurement, just like customer satisfaction surveys.

One company *Ansells* even featured a mystery shopper in its advertising to reassure customers that there was constant checking of service quality.

4.4 A capability and strengths and weakness profile of a competitor should include the following areas.

(a) **Future goals**

(i) What are their stated goals and real priorities?

(ii) How satisfied are they with their present position in the market, and what changes are they most likely to attempt?

(iii) What is the management like? (Strong or weak? United or divided? Risk-taking or risk-averse? Good at change? Locked into a particular strategy?)

(b) **Capabilities**

(i) What are their **core competencies**: what do they do distinctively well?

(ii) What **resources** do they have to build on? (Production capacity, established distribution channels, flexibility and innovation, capital, staff skills and motivation, reputation, brand strength.)

(iii) What are their special **competitive advantages**? (Relationship with key distributors, cheap production, access to government?)

(c) **Current strategy and performance across the extended marketing mix**

(i) **Managerial ability**, ability, loyalty and motivation of employees.

(ii) **Product mix**: product/service quality, diversity, positioning and specifications, new product development, leaders or followers on product design?

(iii) **Operations**: research and engineering capacity, up-to-dateness and development potential of plant and machinery.

(iv) **Distribution channels**: including the effectiveness of the sales force and direct marketing.

(v) **Price strategy**: product/service prices, leaders or followers on price?

(vi) **Financial strength**: cost of sales, debt position and sources of new finance, profitability, ability to develop new products or sustain competition on price.

(vii) **Promotional strategy:** preferred messages and media, 'unique selling points' and promotional platforms or themes, expenditure on advertising, promotion and selling, effectiveness of PR, customer care/service programmes.

(viii) **Organisation**: ability to gather market intelligence and respond flexibly, organisation culture, marketing orientation, efficient processes and systems.

(ix) Customer/consumer **perception** of all the above.

4.5 This data can be used in two main ways.

(a) **A competitor analysis** compares the strengths, weaknesses and capabilities of the competitor with those of the organisation doing the analysis.

(b) **A competitor response profile** indicates:

(i) the competitor's **vulnerability** to environmental forces, downturns in sales and competitor activity (if you can analyse your company's vulnerability to such factors, you can also model that of your competitors)

(ii) the most potentially advantageous **'battle ground'** on which to take on the competitor. This may be a market where the competitor is weak, or a product range which is low-priority for the competitor.

4.6 If you need to gather the same kind of information about your competitors as you do about your own organisation, how is this possible? This is where your wider research skills come into their own.

Where do you get the information?

4.7 The very phrase 'intelligence system' has a ring of 'espionage' about it. The more useful competitor information is, the more sensitive it is, and the more closely guarded it will be: however, by definition, it is also information that competitors will be very keen to obtain!

4.8 However, there are plenty of ethical and completely open sources of information about competitors.

(a) **Competitors' products and services**. If you want to know about the product, you can see it on store shelves (which gives additional information about point-of-sale display, promotion and impact), or buy it for analysis. Members of the organisation might also use the competitor's services and report back on the experience or bring back relevant literature.

(b) **Competitors' promotional and informational literature**. Monitor advertising, point-of-sale information and direct mail packages (put yourself on the mailing list). Public companies also issue annual reports and accounts, which give a wide range of financial and non-financial information, including goals for the future. Don't forget job advertisements and application forms: they give data on personnel policies and capabilities.

(c) **Press/media coverage**. Monitor articles in trade and general press and press releases. Internet databases are an efficient way of running a cuttings search, or a media monitoring agency may be retained to gather relevant clippings for you.

(d) **Exhibitions, conferences and meetings of trade/professional associations**. Network with third parties who know and are willing to discuss competitors, and even competitors themselves. Even if information is tightly controlled, a sense of the organisation's culture, style and staff can be gleaned.

(e) **Internet**. Monitor the competitor's website. How sophisticated is it? What does it offer?

(f) **Sales rep activity**. The competitor's customers and retail outlets may discuss visits and offers made by representatives. Your own reps will be a useful source of feedback.

(g) **Competitors' suppliers**. Suppliers of services or products to the company may disclose some information about their relationship with another, especially if it is openly available. Many retailers and wholesalers get information on competitors' pricing from suppliers.

(h) **Retailers** may be a source of information such as share of sales volume, customer feedback and scheduled promotions.

(i) **Customer research** is often used to elicit information about the customer's experience with, awareness of and attitude to competing products.

(j) **Other secondary sources**. The competitors' directors may be in Who's Who or the **Directory of Directors**. The company may feature in a local history. Advertising may be reviewed in *Campaign*.

4.9 All of the above can be researched via open networking, desk research and field research. Be aware, however, that there are more covert means of gaining information, especially from competitors and their suppliers. People may issue bogus requests for tenders/proposals to get competitors to submit product/service/costings details, or make bogus calls to competitors. Variations on this theme include calls from job seekers, market researchers, and marketing students doing a project, wanting details about the company and its plans.

4.10 There is nothing at all unethical about an employee of a restaurant, say, eating in another restaurant and bringing back impressions of its decor, service, menu and food. But what if the same employee called the restaurant and claimed to be a food journalist preparing a profile for 'The Good Food Guide', in order to get more in-depth information on recipes, or the chef, or the restaurant's plans for the future? Use research strategies you feel comfortable with, in accordance with your organisation's ethical objectives.

Exam Tip

The questions we have just asked in Paragraphs 4.2-4.10:

- *Who are your competitors?*
- *What do you need to know about competitors?*
- *Where do you get the information?*

. . . mirror precisely the requirements of Question 2 on the Pilor Paper.

Action Programme 5

Where would you go for information on competitors' prices?

A simple competitive intelligence system

4.11 Taylor (1997) suggests a simple two-step system for efficient competitive intelligence gathering.

(a) **Use the Internet**. Set up a group of key words (the name of competitors, brand names, prominent figures). You could do database searches yourself, or use a news scanning service, which scans for you. You should also review relevant online databases such as the *Financial Times*' FTPROFILE or AC Nielsen's marketing information.

(b) **Use a network**. Select one individual in every major operating group or department in your organisation as the competitive intelligence specialist for that area. Ask that individual to gather and e-mail you any piece of market intelligence that may be valuable.

Exam Tip

Always remember it is useful to commence any report with a situation analysis, and conclude by bringing all of your information together. Below is a suggested format for a competitor analysis.

A competitor analysis is an analysis of the current competitor situation, which may include the following.

- An overview of your organisation, identity, business role, product and service offering, size and turnover.
- An outline of who your competitors are, comparing them with your own organisation in terms of product and service offers, the size and turnover of the organisation.
- Identification of your own organisation's strengths, and those of the competitor.
- A grid that compares your own organisation with three other competitors, focusing on the marketing mix. Set up headings in the grid that enable you to identify key competitive areas.
  - Price
  - Product
  - Distribution outlets
  - Promotional activity
  - Customer services activity
  - Service levels
  - Customer profile
  - Market share

As an added dimension, look at the broader issues affecting competition, such as PEST factors. How do they affect pricing? How do environmental issues affect packaging?

How does your organisation respond to external forces? How do your ccompetitors respond to the same forces?

From the information you have drawn together, make some key comparisons and conclusions. Fully explain where your organisation could add more value to the product or service proposition.

Identify and recommend some possible tactical activities for the marketing mix to help the organisation be more competitive (not just in the short term, but to sustain the competitive advantage). Don't forget to justify your recommendations.

---

5 Investigating marketing and promotional opportunities

5.1 This area of the syllabus is the application of everything we have covered so far in this chapter and in Part A of this Study Text. It represents one of the key purposes to which customer, marketing and competitor research is put.

5.2 We have already covered the information-gathering process in detail, and will be looking at how it is applied across the marketing mix in specific contexts in Part D of this Text.

5.3 There are many occasions when opportunities arise which are not preplanned and part of some previously agreed marketing strategy. The most frequent type of 'opportunity' is that of being offered advertising space or airtime. On other occasions there may be an approach from another organisation to join in a joint promotion.

Tactical decisions

5.4 Tactical decisions are relatively low-key and made quickly in response to opportunities or changes. However, it is hoped that any tactical decision on whether to engage in an activity should fit in with the organisation's overall direction or strategy. Clearly advertising in an inappropriate journal because it was half price, or having a joint promotion with a company whose reputation is poor, are not good ideas!

'Scorpion' – a tool for assessing opportunities

5.5 The acronym SCORPION can be used as a tool for assessing the merits of a wide range of options, whether this be a change in price, opening a new outlet, renting a poster site, advertising on the back of bus tickets, or anything else for that matter.

Synergy	Is this opportunity one which fits in with what the organisation is trying to achieve? In terms of reputation, branding, market share etc?
Customers	Will this activity positively impact on our customers, or even attract new ones?
Objectives	Does this fulfil any of our business objectives?
Rivals	Is this the sort of activity that would allow us to gain advantage over our rivals?
Profit	Perhaps the most important. Will this make us money?
Information	Do we have enough information on which to base a decision?
Other actions	How well does this stand up against other things we could do with the same amount of money which may be better value?
Needs	Does this match a need we have? Or does it help fulfil our customers needs?

Exam Tip

Using a model such as SCORPION can be very useful in an exam situation as it steers you to making structured, intelligent comments against a set range of criteria. Don't forget, though, that a model by itself is unlikely to be sufficient: you need to be able to ask the questions from the perspective of the particular scenario given!

Action Programme 6

Hall Faull Downes Ltd has been in business for 25 years, during which time profits have risen by an average of 3% per annum, although there have been peaks and troughs in profitability due to the ups and downs of trade in the customers' industry. The increase in profits until five years ago was the result of increasing sales in a buoyant market, but more recently, the total market has become somewhat smaller and Hall Faull Downes has only increased sales and profits as a result of improving its market share.

The company produces components for manufacturers in the engineering industry.

In recent years, the company has developed many new products and currently has 40 items in its range compared to 24 only five years ago. Over the same five-year period, the number of customers has fallen from 20 to nine, two of whom together account for 60% of the company's sales.

Give your appraisal of the company's future, and suggest what it is probably doing wrong.

Action Programme 7

The Needle Works

Your market research questionnaire on educational activities has had a very good response (53%). Research shows that most of your customers are in favour of such an initiative, particularly those in your local region. Direct competitors (smaller craft shops) already run classes which are very popular and inexpensive (under £5 per hour), but do not offer a wide range of topics, do not run very often, and are generally held during shopping hours only, which working customers are unable to attend. Cost and small group sizes are particularly important to potential students, as is the timing/convenience of classes. Expensive classes are accepted by people who want individual tuition and a high-quality class environment or 'celebrity' tutors. Your suggestions of social activities and a membership club were almost unanimously welcomed (95% of respondents).

Draw up a suitable visual representation of these results (plus any detail you want to add) which will highlight a possible opportunity or competitive advantage. Add notes on the factors you would take into account in evaluating the feasibility of the opportunity you identify. Think about all 7 Ps of the extended marketing mix.

Chapter Roundup

- A **marketing audit** is a systematic analysis of the organisation's marketing position and performance. It includes marketing objectives, capabilities and competitive effectiveness.
- Organisational **strengths and weaknesses** are significant if they:
  - are important and relevant to customers and/or
  - affect the organisation's ability to compete
- **External appraisal** is aimed at identifying environmental changes which may represent threats or opportunities for the organisation.
- **Competitor analysis** involves identifying the relative strengths and weaknesses of the organisation, compared to those of competitors and potential competitors. Influential competitors should be profiled in the same way as the organisation's own marketing position and performance.
- There are many open and ethical **sources of competitor information**, including published material, advertising, media coverage, customers, suppliers, distributors and the competitors themselves (products and services).
- **Evaluating a marketing or promotional opportunity** requires the gathering and analysis of information about the objectives of the opportunity, its feasibility (SWOT analysis), cost-benefit analysis and performance measures for control.
- Two techniques for communicating evaluations are **SWOT charts** and **product/position/perceptual maps**.

Quick Quiz

1 What is a 'capability profile'?

2 What questions might be asked to analyse an organisation's competitive effectiveness?

3 What is the purpose of (a) internal and (b) external analysis?

4 Outline the sequence for creating market/environmental intelligence.

5 Who are the 'key' competitors of a business?

6 What information might you gather about a competitor's (a) future goals, and (b) capabilities?

7 What is a 'competitor response' profile?

8 List eight sources of information about competitor activity.

9 What issues should be considered when evaluating the feasibility of a marketing opportunity?

Now try Question 4 in the Question Bank

Action Programme Review

1 This is a useful intelligence gathering tool on *any* marketing organisation. If you are using it, however informally, with a fellow student or someone from an organisation not your own, check for conflict of interests, confidentiality issues and so on.

2 You may be more familiar with the acronym PEST (Political, Economic, Social and Technological). SLEPT adds 'legal' as a separate factor. Additional factors include: interest and pressure groups like professional bodies, the CBI, trade unions, consumers' associations, and the physical environment, ecology and the 'Green' movement. Since we did not specify the 'macro' environment, you might also have listed 'micro' factors such as customers, competitors, suppliers and distributors.

3 (a) Square Wheels' environment is fairly complex, because it operates in so many different countries, but the basic technology is fairly simple - a bicycle is not a complex product.

(b) To identify the political risks in any of the areas mentioned, read a newspaper! Hong Kong reverted to Chinese sovereignty in 1997: but this is unlikely to raise the risk profile of the business, since it already has substantial operations in China, and there is no evidence that the Chinese government is going to nationalise profitable businesses. There may be other risks with the labour force in Tijuana, and problems of economic and business management in Romania.

(c) The implication of population growth is an increased market. However, if accompanied by increases in prosperity, customers may be able to afford other means of transport for commuting (eg motor scooters and cars). The new battery technology may be useful in developing countries, rather than in Europe. In Europe, the changing age structure may affect the use of bikes: fewer young people will buy them, so the aim might be to promote them on the grounds that they offer health-giving exercise.

(d) In ecological terms, the push-bike is energy-efficient, and so is a prime example of an ecologically friendly product. Other issues include energy efficiency in its factories, and how hazardous materials are dealt with.

4 (a) The bank's competitors would include the other banks: indeed, this was the only way the market was perceived for a long time. However, building societies have now emerged as a major competitor in the wider 'financial services' sector, follows by supermarkets and retailers offering financial services (advice, loans, insurance, cash).

(b) Similarly, petrol companies were so busy competing among themselves that they were wrong-footed by supermarkets, who now sell petrol at out-of-town stores as part of a larger package of services.

5 Price information is available from a variety of sources. Most manufacturing firms get the data from customers. In retail, prices are readily available at point of sale and in price listings, advertisements and catalogues, as well as from customers and suppliers. Many firms use sales agents to monitor prices. There may also be feedback available from competitive tendering.

6 A general interpretation of the facts as given might be sketched as follows.

(a) Objectives: the company has no declared objectives. Profits have risen by 3% per annum in the past, which has failed to keep pace with inflation but may have been a satisfactory rate of increase in the current conditions of the industry. Even so, stronger growth is indicated in the future.

(b)

Strengths	**Weaknesses**
Many new products developed. Marketing success in increasing market share.	Products may be reaching the end of their life and entering decline. New product life cycles may be shorter. Reduction in customers. Excessive reliance on a few customers. Doubtful whether profit record is satisfactory.
Threats	**Opportunities**
Possible decline in the end-product. Smaller end-product market will restrict future sales prospects for Hall Faull Downes.	None identified.

(c) Strengths: the growth in company sales in the last five years has been as a result of increasing the market share in a declining market. This success may be the result of the following.

- Research and development spending
- Good product development programmes
- Extending the product range to suit changing customer needs
- Marketing skills
- Long-term supply contracts with customers

- Cheap pricing policy
- Product quality and reliable service

(d) Weaknesses:

(i) The products may be custom-made for customers so that they provide little or no opportunity for market development.

(ii) Products might have a shorter life cycle than in the past, in view of the declining total market demand.

(iii) Excessive reliance on two major customers leaves the company exposed to the dangers of losing their custom.

(e) Threats: there may be a decline in the end-market for the customers' product so that the customer demands for the company's own products will also fall.

(f) Opportunities: no opportunities have been identified, but in view of the situation as described, new strategies for the longer term would appear to be essential.

(g) Conclusions: the company does not appear to be planning beyond the short term, or is reacting to the business environment in a piecemeal fashion. A strategic planning programme should be introduced.

(h) Recommendations: the company must look for new opportunities in the longer term.

(i) In the short term, current strengths must be exploited to continue to increase market share in existing markets and product development programmes should also continue.

(ii) In the longer term, the company must diversify into new markets or into new products and new markets. Diversification opportunities should be sought with a view to exploiting any competitive advantage or synergy that might be achievable.

(iii) The company should use its strengths (whether in R & D, production skills or marketing expertise) in exploiting any identifiable opportunities.

(iv) Objectives need to be quantified in order to assess the extent to which new long-term strategies are required.

7 You may have come up with a different way of representing a different opportunity, but as an example:

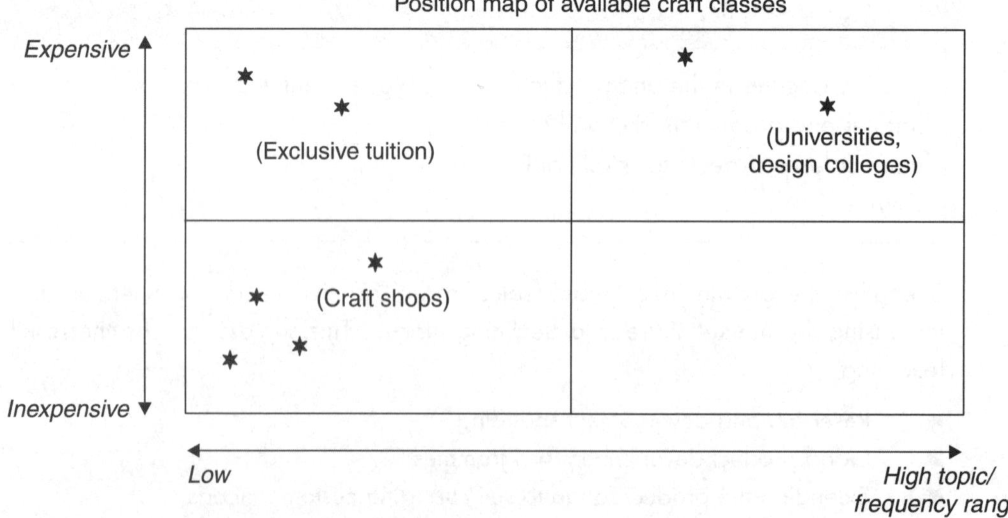

Strengths	Weaknesses
Quality premises Strong customer loyalty Finance/size Networks Customer database	High overheads Staff availability evenings
Opportunities	**Threats**
Evening classes Wide topic range Large/frequent programme Membership Club	Competitor classes cheap Local area at night: perception of elderly customers? Customer demand for small class/low cost

Your notes might include observations such as:

(a) There is an apparent opportunity for a reasonably-priced programme offering a wide variety and high frequency of classes: demand seems to be supportive.

(b) The apparent opportunity for evening classes. However, other factors include the threatening perception of the city at night, particularly for an elderly customer group and the costs of staffing the premises after hours. An alternative proposal - lunchtime short classes - might be advisable.

(c) The mathematics of small class numbers and low cost does not immediately add up, given the need to pay tutors per hour. The quality of the premises might allow a higher price, relative to competitors. The 'club' activities could be pursued in larger numbers to support small class rolls.

(d) The Needle Works' strengths in database and customer loyalty provide cost-effective access to the target market, and the Club and class programme support each other.

Answers to Quick Quiz

1. A description of the potential ability of an organisation to operate in its markets in terms of its assets, skills, knowledge, reputation, management, infrastructures and attitudes.
2. A full list of questions relating to competitive effectiveness is found in Section 3 of Paragraph 2.4.
3. Both internal and external analyses are vital information gathering tools if an organisation is to fend off challenges and exploit opportunities. SWOT analysis deals with both aspects: the strengths and weaknesses identified are a good indication of how fit the organisation is to deliver its objectives or respond to changes in the market place. The perceived opportunities and threats enable the organisation to deal early with potential problems from the macro environment and to profit from new openings in the market.
4. This is shown in the flow chart in Paragraph 3.2
5. Key competitors are those who have already established a large or growing market share, highly differentiated product and a capability profile that allows them to capitalise on opportunities.
6. Future goals: their stated goals; satisfaction with present position and market share objectives; their management style /culture particularly how innovative, responsive and united they are. Capabilities: what they do very well with what level of resources; untapped resources; main competitive advantages.
7. A competitor response profile indicates the competitor's vulnerability in relation to environmental and market forces, and suggests in which arenas you might successfully compete.
8. A full list is provided in Paragraph 4.8.
9. A full feasibility test is given in Paragraph 5.5. SCORPION is a useful mnemonic.

Part B

Building and developing relationships

Working with Others

5

Chapter Topic List	
1	Setting the scene
2	The marketing function within the organisation
3	Roles and relationships at work
4	Interpersonal skills and managing others
5	Working effectively in teams

Learning Outcome

☑ Develop relationships inside and outside the organisation

Syllabus References

☑ Describe the structure and roles of the marketing function within the organisation

☑ Build and develop relationships within the marketing department; working effectively with others

☑ Describe techniques to assist in managing your manager

Key Concepts Introduced

- Co-ordination
- Politics
- Discrimination
- Interpersonal skills
- Rapport
- Co-operation
- Conflict
- Team

1 Setting the scene

1.1 How might you describe a 'good working relationship'? A precise definition would include different things for different for different people, but there are two main components.

(a) **Good working**

A good working relationship allows or facilitates work **transactions**, the completion of **tasks** and the fulfilment of **objectives**.

(b) **Good ... relationships**

A good working relationship allows or facilitates ongoing and mutually satisfying **interpersonal relations**.

Elements in (a) might include prompt and willing service, co-operation and co-ordination, communication, expertise, teamworking skills and mutual reward or benefit.

Elements in (b) might include politeness, friendliness, trust, openness, the ability to resolve conflict and respect.

1.2 A working relationship can be established with anyone with whom you come into contact for the fulfilment of a transaction or task: colleagues, suppliers, customers or clients.

1.3 In this chapter, we will look at working relationships within the marketing department and between the marketing department and the rest of the organisation. In the chapters that follow, we go on to consider relationships with customers and visitors, suppliers of services, partners in the supply chain, and finally the wider business and social community.

1.4 On completion of this chapter you should be able to:

- analyse the structure and culture of the marketing function and its relationship to the organisation as a whole
- identify key roles and relationships in the marketing department
- understand what is required to build and maintain effective working relationships
- appreciate the need to meet commitments to others within agreed timescales
- suit your methods of communication and support to the needs of colleagues
- handle disagreement, conflict and change within a team

1.5 Many of the general principles of building relationships are discussed in this chapter. Interpersonal skills, conflict management and team roles and dynamics will be relevant to customer and supplier relationships too. This section of the Text links closely with your *Customer Communication* Studies.

2 The marketing function within the organisation

The role of the marketing assistant

2.1 When the syllabus for *Marketing in Practice* was being researched, the role or job title most closely related to it was that of marketing assistant. Although by no means a senior role, this job involves a variety of tasks, relationships and responsibilities.

The role can sometimes be an extension of a secretarial job, and a position as secretary to the marketing manager is often the route in to a career in marketing.

There is no standard job description for a marketing assistant, although it is likely to involve:

- Advertising, but not with large budgets
- Organising events, such as exhibitions, stands or conferences
- Some responsibility for budget administration

The above are recognisable as sections of the MIP syllabus, and as such feature in each exam set so far.

However, there is often a very 'ad hoc' element to such jobs, meaning every day is different and you get called on at short notice to undertake a variety of projects.

The organisation of marketing

2.2 **Kotler** *et al* (1999) note that there has been both an absolute and a relative rise in the importance of marketing in the organisation.

(a) The **responsibility** of marketing has increased due to the increasingly complex environment, the slow-down of demand in existing product fields and the rise in competition.

(b) Companies have been forced to move from a **product orientation** to a **marketing orientation**, making marketing one of the critical management functions.

Kotler suggests that as a business grows, it moves from basic functions (finance, production, sales) to an increasingly evolved view of marketing: Figure 5.1.

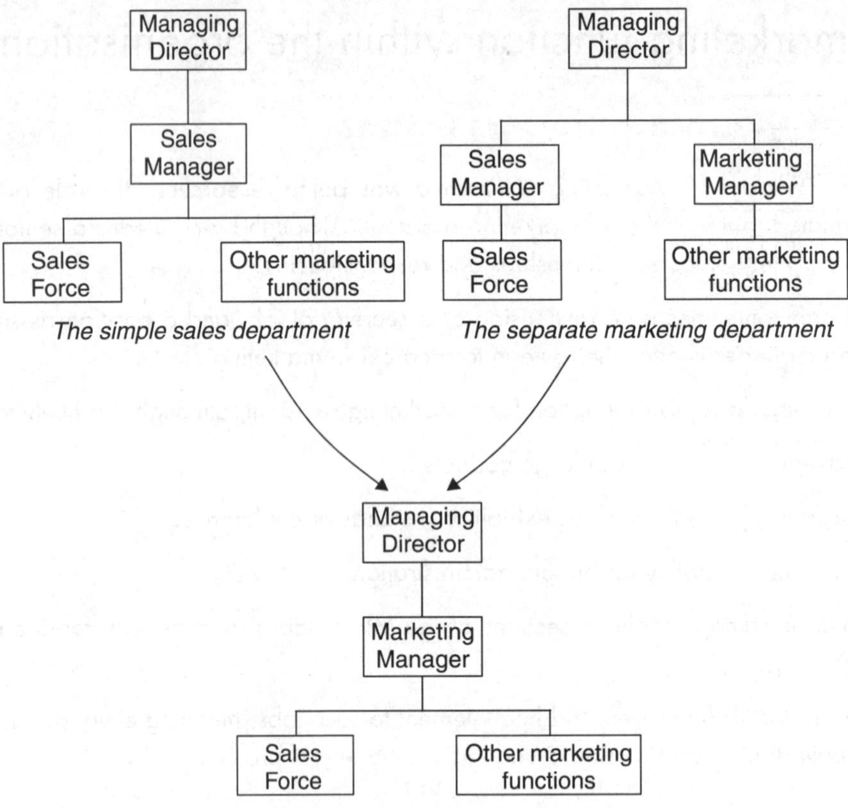

Figure 5.1: The evolution of marketing organisation

2.3 Of course, organisation structures are more complex than that, and the precise relationship of the marketing function to other functions (such as production, finance, human resources, research and development) will depend on whether the organisation is structured by function, geographical/national territories or more marketing oriented divisions by market or product.

2.4 **Product management** or **brand management** systems have become popular with organisations producing a range of products. This is a type of **matrix organisation**, which overlays functional management with resource management: Figure 5.2. Product or brand managers have several responsibilities.

- Developing **marketing plans** for their product/brand
- Developing **promotional campaigns**
- **Stimulating support and interest** among the salesforce and distributors
- **Gathering feedback** on the product/brand's performance
- **Initiating product improvements** to meet market needs

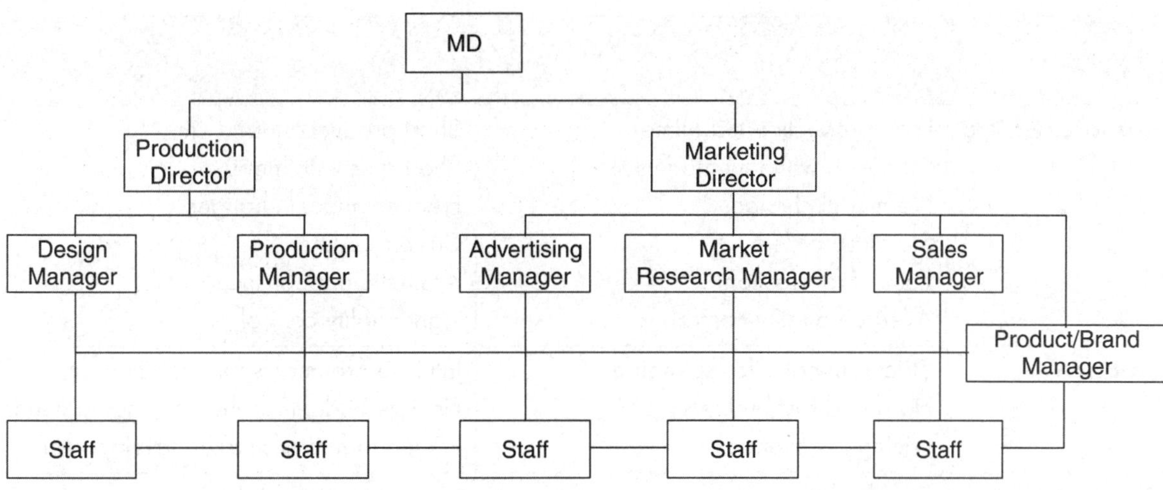

Figure 5.2: A matrix structure

Interdepartmental relations

2.5 'In principle, business functions should mesh harmoniously to achieve the overall objectives of the firm. In practice, departmental interfaces are often characterised by deep rivalries and misunderstandings... Some inter-departmental conflict stems from differences of opinion about what lies in the best interests of the firm; some from real trade-offs between departmental well-being and company well-being; and some from unfortunate departmental stereotypes and prejudices'. (Kotler, 2002).

2.6 The **marketing concept** is designed to foster a deeper appreciation by all departments of the value and benefits of a **customer orientation**, but how much influence should marketing have over other departments to bring about co-ordinated effort in customer service, say, or product development? Other departments naturally stress their own special contribution to company goals, and view problems and opportunities in the light of their own expertise and culture.

2.7 Kotler *(ibid)* summarises the potential for conflict as follows.

Other Departments	Their Emphasis	Marketing Emphasis
R & D	Basic research Intrinsic quality Functional features	Applied research Perceivable quality Sales features
Engineering	Long design lead time Few models Standard components	Short design lead time Many models Custom components
Purchasing	Narrow product line Standard parts Price of material Economical lot sizes Purchasing at infrequent intervals	Broad product line Non-standard parts Quality of material Large lot sizes to avoid stockouts Immediate purchasing for customer needs

Other Departments	Their Emphasis	Marketing Emphasis
Manufacturing	Long production lead time Long runs with few models No model changes Standard orders Ease of fabrication Average quality control	Short production lead time Short runs with many models Frequent model changes Custom orders Aesthetic appearance Tight quality control
Finance	Strict rationales for spending Hard and fast budgets Pricing to cover costs	Intuitive arguments for spending Flexible budgets to meet changing needs Pricing to further market development
Accounting	Standard transactions Few reports	Special terms and discounts Many reports
Credit	Full financial disclosures by customers Low credit risks Tough credit terms Tough collection procedures	Minimum credit examination of customers Medium credit risks Easy credit terms Easy collection procedures

2.8 So what can you do as a member of the marketing department to overcome such obstacles to co-operative working? You may not be able to influence orientation or policy but you will be involved in communication and co-ordination.

2.9 The following paragraphs suggest some brief guidelines for working with individuals and teams from other departments.

Networking

2.10 The more you have contact with people in other functions, learn what they do and show that you appreciate their problems and capabilities, the more likely you are to develop co-operative relationships.

(a) Attend organisation-wide and interdepartmental events and meetings.

(b) Join quality circles and other multi-disciplinary teams and committees that focus on joint objectives.

(c) Use your contacts in other departments to arrange visits and briefings so you learn about each other's functions.

The internal customer concept

2.11 As the term suggests, the internal customer concept implies the following.

(a) Any unit of the organisation whose task contributes to the task of other units (whether as part of a process or in an advisory or service relationship) can be regarded as a **supplier of a service** like any other supplier used by the organisation.

(b) **Customer choice** operates within the organisation as well as in the external market environment.

(c) The unit's objective thus becomes the efficient and effective identification and satisfaction of customer needs, wants and expectations within the organisation as well as outside it.

(d) The unit must 'create, build and maintain mutually beneficial exchanges and relationships' within the organisation, as well as outside. In other words, customer relations are important internally, too.

Action Programme 1

Who are the internal customers of the marketing function? What are their needs/expectations?

Internal promotion and communication

2.12 Every organisation has a major internal target audience for its promotional message. The PR function includes employee relations. These are important for various reasons.

- **Public relations**, since employees are also representatives of the company
- Employee **morale and productivity**
- **Innovation** and **quality control**

2.13 As a marketing communicator, you should recognise the importance of getting production staff excited about an upcoming launch (which might soften the blow of the launch deadlines) and encouraging branch managers and sales staff to feel energised by your marketing support of their efforts. You may have to brief front line staff on customer likes and dislikes.

2.14 Be prepared to use a wide range of internal **promotional media and activities**. This may include meetings, factory tours, presentations, internal newsletters, intranet messages, competitions and suggestion schemes, letters, memos and reports.

Co-ordination

2.15 One of the main purposes of organisational communication is co-ordination.

Key Concept

Co-ordination is 'planning, or taking action to improve, the inter-relationships (especially of timing and methods of communication) between a member of various activities, which contribute to the achievement of a single objective, so that they do not conflict and the objective is achieved with a minimal expenditure of time and effort.' *(Dictionary of Management)*

2.16 You need to ensure that departments whose work depends on yours, or on whose work yours depends, are kept informed.

- **Plans and schedules**
- **Changes** to plans and schedules
- **Feedback** on the results or completion of plans and schedules

2.17 This may seem like common sense. It seems obvious that you should check with the design or production department before you advertise product specifications, and inform them of the

planned date of a new product launch, and monitor their readiness as the date approaches. Failure to monitor progress, adjust plans and communicate between units are common problems, and sources of conflict and chaos.

3 Roles and relationships at work

Roles

3.1 **Roles** are sometimes described as parts that people play (like actors) or hats that people wear.

- People adopt different roles in different circumstances
- Roles define 'who a person is' in these circumstances and in relation to others
- Roles have certain signs or characteristics associated with them, so that a style of behaviour is expected of a person in a given role

3.2 In the marketing department, you adopt your '**work role**', as opposed to your role as student, member of a family, sports enthusiast (or whatever). Within your work role may be more specific roles, such as co-ordinator of marketing activity, event organiser, assistant to your superior and colleague to your peers – depending upon what function you are performing and what other people require and expect from you.

3.3 There are important skills in working with others.

- Identifying what roles other people are in, and what your role should be
- Identifying the behaviours and role signs expected of you in a given role

This will help you to avoid inappropriate behaviours such as over-familiarity in a professional context, lack of leadership in an authority role or insubordination in a subordinate role.

Structural relationships

3.4 Roles exist **in relation to each other**. In the work environment, there are three basic relationships between roles.

- **Subordinate role** working for and reporting to others
- **Equal or peer role** working with others towards a shared goal
- **Authority role** with people working for and reporting to you

These are essentially relationships of **power, authority** and **influence**. Within this structure, there are also **functional** relationships.

3.5 Authority and functional relationships are built into the formal structure, communication and procedures of the organisation. Its **culture** dictates the way in which these relationships are regarded and expressed.

3.6 Structural relationships shape two key aspects of working with others.

(a) **The scope and limits of authority**

Each person and team needs to know what areas they have authority over, and how far that authority extends. For example, you may have responsibility for controlling local advertising, but refer national advertising decisions to your boss.

(b) **Co-ordination and communication**

Since your work objectives will be achieved for or through other people, you need to ensure an efficient flow of work, resources and information towards overall objectives. Your plans and schedules need to dovetail with those of other individuals and teams with whom your work is linked.

3.7 **Politics** flows from **authority relationships** in an organisation.

Key Concept

Politics are activities concerned with the acquisition of power and the exercising of influence in relation to others.

Organisations are political systems.

(a) Individuals have their own **agendas**, priorities and goals.

(b) They compete for their share of the organisation's **limited resources**, power and influence.

(c) They form **cliques**, alliances, **pressure groups** and blocking groups centred around values and objectives which may be opposed by others.

Interpersonal relationships

3.8 Overlaid on structural factors in relationships, there are interpersonal or human factors such as individual personalities, interpersonal skills, whether people have rapport, personal differences, attitudes and values, perceptions, communication and communication barriers and group behaviour.

3.9 When we talk about **building relationships**, we are mainly talking about developing rapport, trust and effective communication, which, although complicated by structural factors and politics, are essentially **interpersonal skills**.

Contractual and legal relationships

3.10 Some aspects of work relationships are covered by **contract, law and regulation**.

3.11 You have a general duty, for example, of **faithful duty to your employer** under your contract of employment.

- Duty to obey lawful and reasonable orders
- Duty to use skill and care
- Duty not to disclose confidential information

You also have specific responsibilities, under **health and safety legislation**, to work in such a way as to avoid injury to yourself and others.

3.12 Similarly, there are laws and regulations covering how your employer should treat you, including disciplinary situations, dismissal and redundancy, grievance handling, health and safety, working terms and conditions (pay, holiday entitlements).

3.13 Among the formal aspects of work relationships, you should be aware that you have responsibilities under **equal opportunities legislation** not to **discriminate** or show prejudice against people on grounds such as sex, race or disability. This applies to how you deal with colleagues and members of the public.

Key Concept

Discrimination is giving less favourable terms or treatment to a particular individual or group because of some characteristic that they are assumed to have, or some category to which they are assumed to belong.

3.14 There are **legal provisions** against **discrimination** in the UK.

(a) The **Sex Discrimination Act** 1975 outlaws certain types of discrimination on the grounds of sex or marital status (that is, whether the person is single, married or divorced).

(b) The **Race Relations Act** 1976 outlaws certain types of discrimination on grounds of colour, race, nationality or ethnic origin.

(c) The **Disability Discrimination Act** 1995 outlaws certain types of discrimination on grounds of physical or mental disability.

(d) The **Employment Equality Regulations** 2003 outlaw discrimination and harassment on the grounds of sexual orientation and religious belief.

3.15 There are **two types of discrimination** under the Acts.

(a) **Direct discrimination** occurs when one interested group is treated less favourably than another.

(b) **Indirect discrimination** occurs when requirements or conditions are imposed, with which a substantial proportion of the interested group could not comply. If you were serving a queue of people and gave a discount only to those who could say 'Happy Christmas' to you in Welsh, you would be guilty of indirect discrimination.

3.16 Another current issue in the workplace is **sexual harassment**, which has been ruled to be unlawful sexual discrimination. With the new regulations on sexual orientation and religious belief, a wider range of jokes, 'banter' and potentially harassing behaviours in the workplace will have to be addressed. All employees (and marketers) must recognise the increasing diversity of the workforce (and consumer base) in this regard.

Action Programme 2

Find out what policies your organisation has to define the relationships, rights and responsibilities between its individuals and groups. Check

- the organisation or office manual or handbook
- your contract of employment
- policy statements and notices to staff
- the personnel or human resources department

Recognising 'key relationships'

3.17 You cannot invest the same amount of time and energy in every person you deal with, and the fact is that some individuals and groups will be more useful or necessary to you in accomplishing your personal and work goals than others. We are not saying you should not bother with social or friendly relationships, or that you need to become a manipulator of people! In your work role you need to establish effective **working relationships**.

Exam Tip

Developing relationships inside and outside the organisation is one of the learning outcomes of this syllabus. The June 2003 case study set you up in a team at a radio station, including marketing management, sales team and shared administrative assistants: you are involved in event organising, and collaboration with other local media. In this complex scenario, you are asked to identify your 'key contacts' and how you can build effective working relationships with them.

A slightly different aspect was set in December 2003, addressing particular difficulties likely to be experienced in a setting where the management committee are unpaid volunteers and your own appointment is part time.

The examiner noted that 'there is no easy mnemonic or framework here, and candidates needed to really think about what the issues might be'. He also reminded candidates that ways to build relationships or overcome difficulties 'needed to be practical and low cost': resist the temptation to have daily meetings or weekly parties!

3.18 There are some key individuals with whom you need to manage your relationship with particular care.

(a) **People on whom you rely for information** or input to your own work, in order to fulfil your objectives

(i) **People whose work precedes yours in the flow of work or project sequence**. For example, the market researcher who has to gather and supply data before you compile a report and recommendations.

(ii) **People to whom you have delegated tasks: that is, people through whom you get things done**. This includes subordinates and colleagues as well as agencies to whom you contract aspects of a task. For example, the office assistant you rely on to get your reports typed, copied and bound for the departmental meeting.

(iii) **People with whom you must collaborate in order to complete a project**. You may not have delegated or contractual authority over other people involved in a project: relationships will be key to co-ordination and co-operating. A product launch, for example, will involve many units of the marketing and production functions: who can you talk to for progress checks?

(iv) **People who have information or expertise you regularly require**. Sources of expert knowledge and advice need to be identified and cultivated. For example, the information technology officer who can be relied on to get the system working again when it has crashed on the morning when a report is due.

(b) **People who have authority over you and your work**

Your relationships with your team leader, immediate boss and department head are vital.

(i) They control your salary and career prospects, and the quality of your working life in general.

(ii) They set the objectives and give the instructions that define your work.

(iii) They control access to the resources (budget, information, staff, space), that you need to do your job.

(c) **Other people who can mobilise influence and resources on your behalf**

In Chapter 8 we discuss the importance of **networking**, both within and outside the organisation. It is important to build relationships with powerful allies, supporters, information sources and controllers of budgets. Not all influential people are in high positions of authority. A personal assistant may know more than anyone, and have access to the right people.

3.19 These relationships should be particularly cultivated, on a regular basis, or at least for the duration of the project to which they are key. We discuss how they can be built and developed in the next section.

Working with anybody

3.20 Having said all the above, it is also important not to neglect or destroy relationships with non-key players. Without people like receptionists, telephonists, post room staff, maintenance and security staff, your job would be a lot harder!

Action Programme 3

The Needle Works

As a result of your market research and competitor comparison (Chapters 3 & 4), you have drafted a recommendation that The Needle Works set up an educational and activities programme, for submission to Albert Smith. Thinking about the history and culture of the business, and about how the programme would need to be organised, it occurs to you that Albert will not be the only 'key player' in the decision-making and implementation processes.

Make a list of who has influence, and in what area. Whose support and input might you require to get your programme (a) approved and (b) up and running?

Marketing at Work

What 'type' of people are you likely to find in your marketing department? Have you geared your relational style to the stereotypical marketing person: extroverted, creative, fast-talking, enthusiastic?

Marketing and the Small Firm asked small firms which skills they considered most vital for *effective* marketing.

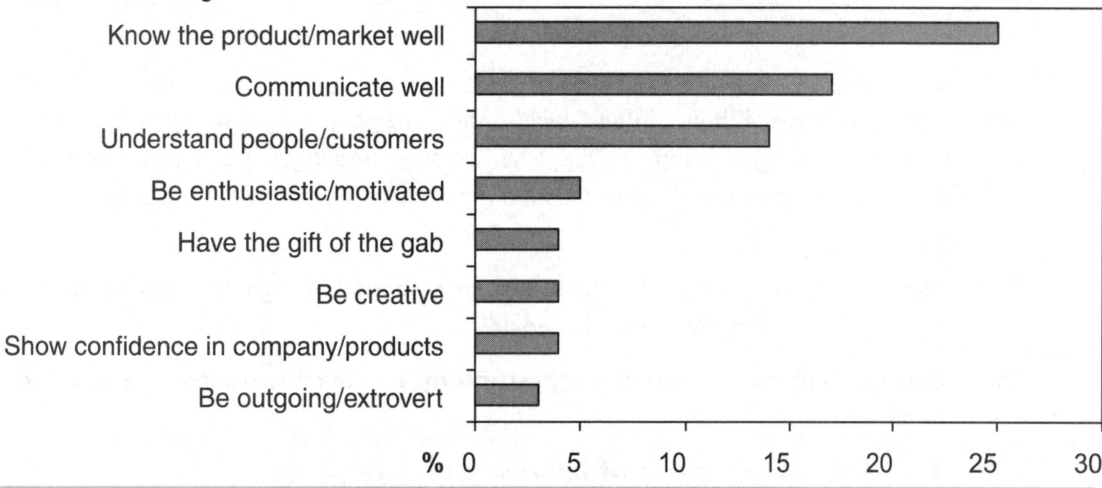

4 Interpersonal skills and managing others

Key Concept

Interpersonal skills are skills used in establishing and maintaining relationships between people. They are essentially communication skills, used in an interactive situation such as a face-to-face or telephone discussion.

4.1 **Interpersonal skills** include:

- The ability to build **rapport**, or a sense of relationship, with another person
- The ability to **persuade** or **influence** another person
- The ability to gain the **trust**, **confidence** and **co-operation** of another person
- The ability to **resolve conflict or disagreements**

4.2 Obviously, these are not things you can really learn in a book. You need to develop your communication skills, and to practise applying and adjusting them in every interaction that you encounter, until you consistently get the results you want.

4.3 We will look briefly at each of the areas listed in Paragraph 4.1 above: they are the building blocks of relationships.

Building rapport

Key Concept

Rapport is the process of establishing and maintaining a relationship of mutual trust, understanding and responsiveness between two or more people.

4.4 **Rapport** is the sense of 'being in tune with' another person, or 'getting on' with them. Building rapport is like building a bridge to the other person: creating a point of understanding and contact, on which meaningful communication and relationship can be based. So how is it achieved?

(a) Matching, or mirroring, the other person's non-verbal signals: posture, gestures, eye contact and volume and pace of speaking.

(b) Demonstrating **respect and understanding** for the other person's viewpoint, emotions or culture.

- Talking about **topics of interest** to the other person
- Using a **vocabulary** the other person shares
- **Empathising** with the person's feelings
- Wearing **clothes** and adopting **manners** which will not alienate the other person
- Appreciating the person's views, even if not agreeing with them

Influence

4.5 Influencing is a process whereby some form of 'pressure' is applied to change other people's attitudes or behaviours. Gillen (1999) distinguishes between what he calls:

(a) **Manipulative** influencing, using tactics designed around dishonest logic or negative feelings. This is a 'push' approach which attempts to dismiss, override or get around the other person's point of view

(b) **Positive** influencing: 'non-manipulative, persuading behaviours that demonstrate that you are treating people openly, honestly and respectfully'. This is a 'pull' approach which:

- attempts to understand the other person's point of view
- attempts to help the other person to understand your point of view
- invites or leads the other person to appreciate or agree with your point of view (through persuasion)

4.6 In addition, influence may be exerted through **power**. Power is an aspect of the relationship between people: how the power holder is perceived by others and what (s)he is able to offer them. French and Raven (1958) classified power as follows.

(a) **Legitimate power**: the ability of a leader or manager to exercise authority, based on his or her position in the organisation.

(b) **Expert power**: the ability of a leader to exert influence based on others' recognition of his or her knowledge or expertise in an area in which they need help.

(c) **Reward power**: the ability of a leader to exert influence based on access to, and control over, resources which others value (pay, assistance, information, contacts and so on).

(d) **Referent power**: the ability of a leader to exert influence based on his or her 'charisma' or leadership qualities.

(e) **Coercive power**: the ability of a leader to exert influence based on his or her ability to apply negative sanctions if people don't comply.

Trust and co-operation

4.7 Rapport and **influencing skills** can be used to facilitate encounters. In order to develop a relationship, further investment is required.

4.8 Cultivating a relationship is a bit like cultivating a garden: it requires regular time, effort, nourishment and creativity, even at work, where you might think that sharing an office all day would be sufficient!

(a) **Keep in contact**. Communicate regularly. (This may be a challenge in 'virtual' teams which do not share office space, or with part-time workers.)

(b) **Be dependable**. Trust is built on trustworthiness. Don't let people down, break promises or violate confidentiality.

(c) **Showing willing**. Offer or agree to give information, collaboration, help or support whenever appropriate. This builds up a credit bank of co-operation.

(d) **Utilise social and informal opportunities**. Lunch breaks, after-hours activities, even a quiet chat over the coffee machine, are designed to allow colleagues to get to know and trust each other as people, building a relationship that will benefit co-ordination and communication at work.

(e) **Avoid or mend conflict**. Unresolved personality clashes, hostilities and rivalries ruin working relationships.

(f) **Maintain appropriate roles.** However friendly you get with people outside work, or in informal situations, remember to behave appropriately in business contexts.

Managing conflict and disagreement

Key Concepts

Co-operation is working or acting together.

Conflict is the clash or opposition of opposing 'forces', which may include the interests, opinions or beliefs of individuals or groups. Conflict often arises at work from competition for scarce resources and power, the incompatible goals and priorities of individuals and teams, lack of communication, and incompatibility of individual or team personalities or styles of working.

4.9 One useful model of conflict resolution is the **win-win model**. This states that there are three basic ways in which a conflict or disagreement can be worked out.

Method	Frequency	Explanation
Win-lose	This is quite common.	**One party gets what (s)he wants at the expense of the other party**: for example, Department A gets the new photocopier, while Department B keeps the old one (since there were insufficient resources to buy two new ones). However well-justified such a solution is (Department A needed the facilities on the new photocopier more than Department B), there is often lingering resentment on the part of the 'losing' party, which may begin to damage work relations.
Lose-lose	This sounds like a senseless outcome, but actually **compromise** comes into this category. It is thus very common.	**Neither party gets what (s)he really wanted**: for example, since Department A and B cannot both have a new photocopier, it is decided that neither department should have one. However 'logical' such a solution is, there is often resentment and dissatisfaction on both sides. (Personal arguments where neither party gives ground and both end up storming off or not talking are also lose-lose: the parties may not have lost the argument, but they lose the relationship ...) Even positive compromises only result in half-satisfied needs.
Win-win	This may not be common, but working towards it often brings out the best solution.	Both parties get as close as possible to what they really want. How can this be achieved?

4.10 It is critical to the **win-win** approach to discover what both parties really want. For example, Department B may want the new photocopier because they have never found out how to use all the features (which do the same things) on the old photocopier because they just want to have the same equipment as Department A or because they fear that if they do not have the new photocopier, their work will be slower and less professionally presented.

4.11 There are important questions in working towards win-win.

- What do you want this for?
- What do you think will happen if you don't get it?

These questions get to the heart of what people really need and want.

In our photocopier example, Department A says it needs the new photocopier to make colour copies (which the old copier does not do), while Department B says it needs the new copier to make clearer copies (because the copies on the old machine are a bit blurred). Now there are options to explore. It may be that the old copier just needs fixing, in order for Department B to get what it really wants. Department A will still end up getting the new copier but Department B has in the process been consulted and had its needs met.

Action Programme 4

Suggest a (i) win-lose, (ii) compromise and (iii) win-win solution in the following scenarios.

(a) Two of your team members are arguing over who gets the desk by the window: they both want it.

(b) You and a colleague both need access to the same file at the same time. You both need it to compile reports for your managers, for the following morning. It is now 3.00pm, and each of you will need it for two hours to do the work.

(c) Manager A is insisting on buying new computers for her department before the budgetary period ends. Manager B cannot understand why - since the old computers are quite adequate - and will moreover be severely inconvenienced by such a move, since her own systems will have to be upgraded as well, in order to remain compatible with department A. (The two departments constantly share data files.) Manager B protests, and conflict erupts.

Managing your manager

4.12 Green (2002) sets out some advice on getting the most from your working hours. He lists three common problems.

- Allowing the **'urgent'** to squeeze out the **'important'**
- Ineffective **planning and prioritising**
- Failing to **link** medium-term goals with long-term plans

4.13 Green's key advice is to **focus on what is important**. Speak to your boss to **agree what is expected of you**, and then **safeguard the time available for priority tasks** by employing some of the following tricks:

- Explain to your boss the value of having some uninterrupted time each day
- Agree ground rules for what you can and cannot be interrupted with
- Do not be afraid to say 'no', or perhaps schedule a task for another time
- Use voicemail
- Limit the number of times you check your e-mail each day
- Find a quiet office for an hour or two if you work in an open plan environment

5 Working effectively in teams

Key Concept

A **team** is a small number of people with *complementary skills* who are committed to a *common* purpose, performance goals and approach for which they hold themselves basically accountable.

5.1 The basic work unit of organisations has traditionally been the **functional department** (such as marketing or sales). In more recent times, businesses have adopted smaller, more flexible and responsive units: teams. **Teamworking** allows work to be shared among a group, so that it gets done more quickly and with a sharing of skills and information, while allowing people to keep sight of the 'whole' task. Teams are particularly effective for increasing communication, generating new ideas and evaluating ideas from different view points.

(a) **Brainstorming groups** generate creative ideas for problem-solving, or innovative promotional campaigns.

(b) **Quality circles** draw people together from different disciplines to share ideas about quality issues.

(c) **Project teams** can be set up to handle particular tasks or projects, cases or customer accounts or product launches.

(d) **Study and discussion groups** explain issues from different points of view.

(e) **Team briefings** present information and instructions.

5.2 **Belbin** (1993) drew up a list of the necessary functions which must be performed to keep a team functioning effectively.

Member	Role
Co-ordinator	Presides and co-ordinates. Balanced, disciplined, good at working through others.
Shaper	Highly strung, dominant, extrovert, passionate about the task itself, a spur to action.
Plant	Introverted, but intellectually dominant and imaginative. Source of ideas and proposals but with disadvantages of introversion.
Monitor-evaluator	Analytically intelligent. Dissects ideas, spots flaws. Possibly aloof, tactless - but necessary.
Resource-investigator	Popular, sociable, extrovert, relaxed. Source of new contacts, but not an originator. Needs to be made use of.
Implementer	Practical organiser, turning ideas into tasks. Trustworthy and efficient, but not excited. Not a leader, but an administrator.
Team worker	Most concerned with team maintenance - supportive, understanding, diplomatic. Popular but uncompetitive - contribution noticed only in absence.
Finisher	Chivvies the team to meet deadlines and attend to details. Urgency and follow-through important, though not always popular

The **specialist** joins the team to offer expert advice when needed: legal experts, PR consultants or design consultants.

5.3 Effective teams therefore need a mix of people.

- In order to get things done
- To get along with other people

Action Programme 5

The Needle Works

What difficulties can you anticipate in building working and supplier relationships at the Needle Works? How might these be overcome?

Team decisions

5.4 **Group decision-making** can be of benefit.

(a) **Pooling** skills, information and ideas - perhaps representing different functions, specialisms and levels in the organisation - could increase the quality of the decision. Groups have been shown to produce better evaluated decisions than individuals working separately. Even the performance of the group's best individual can be improved by having 'missing pieces' added by the group.

(b) **Participation in the decision-making process** makes the decision acceptable to the group, whether because it represents a consensus of their views, or simply because they have been consulted. Acceptance of the decision by the group may be important if it affects them, and/or they are responsible for carrying it out.

5.5 There are however problems in group decision-making.

(a) Group decisions take **longer** to reach than individual decisions - especially if the group seeks **consensus** by working through disagreement.

(b) Group decisions tend to be **riskier** than individual decisions.

(i) **Shared responsibility** blurs the individuals' sense of responsibility for the outcome of the decision.

(ii) **Contradictory information** may be ignored, to protect the group's consensus or pet theories.

(iii) **Cohesive groups** tend to feel infallible and they get over-confident.

(iv) Group cohesion and **motivation** may be founded on values like innovation, boldness and flexibility - which support risk-taking.

Factors in team performance

5.6 Some of the factors affecting the performance of teams are as follows.

(a) **Co-operation and conflict resolution.** Since teams are made up of a number of individuals, it is important that they all get on and work well with each other. Two team members who are hostile or non-communicative are likely to have a negative effect on the whole team.

(b) **Clearly defined goals and responsibilities**. Teams should be **briefed** on a regular basis so that they know what is expected of them. The goals of individual team members should if possible be made to coincide with those of the group as a whole. This is known as **goal congruence**.

(c) **Clear and regular feedback**. The team must be given information of progress and results so that it can learn, correct or adjust its performance – or celebrate.

(d) **Group motivation**. As with individuals, if teams are encouraged to work hard, and rewarded for doing so, then this is likely to have a positive effect on performance.

(e) **Communication**. In general, the greater the communication between team members and team leaders, the greater and more effective the performance.

Action Programme 6

What teams are you currently a member of? What makes them feel like 'teams', rather than just groups of people? See if you can identify which of Belbin's team roles are fulfilled in your team, and where there are gaps which need to be filled.

Chapter Roundup

- People adopt a number of different **roles** and relate to each other in those roles, as well as interpersonally.
- **Relationships in work organisations** are structural (based on authority and function), interpersonal (or human) and contractual/legal.
- **Key relationships** are those with people whose information, input or authority are essential to your working effectively with different people in different contexts. They include rapport building, influencing, building trust and co-operation and managing conflict and disagreement.
- **Teams** are particularly useful where the sharing and testing of ideas is required. There are many different roles and styles of contributing in teamworking.
- Interdepartmental **conflict** stems from genuine clashes of emphasis as well as prejudice and politics, and the marketing department needs to exercise internal promotion and employee relations in order to integrate its activities with those of other departments.

Quick Quiz

1 Give one example of incompatible emphases between marketing and another department.

2 What is the internal customer concept?

3 Give three examples of the benefits of internal promotion/member relations.

4 How can an awareness of 'role sets' and 'role signs' help you to work with others?

5 Why is there 'organisational politics'?

6 Give four examples of legal, contractual or policy provisions governing interpersonal behaviour at work.

7 Give six examples of 'key players' in your job situation.

8 What are the sources of power or influence in an organisation?

9 List five steps you can take to cultivate relationships.

10 List Belbin's team roles.

Now try Question 5 in the Question Bank

Action Programme Review

1 (a) Senior management and shareholders, who expect the strategic objectives of the organisation to be met through effective and efficient marketing activity.

(b) The production function, which expects to be given practicable product specifications and production schedules and expects its efforts to be justified by the success of the product in the market place - to feel that output is being effectively 'sold'.

(c) The accounting and administrative function, which expects clear and accurate budgets, forecasts and records of expenditure, sales and so on, for the required financial control and reporting and record-keeping systems.

(d) The members of the organisation as a whole, who expect to be given information - and particularly 'good news' - by the organisation, to be able to feel pride in the organisation's image to the outside world, to identify with it and to feel that the marketing function is 'getting it right' and that:

(i) they are not wasting effort on a product that nobody wants; and

(ii) their efforts are being properly communicated to the market: the marketing 'does justice to' the products/organisation they are committed to.

2 Your findings might have included a wide range of policies from dress codes to passive smoking, sexual harassment, age discrimination, the rights of gays and lesbians, discipline and grievance, general conduct in the work place and so on. If no such policies were accessible, how are 'norms' of roles and relationships defined in the organisation?

3 Albert Smith has the organisational authority to approve your recommendation. However, Mr and Mrs Smith still exercise informal cultural and expert power in the business, as the founders - and heads of the family. You are likely to have to get their support. Mrs Smith will be

particularly important as a source of expert knowledge and experience, as you develop your programme - and also of contacts, since you will need to source teachers. It is not clear how the programme would be organised, or under whose authority: it may well come under the umbrella of 'Administration' once it has been launched, so you will need to get Amy Chan's support and involvement at an early stage. It is also worth bearing in mind that the Sales Assistants - in their front line role - will be the ones who promote, explain and welcome people to the programme, so you will need to involve and educate them - probably through their senior.

4 (a) (i) **Win-lose**: one team member gets the window desk, and the other does not. (Result: broken relationships within the team.)

(ii) **Compromise**: the team members get the window desk on alternate days or weeks. (Result: half satisfied needs.)

(iii) **Win-win**: what do they want the window desk for? One may want the view, the other better lighting conditions. This offers options to be explored: how else could the lighting be improved, so that both team members get what they really want? (Result: at least, the positive intention to respect everyone's wishes equally, with benefits for team communication and creative problem-solving.)

(b) (i) **Win-lose**: one of you gets the file and the other doesn't.

(ii) **Compromise**: one of you gets the file now, and the other gets it later (although this has an element of win-lose, since the other has to work late or take it home).

(iii) **Win-win**: you photocopy the file and **both** take it, or one of you consults his or her boss and gets an extension of the deadline (since getting the job done in time is the real aim - not just getting the file). These kind of solutions are more likely to emerge if the parties believe they **can** both get what they want.

(c) (i) **Win-lose**: Manager A gets the computers, and Manager B has to upgrade her systems.

(ii) **Compromise**: Manager A will get some new computers, but keep the same old ones for continued data-sharing with Department B. Department B will also need to get some new computers, as a back-up measure.

(iii) **Win-win**: what does Manager A want the computers for, or to avoid? Quite possibly, she needs to use up her budget allocation for buying equipment before the end of the budgetary period: if not, she fears she will lose that budget allocation. Now, that may not be the case, or there may be other equipment that could be more usefully purchased - in which case, there is no losing party.

5 Some of the potential areas of difficulty you may have noted are as follows.

(a) The family involvement in the business: there may be a tendency to under-communicate with other staff because family members know each other so well (and because power is concentrated in the family). You will need to be assertive in ensuring that your expertise is heeded and valued. Your role may also involve ensuring that information flows to non-family members of the team.

(b) Part-time sales assistants: particular efforts will have to be made to keep part-timers 'in the loop' as things change, and to help them to feel part of the team. Staff meetings will be difficult, as members will be in the store at different times. Notice boards – and a communicative management style – may be used, and occasional staff get-togethers arranged.

(c) Two worksites: factory staff may feel quite separate from store staff. Measures may have to be taken to bring them together: for example, site visits or all-staff quarterly meetings. A staff bulletin or news sheet might also be used.

(d) The prospect of external trainers/demonstrators: relationships will need to be set up and managed so that they are involved (and therefore dependable), informed (so that they project the right image, and promote the right products for the firm) and able to co-operate with store staff. Regular phone, email or newsletter contact, plus face-to-face meetings when they are in-store may be used to maintain contact.

6 What makes a team feel like a team? Perhaps a name, behavioural or dress norms, shared stories and successes (or heroic failures), 'badges' of some kind, its own space: there are many ways of building a team identity. As for the Belbin roles, you may have noticed that an individual can play more than one role.

Answers to Quick Quiz

1 Kotler's conclusions are listed in Paragraph 2.7.

2 Your internal customers are anyone in the organisation whose work is affected by your own. It is your role to develop relationships, satisfy colleagues' needs, market your competence and communicate with them as effectively as with customers external to the organisation.

3 By creating excitement about the company's objectives and projects, you create personal motivation in staff and 'buy in'. By creating involvement and pride you increase the company's productivity and quality. Being informed helps make staff realise their contribution to the bigger picture and can help the organisation pull together by removing some of the inter-departmental friction (which Kotler describes).

4 Professional behaviour is appropriate to your role or roles. Understanding what others expect from you will prevent you from making mistakes.

5 Organisations are political systems. Individuals have their own goals, and have to compete with others for the organisational resources to achieve them. Individuals can form interest groups in order to exert more power in influencing the outcome of decisions which may be based on self-interest rather than the company's well-being.

6 You have a contractual obligation to show 'loyal duty' to your employer. There is legal enforcement of indirect and direct discrimination through the Race Relations, Disability and Sex Discrimination Acts over the previous three decades. Many companies issue a policy against bullying, harassment and discrimination.

7 This will depend on your own circumstances. Remember that key relationships are those which impact on you most directly.

8 Legitimate power, expert power, reward power, referent power and coercive power.

9 Refer to Paragraph 4.8.

10 Refer to Paragraph 5.2

The Front Line Role

6

Chapter Topic List	
1	Setting the scene
2	Receiving visitors
3	Assisting visitors
4	Dealing with difficult customers
5	E-relationships

Learning Outcome

☑ Develop relationships inside and outside the organisation

Syllabus References

☑ Explain the 'front line' role; receiving and assisting visitors, internal and external enquiries

☑ Explain the concept and application of e-relationships

Key Concepts Introduced

- Customer care
- Confidentiality

1 Setting the scene

1.1 Business organisations are increasingly recognising two things about customers.

- They have an ever-widening **choice** of products and services available to them
- **Service** is of major importance in winning and retaining customers

Key Concept

Customer care is: 'the management and identification of 'moments of truth', with the aim of achieving customer satisfaction.' (Thomas, 1986)

1.2 **Customer care is everybody's job**. Every individual and team in an organisation contributes to the products, services or general impression of the organisation that customers, clients and visitors take away with them. All employees who come into contact with people from outside the organisation are ambassadors of the organisation.

1.3 This is particularly true of those employees who have responsibilities which put them regularly in contact with customers and clients. Again, do not think just in terms of sales and delivery people. Your job as a marketing assistant may be a 'front line' customer contact position.

- Assisting in the **reception** of visitors to the premises, or to your department
- Answering **enquiries** from customers, or members of the public
- Providing **information** about the organisation's products and services
- Handling **complaints** or **queries** from customers about products or services

1.4 On completion of this chapter you should be able to:

- greet visitors promptly and courteously
- identify and match the needs of visitors to appropriate products, services or personnel
- describe (and promote, as appropriate) the structure, products or services of the organisation to visitors
- suit your methods of communication and support to visitors' needs
- keep complete, legible and accurate records of visits
- follow established procedures for dealing with awkward or aggressive visitors

Marketing at Work

According to the *Citizen's Charter Complaints Task Force* (*Putting Things Right*), it is much more cost effective to handle customer complaints at the front line than to pass them on for review by staff higher up the organisation. According to the survey, the following public sector organisations reported these costs per complaint.

	Handled informally by front line staff	*Formally reviewed by senior staff*
NHS Trust	£3.45	£370
Local Authority	£17	£110
Inland Revenue	£30-70	£78-£650
Electricity company	£5.10	£80-£140

Exam Tip

This element of the syllabus may form part of a skills audit in your workplace. You may need evidence of your ability to greet visitors in the workplace, determine their needs and, where appropriate, meet their needs, either personally or through appropriate persons. If you still think customer service 'isn't your job', you will at least have to make it your job to this extent!

2 Receiving visitors

2.1 There are many general rules on dealing with people, such as **effective oral and non-verbal communication,** and **courtesy**. These should of course be applied when dealing with anybody with whom you came into contact in the course of business.

2.2 Dealing with visitors to the workplace involves **direct interpersonal contact**. Personal contact is the most **direct** and **flexible** way of communicating.

(a) **Each party gets an overall impression of the other**: hearing and seeing aid interpretation, and help to confirm it through feedback.

(b) **Personality can be brought into play**, especially in persuasive contexts encouraging customers to buy or reassuring them that their business is being dealt with efficiently.

(c) **Immediate exchange is possible**: question and answer, action and reaction, feedback and modification.

(d) **Greater sensitivity is encouraged**: tact, trust, understanding, sympathy or co-operation can be exchanged in face-to-face situations.

2.3 We discuss some of the 'practical PR' skills involved in dealing with people, and how they affect the organisation's image, in Chapter 8. Here, we discuss some of the human, procedural and legal aspects of the front-line reception and assistance role.

Greeting people

2.4 First impressions are vital: if you do not get it right first time you may never deal effectively with that person.

(a) **Smile**. It actually takes fewer muscles to smile than to frown, so give your face a rest! Forget about your own troubles and concentrate on the matter in hand.

(b) **Make eye contact**. Don't gaze intently into people's eyes - in some cultures, this is threatening and uncomfortable - but don't keep looking down or away, otherwise they will think that you are not interested in them and they may not trust you.

(c) If the visitor offers to **shake hands** with you, never decline the offer.

2.5 If you are greeting somebody you know you must **gauge the formality** or otherwise of your greeting according to your relationship to date. **Do not be overfamiliar**, but make sure that you use their name once or twice (their first name if the relationship has developed that far).

2.6 Remember that pleasantries ('How are you?', 'Did you have a good journey?') are useful in establishing rapport, but do not waste time in getting down to business. (If clients are inclined to gossip do not cut them dead, but say 'Well, what can I do for you today?' at the earliest opportunity.)

Receiving external visitors

2.7 These are certain standard **reception procedures** which should be carried out when receiving all visitors. These may be summarised as follows.

- Greet the visitor politely
- Sign the visitor in for identification, security and safety purposes
- Notify the person that (s)he has come to see that the visitor has arrived
- Stay with the visitor until (s)he is collected
- Direct the visitor to the office of the persons he has come to see

2.8 Here are some further guidelines whether you are on reception duty or welcoming a visitor to a meeting.

(a) **Don't keep visitors waiting unnecessarily.** They should be made comfortable whilst waiting.

(b) **Greet visitors by their name** (if known) and with a handshake.

(c) If dealing with **sensitive or personal matters**, wait until you are behind closed doors before beginning such discussions.

(d) **Direct visitors** to the office or interview room where the meeting is to be held.

(e) **Maintain a courteous and interested tone** during all dealings with external visitors.

(f) If you have to take a **phone call** whilst waiting with a visitor, or whilst in a meeting with one, keep it very brief.

Action Programme 1

Consider the following scenario in the Customer Service office of Baddley & Co Bank.

MRS WEAVER: [*Timidly, glancing at her watch*] Um...excuse me...that young man knows that I've arrived, doesn't he?

RECEPTIONIST: [*Not looking up*] Oh yes. He said he'll be along in a minute.
[*Several minutes pass by*]

PETER:	[*Ambling out of the reception area and winking at the receptionist.*] Ah. Mrs...um. I see you've found some magazines! Would you like to finish reading that?
MRS WEAVER:	[*Putting down* Banking World *and looking rather frightened.*] Hello. I had an appointment to see a Mr Benton. I hope I'm...
PETER:	That's me - you can call me Peter. Mrs...[*flicks through file*] Weaver, ah yes, that's right - problems with loan repayments. Would you like to come this way?
	[*PETER walks quickly down the corridor, pausing half way down to check that MRS WEAVER is following.*]
PETER:	[*In doorway, to three junior staff in suits, smoking and laughing*] Could you clear out for ten minutes, please guys: I've got an F104.
	[*MRS WEAVER arrives in the room. The three 'guys' pick up their papers, put out their cigarettes and leave. PETER leans his head out of the door before closing it and makes an inaudible remark which is greeted with loud laughter.*]
PETER:	Well Mrs Weaver. How can we help you?
MRS WEAVER:	Well actually *you* wrote to me and asked me to come in and see you. I'm sorry.
	[*The phone rings.*]
PETER:	Oh, put him through. John! How are you? How's business?... Yes I did ring you, its about that ten grand you were after. I just wanted to say, no problem mate. Yes, I thought you'd be pleased. How's Caroline? [*Lengthy silence while PETER listens to the person on the other end of the line.*] I'm sorry... I had no idea, mate. So it's completely... um... there's no chance of you getting back together? ... Well, give it time, you know what they say. Look, I've got to go - I'll see you Friday, OK? Bye.
	[*Peter now looks down at the file on the table and leafs through it for some time.*]
	Now then, Mrs Weaver...

Peter clearly does not deal with Mrs Weaver very well. What criticisms would you make of his handling of this case?

Ascertaining visitors' needs

2.9 If you are receiving visitors it is your responsibility to **ascertain their needs**. You need to find out:

- What they want or need
- Whether your organisation can help them
- What information they require
- Who they need to see

2.10 **Put yourself in your client's position**. Imagine you are in his or her business: what does (s)he need to know about the products and services you offer? Can you describe the essential features that persuaded you to buy your most recent major purchase?

2.11 We shall now consider the different types of enquiry which visitors may be armed with, and how best to deal with them.

3 Assisting visitors

General guidelines for assisting visitors

3.1 There is a balance between what you can reasonably be expected to know about your organisation and knowing the **limits within which you are able to deal with enquiries**. Nevertheless, the way that you deal with visitors and their enquiries is crucial to the success of the relationship and of your organisation.

Action Programme 2

The Needle Works

You have recommended an 'open evening' for regular customers in the refurbished showroom, partly as a public customer contact exercise and partly to show off the new knitting department. You have organised a festive in-store display, a string quartet and a buffet and drinks, with waiter service. Albert Smith wants you to attend on the evening itself because you are frequently the first point of contact with clients on the telephone, and because you organised the open evening, and might be needed to supervise arrangements. You know that your presence will (thanks to excellent pre-planning) not be required once things have been set up. You will not be paid to attend. You had arranged to see some friends that evening.

Who will gain if you attend the open evening and in what ways?

3.2 There are many positive things that you can do to provide a good service to visitors.

(a) Be **polite**, interested, warm and friendly, but not over-familiar or disrespectful.

(b) Be as **helpful** as you can within the bounds of your responsibilities.

(c) If you cannot help but somebody else in your organisation can, then **put the customer in touch with that person** as soon as possible (there is more on this below).

(d) Make your customers trust you by **doing what you say you will do** promptly and efficiently.

(e) **Do not promise to do something that you do not have the ability or authority to do.**

(f) **Do not criticise your own organisation** in response to complaints or difficulties, whatever your personal feelings about it. You will only make things worse by whinging to outsiders.

(g) **If you make a mistake, apologise and put it right straight away**. Be aware that what may seem a minor, unimportant slip to you may have seriously inconvenienced or distressed your customer.

Meeting visitors' information needs

3.3 If a visitor or caller requests **information about the products or services of the organisation**, you may well have the information to hand, although the degree of knowledge you need to have will depend on the nature of your involvement and the complexity of the organisation's activity.

3.4 Be sure that you can give an answer to the following questions.

(a) What does your organisation do? What does your own department do, and what other departments are there?

(b) Does your organisation supply to other businesses, to domestic clients or to both? Does it export its product or services?

(c) Is there a brochure describing your organisation's products/services? There may be many such brochures - are you aware of all of them?

(d) What new products or services are going to be introduced? Are the old versions to be discontinued?

(e) Do you know where your organisation's branches are, in relation to major towns?

(f) Is your organisation part of a larger group or does it have smaller subsidiaries? What are their names and what do they do?

(g) Who are your organisation's major competitors? How are your organisation's products/services different from theirs?

(h) If you did not know the answer to a question about your organisation, who could help you or deal with the query?

Exam Tip

Learn as much as you can about your organisation's business: it will make you more effective in your job and it will help your prospects. You will learn by experience from doing your own job and you can also learn by talking to colleagues, especially those who are more experienced than you are. You could also glance through trade journals - even if the detailed articles are too complex or specialised for you, the advertisements will be very informative.

3.5 **Asking other people** is an acceptable option. Recognise your own limits and get help. You should have a telephone list of departments and individual colleagues you can consult. Use your common sense

- Who is the most appropriate person to consult?
- When and how to consult them?

3.6 Also, while you are conducting your information search, remember to **keep the enquirer informed**. ('I'm just calling the production department. I won't be a moment.')

3.7 **Referring the enquirer direct to the expert** is a legitimate option. There are four ways of doing this.

- Directing the visitor to the **appropriate department**
- **Calling the appropriate department** to arrange an appointment
- **Putting the enquirer though by telephone** to the appropriate department
- Calling or **paging the appropriate person** to come to meet the visitor

To whom should you give information?

3.8 Whether or not you give **information** about your organisation's products or services in response to unsolicited queries depends very much upon the sort of product or service that you supply. You may, for example, need to know something of the circumstances of prospective customers to determine whether its products or services are suitable for that customer's needs. We shall return to this point in a moment.

3.9 In cases where the product/service is more limited in its availability or more sensitive in its nature, the organisation may require certain **formal checks** to be carried out to verify an enquirer's **identity** and **eligibility** to receive information.

(a) Some companies operate a policy of replying **only in writing** to requests for information that could be sensitive.

(b) Banks, for example, will not tell you your own bank balance unless you have agreed some **password** known only to you and them in advance.

3.10 **Less formal checks** are carried out all the time, sometimes even unintentionally.

(a) If a known client rings up and asks for certain information and you agree to ring back with the details, you are verifying that the caller was who he said he was simply by ringing the number you have on record.

(b) You may get calls or written requests that your instinct tells you do not ring true - the address may be too suburban for a business-related product, say, or the amount ordered may be improbably large. Your organisation probably has a policy to deal with such incidents, perhaps asking for written confirmation or payment in advance.

(c) You can carry out informal identity checks by looking people up in trade directories or Yellow Pages.

Confidentiality

3.11 The information you give out will also be limited by the principles and procedures of **confidentiality**. You do not expect the staff of your bank to discuss your personal financial circumstances with anybody who happens to walk into the branch. Everybody has a right to expect the organisations that they deal with to respect the privacy of their affairs.

(a) **Do not discuss the detailed affairs of one client with another**. You might sometimes need to say 'I dealt with a very similar case last week, and the way we solved the problem there was...', but you should never give names or other details that would identify one client to another.

(b) If you are asked for the **names of some of your other customers** - for example, if a potential customer wants a second opinion on the worth of your products - make sure you get permission from the other customers to use them as **references**.

(c) **Within your organisation use the 'need to know' principle**. If people in other departments do not need to be given all of the information that you possess about a particular client, do not give it to them. There may be organisational rules that forbid certain information from being passed between departments.

Key Concept

Confidentiality is the keeping of information, given 'on confidence' to particular parties, between those parties: not disclosing information to those not authorised to have access to it.

3.12 Do not forget that the **affairs of your own organisation are confidential**. Do not gossip about your organisation to clients, or malign your colleagues.

4 Dealing with difficult customers

4.1 You will encounter **awkward or aggressive people** no matter how hard you try to please them or how well you do your own job. Some people seem to like complaining over the smallest thing and some are simply having a bad day and your organisation's slip is the last straw.

4.2 In many ways dealing with customers who are upset or angry is like dealing with difficult colleagues. Here are some guidelines.

(a) **Be calm and polite**. If you speak in a fairly low, slow tone of voice, and keep your body fairly still (even if you are speaking to them on the phone), you can usually calm the other person down.

(b) **Listen** to what they have to say, and let them know you are listening (nod in face-to-face encounters; say 'yes' or 'I see' on the phone). Repeat back the substance of their complaint, to demonstrate that you have understood the problem from their side.

(c) Deal with **the problem, not the person** - and get the complainers to do the same. Try to make them see you as the person who can get their problem put right, not the person who caused it in the first place. Take detailed notes of all relevant facts.

(d) Use a **win-win approach** (see Chapter 5) to show your willingness to be constructive and creative in getting the complainer what he wants if at all possible.

(e) **Do not grovel, apologise or give way too readily**, however. The customer might have a valid complaint - or might not. (He may even be 'trying it on', to get a rebate or discount, say.) This situation is rather like a car accident: get each others' details but don't admit liability! Don't agree or disagree with the visitor during the confrontation: listen, be sympathetic but firm, and say that you will make sure that the complaint is investigated immediately.

(f) **Follow through** on any investigation or action you promise, and keep the person informed of progress and outcomes.

4.3 There may be an organisational policy for dealing with difficult people, for example handing over people who start to get difficult to a **more senior person**. If so, follow the rules in your organisation.

5 E-relationships

E-relationships with customers

5.1 Marketers can take steps towards promoting **effective e-relationships with customers** in the Internet age. We look at relationships with suppliers in the context of **'e-procurement'** in the next chapter. You will probably notice that the principles which are explored would hold true for 'offline' customers as well, and that human interaction will never be fully replaced.

Improve customer interaction

5.2 The first thing for the organisation to do is to **upgrade the interaction with its existing customers**.

(a) Create **automated responses for the FAQs** (Frequently Asked Questions) posed by customers, so that customers become conditioned to electronic communication.

(b) Set **fast response standards**, at least to match anything offered by the competition.

(c) **Use e-mail** in order to confirm actions, check understanding, and reassure the customer that their business is being taken forward.

(d) **Establish ease of navigation** around your website and enhance the site's 'stickiness' so that there is a reduced likelihood that customers will wander away.

Marketing at Work

A study conducted by Rubic Inc in the USA ('Evaluating the 'Sticky' Factor of E-Commerce Sites') found that the majority of websites fail to communicate effectively with customers. Only 40 per cent had a strategy of personalisation for their e-mail messages to customers. When customers responded to follow-up offers, only one quarter of websites recognised the fact that they were dealing with a repeat customer. Forty per cent of e-mail enquiries went unanswered despite promises of replies within two days.

Understand customer segments

5.3 The organisation should **understand its customer segments** and the likelihood that they will be receptive to the Internet.

(a) Some will be **eager** to transfer to the new technology, others will do so **if persuaded**, and residual groups will prefer to **remain as they are**.

(b) Efforts should be made to **automate** the provision of customer service to **low-value customers**.

(c) The organisation should establish **personalised service relationships** with high value customers.

Understand service processes

5.4 The organisation must **understand its customer service processes** in order to see those which can safely be put on to the Web, and those which have to be delivered in other ways.

(a) This analysis is essential for addressing such questions as: Which of these processes is appropriate for automation? Which of these processes will work better if put on the Web?

(b) Customers are often conscious about time and timeliness. Getting on to the Internet sometimes takes longer than a telephone call, so the customer will want more value from the process.

(c) Remember that a short simple transaction is often better conducted over the telephone!

Define the role

5.5 The organisation needs to **think about how much live interaction with its customers is needed**.

(a) Live interaction may be very useful if there is scope for cross-selling and the conversion of enquiries into sales. It is essential for customers who have a strong **preference** for human contact.

(b) The availability of service supplied by human intervention can also be appropriate if the organisation needs to build **trust** (eg it is a new brand) and secure **information** from the customer.

(c) **E-mail may not be sufficient as a communication route**, especially if it involves a delay before replies are forthcoming.

Deal with the tidal wave

5.6 There is much evidence that offering an Internet-based service can lead to a major increase in customer interaction, and so organisations need to develop strategies for this. This might involve:

- Ensuring sufficient **capacity** is available
- Using **user-friendly** technologies
- Ensuring facilities can adjust if demand rapidly outstrips supply

Marketing at Work

Many banks offer all four; some have single-channel accounts (phone or Internet only), whilst others (like **egg**) allow constrained choice: **egg** (the Internet and telephone banking arm of the Prudential Assurance Company) will allow telephone and Internet customer interaction, but only permits new customers to enrol via the web.

One reason why Charles Schwab (specialists in stock and share dealing) is able to charge much bigger fees than some of its rivals is that it combines an online service with a low-cost branch network and a telephone service. They have recognised the web has certain virtues and weaknesses. The web is lousy if you have a complex question. Likewise, it does not allow for people's need for relationships. Not everyone feels happy about sending a cheque to a broker they have never seen.

Exploit the Internet

5.7 The organisation should exploit the Internet in order to create new **relationships** and **experience** for customers.

(a) E-mail marketing can be used to give product and offer updates.

(b) E-zines and newsletters can be used to make regular value-added contacts with customers.

(c) The corporate website should be designed to prompt multiple visits: offering new/updated content; entertaining interactive features (eg quizzes and testers, games etc); helpful links and database/search features; special offers and so on.

(d) Special areas of the website may be set up for key account customers, or to customers who choose to register as 'members' (thereby giving permission for relationship marketing), with special offers, facilities or perceived exclusivity.

(e) Virtual communities of customers can be set up (using discussion groups, message boards and so on) to create word-of-mouth promotion and referral, elicit feedback and enhance the 'stickiness' of the website.

(f) Self-service elements (database searches, e-commerce transactions) can be used to empower customers and cement relationships: eg an online grocery store which allows past shopping lists to be saved for next time, making recommendations and offers on previously bought items etc.

(g) Web links and banner advertisements can be used to provide added value to customers through collaborative promotions and referrals.

5.8 Other ICT tools for relationship marketing include mobile phone text-messaging, which has become a key promotional tool in the youth market in recent years.

E-relationships within the organisation

5.9 Many organisations now operate using 'virtual' teams: interconnected groups of people who may never be present in the same office – and may even be on different sides of the world – but who share information and tasks, make joint decisions and fulfil the collaborative functions of a 'physical' team.

The development of ICT has enabled communication and collaboration among people in different locations via:

(a) Teleconferencing, videoconferencing and webcasts, allowing 'virtual' meetings.

(b) Locally networked PCs and the World Wide Web, with email, instant-messaging, shared access to databases and so on, allowing fast, interactive communication and data sharing.

(c) Meeting manager systems, with electronic 'white boards' (for making notes), bulletin boards and data sharing. Virtual meeting participants can use teleconference lines to talk to each other, while showing charts and data on their PCs.

(d) Intranets, or employee-only areas of the corporate website, allowing online handbooks, journals, staff information and so on to be exchanged.

5.10 'Virtual teams may be composed of full-time or part-time employees. They might have a global reach, or involve combinations of local telecommuting members and more traditional in-house workers. A senior executive might be on one planning committee for a product release, for example, another for identifying minority vendors, another to study relocating a plant, and another to evaluate software tracking. He may deal with key players who not only are out of the country but also are working for another company, or perhaps as suppliers who are on the virtual team to add information and technical support.' (Solomon, 2001)

5.11 Localised virtual teams have been used for some time in the form of 'teleworking': the process of working from home, or from a satellite office close to home, with the aid of computers, facsimile machines, modems or other forms of telecommunication equipment. The main benefits cited for such work include savings on office overheads and the elimination of the costs and stresses of commuting for employees.

5.12 More recently, however, the globalisation of business, the need for fast responses to marketplace demands and the increasing sophistication of available technologies has brought about an explosion in global virtual teamworking. More and more organisations are attempting to conduct business 24 hours a day, seven days a week, with people on different continents and in different time zones. Electronic collaboration allows organisations to:

- Recruit and collaborate with the best available people without the constraints of location or relocation. A team can 'co-opt' a Specialist when required, from a global pool of skills.
- Offer more scheduling flexibility for people who prefer non-traditional working hours (including the handicapped and working parents, for example).
- Maintain close contact with customers throughout the world.
- Operate 24-hour 'follow the sun' working days (for example, for global customer support) - without having to have staff on night shifts.

Marketing at Work

Is virtual team working all about the technology? Charlene Marmer Solomon (Managing Virtual Teams, *Workforce*, June, 2001) argues otherwise.

'Effective managers of virtual teams understand critical non-technological skills. "Trust is a very important component of virtual teams," says Lynn Newman, an associate professor of organisational studies at the California School of Professional Psychology in Los Angeles. "Managers have to trust that people will perform when they're away from direct supervision. Individual team members need to develop trust across different media, such as e-mail and telephone, which may be difficult to do."

'One of the reasons developing trust is so crucial is that teams are formed to create knowledge. Problems often arise when people work across cultures and have different perceptions of projects. They have to be able to trust each other and the leader if they are going to get the job done effectively.

'Developing a productive virtual team begins with selecting the right people. A successful team member is self-motivated and doesn't need a lot of detailed instructions or structure. Ideally, he or she is a strong communicator, a quality that helps counter-balance the anonymous nature of technology. In addition, Newman recommends people who are adaptable, technically self-sufficient and results-oriented.

'Teams need tools - as well as leaders - to create shared knowledge or shared vision. When a team has a meeting, whether a teleconference, videoconference or face-to-face encounter, the leader must be explicit about goals. "People may have gone off on tangents, and it is at this point that the facilitator keeps the team aligned in terms of the goals and continues to recognise the knowledge sharing," Newman says. "When people are creating knowledge, keeping people up-to-date on where the group is at the moment is key. You need shared understanding of how far they've come and what the group knows as a whole."

'Managers should set up regular virtual meetings to share expectations and debriefings. It is their task to frame the team's objectives so members clearly understand their roles. They emphasise the consequences of team decisions and provide ongoing monitoring and honest feedback about how the team is doing.

'Virtual teams offer an opportunity to work with the best talent throughout an organisation. But to accomplish this, managers must actively work to create a sense of connectedness and shared space, to use technology effectively and to know when to forgo technology for personal communication.'

For reflection:

How does your own experiences of virtual team working reflect the management challenges discussed in this article?

Chapter Roundup

- A **visitor** is a person who visits a person or a place. **Internal** visitors are the other people who work in your organisation, whereas **external** visitors include customers and clients (those people who do not work in your organisation).
- Whatever type of visitor you are receiving, you should always be **polite**, **courteous** and display **good manners**.
- You may receive **routine** or **non-routine** enquires in your place of work; it is important that you are able to deal with them in the proper manner. Make sure that you are familiar with the guidelines covered in this chapter and with your organisation's practice. Always use your common sense when dealing with visitors.
- **Confidentiality** should always be maintained where considered necessary. The affairs of your own organisation and its clients are confidential and should not be disclosed to others unless the circumstances are appropriate.
- Marketers can take steps to improve **e-relationships** with customers and employees.

Quick Quiz

1 What sort of information does a visitors' signing-in book usually record?

2 What are the guidelines that should be followed when dealing with external visitors?

3 What can you do in order to create a good impression when greeting visitors?

4 What options do you have if you do not know the answer to an enquiry?

5 Outline a procedure for dealing with awkward or aggressive visitors.

6 What is an e-relationship?

Now try Question 6 in the Question Bank

Action Programme Review

1 Peter (and the organisation generally) handle Mrs Weaver badly from start to finish.

(a) Mrs Weaver is kept waiting for some while after the appointed time before she receives any attention. Even the receptionist is offhand with her.

(b) When he does arrive Peter does so in a very unbusinesslike manner. He does not greet Mrs Weaver by name. He does not apologise for being late.

(c) His tone of friendliness ('you can call me Peter') is belied by his complete lack of interest in Mrs Weaver's case.

(d) He is quite oblivious to any desire that Mrs Weaver may have for her business to be handled confidentially. He blurts out her financial problems in front of the receptionist.

(e) He is most discourteous in not showing Mrs Weaver the way to the interview room. He should have let her go first and made some attempt to put her at her ease.

(f) He is more polite to the three juniors who appear to be wasting time than he has so far been to his customer. He becomes conspiratorial in referring to her, mysteriously, as 'an F104'. This tells Mrs Weaver that the organisation regards her as a number and that her case, however harrowing its circumstances may be, are about to be swallowed up by bureaucracy.

(g) Peter's private joke with his colleagues may have nothing to do with Mrs Weaver, but by now she is likely to be feeling that, when the organisation is not being seriously inconvenienced by her, it regards her as a laughing matter.

(h) Once more Peter's lack of preparation is shown by his 'How can I help you?'

(i) He should not have accepted the telephone call - it could have been diverted to a colleague or he could have called back later.

(j) The organisation's time and Mrs Weaver's is wasted by the discussion of the caller's domestic circumstances. Mrs Weaver will hardly be able to feel that her own affairs are being handled confidentially if Peter is prepared to have conversations about his friend's circumstances in front of her.

2 (a) You can gain from the evening in a number of ways.

(i) You may learn more about The Needle Works - about its overall aims and the way its various services are linked and complement each other. This will help you to market it more effectively.

(ii) You will extend and develop your networks of people within the company. This is valuable networking, PR *and* market research: you are likely to find out more about how your customers view The Needle Works and its services.

(iii) You will get feedback on your organisation of the open evening: both positive (hopefully) and negative (indicating areas of learning and improvement) which is good market research.

(iv) Albert will be impressed by your loyalty to the company: good personal 'PR', enhancing your image with a person of influence in your workplace.

(v) You will get a free meal!

(b) The Needle Works and its customers will gain in the following ways.

(i) You will have gathered information that will make you more effective in tailoring the marketing message to the customers.

(ii) Your customers will be able to put a face to your name. They will feel more comfortable when dealing with you over the telephone or receiving direct mail from you.

(iii) Your customers may be inclined to use a wide range of the company's services, if they are dealing initially with a known quantity. This should be to the benefit of both parties.

Answers to Quick Quiz

1 A visitors' book usually records the visitor's name, the name and department of the person they have come to see and the purpose of their visit. Sometimes signing in procedures include a time of arrival and exit or a car registration number for security and administration purposes.

2 They should be welcomed, asked to sign in, the person they intend to visit should be notified and reception should stay with the visitor until the host is available.

3 Show that you respect their time, their privacy, their comfort and are interested in them. Good manners dictate you should welcome by name if possible and that you should not keep visitors waiting unnecessarily or leave them to their own devices while you deal with other business.

4 Be honest and let the visitor know that you do not know the answer without making excuses. Let the visitor know what you are going to do about it and then do it or check that it has been followed up by a colleague.

5 Remain calm and polite. Listen sympathetically to the problem and try to solve it. Reason, rather than react. Is it the fault of your organisation or is the complaint unreasonable? Either way, negotiate an outcome that is positive for both sides without appeasing the complainant with unwarranted apologies. Let the complainant know what you are going to do and when and make sure that the action is undertaken.

6 An e-relationship is one maintained by electronic contact through an Internet site.

7 The Supply Chain

Chapter Topic List	
1	Setting the scene
2	Collaborating and negotiating
3	Suppliers of marketing services
4	Working with advertising agencies
5	Working with distribution channels
6	E-procurement

Learning Outcome

☑ Develop relationships inside and outside the organisation

Syllabus References

☑ Explain the supplier interface; negotiating, collaborating, operational and contractual aspects

☑ Explain how the organisation fits into a supply chain, and works with distribution channels

☑ Explain the concept and application of e-relationships

Key Concepts Introduced

- Collaboration
- Brief
- Push
- Pull

1 Setting the scene

1.1 In many ways, relationships with suppliers and distribution channels are the same as those with colleagues, customers, visitors and other business contacts and require many of the same features. We will not be dealing again in detail with the 'human' aspects of relationships in this chapter.

1.2 In other respects, however, relationships with suppliers and distributors are different to those with colleagues and visitors. As business relationships, they raise a number of other issues.

(a) They involve dealings with other business organisations which have their own aims and objectives which may or may not be in harmony with yours.

(b) They involve dealings with representatives of other business organisations, who have a dual responsibility to you (as client) and (primarily) to their employers.

(c) They are governed by legal terms and constraints, expressed in contracts.

(d) They are subject to commercial and competitive pressures: if one party is not satisfied, they can break the relationship.

(e) They are shaped by the operational requirements of the work for which the relationship was formed.

1.3 In this chapter, we will look primarily at the **operational**, **procedural** and **contractual** aspects of working with the supply chain, particularly from the point of view of the marketing department's relationships.

(a) **Suppliers of marketing services** (advertising agencies, PR consultancies, creative freelancers)

(b) **Retailers and other distribution channels** which require marketing support. (If you're in the marketing department of a retail outlet, say, you can consider this section 'in reverse'!)

1.4 On completion of this chapter, you should be able to:

- negotiate and collaborate with suppliers of marketing services
- appreciate the interpersonal, procedural and contractual aspects of working with suppliers
- liase with advertising agency account executives to co-ordinate a range of marketing operations
- appreciate the role of marketing support, collaboration and co-ordination with distribution channels

1.5 First, we will look in general terms at two aspects of business relationships: **collaborating** and **negotiating**.

2 Collaborating and negotiating

Collaborating

Key Concept

Collaboration simply means 'working with', but is used in the stronger sense of working *jointly* or sharing tasks and responsibility with another party.

2.1 There are **three main elements** to collaborating effectively with other business organisations and their representatives.

- Contracts
- Systems and procedures
- Purpose

Contracts

2.2 In basic terms, a contract or **legally binding agreement** exists between two parties if there is:

- The **intention to create a legal relationship** (as opposed to a purely personal one)
- **Offer and acceptance** (agreeing to supply or receive goods or services)
- **Consideration** (some payment given or promised for the goods or services to be supplied)

2.3 This covers most of the transactions you will come across in marketing activity. A contract does not have to be a formal legal document: it can be a letter, or even a strong **verbal understanding** (as long as the three basic elements can be proved). Be aware that when you ask a designer or printer to do work for you and they agree to do so, and you negotiate a price, that you are entering into a contract.

2.4 A contract may set out **express terms**, or clearly stated terms.

- Delivery/completion dates
- Description of the goods/services to be provided
- Quality standards below which the goods/services will not be accepted
- The amount to be paid, and when, and what it covers and does not cover
- Any conditions and caveats either party wishes to impose: for example, that they will not be liable for errors arising from faulty components or information provided by the other party; that in the event of cancellation of the project, they will be paid for all work done up to the date of cancellation.

Action Programme 1

Get hold of a copy of the terms and conditions of any service supplier you may do business with. (Printers often put them on the back of quotation stationery: advertising media with their rate card. You can find them in Photo Library catalogues and order forms. Use your research skills.) Note the main issues covered by contract terms and identify areas where your procedures and practices may need adjusting to comply more securely.

2.5 A contract also has **implied terms**, which are 'understood' from the context of the business relationship. If not expressly stated, for example, it is still implied that goods and services should be of reasonable quality, provided to specification and within a reasonable timescale.

2.6 When working with other organisations, it is helpful to exchange a contract, letter or purchase order.

- Which is in **writing** (even if only to confirm a verbal agreement)
- Which **defines the products/services** to be supplied, and the delivery schedule
- Which **defines the division of responsibility** between the parties
- Which confirms the negotiated **terms and conditions for payment**

Systems and procedures

2.7 The procedures to be followed will be dictated by the particular task or project in hand. Be aware that simply following recommended procedures correctly and efficiently is a major element in working smoothly and successfully with other organisations, who have usually developed ways of working for a reason!

2.8 In general, however, a **systematic approach** to collaboration should include the following.

(a) **Clear and specific briefing on requirements**. Be clear what you want suppliers/collaborators to do for you. Objectives, schedules, budgets and job specifications make everyone's job easier.

(b) **Joint planning**. The brief sets out what you want to achieve: how you get there (together) is best decided collaboratively, since the other party has input to offer, and their own aims, procedures and constraints to take into account. Define clearly the scope and limit of everyone's activity, and establish how to implement any recommendations agreed on.

(c) **Negotiation of terms**. (This will be discussed in more detail below.)

(d) **Sharing of information and resources**. Helping others to help you requires the provision or availability of any information, materials and other resources they may require. (A designer working on an ad for example, may require product samples, catalogues, existing corporate literature, corporate identity specifications and contacts with the company's printers.)

(e) **Monitoring, checking and approval**. Liaison and accountability is the way to ensure your objectives are met. Collaboration with marketing service providers requires submission of plans of work for checking and approval by the client at each stage of the process. If this is not built into the procedure, initiate it yourself.

(f) **Exchanging feedback**. Developing on-going relationships requires mutual adjustment. Regular feedback meetings allow both parties to reinforce positive aspects, identify and solve problems and celebrate collaborative successes. Balance constructive criticism and complaints.

(g) **Paying debts.** Nothing sours a commercial relationship like non-payment or persistent late payment. Accounts departments may resist for cash-flow reasons, but be prepared to champion legitimate demands.

Purpose

2.9 Here, we are referring to more than the job specification or task objectives which govern the activity of a relationship. If you want to develop an effective collaboration, consider what it is for: what is the purpose of collaborating rather than doing the work yourself?

(a) Your purpose in retaining an advertising agency or other consultancy service is to take advantage of the expertise, experience, contacts, facilities and synergy they offer. Your organisation is paying for specialist skills and objectivity and wide experience which it ignores to its loss – and to the detriment of the professional relationship. Moreover, it is unfair to force a supplier to perform against his judgement and advice especially if, as in the highly visible world of advertising and PR, it may affect his reputation in the industry.

(b) Your purpose in working with retail outlets, wholesalers, sales representatives and other distribution channels is to motivate them to stock and sell your products ('**push**') and/or to support them by promoting products to consumers ('**pull**').

Marketing at Work

Quinn (1988) tells the story of an advertising agency which has a major banking organisation as its client. The bank 'had a habit of running its agency like it would run any other department of its organisation, and the agency let it' (because it was frightened of losing a multi-million pound account). A UK television campaign was being planned, when the bank called in the agency to show them an American TV ad, which bank executives had seen and fallen in love with. In spite of the agency's opposition, the bank insisted that the campaign simply be re-shot in the British idiom. The agency argued that what works for US audiences (especially in terms of humour) does not work with British audiences. They were overruled, and though they did their best, the campaign was a disaster: the bank lost its claimed number one market position within weeks.

Negotiating

2.10 **Negotiating** is, simply, a process whereby two parties came together to confer with a view to concluding a jointly acceptable agreement. Gennard and Judge (2003) suggest that this process involves two main elements:

- **Purposeful persuasion**: whereby each party attempts to persuade the other to accept its case by marshalling arguments, backed by factual information and analysis.
- **Constructive compromise**: whereby both parties accept the need to move closer toward each other's position, identifying the parameters of common ground within and

between their positions, where there is room for concessions to be made while still meeting the needs of both parties.

2.11 Such an approach can be applied to a number of different situations.

- Agreeing **contract terms**. For example: negotiating price, specifications and trading terms for purchase contracts; negotiating terms and conditions in employment contracts; and negotiating industrial relations agreements.
- **Conflict resolution**: reducing resentment and preserving relationship, by allowing both parties to obtain at least some of their desired outcomes;
- **Group decision-making** and **problem-solving**: integrating different viewpoints and interests so that the decision or solution is high on quality (from diverse relevant input) *and* acceptability (from joint consultation and commitment), enhancing the likelihood of effective implementation. People are increasingly expecting to participate in decisions that affect them, particularly at work.

2.12 Dobler *et al.* (1990) define negotiation in the purchasing context as: 'a process of planning, reviewing and analysing used by a buyer and a seller to reach acceptable agreements or compromises [which] include all aspects of the business transaction, not just price.'

- They cite five major objectives in commercial negotiation:
- To obtain a fair and reasonable price for the quality specified
- To get the supplier to perform the contract on time
- To exert some control over the manner in which the contract is performed
- To persuade the supplier to give maximum co-operation to the buyer's company
- To develop a sound and continuing relationship with competent suppliers.

The negotiation process

2.13 The following figure (Figure 7.1) is a general overview of the negotiation process.

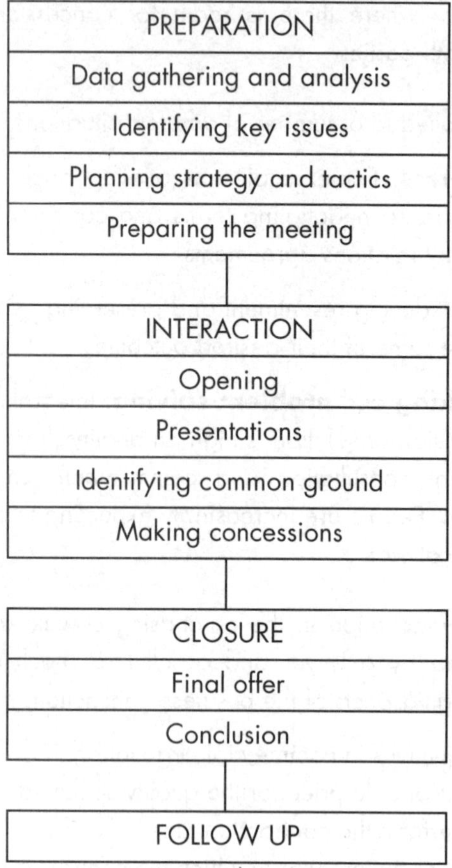

Figure 7.1: The negotiation process

Marketing at Work

In general, Asian cultural preferences in relation to conflict and negotiation reflect their collectivist values and high-context communication styles. Research into conflict strategy and face by Ting-Toomey *et al.* (1991) found that Asian subjects tended to use mutual face-saving strategies, including given others room to manoeuvre in negotiation, allowing them to recover face. They used consensus-seeking, integrative strategies. American subjects, in contrast, tended to focus on saving their own face (interpreted in a more individualistic sense as pride, reputation and self-respect), adopting control-focused and win-lose conflict/negotiation strategies.

Negotiating strategies

2.14 The aim of negotiating is not to get the best position for yourself or your organisation at the expense of the other party (a **win-lose outcome**). This can cause resentment, under-motivated performance by the 'losing' collaborator, or even the breaking of the relationship.

2.15 A basic **'win-win' approach** to negotiating (Cornelius & Faire, 1989) is as follows.

(a) **Map out**, in advance, what the needs and fears of both parties are. This outlines the psychological and practical territory.

(b) **Define your desired outcome** and estimate the worst, realistic and best case scenarios. ('If I can pay £500, it would be ideal, but I'd settle for £600. Above £700, it's just not worth my while.') Start with the best case and leave room to fall back to the realistic case. Keep your goal in sight.

(c) **Look for mutual or trade-off benefits**. How might you both gain (for example, by getting a higher discount in return for longer or pre-booked series of ads or providing camera ready copy)? What might be cheap for you to give that would be valuable for the other party to receive, or vice versa?

(d) **Spell out the positive benefits** to the other party and support them in saying 'yes' to your proposals by making it as easy as possible. (Offer to supply information or help with follow-up tasks, for example.) Emphasise areas of agreement and common ground.

(e) **Overcome negativity** by asking questions

- What will make it work for you?
- What would it take to make this possible?

(f) **Overcome side-tracks** by asking questions such as: ' How is this going to get us where we want to go?'

(g) **Be hard on the problem but soft on the person**. This is not personal competition or antagonism: work together on problem solving (eg by using flip chart or paper to make shared notes). Show that you have heard the other person (by summarising their argument) before responding with your counter argument.

(h) **Be flexible**. A 'take it or leave it' approach breaks relationships. (However, saying 'no' repeatedly to sales people is a good way of finding out just how far below the list price they are prepared to go!) Make and invite reasonable counter offers.

(i) **Be culturally sensitive**. Some markets thrive on 'haggling'. Some cultures engage in a lot of movement up and down the bargaining scale (eg Asian and Middle Eastern), while others do their homework and fix their prices (eg German). In the former cultures, much emphasis is placed on building relationships and extending hospitality before getting down to terms.

(j) **Take notes**, so the accuracy of everyone's recollection of what was proposed and agreed can be checked.

(k) Summarise and **confirm the details** of your agreements to both parties (by memo, letter, contract) and acknowledge a mutually positive outcome.

2.16 **Experience**, **knowledge** and **expertise** count in negotiation: they add up to bargaining power, which is important even in a win-win approach. If there is someone in your department who has experience in a particular field (such as advertising sales), or your organisation retains an agency or consultancy, be prepared to let them handle negotiations for you.

Action Programme 2

Get together with fellow students (or friends) in pairs or teams to prepare and role-play a negotiation.

You are looking to purchase advertising space in (any appropriate) magazine for a colour advertisement for your product. You have not previously advertised in this magazine, but have identified it as one which is targeted for your market and high circulation: it could be the key to your up-coming campaign. The copy deadline for the next issue is approaching and the magazine had an unsold colour page which it needs to fill. Rate card price for the colour page is £2,000 (£2,800 for the inside front cover, £2,500 for the inside back cover highly contested positions), which you would love to secure. Standard discounts include 10% media buyer's commission, 10% for a series of six ads. You pay 5% extra for bleed colour (running off the page edge). You and the magazine representative(s) should separately (without telling each other) decide what your necessary outcomes are: you should decide what you have to spend from your space budget, and how many ads you think you will need; the magazine rep(s) should decide that the minimum price they will accept, given their need to see space filled. Negotiate a deal!

If you really can't find role-play partners, make notes on the possible strategies, win-win potential, and best-realistic-worst positions for all participants.

3 Suppliers of marketing services

3.1 There are a number of reasons why you might want to use external marketing services, rather than plan or carry out marketing activities in-house.

(a) Professional marketing agencies **specialise** in communications, media and consumer trends, and stay **up-to-date**.

(b) They have wide **experience** with a range of clients, which they can bring to bear on problems and opportunities.

(c) They supply specialist organisational and creative talent with **specialist facilities** (for example, for filming, sound recording and editing).

(d) They are **objective** about the client's needs and position, and may be better able to view the product from the consumer's point of view.

(e) The **cost** of using external services, past a certain level of sophistication, is usually cheaper than attempting to perform the same functions in-house.

3.2 In the last few decades, marketing techniques have increased dramatically in range and complexity. Standard '**above-the-line**' marketing (where media space is paid for), handled by large advertising agencies, has been augmented by '**below-the-line**' (promotional) activities. Agencies specialising in sales promotion, direct marketing and PR have sprung up as independent operations and divisions of large advertising agencies. Many companies now use more than one agency to handle a **portfolio** of techniques above- and below-the-line, or to cover **local and on-going** work as well as **national strategic** campaigns.

3.3 We will discuss the various marketing techniques (above- and below-the-line) in Chapters 12 – 14. Here we will briefly outline some of the **service providers** with whom you may have to deal.

Market researchers

3.4 Market researchers can be commissioned to gather and analyse information on any aspect of the business, market or environment, as discussed in Chapter 3.

Advertising agencies

3.5 Advertising agencies are still the most commonly used marketing service. Agencies come in a range of sizes and specialisms to reflect the increasingly fragmented and diverse range of media.

(a) '**Media only**' service (where the agency selects schedules and books advertising space at a discount, which is in part passed onto the client)

(b) '**Full service**' (where the agency creates the whole campaign from concept through production to press/air).

3.6 Many larger, integrated agencies now have divisions specialising in various areas.

- Sales promotion
- Direct marketing
- Public relations
- 'New' media (Internet, CD-ROM)
- Design

3.7 We will discuss relationships with advertising agencies in detail in section 4 below.

Promotion agencies

3.8 **Promotional activities** – collaborations between brands, competitions and incentives – have been a huge growth area in marketing. Some agencies specialise in these areas.

- Sourcing promotional incentive products and merchandise
- Devising links and negotiating deals between brands
- Organising competitions
- Designing and producing promotional packaging and information material

3.9 **PR consultancies** handle several areas.

(a) **Media or press relations** (keeping the media informed, in order to manage the company's portrayal and secure 'free' coverage of product/service information)

(b) **Corporate relations** (promoting a corporate image to the public, market and business world, through a range of PR techniques)

(c) **Marketing support** (promoting specific products or services via publicity, events, press coverage and so on)

(d) **Government relations** (lobbying on behalf of the company's interests)

(e) **Community relations** (targeted at the general public or local residents, via communication and social programmes, community involvement, sponsorship etc)

(f) **Financial relations** (communicating with shareholders, financial media, the Stock Market)

(g) **Employee relations** (communicating with staff)

3.10 PR agencies are less easy to manage than advertising agencies, because their activity and output is often less tangible. The major cost is their time plus expenses. In order to make cost effective use of their services you need to consider the following.

- Set clear **objectives** for the on-going PR plan or specific project
- Set a project **fee** where possible
- **Brief** comprehensively
- **Monitor activity** perhaps via an independent cuttings or media monitoring agency
- Monitor expenditure

Direct marketing services

3.11 **Direct marketing agencies** (and separate specialists) offer a range of services from database and mailing list development, analysis and segmentation to telemarketing, direct mail package design, copy writing, mailing and fulfilment.

Brand identity

3.12 There are specialist agencies which perform specific brand-related services.

- Design and produce product **packaging** and display
- Orchestrate the up-dating of **brand identity** and style
- Research, devise, market-test and register **brand names**

Sponsorship

3.13 Agencies undertake negotiations

- **Sponsorship agreements**
- **Product endorsements** by celebrities
- **Product placement** (the inclusion of branded products in films or TV programmes)

Creative service

3.14 Agency, freelance and corporate help is available.

- Design and layout, artwork and illustration
- Concept development and copy writing
- Print buying and print production
- Photography
- Film, video and audio production
- Web-page design

Action Programme 3

Go out and buy or borrow a copy of *Campaign* (the journal of the advertising industry) and *Marketing Week*. Browse through them: you can ignore the 'who's moved where' and 'who won what account' material, but you will gather lots of useful ideas on the kinds of services and consultancies that are out there, and what they are doing. Add any interesting details to your list of potential useful contacts.

Other services

3.15 In addition to all the above, the marketing department may deal with many providers of services related to promotional events and activities.

- Event organisers, venue managers, hotel/restaurant staff
- Exhibition organisers, stand constructors and removalists
- The Royal Mail and mailing houses
- Model agencies, prop/costume hirers

4 Working with advertising agencies

4.1 Most companies which advertise use an advertising agency:

- for national or international campaigns
- for consumer markets

In addition, large agencies offer a wide portfolio of marketing and corporate/brand identity services which may be utilised as a full-service package.

4.2 However, some companies prefer to arrange their own advertising.

(a) **Issues to consider in adopting a 'do it yourself' approach**.

Factors to consider	Questions	Directions
Experience	Do I know about advertising?	If 'yes', do-it-yourself is a possibility.
The task	Is it simple?	If simple, do-it-yourself is a possibility.
	Am I sure what it is?	If 'no', you probably need an agency.
Money	Would my account interest an agency?	Probably!
Confidence	Do I need a second opinion?	If 'yes', try an agency.
Workload	Is there likely to be a lot of detail?	If 'yes', try an agency.
People	Do I have people who can do it in-house?	If 'no', try an agency or specialist.

(b) **Advantages and disadvantages**

	Agency	Do it yourself
Advantages	Skills Experience Outsider's point of view You can learn from other's mistakes.	Everything in your control Full understanding of your problems Learn as you go along May be faster and cheaper
Disadvantages	Lack of specific knowledge of your business Cannot devote all their time May do a poor job for a small client Probably expensive	Easy to make mistakes Lack of required skills Lack of specialised know-how Limited view – no outside knowledge

Adapted from Wilmshurst (1999)

Exam Tip

The Pilot Paper covered a range of agency issues, including:

- What should be covered in an agency brief (with sample briefing document)
- What problems are likely to arise with a new supplier (especially in a specialised, international market) and how they can be overcome.

In December 2002, you were asked to evaluate a new advertising strategy from the point of view of relevant 'stakeholders': the agency required to carry out the strategy would be one of these 'stakeholders'!

It may not always be stated in a scenario whether the firm has engaged an agency: you may wish to consider engaging one, as one of the tools that may be appropriate in the context given.

Selecting an advertising agency

4.3 If you are using an agency for the first time, or are changing agencies, it is useful to have a list of section criteria such as the following:

Size	Is the agency's size/status comparable to our organisation
Creativity	Do these people do creative imaginative work (if that is what we want)?
Full service	Can the agency source all our needs eg print, TV conference organisation?
Experience	Do they have suitable experience, as an agency, and as individuals?

Confidentiality	Do they work for our competitors?
Location/logistics	Are they nearby if this is necessary?
Personal factors	Can we work with them?
Billing/admin arrangements	Are they to our satisfaction?

4.4 Most firms retain their advertising agency after a careful selection process and with the intention of an on-going relationship. Involvement in a firm's marketing is a more 'intimate' relationship than providing legal or financial advice: the agency will be communicating for the company, so it has to 'immerse' itself in the company's culture. It would be impossible to brief and acclimatise a different agency to this extent for each campaign.

4.5 The agency will appoint an '**account executive**', who liaises with the appropriate person (marketing assistant or advertising co-ordinator) within the client organisation. These two individuals represent the interface between the two organisations and are responsible for the co-ordination of work traffic between them.

Briefing the agency

4.6 The **agency brief** is the initial and most important stage of any project undertaken. The planning and creative teams of the agency need initially to get to know the client, its products, brands, market and customers, and its culture, style, self-image and designed image.

Key Concept

A **brief** (in advertising agency terms) is 'an interpretation of a given market in relation to the product, plus every usable detail about the features and benefits of that product.' (Quinn, 1988)

4.7 A comprehensive **brief** will include the following details.

(a) **The product**, including its design and marketing history, and current 'life cycle' stage, its technical specifications, pack sizes, shelf-life, packaging/distribution arrangements and associated after-sales services.

(b) **The market**: who uses the product, how, when and why, how it is distributed (via wholesale, retail or direct selling), the product's current and desired market share, pricing and discount/margin policies for the product, and sales strategies.

(c) **Previous advertising**: the previous advertising budget (if any), competitors' advertising spend, breakdown of spend above- and below-the-line.

(d) **Current advertising policy**: budget available, desired image for the product and company, objectives of advertising.

(e) The brief may also contain the company's current ideas about the theme for advertising: what it believes is the key concept or **unique selling proposition (USP)** of the product or brand.

4.8 The brief is usually given to the agency account executive who relays it to the relevant agency personnel.

4.9 An example of a proforma for an Adverting brief is set out below.

ADVERTISING BRIEF
Agency
Briefing date
Company
Contact name
Project name
Project description
Budget
Key deadlines
Company background
Business objectives
Background to the brief
Communications objectives
Target audience
Proposition

4.10 Here are some brief notes as a simple aid to filling in each section.

(a) **Project name and description**

Give the project a meaningful name to refer to. The specifics of the product along with the style (punchy, slick and so on) are needed.

(b) **Budget**

You need to be **clear** about what the **budget** covers. For example, how many new photographs need to be shot? This will have a bearing on the production costs. The budget for media will determine the choice for media selection. The agency can alter the **resources** according to the job. All budgets need to be agreed **formally** before proceeding.

(c) **Key deadlines**

List important key deadlines and ask the agency to draw up a timetable for presentation of design concepts, proofs, final proofs and so on.

(d) **Company background**

A brief description of the company will assist the agency in getting a '**feel**' for an appropriate design.

(e) **Business objectives**

This will help the agency position the campaign (or whatever the project involves).

(f) **Background to the brief**

For example, is this a complete **redesign**, or just a **freshen up**? You need to be clear.

(g) **Communications objectives**

The **primary** objective may be to increase sales. This can be incorporated in the design.

(h) **Target audience**

The agency needs a **full description** of the characteristics of the audience. This will enable them to design the campaign (or whatever) with them in mind.

(i) **Proposition**

Be clear what the **USP** is. For example, you cannot have high quality, cheap products, top brands and commodity goods all in the same catalogue. With a clear picture, the agency will be able to **focus** on producing what is required without constantly referring back to the client.

Who's who in the agency?

4.11 Each agency may be structured in different ways.

(a) The simplest form of **agency structure** is as follows (Figure 7.2).

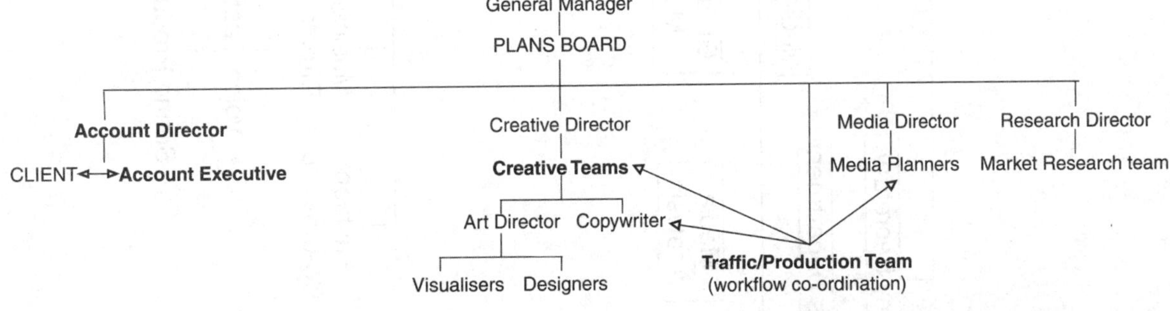

Figure 7.2 Simple agency structure

- The **account executives** service the clients on a day-to-day basis
- The **account director** monitors work on given accounts
- The **creative team** 'produces' the ad

- The **traffic/production team** plans and schedules agency workflow, monitors progress against deadlines and 'chases' work

(b) A large full service agency might look more like the organisation chart below: Figure 7.3.

- Board of Directors
  - General Manager
    - Research Director
      - Market Surveys
      - Psychological Research
    - Plans Board
    - Account Directors
      - Account Executives
    - Creative Director
      - Creative Groups
        - Creative Supervisor
          - Art Director
          - Copy Writer
            - Fashion Co-ordinator
            - Musical Director
              - Voice Casting
              - Sound Production
            - Television Producers
              - Casting
              - Wardrobe
            - Art Studio Manager
              - Studio Artists
              - Art Buyers
            - Press Production
              - Typesetters
            - Print Production
              - Printers
            - Despatch Department
    - Media Director
      - Group Media Manager
      - Media Analysis
      - Checking Department
    - Company Secretary
      - Accounts Department

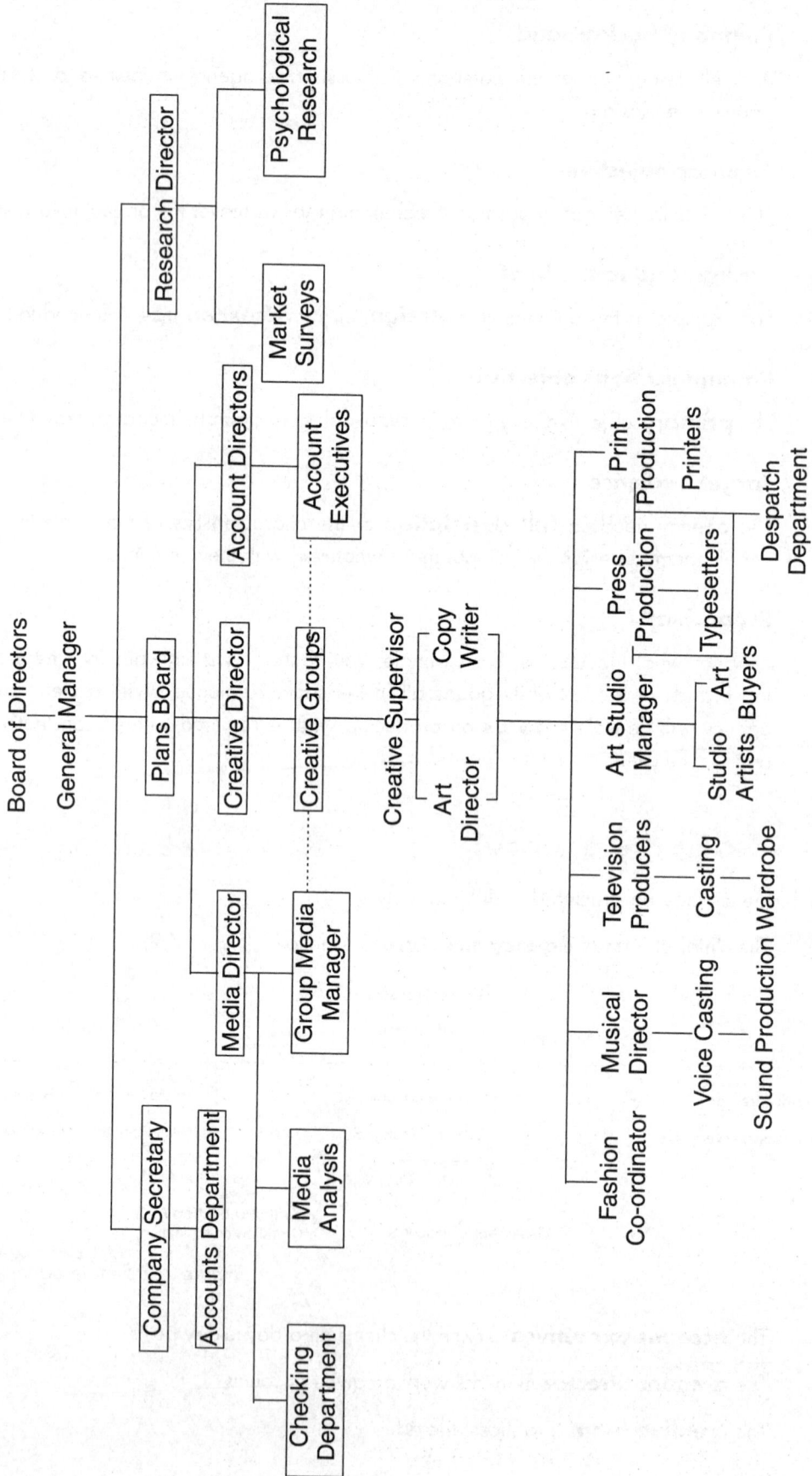

Figure 7.3: Large agency structure

Flow of work through the agency

4.12 The flow of work through the agency can be depicted as follows: Figure 7.4.

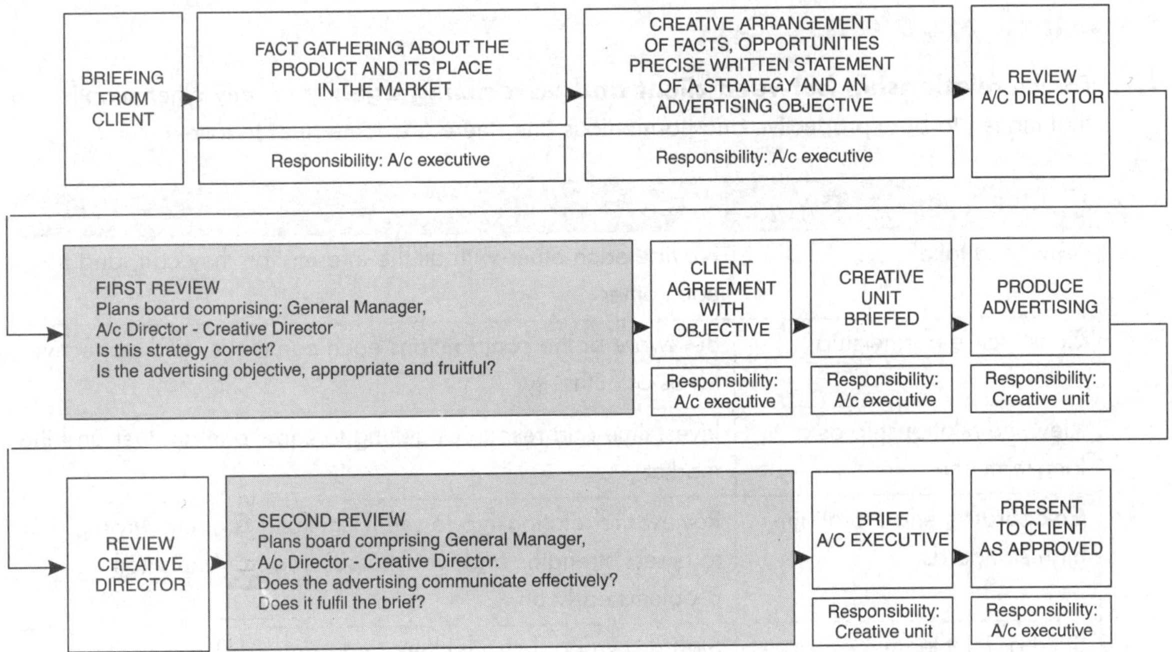

Figure 7.4: Agency work plan
(*Source:* Hearne, 1987)

4.13 Note the **client's responsibilities** implied by the above flow-chart.

(a) The advertising co-ordinator (or marketing department head) briefs the agency.

(b) The marketing department head approves the agency's assessment of the advertising objective, strategy, schedule and cost estimates.

(c) The advertising co-ordinator provides the agency with all available materials and information to help the creative team to produce effective ads.

(d) The advertising co-ordinator is the first one to see work that comes back from the agency at each stage of production (copy, story boards, sketches), and will probably check, correct and recommend any necessary changes before the ad is finally approved by the marketing department head.

(e) The ad is returned to the agency for typesetting, final art, filming and sound production.

(f) The advertising co-ordinator carries out final checks, and gets final approval before giving the agency clearance to release the ad to the media.

Agency costs

4.14 Advertising agencies traditionally charge the following fees.

- A fee for **advice/creativity** (usually around 15% of the value of the media space booked)
- **Design and production** costs, marked up by an agreed percentage

Commission or media discounts raise issues of conflict of interest. Many services are now fee-based: hourly, per project, or hourly up to an agreed maximum per project. This gives greater accountability. Production costs should still be separately budgeted, monitored and accounted for.

Avoiding problems

4.15 For the **relationship between client and advertising agency** (or any other supplier, for that matter) to be a productive and harmonious one, there are some rules to follow.

Behaviour	How?
'Give and take'	Provide each other with all the information they can, and trust each other
Constructive partnership	Be aware of the contributions each can make, and respective levels of authority
View the relationship as a long-term one	Invest time and resources getting to know one another and the market
Co-operative effort to attain high standards	Review the relationship to see if anything is going wrong, and to assess strengths and weaknesses and iron out small problems early on
Build a 'joint team'	Staff drawn partly from client and partly from agency to manage the relationship
Clarity of costs	Agree remuneration in writing

4.16 An IPA (*Institute of Practitioners in Advertising*) booklet 'Getting the most out of the client-agency partnership' suggests the following checklist of questions.

1. Are the client's **corporate objectives**, and the **marketing objectives** that derive from them, entirely clear to both parties? Have the marketing and communications tasks been quantified, together with their financial and profit implications?
2. Are the marketing and communications planners fully informed about **relevant factors in the commercial environment**, particularly:
   - Actual and potential customers
   - Product advantages and limitations
   - Competitors
   - Current or predictable marketing problems
   - Product and marketing development plans?
3. Has sufficient **lead-time** been allowed for planning purposes?
4. Has the agency's **creative policy** been fully thought through and discussed in relation to the defined communications tasks?
5. Do the various creative manifestations (whether advertisements in paid media, explanatory literature, direct mail shots, audio-visual and other sales aids, exhibition stands or press publicity) **express the policy** effectively?
6. Have the **media plan and budget** been fully thought through and discussed? Are both agency and client convinced that they are as cost-effective as available information will permit?

7 If **results** is one area or another have not come up to expectations, has there been a serious effort to find out *why*, instead of shrugging it off or explaining it away?

8 Is there sufficient readiness not just to change for change's sake, but progressively to **improve performance** within an agreed long term policy?

9 Is the level of **financial and administrative control** satisfactory on both sides?

10 Is the level of **client-agency communications** – in both directions – as good as it should be?

11 Is there **mutual understanding and respect** between the individuals working on the account, on the client and on the agency side?

5 Working with distribution channels

5.1 We will be discussing 'place' as part of the marketing mix and the evaluation and management of distribution channels in Part D of this Study Text. Here we will briefly discuss distribution channels as another category of working relationship. Once again, all the interpersonal aspects already covered (collaborating, negotiating, courtesy, communications skills) apply.

Points in the chain of distribution

5.2 Potential distributors with whom the marketing department might deal include the following.

(a) **Retailers**: traders operating outlets which sell goods directly to consumers. These may be large or small, independent or part of a chain or co-operative, specialist or variety.

(b) **Wholesalers**: intermediaries who buy in and stock a range of products to sell on to other organisations such as retailers. Economies of scale allow them to buy and sell at discount prices.

(c) **Distributors and dealers**: intermediaries who contract to buy goods and promote and sell them to customers at a profit. They usually specialise in a particular product or brand.

(d) **Agents**: intermediaries who sell goods on the manufacturer's behalf, earning commission on the sales.

(e) **Franchises**: independent organisations which in exchange for an initial fee and a share of sales revenue are allowed to trade under the name of the parent organisation.

(f) **Direct sales service providers**: telemarketing agencies and TV/Internet/direct mail marketing agencies. These functions may be carried out within the sales and marketing department of the organisation.

Factors in relationships with distribution channels

5.3 In working with **distributors**, the marketer needs to bear in mind the following points.

(a) **The independent commercial objectives of the distributor**. Distributors are business organisations with their own requirements for efficiency and profitability. They do not stock products or run promotions as a 'favour' to the supplier!

(i) You need to negotiate and contract terms.

(ii) You need to promote the benefits of the product or collaboration to the distributor. We will discuss this further below.

(iii) You need to work efficiently and with professionalism in order to maintain the working relationship.

(b) **The distributor's relationship with competitors**. Bear in mind that a retailer or wholesaler may well be stocking and promoting competing products. You will need to be discreet to differentiate your product and promotions, and to be aware of opportunities to gain useful market intelligence.

(c) **The distributor's knowledge of the consumer**. Distributors are in the front line of contact with consumers. Be prepared to seek and respect their research or sense of what will work in terms of product and promotion.

(d) **The distributor's power in the market**. Major distributors have considerable buying power over suppliers, and good working relationships must be preserved with them, usually at the expense of autonomy and control over promotions. A major distributor may ask for exclusive rights to sell a product, or ask to sell it under an 'own brand' label. It may control all point-of-sale and media promotions regarding its sale of the product, charging a fee for promotional space and collaboration.

(e) **The mutual benefit of promotional collaboration**

(i) If the supplier promotes the product to consumers through PR, advertising and consumer incentives, the distributor selling the product to consumers will benefit.

(ii) If the distributor promotes the product to consumers – through advertising its availability through the distributor, or through in-store display and incentives -the supplier will benefit.

'Push' and 'Pull' activity

5.4 In terms of marketing activity, the supplier will be involved in both **'push' and 'pull' promotion**.

Key Concept

'**Push**' or '**sell in**' techniques are designed to promote the product to the distribution network in order to get the product into the market place.

5.5 Unless the supplier has its own distribution outlet, it has to persuade distributors that stocking and selling the product will be worthwhile using various methods.

(a) **Trade advertising and promotion**, focused on the product's sales potential and the marketing support offered by the supplier.

(b) Offering **incentive** discounts or sale-or-return terms, to reduce the distributor's risk.

(c) Offering product **support**, such as guarantees, efficient after-sales, exchange or repair service, in-store stock checking and maintenance.

(d) Offering **marketing/promotional** support, such as point-of-sale display materials, sales force incentives, joint promotions and the demonstration of an aggressive 'pull' campaign.

Key Concept

'**Pull**' techniques are designed to promote the product to the consumer, so that forecast or actual enquiry/sales volume encourages distributors to stock and re-stock the product.

5.6 **Pull** or **sell through** is achieved through the range of promotional methods: consumer advertising, promotional incentives, merchandising, packaging and PR: Figure 7.5.

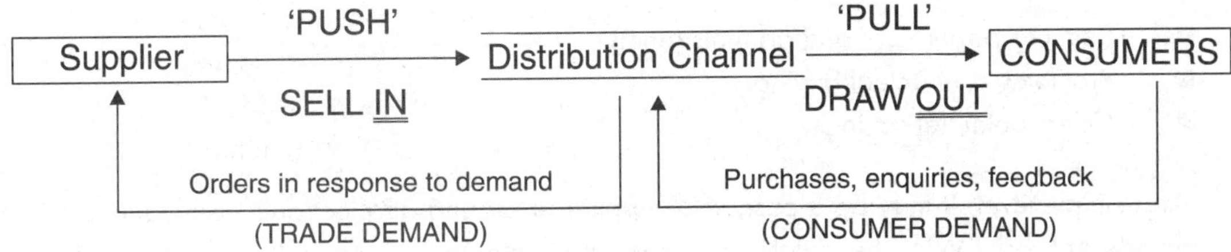

Figure 7.5: Promotion through the supply chain

Marketing at Work

IBM established the IBM Gold Logo Dealer award scheme, as a non-monetary incentive scheme for dealers. A number of computer dealers who exceed incentive-level volume and quality targets are annually awarded the title, which they are allowed to display on signage, stationery, advertising and so on. As if the recognition and prestige were not enough, surveys showed that *consumers* value this award and most major dealerships say it boosts their sales.

On the other hand, MacNamara (1993) tells of another major computer manufacturer who wanted to offer a new car or holiday to the dealership sales rep who sold the most machines. A communication audit was carried out to test dealers' responses – 'thank goodness', says MacNamara, because many dealerships refused outright to support such a supposed 'push' technique. 'If our customers know we are in the running to get a new car or holiday for selling them a certain brand of computer, they will question our motives. It will jeopardise our credibility! In other words, 'push' can *damage* 'pull': information-sharing, monitoring and feedback saved this set of supply chain partnerships.

Action Programme 4

The Needle Works

The craft field seems to be characterised by small specialist suppliers: Mrs Smith sells equipment and accessories, patterns, books, magazines and kits from many different designers and manufacturers, locally and overseas. However, there is one major UK manufacturer of yarns, called Threadlines: they have a high profile in the market, and many needlework and knitting patterns specify their wool and threads as a guide to colour, amount required and so on. You carry an extensive range of Threadlines stock, which does well for you – and for Threadlines, since The Needle Works is the largest independent outlet for its products.

Write a memo to Albert Smith, the General Manager, and copied to Mrs Smith, suggesting some ideas for a collaborative promotion between the Needle Works and Threadlines. Emphasise the benefits to the former, but describe the benefits which could be offered to the latter, as an incentive to them to support the promotion.

6 E-procurement

6.1 **Business-to-business e-commerce** dwarfs the business-to-consumer variety. 'E-procurement' (buying business goods and services online) has the following benefits.

- Reduces paperwork and administration
- Promotes contractual buying
- Offers potential savings

6.2 'At a simple level, it may be a case of a supplier preparing an electronic catalogue to sit on the buyer's network. With the catalogue freely available to anyone authorised to access it, the buying process is simplified, and the incentive to buy out of contract, with the consequent loss of discounts negotiated between buyer and seller, is removed. And in the process, much of the time consuming interaction between seller and buyer, in the way of phone calls, faxes and hard copy orders, is removed, saving time and streamlining the admin.' (Murphy, 2000)

Marketing at Work

Companies using e-procurement

- General Electric – via its Trading Partner Network of electronic supplier catalogues
- In early 2000 in the US, companies including Kelloggs and Prudential Insurance formed a $17 billion Internet buying group
- Sainsbury's Efficient Consumer Response initiative uses an Internet-based system to share information between the retailer and its suppliers, allowing better estimation of required stock levels.

Action Programme 5

Follow David Murphy's advice and enter the word 'e-procurement' in a search engine to get yourself started . . .

6.3 The Internet has enabled business buyers of goods and services to take advantage of:

(a) A wider choice of suppliers, including international and smaller suppliers they might not otherwise have access to.

(b) Savings in procurement costs, through electronic transaction processing, documentation exchange and information search.

(c) Low inventory and efficient stock turnover (such as Just In Time supply systems), because of quicker order turnaround times.

(d) Improved relationships down the supply chain, thanks to data sharing. The Internet makes it possible to set up 'virtual partnerships' between customers and suppliers.

Chapter Roundup

- **Supply chain relationships** require interpersonal and business skills. As well as the human aspects discussed in other chapters, they involve:
  - contracts
  - systems and procedures
  - in the context of business objectives or purpose
- **Collaboration** involves the structuring of the relationship and the co-ordination of effort and resources.
- **Procedures for collaborative working** should include:
  - briefing
  - joint planning
  - negotiation of terms
  - sharing of information and resources
  - monitoring, checking and approval
  - feedback
  - payment
- **Negotiating** is a bargaining process through which commitments and compromises are reached, which are acceptable to both parties. A 'win-win' approach builds relationship more effectively than a 'win-lose' approach.
- There are many **suppliers** of marketing-related services, providing advice on or implementation of market research, advertising, promotions, PR, direct marketing, brand identity, sponsorship, creative process and many more areas.
- The most important aspects of **working with an advertising agency** are:
  - the agency brief
  - checking and approving work-in-progress
  - taking the advice offered
- **Distributors** are commercial organisations which have their own objectives. 'Push' and 'pull' techniques (aimed at 'selling in' and 'selling through') should be carefully planned and negotiated to the mutual benefit of supplier and distributor.
- **Information sharing** is crucial to the success of supply chain partnerships.

Quick Quiz

1 What are the three basic requirements for a contract to exist?

2 Outline the importance of (a) monitoring and (b) feedback in supply relationship.

3 Why should you take the advice offered by an advertising agency or other external marketing consultancy?

4 What is a 'full service' advertising agency?

5 How can an organisation ensure that it makes cost-effective use of a PR agency?

6 What should the 'brief' to an advertising agency contain?

7 Describe the flow of work to, through and from an advertising agency.

8 Give five examples of types of distribution channel.

9 What are 'push' and 'pull' techniques? Give three examples of each.

10 What is e-procurement?

Now try Question 7 in the Question Bank

Action Programme Review

1 Depending on what service you chose, terms may cover such issues as: delivery, variations of quality/quantity, payment dates and penalties, responsibility for additional costs, liability (for loss or destruction of property, problems, costs etc), ownership of materials, cancellations and delays, copyright ownership and rights, disclosure of information. Do take seriously the part of the exercise where you evaluate your own procedures in the light of contract terms. Just as an example, if you routinely ask printers or reprographics houses for the films of an ad or leaflet 'back', so you can use it again elsewhere, you might notice that your contract with them specifies that *they own* the films they have produced for you: you will need to state in your initial job contract that you want them at the conclusion of the job.

2 Do this exercise: it's useful – and great fun. In the marketing scenario, you may have come up with trade offs gaining you extra discount, free bleed, guaranteed cover positions etc in return for a pre-booked series.

3 Get into the habit of doing this regularly.

4 Your answer should be in proper memo format (and don't forget to 'c.c: Mrs Smith'). Your suggestions may have included activities such as: a one-off 'Threadlines' promotion in store, with exclusive window space and displays for two weeks, the cost to be offset by a 5% extra trade discount during the promotion. Threadlines to provide demonstrators of needlecraft or knitting in-store as PR and to draw customers in – with the understanding that they would use and promote Threadlines materials; joint advertising ('Threadlines – available from the Needle Works') in the local region; or Threadlines financial contribution to a Needle Works mail order catalogue or direct mail campaign in return for exclusive promotion of their materials. Benefits to the Needle Works would be extra sales of Threadlines materials at extra discount, sharing the costs of wider promotion and PR, and building on Threadlines' existing customer base and name to boost the Needle Works' own. Benefits to Threadlines would include increased pull-through, advantage over competitors through exclusivity, good relations with major distributor.

5 Your own research.

Answers to Quick Quiz

1 The intention to create a legal relationship; offer and acceptance and consideration.

2 Monitoring ensures that your objectives are being met at every stage of the process. Feedback is necessary to developing an ongoing working relationship and overcome problems.

3 Agencies specialise in communication and media and they are up-to-date. They have wide experience, objectivity, specialist knowledge and expensive production facilities.

4 A full service agency takes control of the whole campaign from concept through to press/air.

5 Ensure cost effectiveness by: setting clear objectives; negotiating a project fee; briefing fully; monitoring activity and expenditure.

6 Background to the company, market information and previous advertising strategies, campaign objectives, desired image, relevant policies, ball park budget.

7 This is summarised in the diagram in Paragraph 4.12.

8 Your answer may have included: retailers, wholesalers, distributors, agents and franchises.

9 Push techniques work through promoting a product to the distribution network to get access to the market. Pull techniques promote direct to the consumer who put pressure on the distributors to stock the desired goods.

10 E-procurement, quite simply means buying goods and services online.

8 Practical PR Skills

Chapter Topic List	
1	Setting the scene
2	Representing the organisation
3	Networking
4	Becoming your own PR agent

Learning Outcome

☑ Develop relationships inside and outside the organisation

Syllabus References

☑ Represent the organisation using practical PR skills, including preparing effective news releases

☑ Use networking skills in the business world

Key Concepts Introduced

- Public relations
- Crisis communication
- Issues management
- Networking

1 Setting the scene

Key Concept

Public relations is 'the planned and sustained effort to establish and maintain goodwill and mutual understanding between an organisation and its publics' (*Institute of Public Relations*). It involves a range of corporate activities such as publicity, press/media relations, lobbying or representations to government and trade bodies, community projects and communicating with consumer groups. In its broadest sense, however, PR is simply the interface of groups in society: marketing organisations interface continually with their members, with the public, with consumers, with suppliers, with competitors and with governments.

1.1 All contact a company has with its outside world is communication of some sort. Some examples are shown in Figure 8.1 below. Your organisation may have a PR, Corporate Affairs, Public Affairs, Community Relations, Media Relations or Public Information department. It may employ an **external PR agent** or **consultancy** to perform these functions.

Figure 8.1: A company's target audiences

1.2 The organisation's **image** is an important factor in whether it attracts and retains **members**, whether **consumers** buy its products/services, whether the **community** supports or resists its presence and activities and whether the **media** reports positively on its operations. **Publicity** may create an image - but an image also creates publicity.

1.3 Since an organisation will inevitably project an image in its dealings with the outside world, and the costs of a negative image can be high, it makes sense to manage the messages being projected.

1.4 You are 'doing PR' when you send press releases or supply editorial articles, greet and assist visitors, deal with suppliers and distributors, design and send promotional messages or organise and participate in marketing activities. Talking to people may seem like common sense, but there are **principles** to be learned and **skills** to be developed. We draw attention to some of them in Section 2 of this chapter.

Exam Tip

PR skills may be examined via the case study, in which you might decide to draft a press release or editorial/advertorial as part of your marketing strategy in the given scenario. They may also be included in a basic skills or communications audit, so each time you draft PR-related documents or recommendations, keep a copy for your portfolio.

1.5 Projecting a positive image is essentially a process of **influence**. In Section 3, we discuss how circles of influence can be progressively widened, through **networking** in the business world. In Section 4, we suggest how networking and other PR skills can be used on your own behalf: how you can manage your own image and widen your circles of communication and influence to further your professional development.

1.6 On completion of this chapter, you should be able to:

- identify situations in which you represent the organisation
- plan, identify and exploit opportunities to present a positive image of the organisation
- establish and build a network of business contacts of use to yourself and the organisation

Action Programme 1

According to Wilmshurst (1999), public relations has seven stages. These are listed in the table below. For each stage, think of an applicable example from your own work experience or organisation with which you are familiar.

1 State the problem or aim	
2 Research	
3 Identifying the publics	
4 Select the media	
5 Monitoring	

6 The future	
7 Maintaining financial checks	

2 Representing the organisation

When do you represent your organisation?

2.1 You need to be able to recognise situations in which you **represent** your organisation, because in those situations your behaviour, attitudes and messages have PR consequences for the organisation.

The word **represent** means:

- to stand as an equivalent or substitute for someone/something
- to portray or act as a picture or expression of someone/something
- to exemplify or typify the characteristics of someone/something
- to act out the part of someone/something.

Action Programme 2

Before you read further, brainstorm your own list of situations in which you might represent an organisation, individually or in a group. (A group brainstorming session allows you to practise a range of interpersonal, planning and creative skills.) Go through your list and give examples of how you could create a positive or negative image in each situation. If you are in a group, role-play any examples that sound interesting: let observers and participants comment on the PR impact of different behaviours.

2.2 The following table suggests some of the contexts in which you might represent your organisation, as a marketing professional.

Context	Example	Affects image of
You **exercise authority** delegated to you by the organisation	You discipline or instruct a subordinate You make a contract with a supplier	Organisation's attitude to employees Organisation's integrity/professionalism
You **issue communications** on behalf of the organisation	You write or approve advertising copy, press releases, editorial articles	The organisation's products/services, aims - or whatever the topic of the message
You **identify yourself** as a member of the organisation	You sign your name to a communication on a company letterhead, or answer the telephone with the company name	Whatever what you say or do implies about the organisation.

Context	Example	Affects image of
	You present a business card You tell someone informally whom you work for	
You are **associated in people's minds** with the organisation	You handle a customer complaint You give a presentation You are on the organisation's stand at an exhibition	The organisation's attitude to customers/quality The organisation's expertise

2.3 In many of these situations, you would be strongly aware of representing the organisation: they might take place in the work environment, or you might be acting clearly in your professional role.

2.4 So how can you **manage the organisation's image** in all these circumstances? We will consider some basic principles.

Awareness

2.5 The first step in image management is **being aware that you are projecting an image**.

2.6 Be aware of the **attitude** implied by words, behaviour and work outputs.

- A positive attitude towards your **work** and the organisation you work for
- A positive attitude towards the **products and services** of the organisation
- A positive attitude towards your **customer, supplier, distributor or colleague**
- A positive attitude towards **yourself, your rights and responsibilities**

Consider what you would assume about the attitude of someone who missed deadlines, issued advertising copy with errors or misleading promises, failed to return telephone calls, worked in an untidy or unhygienic environment, or spoke disrespectfully to you or about you. Consider what you would assume about the organisation that person represented.

Integrity

2.7 **Illegal dishonest or unethical behaviour** (not to mention its legal consequences) creates powerful negative PR, in the business and wider community - and within the organisation itself.

(a) **Abide by law and regulation in the areas of your responsibility**.

Find out as much as you need to about contracts relating to the sale of goods and services, truth in advertising and product labelling standards, discrimination, defamation, health and safety at work and sexual harrassment.

(b) **Abide by the terms of contracts**. Remember that letters and verbal agreements as well as legal documents may constitute a binding arrangement.

(c) **Keep your promises**. Promises may not be legally binding, but going back on them repeatedly destroys trust, breaks relationships and loses co-operation.

2.8 The boundaries of what constitutes **ethical behaviour** by a corporation are extremely flexible. The organisation may want to project a positive image.

(a) **Fairness** is important in dealings with business contacts, employees and customers. For example, adjusting complaints when not legally obliged to do so, or negotiating non-exploitative terms with suppliers and employees.

(b) **Social responsibility** may include not using anti-social promotional messages, being environmentally friendly and promoting positive images of minority groups.

(c) **Respect for cultural differences**, especially when doing business overseas is fundamental. Attitudes to the role of women, the exchange of gifts, religious beliefs and other customs and taboos should be carefully researched in international markets.

Professionalism

2.9 What is understood by the term 'professionalism' will depend on the context and culture of the organisation. In terms of practical PR, we suggest three dimensions of professionalism that create a positive image.

(a) **Courtesy**. This is a bare minimum requirement of all business communication. However adversarial, competitive, tense or hurried the interpersonal situation, rudeness is simply unprofessional.

(b) **Expertise**. Professionalism implies a level of competence which justifies financial remuneration. Incompetence is bad PR. Work out what range and standard of performance people are reasonably entitled to expect from you, and ensure that you can achieve it.

(c) **Efficiency**. Transactions take time, and invariably cost someone money. Professionals place a value on their time, energy, money and other resources, and recognise that others do the same. Be organised, prompt to appointments, deadline driven and budget conscious.

Action Programme 3

Imagine that your manager has asked you to give a presentation to Customer Services Staff entitled: 'Conveying Professionalism: Everyday PR'. Prepare a visual aid which illustrates the main points of your presentation. (If you are in a study group, you may even take the opportunity to give this presentation: useful experience for your portfolio.)

Discretion

2.10 When you represent the organisation, even informally, to people outside the organisation, you need to be aware of the need for discretion. 'Leaks' of information can be used for good or bad PR.

(a) Some information from within the organisation will be covered by laws or agreements of **confidentiality**. You may be required by contract, for example, not to disclose information about product development or promotional plans. Personal details of employees and market research subjects are confidential under the **Data Protection Act**.

(b) Another category of sensitive information is anything **negative** that you know about the organisation.

Crisis and issues management

Key Concepts

Crisis communication is public communication in the face of a potential PR disaster, through which the organisation initiates damage control, to minimise or counter the negative PR effects.

Issues management is an on-going process of being aware of potential controversies and sensitive matters in relation to the business, and initiating communication programmes which can defuse or head off issues before they become crises.

2.11 Examples of **PR crises** include the withdrawal of a product from the market due to unforeseen safety defects, an ecological disaster such as the running aground of an oil tanker, or the enforced withdrawal of an advertising campaign deemed offensive by complaints to the Advertising Standards Authority.

2.12 Effective crisis communication involves the following.

(a) **Planning**: being aware of areas of risk, identifying audience groups that will need to be communicated with, and preparing a response

(b) Recognising and **responding** to the likely level of public concern

(c) **Explaining** what has happened (telling the organisation's 'side of the story'), demonstrating openness and giving consistent messages (which includes keeping employees informed)

(d) Showing that the organisation **cares** about the problem. (A rule of thumb is: talk about people first, the environment second, property third and financial consequences fourth)

(e) **Demonstrating** that steps are being taken

(f) Using independent, authoritative **'champions'** who could speak out in support of the organisation

2.13 Examples of issues which require careful handling include **public concerns** about food additives, the environment and ethical investment. **Issues management** endeavours not just to fight fires as they arise, but to initiate communication, express general responsibility and openness, educate the public in the organisation's position and establish networks of goodwill and political support.

2.14 An article in *Marketing Business*, June 2000, lists out the 'do's' and 'don'ts' of crisis management. Some examples:

Do	Don't
■ Move swiftly ■ Be proactive ■ Be honest ■ Get senior executives to respond	■ Be complacent ■ Hide ■ Lie ■ Attribute blame elsewhere

Press releases

2.15 The press release is one of the most frequently used tools of public relations, aiming to achieve **advantageous press coverage**. The content and format of press releases were covered in detail in the *Customer Communications* module.

Exam Tip

Even if you are not asked to *draft a press release* to promote a product launch or event (as you may be), don't neglect a press or media release as one option for *'using the promotional mix'* or supplementing an advertising budget, or building relationships (with the media).

2.16 An example of a press release is set out below.

PRESS RELEASE

10 March 2003

WWF HONG KONG LAUNCHES NEW ECOWOODASIA WEBSITE TO GENERATE INTEREST AND FACILITATE INFORMATION FLOW ON FOREST CERTIFICATION

World Wide Fund For Nature Hong Kong (WWF Hong Kong) today launches a new website at www.ecowoodasia.org to generate interest and facilitate information flow on forest certification. We believe that this new website can provide useful information on certification and serve as a platform for exchanging opinions.

Forest certification may seem an irrelevant topic to Hong Kong people. Yet our daily lives are closely related to the forests - wooden furniture, office paper, toilet tissue, newspapers and magazines are probably all made from wood fibre. Every year we import approximately 7.8 million cubic metres of timber, which rank amongst top 20 in the world. This implies that Hong Kong has a vital role to play in conserving world forest resources.

WWF Hong Kong takes the lead in promoting credible certification schemes such as Forest Stewardship Council (FSC) certification and generating market demand on certified forest products by setting up EcoWood@sia. It is a voluntary group comprising of visionary companies which support credible certification schemes such as the FSC. Yet only a handful of people understand certification. "Web-based information tool like the EcoWood@sia website, is powerful and effective to get the message across. It is bilingual in Chinese and English and can reach thousands of audience in different sectors," says Joyce Lam, EcoWood@sia Coordinator.

This new website is an interactive web-based information tool for anyone interested in certification. It not only contains information on forest certification and EcoWood@sia, but also invites stakeholders to share their views and suggestions on certification issues. The site includes sections on "web polling" and "forum" where people can express their opinions and initiate discussions. "We believe that this new website can further spark off interest in certification among other Asian regions such as China and Taiwan, where awareness on certification is growing," says Joyce Lam.

- END -

For further information, please contact Joyce Lam, Programme Officer of WWF Hong Kong at (852) 2526 1011 [tel.], (852) 9738 2930 [mobile], (852) 2845 2734 [fax], jlam@wwf.org.hk [e-mail], or visit EcoWood@sia website at www.ecowoodasia.org

Notes to Editors

1. Forest Stewardship Council (FSC) The FSC is an independent, non-profit international organisation supporting environmental appropriate, socially beneficial and economically viable forest management. The FSC accredits certification bodies which are responsible for certifying forests according to Council's Principles and Criteria.

   http://www.fscoax.org

[posted at www.wwf.org.uk/pdf/references/pressreleases_hongkong]

Action Programme 4

(a) What is 'newsworthy' about the news release shown above?

(b) How does the press release appeal to its dual audiences?

(c) What other features of positive PR does it demonstrate?

Good news

2.17 The opposite of suppressing bad news is spreading good news. The purpose of all promotional communication is, essentially, to spread a positive message about the organisation, its products and services. Formal PR activities seize a range of opportunities for good news spreading, many of which do not overtly 'sell' anything: **networking** and lobbying, press and media releases, editorial articles and interviews, sponsorship and customer newsletters provide examples.

2.18 You can contribute informally. If you are drafting a letter to customers, for example, take the opportunity to inform them of any recent or on-going successes. Generate positive '**word of mouth**' in your dealings with people: a very powerful tool, because it works through personal communication networks.

3 Networking

Key Concept

Networking is identifying, establishing and maintaining personal contact with individuals and groups who may be able to provide information, referrals or resources for one's business or personal development.

3.1 The importance of **networking** is reflected in the saying: 'It's not what you know: it's who you know'. Networks of contacts may be used for all sorts of reasons.

- **Market research**, or intelligence gathering about an industry and how it operates
- **Sourcing particular items** of information
- **Locating** service providers and collaborators, through recommendation
- **Self-promotion**, or raising awareness of your identity and services
- **Gathering sale prospects** or 'leads', recommendations and referrals (known as 'network marketing')
- **Establishing yourself** in the industry/professional 'community'
- **Widening your circle** of communication and influence

3.2 'Using' contacts can sometimes be perceived in an unpleasant light. However, business dealing through personal relationships has a long and natural history: people are more likely to support the known than the unknown, especially if it comes with a personal recommendation. Business networks in particular are understood to be mutually beneficial. Everyone involved has the opportunity to gain from the relationship.

Marketing at Work

The CIM advises you as a student to list the individuals and groups that you have contact with in your organisation and sphere of work. Which ones are particularly useful? Do you have their business card?

Your list may include:

- Departmental colleagues
- Colleagues in other divisions
- Customers/end users
- Suppliers
- External agencies
- Subcontractors
- Media editors/journalists
- Competitors
- Professional institutes
- Local business networks
- Trade associations

You will also meet useful contracts when you attend conferences, seminars, meetings, exhibitions and training courses.

Making contacts

3.3 Formal or targeted contacts can be made in many ways.

(a) **Gathering information**. Each time you identify and tap an expert source of information, regard the person as a potential on-going source to be cultivated.

(b) **Recommendations and referrals**. Each time you make a contact, ask about other people whom it might be useful for you to talk to. (This applies to prospective suppliers, collaborators and clients/customers.)

(c) **Joining organisations and attending events** where people relevant to your aims are likely to gather: professional bodies, training courses, seminars and conferences, trade exhibitions - and also Internet Discussion Groups. Don't forget to regard your own work organisation as a source of contacts. Membership of the 'club' not only opens doors, but reduces the number of doors you have to open to find the right people!

(d) **Secondary sources**. Trade/professional journals, contacts lists and even the Yellow Pages are good sources of leads. Each call can generate both an active member of your network and further personal referrals.

3.4 **Informal or social contacts** should not be underestimated. The people you meet outside work are just as likely to be, or to know, work-relevant contacts. Listen and learn!

Action Programme 5

Making a contact is, initially, simply a matter of intent. Following on from the Marketing at Work example above, for all relevant people you meet or talk to, ensure that you write down core information or collect their business card.

- Their name and contact details
- Their organisation, job title or area
- The nature and date of your latest contact with them

Use a notebook, index card system, electronic organiser or database to categorise and cross-reference your contacts in a range of relevant areas.

Focusing contacts

3.5 Good rapport is not in itself sufficient to create a useful contact: people may be glad to know you, as an individual, but your name will not necessarily come to mind when they are looking for a particular service or asked to recommend someone. Focusing a contact involves linking your name with a relevant 'tag' or piece of information that will enable other people to file you appropriately in their own **contact database**.

(a) **Swap information** about what you do, or (if you are job-seeking, for example) what you are looking for. When making informal, social contacts, this can be done in a casual way, but it helps you to feel out who might be of use to you (and vice versa).

(b) **Exchange business cards**, so that the contact has an aide-memoire immediately linking your name with the relevant organisation if something comes up later.

(c) When seeking referrals or **leads**, give contacts as much information as they need to identify or select relevant prospects, and to jog their memory when things crop up later.

(d) **Gain a profile**. For example, give presentations to business or educational groups in the area of your expertise.

Building relationships

Action Programme 6

The marketer in a front line PR role must possess the following characteristics:

- Skilled communicator
- Good interpersonal skills
- Enjoy networking
- Enjoy meeting new people

How might you use these characteristics to co-operate fully with the media, and achieve your objectives? Think about the following areas of work.

Objective	How can this be achieved via your relationships with media contacts?
■ Produce good copy	
■ Be reliable	
■ Keep yourself informed about events	
■ Be co-operative at all times	

3.6 Contacts can be developed into 'live', on-going relationships by a variety of means, but the following are key principles.

(a) **Follow up**. Maintain **contact, recollection and focus** by 'touching base' every so often. If you encounter someone who might be useful to you, suggest that you meet 'to discuss it' - and do so. Report back to people on the result of any help or information they have given you. Or simply maintain **social contact**: you do not need an excuse to do this, and it can increase the trust and motivation for someone to put opportunities and information your way. If you thought the sending of corporate Christmas cards, and more creative variations on the theme, were a waste of time, think again.

(b) **Reciprocity**. Don't be a user: if you are requesting help, advice or information from a contact, consider what you are able to offer in return, and keep an eye on the 'net balance' over time. It may be a straight swap of information, recommendations or referrals, an incentive or reward, a mutually beneficial collaboration, or simply your recognition and gratitude, with the potential for later 'returning the favour' .

(c) **Pace and lead**. These terms refer to the need to meet people where they are, and build trust, before attempting to influence them. When developing contacts, you need to be open about your objectives, but not pushy. If you are seeking a favour, for example, you might initially approach contacts by stating that you are seeking their 'advice'. You might also ask: 'May I call you from time to time for further advice?'

Marketing at Work

So what is the best way of getting a PR consultant? According to Klesha Handel, who sold her business to a leading PR consultancy:

'Go to the publications, the ones that you are interested in being in, and speak to the journalists. Ask them which consultants they feel good dealing with. It may sound easy, but very few people do it.'

Marketing Business, March 2002

Action Programme 7

The Needle Works

From your organisational efforts so far, on The Needle Works' behalf, you are aware that while you are increasingly able to 'talk the language' of marketing with the various service-providers you deal with, you are not yet fluent in the language of needlecraft. This places a barrier between you and your customers and colleagues. You are also aware that there seems to be a clash of culture between the various Craft Guilds which preserve and promote traditional skills through education and teacher accreditation, and the commercial retailers of craft supplies. There are rumours that the General Secretary of the Needleworkers' Guild disapproves of The Needle Works.

How will you address these issues? What information will you need? What contacts will you pursue, and where? How can you begin to build bridges? Jot down an immediate Action List for yourself.

4 Becoming your own PR agent

4.1 **Image management** and **networking skills** can be deployed on behalf of your organisation, in public relations, customer care, information gathering and relationship-building with suppliers and distributors. However, you should also be aware that they are an element in your own **personal and career development**.

4.2 All the considerations and skills we have discussed in this chapter can be deployed on your own behalf, in order to establish a positive image and relationship with influential people.

(a) Your boss, and other **senior or influential people** in your organisation who could affect your career prospects

(b) The **business and professional community**

- Potential employers
- Sources of information and learning opportunities

Chapter Roundup

- **Public relations 'happens'**, whether an organisation takes active steps to manage its image or not.
- **Key factors** in conveying a **positive image of the organisation** include:
  - awareness
  - attitude
  - appearance
  - integrity
  - professionalism
  - discretion
  - crisis and issue management
  - good news
- **Networking** is the process of making, focusing and maintaining contacts which may be mutually beneficial sources of information and influence.

Quick Quiz

1. Can an organisation *avoid* having a 'profile' or public image?
2. Give six examples of poor image management by an individual.
3. What types of behaviour convey 'professionalism'?
4. What does effective crisis communication entail?
5. Give six examples of sources of contacts for a marketer seeking an advertising agency.
6. What is meant by 'focusing' contacts, and how can it be achieved?
7. Explain what is meant by 'reciprocity' in networking.
8. How might you use networking skills on your own behalf?

Now try Question 8 in the Question Bank

Action Programme Review

1 We have used the example of a customer service department.

1 State the problem or aim	There have been complaints from customers about delayed responses by sales staff. How well are we handling customer queries?
2 Research	The sales manager may ring in to the sales office and pretend to be a customer.
3 Identifying the publics	Having found that service could be improved, and having trained his staff, the sales manager is eager to tell the customers all about it and other employees.
4 Select the media	The company issues advertising flyers, and a company newsletter.
5 Monitoring	The cost of this activity needs to be balanced against the need to improve customer service.
6 The future	How will customer needs change? A website and online ordering may be needed soon.
7 Maintaining financial checks	'It is difficult to quantify the effects of PR, but unless this is undertaken seriously, much money can be wasted.' (Wilmshurst)

2 The main point of the exercise was the brainstorming process, but if you were stuck for ideas, see paragraph 2.2.

3 The following is just our suggestion, which may provide you with a more memorable way of remembering the issues involved.

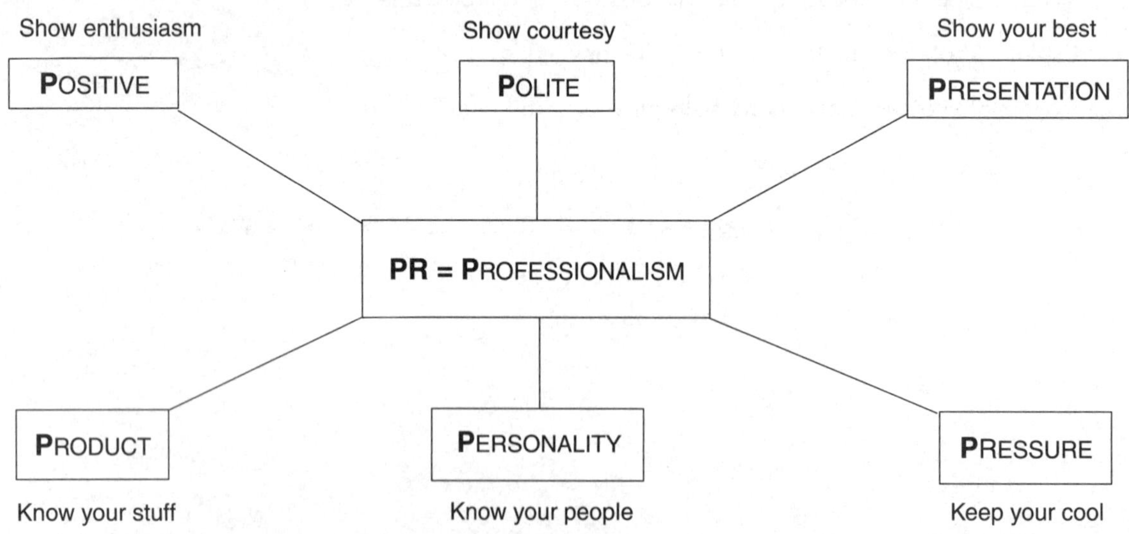

4 (a) The news is *local*, appealing directly to Hong Kong people.
It is current – posted on the day of launch.
It links its subject matter to daily life.

(b) *For the end audience:*
It appeals to people likely to be interested in WWF's activities.
It positions Hong Kong as a world leader, appealing to the local audience.

It appeals specifically to the forestry industry.

For the media audience:

It gives clear date, relevance, information contacts and editorial notes.

It is written in a user-friendly style (with quotes etc) that will make it easy to edit for publication.

5 Marketers deal with a wide range of people and groups in the course of business. Each of these interpersonal encounters should be regarded as a contact, a source of further contacts and the basis of a network.

6

Objective	How can this be achieved via your relationships with media contacts?
■ Produce good copy	Have a clear understanding of the media being used, such as readership profiles for the press
■ Be reliable	Meet deadlines and provide information when asked
■ Keep yourself informed about events	Seek out up-to-date information, with regular contact with your 'network'
■ Be co-operative at all times	Respond appropriately when the media wish to check facts, conduct interviews or visit your organisation

7 Your notes may have included suggestions along the following lines. Joining craft classes (through one of the Guilds, or local education centres) to learn basics and make contacts: membership of societies/groups? Requesting briefings by staff (synergy of technical/marketing input). Chatting informally to customers: identifying Guild members for further contact. Asking Guilds for information (way of making contact + access to info). Request meeting with editors of Craft Journals (discuss possible editorial/advertising + pick brains on market) or request referral to others. Invite Guild Secretary and Committee to launch of Knitting Shop. Contact Guild Secretary to discuss possibility of discount for Guild Members (incentive). Ask Guild Secretary to recommend Guild member to give talk at launch, appreciation evening etc (defer to Guild expertise/credibility).

Answers to Quick Quiz

1. All actions, relationships and physical manifestations – as well as deliberately transmitted communications – convey a marketing message.

2. Your image is suggested by your words, your behaviour and your work outputs: poor image could be conveyed by missed deadlines, carelessly presented work, unfulfilled promises, disrespectful comments about colleagues, untidy environment, or unreturned phone calls.

3. Professionalism: courtesy, expertise, efficiency.

4. Crisis communication is trying to minimise the negative PR effects in the face of an operational disaster.

5. Sources of contacts: trade fairs and exhibitions; word-of-mouth recommendations; specialist press; networking events; suppliers.

6. Focusing a contact involves linking your name with a relevant tag or piece of information that will enable other people to file you appropriately in their own contact database.

7. Reciprocity means offering something back to your contacts for the assistance that you have sought from them.

8. Networking skills, deployed on your own behalf are an invaluable tool in managing your career and personal development. Make friends and influence people!

Part C

Organising and undertaking marketing activities

Planning and Scheduling

9

Chapter Topic List	
1	Setting the scene
2	Objective setting
3	Planning techniques
4	Co-ordinating techniques
5	Measuring and evaluating results

Learning Outcome

☑ Apply planning techniques to a range of marketing tasks and activities

Syllabus References

☑ Identify alternative and innovative approaches to a variety of marketing arenas and explain criteria for meeting business objectives

☑ Explain how marketing makes use of planning techniques: objective setting and co-ordinating, measuring and evaluating results to support the organisation

Key Concepts Introduced

- Planning
- Organising
- Budget
- Deadline
- Activity scheduling
- Time scheduling
- Project
- Network analysis

1 Setting the scene

1.1 One of the learning objectives of the *Marketing in Practice* syllabus is that you should be able to 'apply planning techniques to a range of marketing tasks and activities', and the topic of this section of the syllabus is 'Organising and Undertaking Marketing Activities'.

Key Concepts

Planning is the process of deciding what the 'ends' of activity should be (objective-setting), and determining the most appropriate 'means' of achieving those ends (policies and procedures).

Organising is the process of establishing a framework within which plans can be carried out: determining structures and systems for co-ordinating the human and other resources required.

Planning

1.2 Planning allows individuals and units in business organisations to look ahead.

- The **objectives** for which they are responsible
- What **actions** will serve towards achieving those objectives
- How far they are being **successful** in achieving those objectives

Control

1.3 If planning is the process of deciding what should be done, **control** is the process of checking whether it has been done, and if not, doing something about it. The combined process of planning and control are known as a **control cycle**: Figure 9.1.

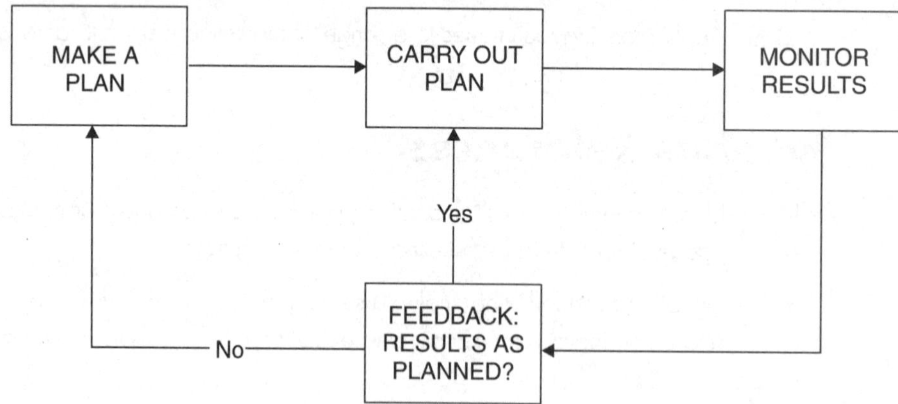

Figure 9.1: A control cycle

1.4 In more detail, the control cycle in management has six basic stages.

(a) **Making a plan**: deciding what to do and identifying the desired results.

- **Aims**
- **Objectives**, which must be achieved for the aims to be fulfilled
- **Performance targets and standards**
- **Specific short-term goals** for key tasks
- **Action plans**, specifying 'what, how, who, when, where and how much'

(b) Carrying out the plan, or having it carried out by subordinates.

(c) Monitoring and measuring actual results achieved.

(d) **Comparing feedback** on actual results against the plans.

(e) **Evaluating** the comparison, and deciding whether further action is necessary to ensure the plan is achieved. If results are worse than planned (negative feedback), the activity will have to be adjusted to get it back on course. If they are better than planned (positive feedback), it may be desirable to maintain the deviation from the plan, or to adjust the plan itself to take advantage of the situation.

(f) **Implementing corrective action** where necessary.

1.5 On completion of this chapter, you should be able to:

- Appreciate the business objectives of marketing events
- Define objectives and set budgets for marketing events
- Utilise a number of simple planning and project management techniques
- Measure and evaluate the results of marketing events

Marketing at Work

Planning and control of CRM programmes

Here are some suggestions from the CIM for *Marketing in Practice* students.

The planning cycle reminds marketers not only of the importance of planning but also the need to evaluate results to examine what went right, and what did not happen as expected. This information should then be used for future planning purposes so activities are more successful.

The planning cycle begins with an analysis of **where we are now**, moving onto **making plans** (with SMART objectives) for where we want to get to. Next comes **implementation** and finally **control** when results are measured and feedback collected for the review process.

This final evaluation is essential in CRM and customer care programmes, for example. Often customer feedback is gathered but not communicated to those who need to act upon it. Research suggests that CRM fails to meet customer expectations 55 – 70% of the time.

CRM programmes need to be carefully planned to ensure the right customers are targeted with the right information and promotions. The internet, e-mail and improved customer databases have made it easier for organisations to achieve this, but people are still required to input the right information and make the right decisions. Effective CRM programmes depend on the company personnel just as much as the electronic tools they use.

Marketing Success, February 2002

2 Objective setting

Criteria for meeting business objectives

2.1 The *Marketing in Practice* syllabus suggests that you should evaluate any potential marketing activity or opportunity (such as the events discussed in Chapter 10 and 11) according to whether it meets **business objectives**.

2.2 In general terms, there are certain attributes of a viable and suitable activity which can be measured and evaluated. Rather neatly, these can all be expressed as 'e' factors.

(a) **Effectiveness**. Does the activity/opportunity fulfil the company's objectives for serving the needs of its owners and its chosen market? Will it, for example, enhance market share, quality or profitability?

(b) **Efficiency**. Does the activity/opportunity allow the organisation to use its resources in such a way as to maximise benefit for cost, or return on investment? Will it, for example, involve low wastage rates, quick response to customer enquiries, completion of products to deadline or high productivity by staff?

(c) **Economy**. Does the activity/opportunity fulfil the company's financial objectives? Will it, for example, bring in the budgeted revenue or contribution, and/or fall within or below budgeted expenditure costs?

(d) **Elegance**. Does the activity/opportunity look and feel 'right' for the company? Will it, for example, enhance the image of the organisation, fit neatly with the market's needs, or create synergy?

(e) **Ethicality**. Does the activity/opportunity fulfil the company's sense of social responsibility and business ethics? Will it, for example, have low impact on the natural environment, make opportunities for minority group employees or promote socially responsible images/products?

2.3 In specific terms, you may well be evaluating the viability and appropriateness of a given event or activity against clearly defined goals and standards set out in the marketing department's policies, plans and budgets.

Setting SMART objectives

2.4 **'Smart' objectives** are:

- **S**pecific
- **M**easurable
- **A**ttainable
- **R**ealistic
- **T**ime-bounded

Examples

Increase sales volume by 5% in the year 2004 – 2005

Achieve and maintain for 5 years a 25% share of the domestic market for product x.

Action Programme 1

List at least five objectives for a product launch, trade exhibition or other marketing event.

2.5 Whatever the specific objective, the important thing is to have a specific objective!

Budgets

2.6 Budgets are, essentially, SMART objectives.

Key Concept

A **budget** is a statement of desired performance expressed in financial terms: expenditure, revenue, profit and so on.

2.7 In practice, overall marketing budgets are often already set, or set based on last year's budget, or set as a percentage of projected turnover for the year. When you are evaluating or planning a marketing activity or event, the limits to your spending will probably be determined.

(a) **Regular or core marketing spend**, which maintains the marketing/selling cycle: catalogues, sales force support, agency retainers, PR.

(b) **Spend on individual products and services**, for launch and/or maintenance marketing.

(c) **Contingencies**. If you are lucky, there may be an amount to be used at the marketing department discretion, for any new or unforeseen opportunities that crop up during the year.

2.8 Main **budgeting control tasks**

- Estimate all the costs involved in the proposed event/activity
- Compare the estimated total cost with anticipated **returns, benefits and objectives**
- Establish that the estimated total cost is within the departmental expenditure budget
- **Monitor actual expenditure** against the budget
- Compare actual total cost against actual returns

Exam Tip

You may be given a number of tasks for which some rate card, fee and other costings are provided, and then asked to draw up a budget. More importantly, you may be asked to assess the viability of various marketing opportunities and options, based on costs and anticipated returns, benefits and objectives. This is usually a feature of the compulsory Part A questions of this paper – so make sure you get some practice!

2.9 Budgeting is covered in Part E of this Study Text. The above paragraphs should enable you to put it in the context of objective setting and control. Always take into account the **cost/budget implications** of any marketing event that presents itself.

3 Planning techniques

3.1 Basic steps in work planning

- The establishment of **priorities** (considering tasks in order of importance for the objective concerned)
- **Scheduling** tasks

Prioritising

3.2 A piece of work will be **high priority** in the following circumstances.

(a) **If it has to be completed by a deadline**. The closer the deadline, the more **urgent** the work will be.

(b) **If other tasks and people depend on it**: if the scheduling of advertisement media depends on a market research report, the first task will be to compile or obtain the report. Begin at the beginning!

(c) **If it is important**. There may be a clash of priorities between two urgent tasks, in which case relative consequences should be considered: if an important decision or action rests on a task (for example, a report for senior management, or correction of an error in a large customer order) that task should take precedence over the preparation of notes for a meeting, or processing a smaller order.

Key Concept

A **deadline** is the end of the longest span of time which may be allotted to a task: in other words, the last acceptable date for completion.

Scheduling

Key Concepts

Activity scheduling provides a list of activities – or task sequence in the order in which they must be completed.

Time scheduling specifies the timescale or start and end times and dates for each activity in a task sequence or action plan.

3.3 Determining the time that it will take to do a task is easy if it is a **routine task** that you do regularly. Simply keep a note of how long it takes you, on average. With **non-routine** tasks, particularly substantial ones, it can be far more difficult to determine how long to allow. You can ask someone with more experience than you, or you might be able to break the new task down into smaller stages whose duration you can more easily estimate.

3.4 **Time schedules** can be determined by two main methods.

(a) **Forward scheduling** starts with a given starting time/date and adds estimated times for each stage of the task (allowing for some which will be undertaken simultaneously by more than one person) to decide the estimated completion time/date. This method is useful for routine tasks and projects for which no definite deadline has been set.

(b) **Reverse scheduling** starts with the target completion time/date or deadline, and works backwards through the estimated time for each stage of the task, determining the latest start timed for each stage and for the task as a whole, which will enable you to meet the deadline. This is often used in marketing where target dates for conferences, launches and campaigns are already fixed.

3.5 Whichever method is used, bear in mind that **task times will only be estimates**. You may wish to build in some extra 'slack' time.

- You will then be less likely to fall behind
- If you do fall behind on one task, you will have some catch-up time built in

Lists

3.6 Lists are useful ways of identifying and remembering what needs to be done, and of monitoring how far you have got. If you do not do this already, try it once: you will be hooked, and your daily productivity will shoot up.

3.7 **A checklist** is simply a list which allows for ticking or 'checking' off each. Again, it may or may not reflect the order in which you actually perform the tasks. You may simply have a column to put ticks against each task, or you may want to have a space for times/dates on which you started or finished the activity, or even for stages of the activity (for example, where a particular document is at a given date) – or elements of all of these.

As an example, here is a checklist for an advertising manager preparing deadlines for a number of press advertisements.

Ad	*Due date*	*Writer*	*Designer*	*Photo-grapher*	*Film*	*Print*	*Proofed*	*Sent?*
Times	3/9	21/8	22/8	24/8	30/8	-	2/9	✓
Standard	3/9	22/8	23/8	26/8	30/8	-	2/9	✓
A5 classified	7/9	29/8	30/8	-	-	-	4/9	✓
Leaflet A	12/9	10/8	12/8	15/8	-	2/9		
Leaflet B	13/9	2/9	3/9					

Action Programme 2

Suppose you are the advertising manager's assistant. She has fallen ill on the 5th September, and has asked you to take over the ad and leaflet production. 'I've left you my work checklist,' she says. 'You can work from that.' You find on her desk the checklist given as our example above.

(a) What can you tell from the checklist?

(b) What does this suggest about the usefulness of checklists?

(c) What tasks that you have to perform in your own work might benefit from the same approach?

Action plans

3.8 **Action plans** set out a programme of work or action, including time scheduling. Our example of a checklist for an advertising manager was a kind of action plan.

The following is another example, for the writing of a report.

Activity		Days before due date	Target date	Date begun	Date completed
1	Request files	6	3/9		
2	Draft report	5	4/9		
3	Type report	3	6/9		
4	Approve report	1	8/9		
5	Signature	1	8/9		
6	Courier	0	9/9		

Timetables

3.9 The same information could be formatted as a timetable or diary entry. You may already be using such methods to timetable your studies. Timetables and diaries have several benefits.

- Remind you of key times and dates
- Remind you to make necessary advance preparations
- Help you allocate your time effectively

Action Programme 3

Here is a timetable/diary page for the week of the 3rd to 9th September. Enter the schedule given in Paragraph 3.8 as an action plan, as you would do an appointments diary. Consider how you would highlight the due date.

SATURDAY 3	WEDNESDAY 7
MONDAY 5	THURSDAY 8
TUESDAY 6	FRIDAY 9

Week commencing 3 SEPTEMBER

S	S	M	T	W	T	F
3	4	5	6	7	8	9

Charts

3.10 Longer-term schedules may be used to show the following.

(a) The **length of time** to be taken for scheduled events or activities.

(b) The **relationship between events or tasks** – for example, whether they take place at the same time or in sequence. This can be particularly useful for identifying where excessive or clashing demands are being made. You may have scheduled two tasks at once, or scheduled a task over a period when you planned a holiday.

(c) The **relationship between planned and actual** task duration or output.

3.11 The following is a simple example of a **bar chart** in the form of a year planner, in this case, a general plan for a fashion retail outlet.

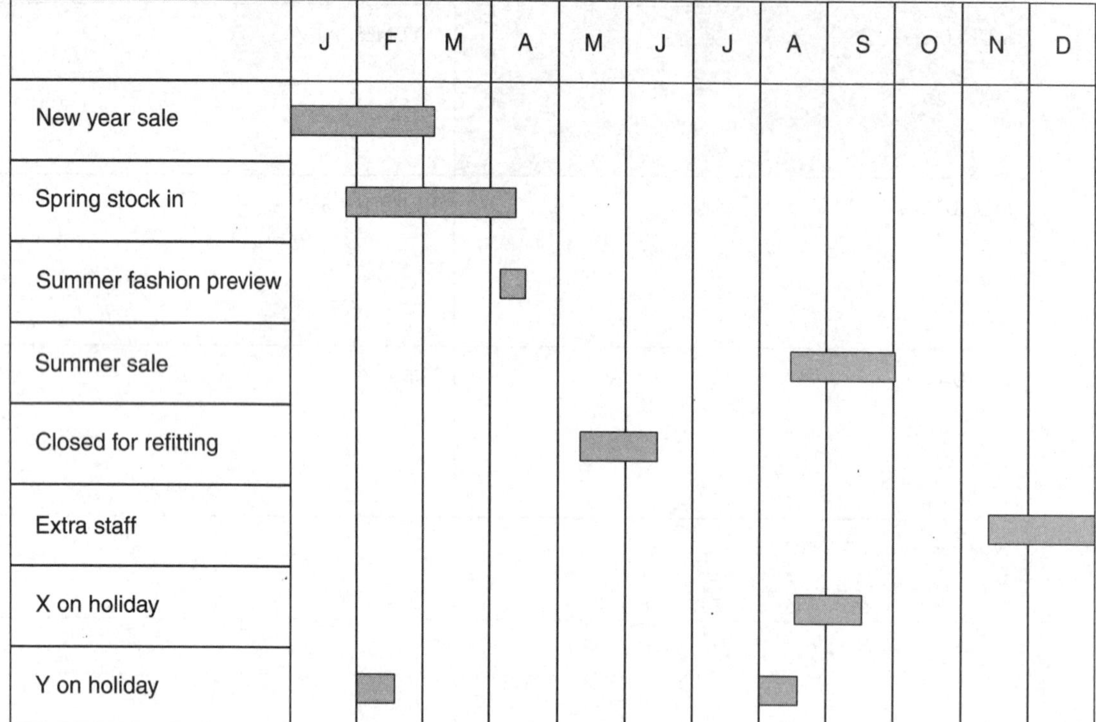

3.12 Another widely-used form of chart, which is used to show **progress** as well as schedule, is the **Gantt chart**, developed by H L Gantt for progressing the building of US Navy ships during the First World War. A Gantt chart is like the horizontal bar chart used above, but each division of space represents both an amount of time and an amount of work to be done in that time. Lines or bars drawn across the space indicate how much work is scheduled to be done and/or how much work has actually been done. The more work, the longer the line or bar.

Exam Tip

The Pilot Paper and December 2002 exam asked you to produce a Gantt chart for the planning of a marketing event. You might also have chosen to use a bar or Gantt chart in December 2003 to illustrate the timing of media bookings as part of your 'media plan'. In general, if you see the word 'schedule', it might be worth asking yourself if a chart such as the one above might be a professional and efficient way of conveying the data.

3.13 The advantage of such a chart is that you can see the **relationship between time spent and amount done**. You can compare amounts produced in one week or month, say, with those in another (by the relative lengths of the bar or line). You can, similarly, compare amounts scheduled to be done with those actually done.

3.14 The information below, about planned work and actual progress, is set out in a Gantt chart.

Day	*Daily schedule (units)*	*Cumulative schedule (units)*	*Work done in the day (units)*	*Cumulative work done (units)*
Mon	100	100	75	75
Tues	125	225	100	175
Wed	150	375	150	325
Thu	150	525	180	505
Fri	150	675	75	580

Daily schedule and work actually done

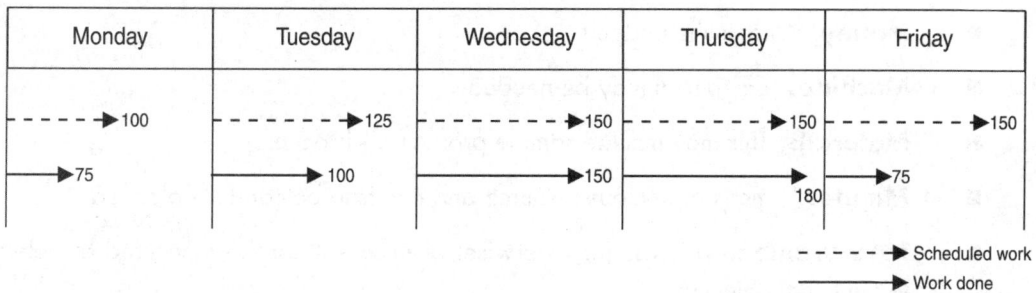

	Monday	Tuesday	Wednesday	Thursday	Friday
Scheduled work	100	125	150	150	150
Work done	75	100	150	180	75

- - - - ▶ Scheduled work
——▶ Work done

Action Programme 4

Look at the Gantt chart above.

(a) What information is clearly shown by the chart? (Is it more obvious how production is doing on the chart than on the tabulated data from which it was drawn?)

(b) What further Gantt chart might be helpful for the manager of this work, which can be drawn from the data given?

(c) Draw the Gantt chart you have suggested.

(d) What information is most usefully provided by this new chart?

SOST + 6M

3.15 One planning technique that may be used for planning marketing events is known as **SOST + 6M's**. It can be represented by a diagram. The points are explained below. We have already covered some of them earlier in this chapter, and this framework provides a useful way of drawing the ideas together.

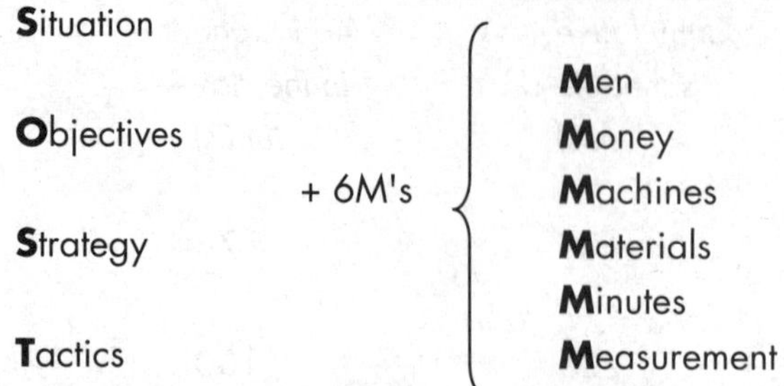

- **Situation**. What are the circumstances the company finds itself in?
- **Objectives**. What are the company's objectives in this situation?
- **Strategy**. How is the objective going to be achieved?
- **Tactics**. What are the operational details of the decided strategy?

3.16 Consideration of the above elements will result in an outline plan, which can be carried out by organising the resources indicated by the 6Ms.

- **Men**, or human resources skills and expertise
- **Money**. What is the budget?
- **Machines**. Equipment may be needed.
- **Materials**. This may include sample products or brochures.
- **Minutes**. Time is a precious resource and needs to be carefully planned.
- **Measurement**. Success (or otherwise) of an event can be measured by referring back to the initial objectives.

4 Co-ordinating techniques

4.1 Co-ordination involves the solving, allocating and scheduling of the various resources and activities required to complete a complex task. In this section, we will look at some of the more advanced techniques used in **project management**.

Key Concept

A **project** is an undertaking, often cutting across organisational and functional boundaries, and carried out to meet specific goals within cost, schedule and quality objectives.

The organisation of marketing activities and events is often approached on a project basis.

4.2 A **project plan** aims to ensure that the project objective is achieved within the requirements of quality, cost and time.

(a) **Breaking the project down** into manageable units of activity, and determining the sequence of, or relationships between, those units or tasks.

(b) **Estimating the resources** (materials, money, time and so on) required for each unit.

(c) **Sequencing and scheduling** each unit in the most appropriate way for co-ordinated performance.

Breaking the task into stages

4.3 Breaking a project down

- Discovering exactly what work must be accomplished
- Determining the resources required
- Sequencing and co-ordinating the work done

This is called establishing a **work breakdown structure** (WBS) for the project.

4.4 The work breakdown can be expressed in a checklist, bar chart, or Gantt chart, as discussed in section 3 above.

Procedures

4.5 Some projects are already set up as a neat sequence of tasks, or **procedure**, reflecting the order in which tasks need to be performed. Where this sequence is not immediately obvious, it can be 'mapped' using a **network**. A simple network shows which activities need to be completed before others. In the example below, the squares or 'nodes' denote activities, and the arrows show logical sequence and precedence.

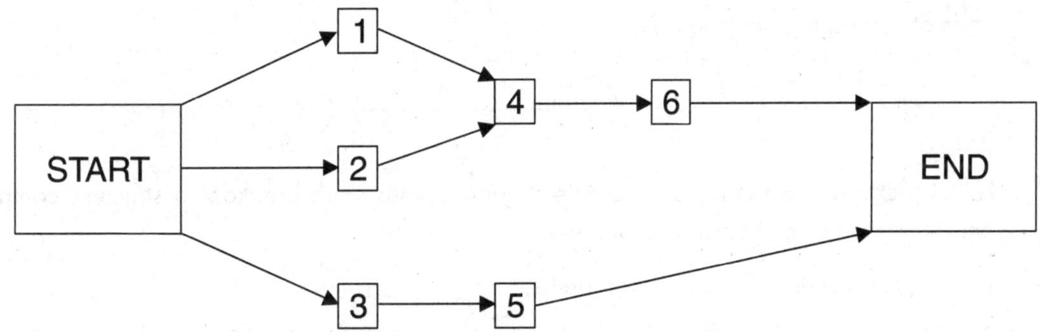

4.6 Consider the diagram above as a plan for going away on holiday.

Activity 1	=	Reserving your holiday place by phone
Activity 2	=	Booking travel insurance
Activity 3	=	Renewing your passport
Activity 4	=	Sending in a completed booking form. (This follows a reservation and requires details of insurance cover.)
Activity 5	=	Obtaining a travel visa. (This can't be done until you have a valid passport.)
Activity 6	=	Collection of tickets (for which you need to have made a written booking).

The advantage of such a method is that (unlike a checklist) it allows you to show where a number of activities need to be done at roughly the same time (like activities 1, 2 and 3 above).

Network analysis

Key Concept

Network analysis is a term for project planning techniques which aim to 'map' the activities in a particular project, and the relationship between them, including:

- what tasks must be done before others can be started
- what tasks could be done at the same time
- what tasks must be completed on schedule if the completion date for the whole project is not to slip: the critical tasks.

4.7 The most commonly used form of network is called an **activity-on-arrow diagram**, because activities are represented by an arrowed line, which runs between one event (start or completion of the activity) and another. Events are depicted by a node, or circle.

Hence in the following example we map activity A, which starts at a certain point (event 1) and ends at a certain point (event 2).

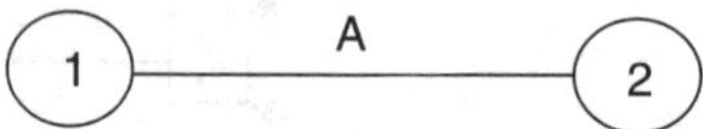

4.8 Let us tackle a more complex example. Suppose your work breakdown structure comprises six activities: we will call them activities A–G.

(a) Activities A and B can start together

(b) You have to have done activity B before you can do activity C

(c) Once activity A is completed, activities D and E can start, at the same time

(d) Activity F follows on from activity D

(e) Activity G will be completed at the same time as activity F, to end the project. However, activities C and E must be completed before G can commence.

Action Programme 5

Do not look at the network diagram below. Read (a)–(e) above again. Working from left to right, draw the network diagram showing activities A–G and events 1–6.

Now uncover our solution.

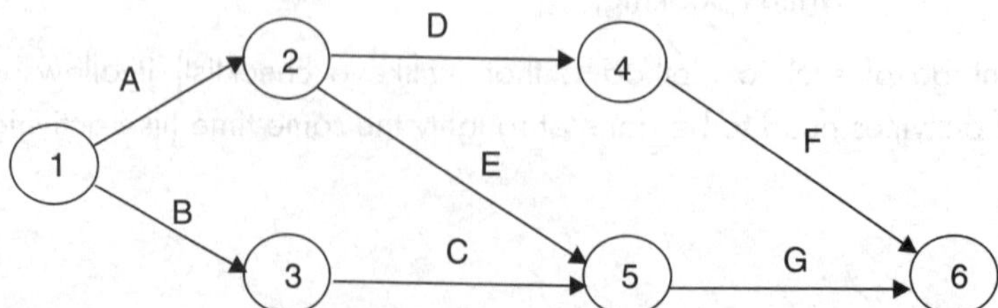

Critical path analysis (CPA)

4.9 More information can be added to a network diagram, to describe not just what happens next, but when it should happen, and how long the whole project will take if each activity takes as long as it is supposed to. This technique is called CPA, or **critical path analysis**. If Activity A takes three days, it is shown like this.

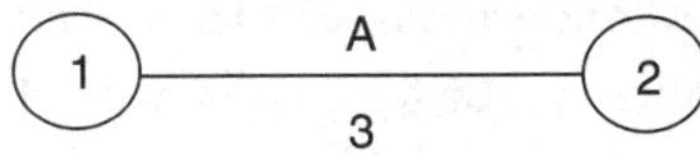

4.10 Let us say, building on our original A-G network, that:

Activity A takes 3 days

B takes 5 days

C takes 2 days

D takes 1 day

E takes 6 days

F takes 3 days

G takes 3 days.

Our network would be as follows.

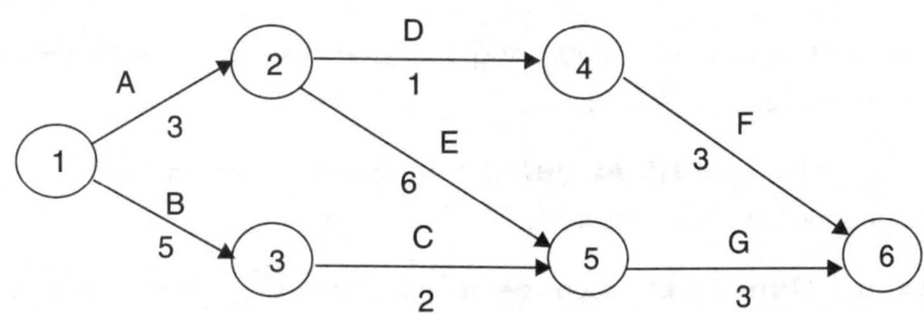

4.11 Let us assume that you have all the resources you need to carry out the above project as drawn: in other words, you have enough workers to do activities A and B at the same time, and so on. The shortest possible time in which you can complete the project is 12 days. See if you can work out why.

Each of the 'routes' of arrows from the first event to the last event is called a **pathway**.

Action Programme 6

List all the pathways in the network in Paragraph 4.10 above, and add up how many days each path will take to reach event 6.

4.12 The shortest possible duration for the project is 12 days. This is the duration of the longest path (AEG), not the shortest! The activities on the longest path determine the deadline for the whole project, because if one of them runs over time, the whole project will run over time. They are therefore critical activities, and the path on which they sit is called the **critical path**. We show the critical path on a network by drawing double or thicker lines between the events on that path.

5 Measuring and evaluating results

Project monitoring

5.1 Control over work must be maintained to ensure that jobs do in fact reach completion, and if those jobs involve various tasks over varying periods, planning will be necessary to keep track of future events, deadlines and results. Systems which provide for this are called **bring forward** or **bring up** systems. Anything which needs action at a later date (and therefore may get forgotten) should be processed in this way.

- Checking on progress of an operation
- Checking completion when the deadline is reached
- Checking payments when they fall due
- Retrieving files relevant to future discussions, meetings, correspondence

5.2 Checklists are useful, as we suggested earlier, for monitoring what has been done and what has not. Diary systems may also be used. A reminder may be put in the diary or timetable for the relevant day, to check 'task x completed?', 'payment received?', 'response received to letter ref: IO/cw2?', 'one week left for revision'. If you use card index or concertina files, you could slip a card or note into the sequence or appropriate date section, for checking on the day.

Evaluating marketing activity

5.3 There are various systems for measuring the effectiveness of marketing activity (which will be discussed in more detail in Part E).

(a) There may be **annual targets** (sales, budgets, expenditure budgets etc) against which performance can be measured.

(b) **Moving standards** (such as monthly sales targets) allow the same performance measurement on an on-going control basis.

(c) **Diagnostic standards** monitor how the market is responding to the marketing activity, to give continuous performance feedback (eg via electronic point of sale information or market research).

Diagnostic feedback

- Monitoring output against the marketing plan
- Measuring volume and/or growth of sales
- Comparing marketing activities (and/or sales) this year against last year
- Monitoring market share, and any year-on-year changes
- Monitoring customer complaints, returns or repeat sales and recommendations
- Gathering research on customer satisfaction, awareness, response to marketing
- Measuring the accuracy of budgets and schedules
- Comparing sales figures (and/or enquiries, size of contacts base and so on)
- Measuring direct responses (coupons returned, calls to response lines)

Chapter Roundup

- **Planning** is the process of deciding what should be done, by whom, when and how. It is essential for co-ordination and control, through which performance is monitored, measured against the plan and adjusted where necessary.
- Five dimensions by which a plan can be **evaluated**:
  - effectiveness
  - efficiency
  - economy
  - elegance
  - ethicality
- **Operational objectives** should be SMART: specific, measurable, attainable, realistic and time-bounded.
- Basic steps in **work planning**
  - prioritising and sequencing tasks (activity scheduling)
  - time scheduling tasks
- **Planning aids** include lists and checklists, action plans and diaries, charts and precedence networks.
- More complex projects may require **network analysis** or **critical path analysis (CPA)** in order to sequence and schedule tasks accurately.

Quick Quiz

1 Give examples of non-operational and operational goals of a business.

2 Define efficiency and effectiveness.

3 Explain what is meant by forward and reverse scheduling.

4 What is the advantage of the Gantt chart for scheduling?

5 What is the 'critical path' in a network diagram?

6 Give three examples of diagnostic standards for evaluating marketing activity.

Now try Question 9 in the Question Bank

Action Programme Review

1 (a) To obtain pricing comparisons with three major competitors with market share over 10%.

(b) To identify five potential distributors and/or agents for our product in South Africa.

(c) To demonstrate our new product to 1,000 potential customers in the UK.

(d) To obtain 500 sales leads in the north-eastern region.

(e) To obtain editorial coverage in two national newspapers or regional newspapers with total circulation of 20 million readers in the 7 days following the event.

(f) To meet 10 new media contacts in television and radio.

(g) To take advance sales orders to a value of £10,000.

(h) To increase the mailing list of potential customers by 2,000 names.

2 (a) Studying the manager's checklist shows that you don't need to worry about the ads: they are finished and sent off. Leaflet A is at the printers, and has been for 3 days: it still needs to be proofed and sent off before the 12th – a week to go. Leaflet B seems to be at the designers – with just over a week to go: it is clearly falling behind and will need watching: in particular, the photography seems to be held up and will have to be dealt with first.

(b) Checklists are particularly helpful in the event that you have to hand a task over to someone else for completion.

(c) You might have suggested shopping lists or things to do in general – or points to be covered in an essay (a very useful planning habit to get into!).

3 The action plan for dealing with the tasks identified in Action Programme 3 is as shown below.

SATURDAY 3 Request files SUNDAY 4 Draft report	WEDNESDAY 7
MONDAY 5	THURSDAY 8 Approve report. Signature to report.
TUESDAY 6 Type report	FRIDAY 9 Courier

Week commencing 3 SEPTEMBER

S	S	M	T	W	T	F
3	4	5	6	7	8	9

4 (a) The Gantt chart shows clearly that production is slightly behind schedule on Monday and Tuesday, spot on on Wednesday, better than planned on Thursday, but well short on Friday.

(b) It would be helpful to see how the cumulative production measured against the cumulative schedule, since daily comparisons are up and down.

(c)

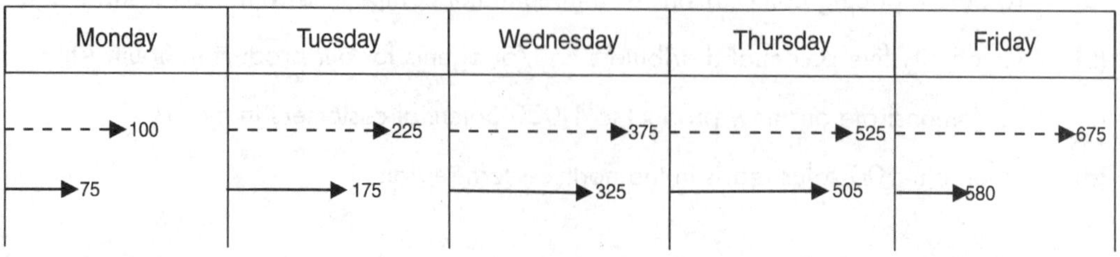

Monday	Tuesday	Wednesday	Thursday	Friday
- - - - ▶100	- - - - ▶225	- - - - ▶375	- - - - ▶525	- - - - ▶675
——▶75	——▶175	——▶325	——▶505	——▶580

(d) It is easy to see that the final weekly total output is well down on schedule.

5 The solution is given in the text.

6 There are three paths, as follows.

ADF = 3 + 1 + 3 days = 7 days
AEG = 3 + 6 + 3 days = 12 days
BCG = 5 + 2 + 3 days = 10 days

Answers to Quick Quiz

1 Stated goals (non-operational) are often not the same as operational (for businesses, usually financial) goals. Operational examples: to increase sales volume by 5% next year; to increase profitability by 10%; to reduce staff absenteeism by half. Non-financial objectives might include: to develop markets in untouched international countries; to gain a reputation as a responsible employer or being environmentally sound.

2 Efficiency – does the organisation operate in such a way as to gain the maximum advantage from all its resources? Effectiveness – does the business achieve what it sets out to do?

3 Forward scheduling starts from now and by estimating the time each task will take arrives at a completion date. Reverse scheduling starts from the date by which the whole activity must be completed and breaks this down into stages by which each subtask must be completed.

4 The key advantage is that you can see the relationship between time spent and the amount done.

5 The critical path (on a network diagram) represents the longest sequence; as this determines the overall project duration, this is the most critical.

6 A full list is given in section (c) in Paragraph 5.3.

Event Management 10

Chapter Topic List	
1	Setting the scene
2	Meetings and conferences
3	Shows, exhibitions and trade fairs
4	Events, stunts and corporate hospitality
5	The international dimension

Learning Outcomes

- ☑ Evaluate and select media and promotional activities appropriate to the organisation's objective, and status and its marketing context
- ☑ Undertake basic marketing activities within an agreed plan and monitor and report on progress

Syllabus References

- ☑ Describe the scope of individuals' roles in marketing; meetings, conferences, exhibitions, outdoor shows, outlet launches, press conferences
- ☑ Identify alternative and innovative approaches to a variety of marketing arenas and explain criteria for meeting business objectives
- ☑ Demonstrate an awareness of successful applications of marketing across a variety of sectors and sizes of business
- ☑ Explain how an organisation should host visitors from other cultures, and organising across national boundaries

Key Concepts Introduced

- Organising
- Conference
- Press conference/news conference
- Publicity stunt

1 Setting the scene

1.1 Just about everything covered in the *Marketing in Practice* syllabus involves organisation! It is the basis for all efficient activity.

1.2 In this chapter, we look at the orderly structure to be developed, and arrangements made, for various marketing activities and events. These range from sales meetings to trade exhibitions to product launch parties and publicity stunts. Essentially, they are opportunities for communication.

(a) **Face-to-face communication** between people involved in the marketing process, such as marketing staff, suppliers, distributors, customers, the media and/or general public.

(b) **Public relations**, including media relations, customer relations and employee relations.

(c) **Personal promotion** of an organisation and its product/services. Often, a first direct encounter – launch or introduction – between a product and its potential market.

1.3 There are three basic dimensions to marketing organisation.

- **How to organise** (planning, co-ordination, administration and control techniques)
- **What to organise** (what aspects of a given event need organising)
- **In what contexts** (what types of event you might be required to organise)

1.4 In this chapter, we address what to organise in a range of contexts. In Chapter 9, we looked at planning and control techniques, or how to organise. One of the key aspects to be organised for any event is the **venue** or where the event will take place. We will tackle this separately, in Chapter 11.

1.5 On completion of this chapter, you should be able to:

- Appreciate the scope of the organisational role in marketing
- Begin organising a range of marketing activities and events
- Evaluate and adopt successful elements of approaches to marketing activities and events
- Appreciate the needs of visitors from other cultures and the challenges they pose for the organisation of marketing events

Key Concept

Organising means 'giving an orderly structure to' or 'making arrangements for' a set of things or events.

Exam Tip

A range of event management tasks may be set in the exam. In the December 2002 exam, it was (a) citing the criteria to be used in venue selection for a 'celebration' event and (b) drawing a Gantt chart for planning the event (some of the requirements of which were given). In June 2003, the focus was on promotion of an event. In December 2003, it was the criteria for choosing a conference venue – and the requirement to appraise the company's own premises for this purpose. You might equally well, in future, be asked to make a report on alternative venues, or draw up guidelines for staff on how to plan the event or exhibition. Think as widely as you can through the issues involved. What difference might it make if (as in the December 2003 scenario) visitors would be coming from overseas?

---

2 Meetings and conferences

Meetings

2.1 Meetings are an organised form of face-to-face communication. In a marketing context, they will mainly include the following.

(a) **Project meetings**, bringing together people involved in a marketing project for briefing, planning, creative brainstorming, problem solving, reporting on progress, or post-project analysis and feedback. Such meetings may be small and relatively informal, involving a working team. If they involve representatives from other organisations or units (interdepartmental management meetings, or meetings with agency executives or consultants, say) they will require greater organisation in order to ensure the efficient gathering of participants and conduct of business.

(b) **Sales meetings**, bringing together the sales team or teams for briefing, motivation, training and/or reporting back from the field. Sales meetings are often used to present new products, marketing plans and sales targets to the sales force, both to inform and (if possible) to enthuse them about the upcoming sales period. Sales meetings are especially important if sales representatives do not work out of the organisation's premises: they offer an opportunity to reinforce team identity and to allow representatives to get to know the marketing team and each other. The venue, dates and frequency of such meetings will require particular attention, in order to avoid disruption to sales activity, and to ensure that information and support are given at the most relevant and helpful time.

(c) **Introduction or 'pitch' meetings**, in which suppliers present their products/services to potential clients/customers. An advertising, PR or market research agency, for example, may make a presentation and show its portfolio to those responsible for selecting and retaining such services. The marketing organisation may hold a similar meeting with retail outlet buyers, to introduce new or existing products.

(d) **Negotiations**. Formal relationships, collaborations and transactions are often conducted face-to-face, in order that mutual benefits can be hammered out with full feedback from all parties.

Organisation of meetings

2.2 Whatever the purpose of a meeting, small or large, formal or informal, the following aspects will need to be organised.

(a) **Venue, date and time**. The convenience of all parties will need to be considered, as well as suitability for the meeting's purpose.

(i) Is the venue equipped with the space and facilities required by the meeting? (This will be discussed in detail in Chapter 11.)

(ii) Is the date timely: does it allow decisions to be reached and action taken by deadlines or target dates?

(iii) The venue will need to be booked (even if it is your company's meeting room).

(iv) Notification of the meeting to participants. Relevant people will need to be informed of the date, time and venue, what they will need to bring with them, how to get there and so on. This may include guest speakers or presenters who will need to be booked and briefed in advance.

(b) **Agenda and objectives**. Some notice needs to be given so that participants know what the meeting is about, what preparation they need to do, what information they need to gather and so on. At the very least, a list of objectives/topics should be available or drawn up at the meeting itself. This may also include a schedule of meeting session times and breaks.

(c) **Preparation of information**. If a presentation is to be given, information will need to be gathered and other material (visual aids, new product samples or prototypes) sourced and collated. Think through the agenda carefully. Most meetings will encourage the asking of questions, so relevant information sources should be available for reference. You may also consider name-tags for larger numbers of participants who do not know each other.

(d) **Facilities**. Depending on the purpose of the meeting, you may need to organise:

- Seating arrangements
- Equipment (TV, video or other visual aids, projectors, flip charts)
- Refreshments
- Other amenities (such as parking or overnight accommodation)

(e) **Follow-up**. Someone needs to take notes of minutes of the meeting, so that follow-up action can be taken. Minutes are also a record and confirmation of what was discussed and so may be circulated to participants along with notes.

Action Programme 1

What information would you need to prepare for a meeting of sales representatives prior to the launch of a new product? (Think about the need to educate and to support/motivate the sales team.)

2.3 If the meeting is held at your business premises, you may have access to many of the facilities required **in-house**. If you are organising a meeting at another venue – a hotel, restaurant or **conference centre**, say – you will need to liaise with the venue staff.

(a) State your **requirements** clearly.

(b) Allocate **responsibility** for sourcing various requirements.

(c) Check that your requirements are being met, according to specification, schedule and **budget**.

2.4 The amount and type of **organisation** required for a meeting will depend on the number of participants involved, the formality or informality of the meeting, the activities to be performed and the facilities required. The **purpose and participants** of the meeting will also dictate the degree of sophistication and presentation required: a departmental team meeting will be less concerned with image-creation and hospitality than a meeting with clients to negotiate a major promotional collaboration. There are many creative opportunities to make a meeting into a PR event, but you need to be aware that 'bells and whistles' cost money, as do external venues and services.

(a) Check the **marketing budget** for general items (such as printing or entertainment) under which some meetings-related expenditure might be allocated).

(b) Check for, or draw up, a budget for regular and important special meetings, such as sales meetings and client pitches. Make sure that you can **justify the expenditure** by anticipated returns (improved sales performance, new accounts).

(c) **Record and monitor** all expenditure on meeting organisation for **budgetary control** and post-meeting evaluation.

Conferences

Key Concept

The term '**conference**' can be used interchangeably with 'meeting'. 'Conferring' simply means 'meeting for discussion'. However, it often implies a much larger gathering of people.

2.5 (a) A **sales conference** is a larger and less frequent version of a sales meeting, involving a gathering of the regional or national sales force, annually or seasonally (prior to relevant selling cycles).

(b) A **trade conference** is a gathering of participants over a day or several days, to attend a schedule of meetings, seminars or lectures, workshops and other activities relevant to their trade or profession.

2.6 The organisation of a conference will cover much the same ground as for a meeting, but the larger number of participants, longer duration and more varied agenda will require more features.

(a) **Longer notice and more comprehensive briefing** on the agenda, schedule and preparation requirements.

(b) **Advertising and promotion** of the conference or invitation to it, if it is open to a wider public.

(c) **Organisation of transport and overnight accommodation** for participants, or guidance on how they can make their own arrangements.

(d) More complex, and long-range **planning and co-ordination** of guest speakers and presentation materials.

(e) Organisation of **social, recreational or educational activities** and presentations, in addition to meetings. This may include dinners and parties, shows and sporting facilities, tours of relevant sites and local attractions and conference merchandise (T-shirts, pens, information packs). These are designed to attract delegates to the conference and to promote the organiser's image and facilities.

2.7 **Hosting or sponsoring a conference** for the trade, or on an issue of relevance to it is a public relations exercise on a major scale. You are perhaps more likely to be called upon to organise attendance at a conference for members of your department, in which case, the basic checklist applies.

- Budget
- Transport bookings/schedules
- Accommodation bookings/details
- Information/preparation/equipment required
- Pre-planned appointments/schedule

Tele- and video-conferencing

2.8 Bear in mind that there are cost-effective long-distance alternatives to face-to-face meetings.

(a) **Tele-conferencing** is a meeting held via the telephone. Modern telephones allow for multi-party link up (conferencing) and also speaker facility, so that all participants in a room can hear and speak. This is a common option for short, relatively informal meetings where travel and associated costs of a face-to-face meeting cannot be justified.

(b) **Video-conferencing**, via live video connection, adds visual and non-verbal communication, effectively allowing a 'face-to-face' meeting without travel time or cost. PC systems also allow data sharing on-screen and via modem, enabling participants to bring to the meeting video, audio, graphic and text information which can be viewed and accessed by everyone.

Press conferences

Key Concept

A **press conference** or **news conference** is a meeting called at a prescribed time and place, to brief journalists and/or issue a statement on a particular subject, and allow journalists to ask questions and take photographs.

2.9 The essential point about a press conference is that you are asking the media to come to you. Such conferences should be used sparingly, being reserved **for genuine announcements of major importance** or newsworthiness. (Journalists become cynical of organisations which call conferences on minor matters or pure self-promotion.) You might consider a news conference if, for example, you were launching a public campaign, releasing a special report or study commissioned by your organisation, or announcing a major policy change.

2.10 Organisation of a press conference includes the following.

(a) **Adequate notice** given to media contacts and news editors. Media invitations or brief press releases should give details of the conference, including a sufficient idea of its subject to act as an incentive to attend.

(b) Selection and set-up of an appropriate **venue**. However attractive your corporate headquarters for PR purposes, consider whether its location will draw the right journalists and have the necessary equipment.

- Powerpoints for TV crews and access to telephone links
- Sufficient seating
- Some form of platform and microphones for spokespeople

(c) Selection and briefing of an appropriate interview co-ordinator or **chairperson**.

(d) Written **briefing material and visual aids** for use and release at the conference.

(e) Provision of **refreshments**.

(f) **Timing** of the conference to suit relevant journalists.

- Not too close to media **deadlines**: late afternoon will usually rule out morning newspapers and TV
- Not too distant from deadlines: Monday morning is unlikely to attract Sunday papers.

(g) Ensuring that evening media coverage is monitored and reported back to the organisation.

3 Shows, exhibitions and trade fairs

3.1 Exhibitions and trade fairs (for example, the Ideal Home Exhibition, the Boat Show or the London Book Fair) offer several opportunities.

(a) **Public relations** (both to visitors and via media coverage, taking advantage of the interest generated by the exhibition organisers).

(b) **Promoting and selling** products/services to a wide audience of pre-targeted potential customers, particularly where demonstrations (eg of technical innovations) or visual inspection (eg clothes or motor cars) are likely to influence buyers.

(c) **Networking** within the industry and with existing clients.

(d) **Testing the response** to new products.

(e) **Researching competitor products** and promotions.

(f) **Researching suppliers' products** and services and making contacts along the supply chain.

Marketing at Work

Exhibition open for Olympic Games contract opportunities

Austrade will be taking a trade mission to Beijing's Stadia China 2004 Exhibition in a bid to gain more 2008 Olympic contracts for Australia.

The exhibition, timed to coincide with the finalisation of the Olympic venue tendering process and the beginning of construction of the new National Stadium for the Games, will target opportunities for sports stadiums and related sports and leisure facilities in China.

Austrade will be providing a Business Matching Centre for Australian companies to position themselves to win more supply contracts.

Business delegations from China's provincial and municipal sports administrations are expected to visit the exhibition. These will include officials from BOCOG, other agencies involved with the Olympic Games and event organisation and the State General Administration of Sports.

Considering exhibiting

3.2 Most industries are catered for by at least one annual or bi-annual exhibition in the UK, as well as internationally. The events themselves are set up by **exhibition organisers** who are responsible for booking and preparing the venue, registering participants and organising seminars and events, issuing catalogues of stand-holders and events, providing stand construction services, organising lounges, amenities and catering facilities, access and parking, power and lighting, promotion and press coverage.

3.3 These are the first steps for the marketing co-ordinator.

(a) **Research** what fairs/exhibitions are **available and relevant**.

(b) **Contact** each show manager or contact person for a 'show pack' or whatever details are available. These should include: how many people attend the show, where from and in what jobs/sectors, who the exhibitors are, what spaces/stands and facilities are available to exhibitors and at what cost, what transport and accommodation is available to exhibitors and at what cost.

(c) **Research the experience**, competence and asset-backing of the exhibition organisers. If it does not look as if they have the money or organisation and communication skills to make a success of a major logistical and promotional exercise, be cautious!

3.4 **Exhibiting is expensive!**

- Site fees, stand construction and display (estimated 66% by the Exhibition Industry Federation)
- Staff costs, including opportunity cost of staff being withdrawn from their normal sales work (22%)
- Promotion and entertainment of visitors (12%)

Marketing at Work

New media is having an impact on the exhibitions industry. The Internet can be used to attract visitors to shows and for post-show marketing via e-mail.

In addition, some exhibitors are using webcast technology to broadcast their shows live on the Internet. While this is not the same as being there, such facilities are still good for communicating useful information about exhibited products, with online visitors able to view just the stands they are interested in.

The director general of the Association of Exhibition Organisers says: 'The growth of exhibitions will go hand in hand with the growth of electronic media'. Visitors can use the Internet to book exhibition tickets, flights, hotel rooms and meetings.

3.5 A **budget** should be drawn up to cover all costs associated with going to the show/exhibition. This should be compared with forecast revenue from the show in order to assess the show's viability. After the event, the show's **profitability** can be evaluated in the same way.

3.6 However, it should be recognised that your objectives for a particular show may not solely be sales revenue. You may want to find a **distributor** in a new international market, or to **raise awareness** of your brand with the trade press, or to **introduce your product** to a new market. Such achievements may take time to 'ripen' into confirmed sales. In the Exhibition Industry Federation survey, the average time to convert an exhibition lead to a sale was seven months, and in some cases, two years or more.

Action Programme 2

(a) Carry out the steps outlined in Paragraph 3.3 for an industry sector you are involved or interested in. Swap information with other students, if available.

(b) Draw up a rough budget for a stand and any facilities and services offered. Compare this (partial) exhibition expenditure with the number and suitability of the target attendees. Would you go ahead with the exhibition?

3.7 At the time of booking a stand or space, you will have to decide on several issues.

(a) The **size** of your site. This will depend on the number and nature of products you wish to display, whether you want entertainment/meeting space for your exclusive use, the relative importance of the particular show, and your exhibition budget.

(b) The **location** of your site. It needs to be accessible for the flow of visitors. It needs to be in a relatively-targeted and labelled sector for your business, among others in your field but not in the shadow of strong competitors.

(c) The **design** and **construction** of your site. Exhibition organisers generally offer a range of basic prefab or modular stand designs and related services which they can have set up for you. If you wish to use their services, you may have to specify your requirements for shelving, lighting, power and telephone points, water/heating facilities, fire extinguishers, floor covering, furniture, flowers/plants and so on. Cleaning services and insurance may also be offered.

(d) The **information** you will provide for the exhibition catalogue, press pack and signage.

Planning and preparation

3.8 Exhibitions can be a huge logistical exercise, taxing your organisational skills to the utmost! They require planning well in advance – and then compress a lot of activity all at once into a very hectic period.

3.9 There are a number of areas in which **advance planning** will pay off.

(a) **Stand design, display and services**. As we mentioned above, specialist stand contractors can set up the structure, fixtures and fittings of a stand to your specifications, but you need to have considered what your needs for display and facilities will be.

(i) What **space** will be required for uncluttered access and vision, and for storage, confidential negotiations and meetings?

(ii) What **furniture** is required for meetings, storage, display?

(iii) What items will you want **displayed or demonstrated**? How will you transport them to the exhibition site? (There are specialist exhibition movers especially for overseas exhibitions, where export regulations must be observed.)

(iv) What decorative items will project the desired **image** of your organisation?

(v) What **stationery** (order books, price lists, visitors books) will you require to do business on the stand?

(vi) What services will you require for operating the stand such as cleaning, rubbish removal, security and provision of refreshments? You will also need to contract with the transporters, constructors and suppliers to dismantle the stand at the end of the exhibition.

(b) **Stand staffing**

Trade show networking and selling is hectic, intense and tiring. You will need to arrange for a rotating roster of stand staff, including a Stand Manager to organise the stand and liaise with exhibition organisers, reception staff, sales staff, technical staff (if the product requires expert demonstration or advice) and multilingual export staff.

(c) **Accommodation and transport for personnel**

A large exhibition can absorb available transport and accommodation even in a major city. If you are outside your home area, ensure that you have booked transport to the exhibition city, hotel or other accommodation and also any hire cars required, well in advance.

(d) **Pre-arranged meetings and visits**

In order to maximise your return on investment, ensure that you hit as many of your target audience as you can. Make a 'hit list' of key customers, suppliers and agents (from your database or from the pre-circulated list of exhibitors and attendees).

(i) Invite them to visit your stand. Give directions, incentives such as prize draws or free samples, and if possible, make definite appointments.

(ii) Supply their details to your sales staff, who can arrange to go and visit them.

Exhibition checklist

- ☐ Book space and pay direct
- ☐ Draft and supply catalogue/signage information
- ☐ Design stand/lighting/fixtures and fittings
- ☐ Order lighting, flooring, furniture, shelving, and storage
- ☐ Order water, power, heating, telecom, drainage
- ☐ Order fire extinguisher, check safety regulations
- ☐ Insure stand and exhibits
- ☐ Organise products/brochures/display materials for exhibit
- ☐ Arrange delivery/export of large items, and return
- ☐ Contract for stand cleaning, plant/flower supply and maintenance, security
- ☐ Plan staffing of stand
- ☐ Plan VIP appearances
- ☐ Arrange transport and accommodation of staff, VIP's
- ☐ Design and prepare promotional literature, signage, incentives to visitors
- ☐ Gather stationery and equipment for use on stand
- ☐ Invite customers/prospects, arrange meetings
- ☐ Arrange for photography, prepare press releases
- ☐ Order stand catering/refreshments
- ☐ Brief stand personnel; prepare task lists, rotas

At the exhibition

3.10 During the **set-up** period before the exhibition, you will work with contractors and your own staff to check that all the structures, fixtures, fittings and services associated with the stand are in place and functioning correctly.

3.11 Day-to-day **administration** of the stand.

- Appointment making, communications, offering refreshments
- Providing information, screening and routing 'serious' prospects
- Distributing leaflets or running competitions
- Recording all visits and sending visitors away with information

Action Programme 3

'The visitors to your stand will form their opinion on your company and its products more by their perception of you, than the stand or its contents.'

Take the time to think about the following issues. What effect could they have on visitors?

Behaviour	Effect on visitors
The way you conduct yourself on the stand	
The way you approach visitors	
The way you describe your product/service	

After the exhibition

3.12 Once an exhibition is finished, the stand will need to be dismantled, and its various components sent back where they came from.

3.13 The most important stage of the exhibition is **follow-up**.

(a) The contact information gained needs to be input to the organisation **database** and immediately utilised, even if it is only an e-mail to thank the contact for the visit.

(b) All promises made during the show (to send out literature or make a sales call) must be fulfilled as soon as possible.

Marketing at Work

Most companies now have a computer-based lead management system. Such a system will ensure that no lead is forgotten, and if you have captured the information electronically at the show you should be able to import it directly into the program. It will store details of every contact with each prospect and enable you to quickly send the client letters. It will remind you of calls, meetings and follow up actions by producing a daily diary or setting off a reminder alarm for outstanding actions each time you log into the system.

Among the leaders in such software are ACT! by Symantec, Achiever by Interactive Software, Caspian by Caspian Partners, Overquota by Cardinal Computers Limited, Goldmine by marketing Answers and Solutions Limited and Win-it from Apex systems.

Keep these leads separate from those generated by other promotional activities, so that when a sale is made you can be sure that it was as a direct result of the show. Depending on the length of your sales cycle you will at some time be able to accurately evaluate the return on your investment.

If the sales cycle is more than three months, you will need to make your decision whether to rebook at the exhibition, based on your sales representatives' evaluation of the prospects. The decision to rebook should also be based on whether your other key objectives were fulfilled. Most exhibitors will only hold your stand open for rebooking for up to three months after the show so if you leave it too long you could miss out on the opportunity. Also if you want a bigger stand or a better located stand you will need to act quickly to get the best opportunities.

4 Events, stunts and corporate hospitality

4.1 Although the territory of **promotional events**, **publicity stunts** and **corporate entertaining** is fairly well trodden, there is room for a high degree of creativity. The syllabus for *Marketing In Practice* requires you to 'develop an awareness of successful applications across a variety of sectors and sizes of business' (including 'alternative and innovative approaches'). Students should share their own experiences and compare and contrast different approaches.

Action Programme 4

Start to develop your awareness now!

(a) Buy, borrow or look in the library for a copy of *PR Week*, plus the trade journal of whatever sector you are interested in. Check the media pages of the reputable newspapers. Start a cuttings file.

(b) Select a major sporting event or venue near you, contact the Corporate Hospitality Department or ticket agency and ask for any information they may have on corporate packages.

(c) Collect any invitations *you* receive to promotional events, (yes, this may mean *joining* those mailing lists you usually avoid) and attend as many as you can.

(d) Swap cuttings and stories with other students.

Product and outlet launches

4.2 **Product and outlet launches** may be accompanied by a range of promotional activities (advertising, special offers, press releases, merchandising), but they are also often the occasion for a social gathering.

- **A preview or private viewing** by press and key clients and contacts, (often used by fashion companies, art galleries and movie distributors)
- A **speech or presentation** by a VIP as the centrepiece of a meal or party
- A **themed party**, reflecting the nature of the product or brand
- An **official opening or unveiling ceremony**

4.3 Hendra (1983) notes that 'good parties have reasons for being: others just shouldn't be.'

The purpose of a launch event may be:

(a) **To attract media coverage**. This is particularly effective if VIP or celebrity guests are present, or if the event itself is newsworthy (unveiling a genuine innovation, or imaginative in its venue or theme).

(b) **To raise the PR or industry profile of the organisation** by inviting a wide range of potential contacts.

(c) **To build relationships with existing customers or clients** by involving them in company celebrations.

(d) **To give key customers or trade buyers a chance to preview and pre-order** new products.

(e) **To reward staff, suppliers and distributors** who have worked on the launch.

4.4 Each event will have its own individual requirements, depending on its purpose, size, budget and style. However, the following will generally need attention.

(a) **Guest list**

Checklists of categories of people to be considered will help to ensure the right mix for the purpose of the event, including general and trade press and media, existing customers, style leaders and celebrities, suppliers and distributors, staff and community figures.

(b) **Invitations**

These should go out weeks in advance, and replies should be requested. In order to estimate numbers, particularly for high profile, smaller and catered events, it may be necessary to follow up those who do not respond. For a large event, anticipate a high dropout rate.

The style of invitations is an important PR exercise in itself: use your creativity to intrigue or impress, or to tie in with the product or event theme.

(c) **Venue**

This will be discussed in detail in Chapter 11.

- Availability
- Suitability/size
- Facilities
- Access
- Budget

(d) **Catering**

Unless you are having a very small informal gathering in your own premises, it is advisable to use professional caterers, or a catered venue. Caterers can supply a wide range of buffet foods and drinks, waiter service and hire of crockery and glasses. Lay out refreshments away from the main exhibition/presentation area, but spread about to keep guests circulating.

(e) **Staffing**

Ensure that you have welcomers and refreshment servers as well as information providers, order takers and an event co-ordinator.

(f) **Photography**

If you cannot persuade a press photographer to be present, or would prefer to control the images yourself, hire a photographer. (An interesting photo with a good caption written on the back may be sufficient to secure a feature in a newspaper or magazine.)

(g) **Promotional material and give-aways**

Depending on the purpose and status of the event, you may wish to make available product catalogues or brochures, samples or themed branded party gifts.

Action Programme 5

The Needle Works

You decide that the opening of the new knitting department needs to be celebrated and promoted with a launch event of some kind. Jot down some ideas on what sort of event you might have; where; whom you invite and how and what you might provide for your guests. For each idea, note what costs will have to be taken into account. Make your ideas as creative as possible, given the need to keep costs fairly low.

Key Concept

A **publicity stunt** is any event calculated to attract the attention of the media. It needs to be amusing or whimsical, unusual, highly visual and of local or topical interest to their audience.

4.5 From the organisation's point of view, a publicity stunt also needs to be relevant to the aims of press coverage: potential customers should remember the **product,** not just the event.

4.6 The organisation of publicity stunts needs to include the following.

- The **event itself** (time, location, participants, props and costumes)
- **Notification** of the public and press/media that the event is taking place

4.7 Other events

(a) **Promotional tours** by artists, recording artists or authors, giving interviews, readings/performances and signing copies of product for sale

(b) **Award ceremonies** and celebrations for staff, or in collaboration with other organisations in an industry

(c) **Public seminars** (or a tour of speaking engagements), promoting an organisation's expertise

Exam Tip

You may be asked for your suggestions for 'other promotional and marketing tools' (as well as advertising) to support a new launch. When given such a wide brief, don't forget 'events' as an option.

Corporate hospitality

4.8 Corporate hospitality involves entertaining an organisation.

- **Building or cementing relationships** with key clients
- **Rewarding and motivating** key suppliers
- Encouraging **networking** and informal communication
- **Showing a presence** at major sporting or cultural events

4.9 Large scale corporate entertaining at sporting and cultural events is often handled by **agencies**, who purchase a block of tickets and sell them on to companies as part of a **hospitality package** including a marquee, box or hospitality room, drinks and food and event programmes. (Larger companies may own a permanent box or block of seats at stadiums and theatres, and use on-site catering services.) For a small company with no particular status requirements, ordinary ticket purchase and on-site catering may be sufficient.

4.10 If you book an event (concert, rugby international, football, golf, tennis) through an agency, the price per head is likely to be high, so you will need to **plan the guest list and attendance** carefully.

- There is likely to be a set number of places which need to be filled: have a reserve list
- Try and find people who will be interesting to each other and of a similar status
- Invite guests verbally at first, to get the date in their diaries: then follow up
- Monitor responses, and invite reserve-list replacements as soon as possible
- Send reminders a week before the event with tickets and details
- Arrange all requirements for transport, parking, accommodation
- Liaise with agency staff to ensure that catering and other services are in hand
- Brief the hosts on the list of guests, their company and position

4.11 There will usually be a separate **budget allocation** for hospitality events. The return on investment on such entertaining is not always readily quantifiable, since there are many other factors in customer loyalty and favour, but there may well be **industry norms and expectations** to live up to.

Marketing at Work

Corporate hospitality (also known as event marketing) needs to become more targeted and focused. Some £330 million is spent on event marketing annually, but it is not necessarily money well spent. A recent survey found that, out of 77 UK companies, only 34% evaluated such events against their objectives, and 72% cited personal management preferences as important factors when choosing what event to stage. Corporate hospitality should instead be regarded as an important part of the marketing mix, and accountable in the following areas:

- Have we seen a growth in business?
- Have we seen improved relationships?
- Have we got direct orders from it?
- Has it opened up new lines of communication?
- Has it been something we can build on?

Marketing Business, April 2000

5 The international dimension

Organisation across borders

5.1 The organisation of international events involves several additional factors.

(a) **Language**

As organiser, you may have to communicate with guests, venues and service providers for whom English is not a first language. You can overcome these difficulties.

(i) Work through an international agency, or branch of your organisation with representatives in the other country.

(ii) Employ a translator/interpreter to prepare or mediate communications or find a colleague who speaks or writes the language in question.

(b) **Currency**

Members of your organisation going abroad for meetings or exhibitions may need to be equipped with appropriate local currency, travellers cheques or credit facilities.

Fluctuations in exchange rates should be taken into account when checking foreign currency expenditure against pound-sterling budgets.

(c) **Travel arrangements**

International travel is more complex.

(i) Travel itineraries, including airport transfers, flexible ticketing options, allowance for checking in times and time differences

(iii) Travel insurance

(iii) Travel documentation. Some countries require travel visas and a letter of confirmation that the person is travelling on company business, as well as a valid passport

(iv) Medical precautions and vaccinations, which need to be planned well in advance of departure

(v) Longer lines of communication. Travellers would be provided with all schedules, itineraries, details of arrangements and if possible local contact numbers in the event of problems

(d) **Import/export arrangements**

Sending products and promotional materials overseas (or receiving them from overseas) for exhibitions and other events can be complicated.

- Customs documentation is required
- Lead time required

International freight services and exhibition consultants may be an option.

(e) **Time differences**

E-mail and fax are the most effective means of communication where events are to be organised in different time-zones.

(f) **Local law and customs**

Check with embassies, trade delegations, consultancy services or local contacts, about such matters as the role and safety of women, consumption of alcohol, dress codes, the content of printed matter, business etiquette and religious sensibilities.

(g) **Distance**

Since you are not on the spot to monitor and supervise arrangements, briefings, instructions and confirmations will be more important when organising events overseas, whether directly or through intermediaries.

Exam Tip

The December 2002 exam asked you to plan a celebration event for all the retailers of a company in Africa. It was up to you to note: (a) The African setting (what constraints may that put on your plans if you are a student from London or Hong Kong?) and (b) the fact that the retailers come from a range of African nations (will they need help with accommodation? what venue will provide ease of access?)

Hosting visitors from other countries

5.2 Similar considerations to those outlined above apply to hosting overseas clients, suppliers or agents who visit your office or marketing events.

(a) Visitors may need your support, as local organiser, with transport and accommodation arrangements, as well as advice on visas and currency requirements.

(b) You may need to provide an interpreter for visitors who are not fluent in English.

(c) Be aware and respectful of the **business and social customs** of your visitors. In the Far East, for example, hospitality requires the host to offer gifts to the guest, and this is not to be interpreted as a bribe. In other countries, 'baksheesh' or 'oiling the wheels of industry' is the norm. Negotiation and conflict resolution styles differ according to culture. Age and gender incur differing degrees of respect. Body language and eye contact have different connotations.

(d) Be aware or ask about **religious or cultural requirements** in regard to diet, Sabbath observance and other matters.

(e) Remember that visitors may be new to your city or country as well as to your organisation, and may welcome scenic as well as factory tours. Opportunities for sightseeing and local entertainment may be highly appreciated.

(f) Be very clear, in advance, whose organisation is responsible for the arrangements and expense of the visit.

5.3 It may be helpful to act as, or appoint, a **permanent host**, guide or liaison person to accompany or keep in regular touch with foreign visitors and to co-ordinate their various travel and business arrangements.

Action Programme 6

Make a list of the (a) corporate areas/cities and (b) tourist sights you would wish an important overseas client to see on a three-day visit to your company/country.

Chapter Roundup

- **Marketing activities** which require **organisation** include meetings and conferences, press conferences, trade shows and exhibitions, launch events, publicity stunts and corporate hospitality.
- **Basic organisational considerations** include:
  - guest list
  - invitation or advertising and response monitoring
  - choice of venue, date and time
  - notification of the purpose/objectives of the event
  - planning of seating, facilities and amenities
  - catering and other services
  - provision of promotional/supporting information
  - booking and briefing of guest speakers/presenters
  - booking of transport and accommodation (if required) of participants
  - budgeting for all of the above
- **International organisation** is complicated by factors including
  - language
  - law and custom
  - import/export requirements
  - currency
  - travel requirements
  - time differences
  - unknown media
  - length of communication lines

Quick Quiz

1 What special considerations apply to the organisation of sales team meetings?

2 What are an 'agenda' and 'minutes' of a meeting?

3 Outline the procedure for calling a press conference.

4 What considerations dictate the desirable size and location of an exhibition stand?

5 What costs of participating in exhibitions need to be budgeted for?

6 Give four examples of events that might be organised for a product launch.

7 What is a 'publicity stunt' and what makes it effective?

8 What is a 'hospitality package'?

9 What are some of the arrangements that need to be made for international travel?

10 Give four examples of cultural differences that might be taken into account when hosting overseas visitors.

Now try Question 10 in the Question Bank

Action Programme Review

1 Information for a sales meeting might include: market research reports, budgets and forecasts, sales support materials (order forms, brochures), new product prototypes and/or samples for demonstration, mock-ups of promotional/ad campaigns, media schedules and promotion/PR plans, training manuals (if required).

2 Just do it! If you struggled to find details of relevant trade shows and exhibitions, did you try trade journals? Perhaps it was the wrong time of year for the exhibition to be advertised. There are also published directories of national and international trade shows and exhibitions. Or, try your local chamber of commerce, or business advisory service. Better yet, tap your networks, or check some websites: practice these research skills!

3

Behaviour	Effect on visitors
The way you conduct yourself on the stand	Will they approach, or stay away?
The way you approach visitors	Will they take the time to listen to you or run away?
The way you describe your product/service	Will they be interested enough to become a firm lead?

4 This is the only way to broaden your thinking.

5 Your ideas might have included aspects along the following lines (but don't let our suggestions limit your thinking).

Venue: In new wool department (opportunity to browse; impact of colour wools, can take pre-orders) – no venue cost

OR

Local tapestry/craft museum? (unusual – but hire cost + staff costs to liaise with curator etc)

Event: Sunday brunch (not evening, to include older customers, out of town customers)

- croissants, sandwiches
- Bucks fizz/orange juice
- catering cost (also crockery/glass hire) *relatively* inexpensive food type
- exhibition of knitted work
- demonstrations

} Supplied *free* by wool manufacturers (promoting own brands)

Invite: Staff (hosts), suppliers, editors of craft magazines, local radio, all regional customers and *all* customers who requested knitting information (even if not expected to come). (Mail costs)

Invitations: Simple card with multicoloured wools knitted through (minimal material cost + staff time).

Gifts/incentives: Prize draw on entry to win a kit. (Cost of kit.)

Introductory 5% discount on launch purchases? (Discount cost.)
Information leaflets

6 Your answer will depend on your organisation and its location. Bear in mind that this is an important client, so (s)he may be worth investing some time and money in entertaining, but also that (s)he is on a business trip.

Answers to Quick Quiz

1 Sales meetings must not interrupt sales activity and should give information and support at an appropriate time.

2 An agenda (Latin for 'things to be done') is a list of various items of business at a meeting. The minutes are a written record of the discussion and/or decisions of a meeting.

3 Give adequate notice and select time appropriate for publication deadlines; select a venue with necessary facilities; brief a co-ordinator; prepare written briefing or visual aids; arrange refreshments; feedback to the organisation afterwards.

4 Size: number and nature of your products; meeting space required; need for prominence. Location: flow of visitors; relative position of competitors; need for prominence.

5 You need to consider site fees, staff costs, promotion and the entertainment of visitors.

6 The four examples given in the text are: presentations, themed parties, an unveiling ceremony and a preview.

7 A publicity stunt is any event calculated to attract the attention of the media. It is effective when it reinforces your message in a novel, entertaining and memorable way.

8 A hospitality package is a set of benefits to enable your customer to best enjoy corporate hospitality – for example, entry to an exclusive enclosure, box seats or hospitality rooms.

9 Language issues, currency, itineraries, import and export arrangements, time differences, local law and customs, and the fact that all of these have to be negotiated at a distance.

10 Four examples of cultural differences you need to consider are religion, social custom, business customs and language.

Venue Selection

11

Chapter Topic List	
1	Setting the scene
2	Venue appraisal
3	Suitability
4	Synergy
5	Making recommendations

Learning Outcomes

☑ Evaluate and select media and promotional activities appropriate to the organisation's objective, and status and its marketing context

☑ Undertake basic marketing activities within an agreed plan and monitor and report on progress

Syllabus Reference

☑ Appraise and select a venue, based on given criteria and make appropriate recommendations

Key Concepts Introduced

- Venue
- Synergy

1 Setting the scene

1.1 As we saw in Chapter 10, the venue of some marketing events in which the company may wish to participate are chosen by external event organisers: trade conferences, shows and exhibitions and some corporate hospitality packages.

In this chapter, we consider the evaluation and selection of a venue for events where this is at the company's discretion: product launches, parties, customer events, publicity stunts, meetings and conferences.

1.2 We will discuss a number of standard and more creative possibilities: you should continue to swap experiences and ideas with fellow students, and to keep an eye out for opportunities yourself.

1.3 Be aware that, like most aspects of marketing, event venues lie on a wide **continuum of possibilities**: from simple to lavish, informal to formal, cheap to astronomically expensive, business-like to exotic. Somewhere along that continuum, the requirements and constraints of a given marketing organisation will be met. From the outset, bear in mind that the most appropriate place for the informal planning meeting of your sales team may be your office meeting room, with no special facilities laid on. The place to celebrate a high status industry award with senior business clients may be the Savoy.

In this chapter, we will help you to evaluate where on the continuum your event falls.

1.4 On completion of this chapter, you should be able to:

- Gather information on venues for a range of events
- Appraise relevant venues for suitability, synergy and affordability
- Make clear recommendations for venue selection
- Liaise with venue management on preparations for the event
- Evaluate the performance and suitability of the venue after the event

2 Venue appraisal

Key Concept

A **venue** is the appointed place for a meeting, concert, sporting fixture or other event.

Gathering venue information

2.1 **Dedicated entertainment and event venues** such as conference centres, large hotels, sports stadia, theatres and exhibition centres promote themselves to event organisers.

- Specialised **directories** and source books for event organisers
- The **catalogues** of hotel and conference centre chains (such as the Forte Group)
- Entries in business directories and yellow pages
- **Information packs** available on request
- Event management **consultants**

2.2 Thinking 'outside the box', however, you might also gather venue information by contacting any potential venue you find interesting: zoos, art galleries, National Trust properties and other such sites will often have information on hire and event management services available. (If not, don't be afraid to break new ground!)

Action Programme 1

Begin to compile you own venue directory file. Make a list of categories that you would find useful (start with your present job, then think beyond): Conference, Prestige, Themed, Sports and so on. As you gather notes and brochures, tag each with the relevant category. (Build towards an index card-file or binder.)

2.3 Once you have gathered, or are aware of, a wide variety of venues, you can match the requirements of a particular event with the attributes of a number of venues to select the best fit.

There are two broad criteria for selecting a venue for a marketing event.

- Suitability
- Synergy

We will look at each in turn.

3 Suitability

Exam Tip

'Criteria for selecting a venue' is a classic exam topic. You should take account of the content of this section and note down its key features as a ready-made checklist.

The examiner also suggests the acronym ASFAB:

- [ ] Access
- [ ] Suitability/size
- [ ] Facilities
- [ ] Availability
- [ ] Budget

'Access' may seem like a small consideration but it featured prominently in the December 2003 scenario, where you were asked to assess the suitability of a small marina as a conference venue. The examiner pointed out that – although students used the ASFAB acronym – they paid insufficient attention to detail. The marina is 'situated at the end of a narrow country lane' – hardly suitable for large equipment trucks or mass vehicular access/parking! If you're going to use an acronym, make sure you take careful account of each point, in relation to the scenario ...

3.1 **Suitability** means **fitness for an intended purpose** and **appropriateness for an occasion**. Your particular event may have many different criteria and constraints: a suitable venue will meet as many of them as possible.

The size or capacity of the venue

3.2 How many people are on your list of guests or participants? How many people does the venue hold? This may be defined by various factors.

- Seating capacity (for example, in a lecture hall, restaurant, theatre or cinema)
- Accommodation capacity (in a hotel or residential conference centre)
- Space and comfort (in a room where people will be standing)
- Accessibility and lines of sight (in a gallery, exhibition hall or shop)
- Safety and fire regulations (which limit numbers, so as to allow emergency exit)

3.3 Cost, atmosphere and PR considerations suggest that you should not select a much larger venue than your numbers require. (A small group of people in a large room feels awkward and looks like a disappointing turnout, even if everyone expected has come.)

(a) Hotels and Conference Centres have meeting rooms and auditoria of various sizes and styles.

(b) 'Private party' areas can be roped or screened off in otherwise public restaurants, theatres or museums.

3.4 The price charged by a large venue may reflect economies of scale, but it may also reflect the wide range of services and facilities available. Do not pay for what you will not use.

The location of the venue

3.5 Where are the majority of your guests/participants based? Will they find the venue convenient to get to? This may not be a critical consideration in the case of a sales meeting, which participants have to attend. However, if you need to **attract guests**, factors concerning convenience will be important.

(a) **Proximity** to where many of your guests are likely to be at the time of the event

(b) **Accessibility**. You will need to evaluate the availability of public transport, road access and parking facilities.

3.6 For a small, special event, however, do not let inaccessibility put you off, if the remoteness of the venue is of benefit in other ways. Minibus or coach hire may be worthwhile to transfer guests to a gathering in a remote country location for golf, or a house-party style event. More innovative alternatives can also be arranged, where the costs of doing the unusual are considered worthwhile.

3.7 The venue should also be located conveniently for the purpose of the event. If you want to show customers a new outlet or showroom, or give suppliers and agents a tour of your plant or warehouse facilities, any associated meetings or entertainment will be most efficiently held at or near the site in question.

The status and style of the venue

3.8 Despite 'star rating' systems, status, style and degrees of comfort and luxury are highly subjective matters. The level of formality of a venue, its comfort and amenities, decor, style of service, dress codes and so on project a powerful image, with which your event will be associated. The image of the venue should be matched to the following.

- The desired image and status of the organisation or the product or brand
- The tastes, age and status bracket of the guests
- The purpose and style of the event (business-like, entertainment, social networking)

Action Programme 2

What sort of marketing events might you hold at:

(a) a branch of McDonalds?
(b) the Ritz tea-rooms?
(c) a country bed and breakfast hotel?
(d) a prominent city night-club?
(e) an outdoor adventure centre?

3.9 Some of the main facilities your event might require include the following.

(a) **Conference/meeting facilities**, including suitable furniture, presentation equipment, staging or sound systems, communications centre and secretarial support services.

(b) **Catering facilities or services**, ranging from drinks and snacks to full-scale buffet or sit-down banquet.

(c) **Accommodation**, for longer conferences and events. Consider what type of accommodation, and what standard of comfort and presentation your guests require.

(d) **Recreational activities**. Conferences are often opportunities to reward staff and to encourage team-building by offering leisure facilities.

(e) **Disabled access** and facilities: ramps, lifts and wheelchair access.

3.10 **Outdoor venues** and events will additionally require attention.

- **Shelter** (especially in the event of bad weather)
- **Toilet facilities**
- **Safety**, for example, if sporting or adventure activities are involved

3.11 The **house rules** of a venue should also be checked. Conference centres owned by church organisations, for example, often prohibit alcohol on the premises. If you require non-smoking, or smoking facilities, you will need to check.

3.12 Bear in mind that any services and facilities lacking from an otherwise ideal venue may be sourced for you by the venue organisers. Event management is a jigsaw puzzle, not just a checklist!

Cost

3.13 All of the above criteria have cost implications. As we discussed in Chapter 9, you need to start the venue selection experience with some clear ideas.

(a) A clear set of **objectives** for your event, including any financial benefits you expect to accrue from it.

(b) An **expenditure budget** in proportion to the financial and non-financial returns expected from the investment.

(c) An **event from concept and plan** which places the venue specification in the context of the objectives and budget.

3.14 The venue is not the only cost of an event. Balance what you need your venue to offer with the constraints an expensive venue will place on the rest of your event budget. If your clients genuinely expect to be entertained at a five-star level, you may have to indulge them. It is however possible to transform the most inexpensive venue into a high-impact event through creativity in concept, decoration and imported services.

This is where synergy comes in.

Action Programme 3

The costs of exhibiting at Trade Fair A and Trade Fair B during August 20XX were as follows.

	Trade Fair A		Trade Fair B	
	£'000	%	£'000	%
Stand design and hire	70	35	50	20
Stand promotion	30	15	125	50
Hospitality and literature	90	45	50	20
Stand staffing	10	5	25	10
	200	100	250	100

Required

Show the costs for the trade fairs in pie charts.

4 Synergy

Key Concept

Synergy is a scientific principle whereby the whole is greater than the sum of its parts. This can be simply put as: 2 + 2 = 5.

4.1 Synergy implies that the venue not only satisfies certain necessary conditions for an effective event, but adds something to the event's effectiveness. In business terms, **the venue itself adds value** and there are several ways in which it can do this.

- Adding **attraction**, or incentive to people to attend
- Adding **impact** or memorability to the event
- Adding **PR/media value**, newsworthiness or media interest
- Adding **association**, linking the organisation, product or brand with the event in the participants' and audience's minds

Creative thinking

4.2 Attraction, impact and PR/media value can be contributed by a venue.

- Originality
- Whimsicality
- Visual impact
- Topical associations or links

Association of ideas

4.3 Synergy often occurs by lateral thinking, so **associative links** or **common themes** between event and venue not only aid originality but help to draw attention and memory to the event/product/brand. Some venues are naturally themed for synergy with products: museums and art galleries for design/art products, for example or embassies for products linked with foreign countries. Other associations may be more specific: showing a pure wool fashion range in a shearing shed or promoting an all-star basketball team at the Planetarium.

Building on relationships

4.4 Another form of synergy is in **building relationships** which enlarge the image or audience of both parties. The venue and event organiser may find possibilities for collaboration on joint PR and promotion, to their mutual benefit. A venue may negotiate a special rate in order to gain from the PR potential of a high profile event.

Building on familiarity

4.5 Synergy may come from familiarity. An event for **existing customers**, for example, might justifiably be held at the company's premises or regular entertainment venue.

- Associations with a history of successful transactions
- The ease and security of familiar surroundings
- The strong projection of corporate image
- The customer's sense of acknowledgement, belonging and involvement
- The customer's habit of making purchases in that environment

4.6 A product or press launch which needed extra impact to attract the media, on the other hand, would require greater originality.

Action Programme 4

Brainstorm, by association of ideas, some possible venues for the following events.

(a) The press launch of a book called 'The Wild West'.

(b) Launch of the new season's designs by an exclusive boutique jeweller to existing high-spending customers.

(c) A party for your sales representative and outlet contacts to celebrate the outstanding success of your 'G.I. Fred' Action Man toy.

(d) A seminar on 'Doing Business in the Commonwealth', sponsored by your organisation for the business community.

---

5 Making recommendations

5.1 You may be asked informally for your thoughts on venues, or you may be required to research and evaluate a number of options for a formal report or presentation.

5.2 Your recommendations should be set out and structured according to whatever instructions you are given. However, a useful general format is as follows.

VENUE SELECTION FOR (EVENT)

Event:	(Brief description of the event type and size, intended audience.)
Objectives:	(Key aims of the event: media coverage, sales generated, leads generated, business transacted, staff rewarded)
Budgetary constraints:	(Total expenditure budget available, if set)

VENUE 1	*VENUE 2* (Alternative option, if required)
Venue: (name)	*Venue:*
Location:	*Location:*
Concept: (Venue type/theme associations, possible synergy)	*Concept:*
Capacity:	*Capacity:*
Style: (Image/status/ comfort level)	*Style:*
Facilities & Services: (relevant to needs of event)	*Facilities & Services:*
Transport/access:	*Transport/access:*
Key advantages: (relevant to needs of event. Opportunity for synergy)	*Key advantages:*
Disadvantages: (facilities/service lacking and needing to be supplied. Any drawbacks)	*Disadvantages:*
Cost: (Estimates based on event plan/brief)	*Cost:*
Recommendation: (Venue 1 or 2, if required)	

Action Programme 5

The Needle Works

Using the above format, write a report or prepare a presentation recommending venue(s) you briefly proposed in Action Programme 5, Chapter 10. Make up any details you wish or take the opportunity to do some live research, if such a venue exists.

5.3 This is the basic data required for a well-argued recommendation. If you were giving a presentation, or submitting a formal report, you might include visual aids.

- Photographs of the venue and its facilities
- Maps showing location, access, parking

You might also submit the full information pack and rate card of the recommended venue.

Exam Tip

One of the proposed assessment tasks for *Marketing in Practice* is a *presentation* to be given on *venue selection* for:

- a product launch and/or
- an event for existing customers.

You might like to practise, or make notes for a variety of such presentations. Research an actual venue and present it as a recommendation to fellow students or to a friend: get feedback on whether you 'sold' your recommendation effectively. Alternatively, give a presentation on 'How to select an event venue': you might want to make this more memorable: try headings such as 'Suitability, Synergy, Size, Status, Style, Site, Service and Safety'! Or ASFAB: Access, Suitability/size, Facilities, Availability, Budget.

Chapter Roundup

- Criteria for appraising the **suitability** of a venue include:
  - size/capacity
  - location: convenience, access, parking
  - status/style/luxury level/formality
  - facilities and activities including business services, accommodation; catering; recreation
  - cost, in relation to purpose of and likely returns from event.
- **Synergy** (2 + 2 = 5) is where the venue itself adds value to the event through:
  - incentive/attraction
  - impact/memorability
  - PR/media value
  - association of ideas to the organisation/product/brand
  - encouraging collaboration
  - building on existing relationships and familiarity

Quick Quiz

1 Where can an event organiser find out about available venues?

2 How is the size or capacity of a venue defined?

3 What does a 'convenient' location involve?

4 Give three examples of special requirements for outdoor venues?

5 Give three examples of qualities of a venue that might attract media interest.

6 Write out a checklist for data in support of a venue recommendation.

Now try Question 11 from the Question Bank

Action Programme Review

1 This will be a valuable resource for your career as well as for assessment of your competence in this area of the *Marketing in Practice* syllabus!

2 The following are just some suggestions to guide your thinking.

(a) A McDonalds might be hired out for a kid's party (PR for charitable donation?) or for an informal cheap sales team lunch meeting (especially if the product was American or pop-culture) – or even for a product launch.

(b) A product launch or preview for older, wealthier customers/clients, or a formal PR seminar/presentation.

(c) Accommodation for sales/marketing staff at a nearby conference or exhibition or a buyer meeting for a new 'bed and breakfast' guide.

(d) Launch party for ABC1 market, celebrities, media: fashion or entertainment product.

(e) Team-building for sales/marketing staff. Inter-corporate challenge (media stunt, charity sponsorship). Press launch for new sports shoes or deodorant?

3

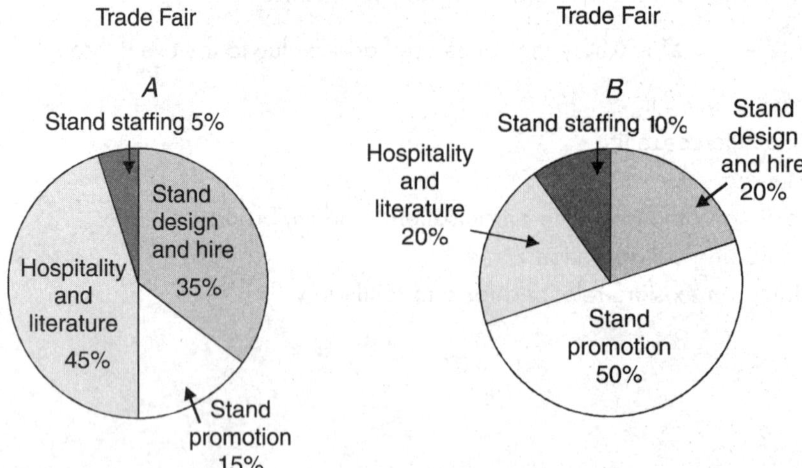

4 Again, these are just ideas: don't let us stifle your creativity!

(a) A wild west theme park, a film set, a rodeo, the bison enclosure at a zoo.

(b) The jeweller's own premises, the Tower of London (crown jewels), the Fabergé section of the V & A Museum, Covent Garden hospitality room.

(c) A paint-ball centre or laserdome (good team-building).

(d) The Commonwealth Centre (in London) or particular country's delegation (eg Australia House) or Tourist Bureau.

5 If you used a live venue, keep this report for your portfolio – it will contain useful information.

Answers to Quick Quiz

1 A full list of information sources is given in Paragraphs 2.1 and 2.2.

2 Your answer should have included: seating capacity, accommodation capacity, standing capacity, accessibility and limits prescribed by fire and safety regulations.

3 A location must be: accessible for staff/delegates; comfortable for your guests; offer all necessary facilities; convey your message – and fall within the budget constraint.

4 These requirements are primitive: toilets, shelter and safety!

5 Media interest will be aroused by: good photograph opportunities (visual impact); originality (newsworthiness to readers); topical associations or links (ties in with other stories).

6 You should refer to the checklist provided in Paragraph 5.2.

Part D

Co-ordinating the marketing mix

Advertising Media

12

Chapter Topic List	
1	Setting the scene
2	Media selection
3	Press
4	Radio
5	Television
6	Other media
7	Advertising on the Internet
8	Media scheduling
9	The printing process

Learning Outcomes

☑ Evaluate and select media and promotional activities appropriate to the organisation's objectives and status and to its marketing context

☑ Undertake basic marketing activities within an agreed plan and monitor and report on progress

Syllabus Reference

☑ Select media to be used based on appropriate criteria for assessing media opportunities, and recommend a media schedule

Key Concepts Introduced

- Advertising
- Above-the-line promotion
- Below-the-line promotion
- Reach
- Frequency
- Ratings
- Banner advertisement

1 Setting the scene

Key Concept

Advertising is 'any paid form of *non-personal* presentation and promotion of ideas, goods or services by an *identifiable* sponsor'. (American Marketing Association).

1.1 **Promotion** is generally divided into broad areas.

(a) **Personal** (direct marketing, network marketing and the use of sales representatives)

(b) **Impersonal**, which can be further divided up.

- **'Above-the-line'** methods, such as media advertising
- **'Below-the-line'** promotions or negotiated sales incentives
- **Point of sale**: promotional messages and displays
- **PR and publicity**: 'free' transmission of the promotional message
- **Informational methods**, such as printed catalogues, brochures and leaflets

Key Concepts

Above-the-line promotion is advertising placed in paid for media, such as the press, radio, TV, cinema and outdoor sites. The 'line' is one in an advertising agency's accounts, above which are shown its earnings on a commission basis, from the buying of media space for clients.

Below-the-line promotion involves product-integral and negotiated sales incentives, such as packaging, merchandising, on-pack discounts and competitions and so on. (Agency earnings on a fee basis are shown below the 'line' in their accounts.)

1.2 In Chapter 13, we will look at below-the-line activities, PR and collaborative sales promotion, and in Chapter 14, the management of informational promotion through printed matter. You should also be able to draw on your studies for the *Marketing Fundamentals* and *Customer Communications* modules.

1.3 In this chapter, we look at **above-the-line advertising media**.

(a) We will start by outlining the general criteria involved in **media selection**

- **Criteria** by which the effectiveness and efficiency of media can be evaluated
- How the major media can be **compared** with each other

(b) We will then look at each of the **major media** in turn, and at how opportunities to advertise in each can be evaluated.

(c) Finally, we will focus on the **scheduling of media**: how to plan the frequency, duration/size and number of advertisement for maximum impact.

1.4 On completion of this chapter, you should be able to:

- appreciate the range of advertising media available
- select and schedule media for an advertising task
- assess media opportunities and make recommendations

2 Media selection

2.1 The general criteria for selecting a medium to convey the promotional message to the appropriate audience are as follows.

- The advertiser's specific **objectives** and plans
- The **size of the audience** which regularly uses the medium
- The **type of people** who form the audience of the medium
- The **suitability** of the medium for the message
- The **cost** of the medium in relation to its ability to fulfil the advertiser's objectives
- The susceptibility of the medium to **testing and measurement**

2.2 The planning of an advertising campaign

(a) The identification of the **target audience**: Who are they? Where are they? Which demographic group do they fall in? What are their interests, media consumption habits, buying patterns, attitudes and values?

(b) The specification of the **communication** or promotional message. What do you need to say, and in what way, in order to impact on the audience in such a way as to achieve your marketing goals?

(c) The setting of **targets**: What is the marketing goal to which the advertising can contribute? What do you expect the ad to achieve and at what cost? What aspects of the audience's thinking or behaviour do you wish to change, and how will you recognise and measure that change if and when it occurs?

Marketing at Work

MacNamara (1993) suggests that this planning process can help you avoid a phenomenon which he calls 'Gotta' advertising. There is a special supplement being published by one of the national newspapers on your field or product group, or a front cover available at short notice at a hugely discounted rate: surely you have 'gotta' take advantage of the opportunity?

Ad hoc advertising is often based on an illusory or irrelevant opportunity: as in sales shopping, it is often possible to be seduced by a 'bargain' – when it is something you would not otherwise buy or need. Media sales people try all sorts of tricks to get you to buy space: even your advertising agency may recommend particular media with their own interests in mind.

The size and type of the audience

2.3 Each medium reaches a certain number and 'type' (demographic group, market segment, interest group) of people. There is a trade-off between the size and relevance of the available audience.

(a) General-interest, national mass-market medium (such as a national newspaper or television) will have the largest **circulation figures**, but may not reach the highest percentage of a particular market segment.

(b) **Segmentation** may be possible through the scheduling and placing of ads in large-scale media (for example, in special-interest sections or supplements in the press, or by programme preference in TV).

(c) **Targeted media** may reach a smaller population, but a higher percentage of the target audience.

- **Local or regional media** (in the catchment area)
- **Specialist magazines** and journals related to the target audience
- Media which fit the **'media habits'** of the target audience

Action Programme 1

Brainstorm a list of media which might be suitably targeted (by factors in the media themselves, or in the media habits of the target audiences) for advertising the following products/services.

(a) A local garage offering car service, maintenance and parts
(b) An up-market restaurant
(c) A software package for use by accountants (based on UK law and regulation)
(d) A new brand of washing powder
(e) A microchip for use in engineering applications

2.4 Hearne (1987) suggests that the effective audience of a medium and therefore the competitiveness of different media is influenced by the following factors.

(a) **Opportunity to use the medium**. The potential audience will not be able to use TV during working hours, or magazines while driving, or cinema over breakfast. Radio in the morning and TV in the evening have bigger effective audiences.

(b) **Effort required to use the medium**. People usually use the medium that will cost them least effort. Print media require the ability to read and concentrate: television is comparatively effortless.

(c) **Familiarity with the medium**. People consume media with which they are familiar: hence the survival of print media, since the education system is still predominantly print-orientated. Electronic media are however gaining ground.

(d) **Segmentation by the medium**. The print media currently has the greatest capacity for segmentation into special-interest audiences. Commercial television segments to a limited extent through programming, and cable/satellite television to a greater extent, through the proliferation of channels. Some media only charge in proportion to the segment you are targeting, which is more cost effective than paying for the full circulation.

Action Programme 2

What opportunity, effort and familiarity issues might you consider when appraising the following media?

(a) A newly launched radio station
(b) Daytime television
(c) Posters on buses
(d) Web pages

2.5 **Media research** is designed to provide advertisers with detailed information on the size and composition of the audience for relevant media and the reading and viewing habits of the different types of people and so on. Media planners (the people in advertising agencies who plan how to deploy the main-media advertising budget) use as much reliable research data as they can obtain. Here are some examples.

(a) The National Readership Survey or JICNARS (Joint Industry Committee for National Readership Surveys) for major newspapers and magazines

(b) BARB (the Broadcasting Audience Research Bureau Ltd) for television

(c) RAJAR (Radio Joint Audience Research) for radio

(d) JICPAS (Joint Industry Committee for Poster Advertising Surveys) for posters

A marketing organisation may wish to commission or carry out its own research into the media habits of its customers and potential customers.

The suitability of the medium for the message

2.6 Certain media 'do' certain things better than others. You might bear this in mind.

(a) **The technical characteristics of the medium**. The success of a medium depends on its ability to identify and offer the benefits which its technical characteristics are best suited to provide: television for images and demonstrations, cinema for fantasy, visual impact, radio for music and participation, print for detailed information.

(b) **The perceived function of the medium**. Media users look to different media to perform different functions in their lives: information/education (world news, local events, specialist instruction) or entertainment (music, sport, escapism, community contact). These perceptions of a medium's functions and strengths will influence the orientation of its audience towards advertising messages.

(c) **The impact/realism of the medium**. One of the strengths of television is the impact to be derived from its realistic merging of sight and sound.

Cost and value for money

2.7 Cost in itself is not a helpful criterion (unless it rules out a medium by virtue of its exceeding the spending budget). What advertisers need to know, in order to compare and evaluate media meaningfully, is the following.

- How many relevant people are reached?
- How many times and how effectively?
- For how much?

2.8 The conventional criteria of value for money measurement is: **cost per thousand people reached** by a medium. If an advertisement in a newspaper with a circulation of 2 million readers costs £7,000, the cost per thousand is £3.50.

2.9 'Cost per thousand' is a common **inter-media comparison**-measuring device. However, it is only a crude measure, which does not take everything into account.

(a) The **targeting or relevance** of the audience reached by different media (or in different issues or time slots)

(b) The **potential impact** of an advertisement in different media (its size or length, colour or black and white, positioning in the publication or programme schedule, proximity to competing ads)

(c) **Extended or repeated exposure** to the ad (if people use the medium frequently, or pass it on to friends)

(d) **Selective exposure** to the ad (for example, people may not read the whole paper or magazine, or may leave the room during TV commercials)

The different media have their own methods of allowing for these factors when promoting their effectiveness to advertisers, and we will look at some of them – such as television ratings – later in this chapter.

Action Programme 3

What is the cost per thousand of the following media, and what other factors would you take into account when comparing them?

(a) The Morning Post (local newspaper): circulation 20,000. Cost per column centimetre: £4.00 and you want a 5c.c. classified ad.

(b) The Weekly (a national trade magazine) circulation 900,000. Cost per colour page (only size available): £2,000 (rate card).

(c) Radio Fab: reaches 30% of its catchment area of 210,000 adults. Minimum package of 20 15-second ads costs £700

Susceptibility to testing and measurement

2.10 **Testing**, or measuring the effectiveness of advertisements is the only sure way to know what 'works' in terms of gaining a response. The same ad run in different media can demonstrate the comparative effectiveness of the media, while different ads (size, position, timing, layout, response methods, headlines) in the same media can indicate the most effective form of the promotional message.

2.11 Some media are better for testing ads than others and if this is important to you, you will need to ask yourself the following questions.

(a) How **quickly** do I want our tests to yield results? (A daily publication produces response more quickly than a weekly.)

(b) How **effectively** does the medium allow me to elicit direct responses? (Will it carry a direct-response coupon, or memorable telephone number?)

(c) Will I be able to **attribute** increased enquiries/sales to their source in a particular ad? (Coded coupons, tracking for example).

Exam Tip

There are a variety of advertisement-focused questions in the examiner's repertoire. Questions include:

- The costing of alternative advertising media/strategies (using data given) to justify a choice (December 2002)
- Producing guidelines for colleagues on 'how to select advertising media' (December 2002)
- Producing briefing notes for radio adspace salespeople, on the advantages and disadvantages of radio advertising compared to newspapers, TV and outdoor media (June 2003)
- Producing a media plan, showing how you could spend a given budget over a given period to best effect, justifying your decisions (December 2003)

This is a core topic: get to grips with the basics – and practise applying/testing them in a variety of contexts.

A general comparison of major media

2.12 The following are some of the ways in which you might usefully evaluate advertising media.

Medium	Advantages	Disadvantages
Newspapers (daily metropolitan/ national)	■ 'Mass' medium: large audience in single exposure ■ Targeted sections (auto, home, computers etc) ■ Reader navigation: seeking news, information ■ Short lead time for production: accept ads 24-48 hours before publication ■ Flexibility of ad size ■ Tangibility of ad (can be torn out and kept) ■ Multiple readers/users ■ Allows detailed information (prices, phone numbers etc) ■ Allows (still) images ■ Allows response mechanisms (eg captions)	■ Circulation does not mean readership: wasted circulation paid for ■ Print/image reproduction of variable quality ■ No exclusivity: ad may be next to competitor's ■ Costs loaded for preferred positions ■ Short life-span of news
Newspapers (local/free)	■ Low cost ■ Geographical targeting ■ High local readership ■ Special sections (especially local real estate, entertainment etc)	■ Circulation of free papers/weeklies not always monitored/audited ■ Variable editorial content ■ Subject to weather and junk mail rejection if letterbox dropped

Medium	Advantages	Disadvantages
Magazines	■ High circulation (major titles) ■ Targeted audiences (special) ■ High quality reproduction (colour photography etc) ■ Potential high prestige ■ Reader motivation (selection, subscription) ■ Long shelf life and multiple use/readership ■ Tangibility, detail, images, response mechanisms (see newspapers)	■ High costs of production ■ Hyper-segmentation (by interest and geography, may be insufficient circulation to support local outlets) ■ Long lead times: copy/artwork required 1 – 3 months before publication, can be inflexible
Television	■ 'Mass' medium: large audience at single exposure, almost universal ownership/access ■ Detailed monitoring of exposure, reach, viewer habits ■ Allows for high degree of creativity ■ Realism: impact of sound + sight + movement ■ High-impact visual images reinforce retention ■ Allows demonstration ■ Flexibility as to scheduling ■ Allows association with desirable products	■ Most expensive of all media costs ■ High production costs ■ Lack of selectivity (except via programming) of audience ■ Lack of opportunity: does not reach commuters/workers ■ Long lead times for booking and production: penalties for withdrawal: inflexibility ■ Passive, unmotivated audience: 'zapping' by video fast-forward and remote controls erodes reach
Radio	■ 'Mass' medium: wide coverage/access ■ Audience selectivity (local/regional) programme style/variety/content) ■ Opportunity: radio is portable – in-home, in-car, on public transport, shops, offices – even jogging ■ Function: high usage for morning news, home 'companionship', background ■ Personal (and potential for participation) ■ Highly competitive costs of air time and production ■ Can be backed by personal DJ promos	■ May be passive 'background' noise: low attention, retention ■ May be 'cluttered' by announcers/DJ promotions ■ Sound only: no tangibility (pressure on retention of message), no shelf-life or 'pass on' circulation, no demonstration, no coupons, limited details
Outdoor media (poster sites bus stops, buildings etc)	■ Flexible: sites, duration of lease ■ Comparatively low cost ■ Opportunity: exposure to commuters, shoppers	■ Difficulty of verification of exposure/response ■ Subject to weather ■ Opportunity: site specific ■ No audience selectivity (except by site)

Medium	Advantages	Disadvantages
Cinema	■ Glamorous ■ High impact (large size, highly visual, loud sound, high quality) ■ Captive audience (no TV 'zap' factor) ■ Can segment by local area	■ High cost ■ Opportunity: site/time specific ■ Poor verification of response ■ Limited number of people reached per exposure
Internet	■ Principally sight, but with sound and colour further possibilities are developing ■ Interactive, permitting direct response ■ Able to track audience movements ■ Message permanent, and can be down-loaded	■ Generally poor viewership ■ Consumer confidence in security low (but improving) ■ Possible to direct audience to information, but can be difficult to gain large audience without support from other media ■ Not yet a mainstream media with broad customer appeal ■ Speed of access depends on sophistication of technological link ■ No universal computing language yet agreed

3 Press

3.1 Press or print media

- **Newspapers**: daily and weekly, morning and evening, national and regional
- **Magazines**, periodicals and journals; general appeal, special interest and trade

Circulation and readership figures

3.2 The **Audit Bureau of Circulation (ABC)** provides audited figures of the actual circulation of major newspapers and magazines. This figure is often the basis of advertising rates. It offers only partial information.

(a) There may be many **more readers than purchasers**. People may pass a publication on to others to read, or it may be perused by many people in dentists' waiting rooms or hairdressers. It is the estimated **readership** that interests the advertiser. The **Readership Survey** publishes the average readership per issue.

(b) Readership data is also available on what **types of reader** consume various publications, with what frequency and in what manner (all the way through or some sections only).

Types of press ads

3.3 Print media offer different types of advertising.

(a) **Classified advertising**. The classified sections of publications offer small spaces for text-only ads. The advantage is that classified space is very cheap, and the publication usually typesets the ad for you. The disadvantage is the difficulty of attracting attention with so much competition and so little space: icons, headline, styles and impactful/incentive copy are required to make an ad stand out.

(b) **Semi-display advertising** allows you to use borders, typographic features and illustrations to attract attention (although on a crowded page, white space and simplicity may be more effective). Small ads in the Yellow Pages are a good example.

(c) **Display advertising** offers further opportunity for creativity: the advertisers design and provide their own artwork or film, constrained only by the technical specifications (size, colour) of the publication. Full-colour magazine ads are a good example. 'Long copy' advertisements break the usual simple visual style of display advertising by including lots of detailed information.

(d) **Advertorials** are advertisements presented as edited copy, in order to take advantage of the perceivably objective authority of editorial matter. Features on health and beauty, advice, house and garden are often advertisements for the products and services 'reviewed' or 'recommended'.

(e) **Loose inserts or 'drop outs'** are printed leaflets (produced by the advertiser) inserted into magazines and newspapers. They usually work out 4 or 5 times more expensive than advertising space – but draw up to 5 or 6 times as many responses as a full-page advertisement.

Marketing at Work

Car manufacturers often use long copy display ads for their cars. Full-page advertisements include detailed technical specifications and engineering drawings of the cars' driving and safety features. Such extensive copy is often effective for very expensive products, because it provides sufficient information to support an expensive purchase decision – and to justify or rationalise the purchase as a 'good' decision, not merely based on desire or snobbery.

Contrast this with purely visual display ads – often with no copy at all.

Press ad rates

3.4 Print media is bought in **column inches** (or centimetres) or standard **page divisions** (quarter, half or full page, or 'junior' page). The cost/rate differs.

- The **size** of the ad
- The number of **colours** in the ad and the production quality of the publication
- **Position** of the ad for which a premium may be charged
- The **readership** number of the publication
- The **potential for readership** targeting or niche marketing
- The **prestige** of the publication and the spending power of its readership.

Positioning press ads

3.5 Media research into **'traffic per page'** (the reading and noting of different pages in a print publication) suggests the following.

- **Early pages** are read more than late pages (depending on editorial content)
- **Right-hand pages** have higher noting scores than left-hand pages

- **Pages opposite relevant or popular editorial content** do better than pages opposite other advertising and less read editorial content.

3.6 **Cover space** is particularly sought after because of its high visibility, and usually also because the covers are printed on better quality paper for colour production. The outside front cover is likely to be most expensive, followed by outside back, inside front (especially if opposite the contents page) and inside back.

Scheduling of press ads

3.7 **Scheduling** (as will be discussed in section 7 below) is a combination of **reach or exposure** (how many of the right type of people see the ad) and **frequency** (how many times people see the ad).

With press advertising, in some circumstances it is generally advisable to repeat an ad more often.

(a) if the ad is **small** (and may not be noticed by all readers at one exposure)
(b) if the publication is **high circulation** (so the ad may not be noticed by all readers)
(c) if the product or ad is **interesting** (and will therefore continue to attract attention)

3.8 Even so, the **law of diminishing returns** operates with repeated exposure: Figure 12.1. As the ad reaches a higher proportion of the relevant audience, more often, the rate of response levels off. Awareness of the company or offer increases with repetition, but the rate of direct response to individual ads (via coupon or response line) falls: the 'easiest' prospects have already been reached.

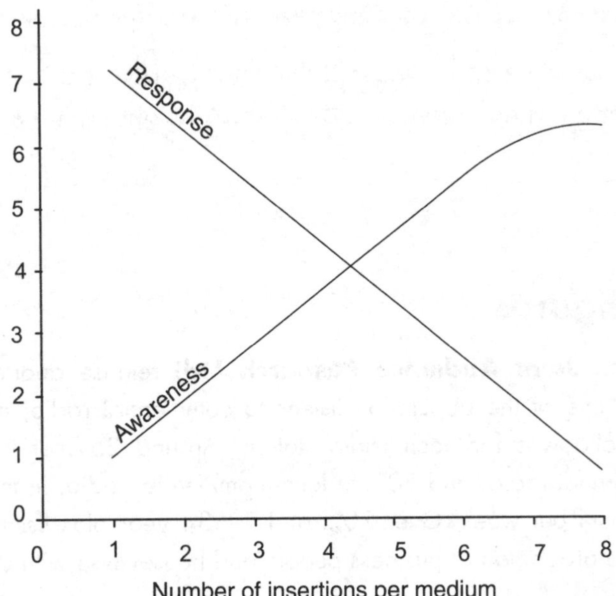

Figure 12.1: The law of diminishing returns

(*Source:* The Institute of Direct Marketing, cited in Jay, 1998)

3.9 The best **time** to place an ad depends on many factors: **seasonal selling cycles** (summer/winter, Christmas), relevant editorial content (special features or supplements), and even different days of the week and times of day (encouraging working hours, evening or weekend purchases).

4 Radio

4.1 The perceived function and image of **radio** is an important factor in the response to radio advertising. Radio is a personal and 'intimate' medium which encourages relationship and trust: according to the Radio Advertising Bureau (www.rab.co.uk), people are more likely to believe what they hear on radio than what they see on television. **Local radio** has a particularly close 'community' image. National radio stations are aimed more at a particular type of listener.

4.2 Radio tends to form the **background** to other activities. This enables it to have a wide reach (since it can be listened to while driving, working, jogging), but also lessens listeners' attention to and retention of advertising messages. The lack of visual images is also a disadvantage, but can be overcome by different techniques: the use of dialogue, mood, drama, humour and curiosity.

4.3 Radio ads are usually bought in series of 15 second or 30 second **'slots'**. Because of the high 'portability' of radio, there may be a wider range of off-peak scheduling opportunities.

Exam Tip

A radio station was itself the subject of the June 2003 paper: it's worth remembering that promotional media also have to promote themselves! The scenario also raised interesting questions about whether other media are 'competitors' – or promotional avenues and potential collaborators. You were asked to consider how the radio station and local newspapers could 'work together' and run 'joint promotions'.

Get used to 'crossing areas of the syllabus'. While you're thinking about how ICT is used in promotion, think how an ICT company might promote itself. And so on ...

Listenership figures

4.4 **RAJAR (Radio Joint Audience Research Ltd)** release quarterly reports showing what percentage/volume of the population listens to commercial radio, at what times and for how long, with breakdowns for each radio station. Around 25% of the UK population listen to national commercial radio, and 50% to local commercial radio, in the course of a week, for an average 15 hours per week. Over 70% of 15 – 34 year olds listen to commercial radio and almost the same proportion of business people and housewives with children.

4.5 Although such figures do not indicate whether people hear or take in any ads that may air during their listening hours, there are several positive indicators that radio can perform well in this respect.

- **Prompted recall of radio ads** is 80% of that of TV ads
- Radio listeners report that they **do not generally switch stations** when ads come on
- An average weight campaign on radio will reach each consumer **four times a week**
- **Talk-back radio** has a high response rate, even late at night

5 Television

5.1 The **Independent Broadcasting Authority (IBA)** controls commercial TV (and radio) in the UK, and licenses a number of regional companies.

5.2 Because of the **high exposure**, **glamour** and **audio-visual impact** of television, it has become the favoured medium for launching new products, raising brand awareness and building brand loyalty, re-positioning brands and also motivating the employees and supply chain partners of the advertising organisation. (This perception is encouraged by advertising agencies, whose **commission** on TV airtime is many times higher than on print space and other media.)

5.3 A major recent trend is in the development of **direct response TV advertising**, in which the viewer is given a telephone number and invited to call for more information or to place an order. This used to be perceived as down-market and American, but research now shows that it promotes an image of the organisation as organised, financially sound and willing to be readily accessible to customers. Direct response advertising has also enabled detailed measurement of the effectiveness of ads on different stations, at different times, in different formats.

Viewership figures

5.4 As with radio, it is a complex matter to access not just how many sets are owned and switched on at particular times, but how many people are actually watching – let alone consciously taking in what is being transmitted.

5.5 The size of the television audience for a given programme (and advertising) is measured in **ratings**: rating points, or **TVRs**. One TVR point represents 1% of all homes which have a TV set in the region to which the programme is broadcast. Ratings are used by TV stations to monitor the popularity of their programmes, and to set advertising rates. The advertiser pays for the number of TVRs allocated to given advertising spots.

(a) A programme with 20 TVRs is seen by 20% of homes with a TV. This is the number of people who will (in theory) see an ad once.

(b) If you placed an ad in four programmes, each with a rating of 20 TVRs, you would achieve 80 TVRs. However, some homes might have seen the ad all four times, while others may have missed it altogether. You need to distinguish between **reach** and **frequency** (the number of times the ad is run, and therefore the number of **opportunities to see it, or OTS**).

(c) **Gross Rating Points (GRPs)** are a measure of probable reach multiplied by probable frequency. If you buy 280 GRPs, about 70% of households should have four opportunities to see your ad.

(d) **Target Audience Rating Points (TARPs)** measure reach and frequency against specific demographic audiences, across a wide range of criteria (geographic, gender, age, socio-economic bracket). These are the most effective guide for advertisers, since they allow the media planner to devise a schedule which will deliver the largest relevant audience for the available budget: the gross cumulative exposure of the campaign to the target audience can be assessed on the standard cost-per-thousand basis.

Key Concepts

Reach refers to the size of the audience which is exposed to an ad, both net (number of people reached) and gross (including cumulative multiple exposures)

Frequency refers to the number of times an ad is run, opportunities to see (OTS) the ad; or 'impacts'

Ratings are measurements of television audiences, which multiply reach by frequency (or OTS) to give the probable coverage and repetition of an ad, with (TARPS) or without (GRPs) breakdown by demographic criteria.

5.6 The lowest cost per thousand is not necessarily the best schedule: One recommendation is the purchase of at least 250 – 300 TVRs, giving 70% coverage and a minimum of 4 OTS, in order to make a TV campaign worthwhile.

5.7 Statistically valid and helpful for comparison as ratings are, they still give only limited information: they count 'pairs of eyes' not responsiveness to ads. Detailed **qualitative media research** is required to indicate people's media habits.

- **Leaving the room** during commercial breaks
- Using the **remote control** to change channel to avoid ads
- **Videoing** TV programmes and fast-forwarding through commercial breaks

Further testing will be required to gauge **awareness and recall** of specific ads.

Marketing at Work

Few would dispute that the giant supermarket chains are gripped by a collective megalomania. Not content with consigning independent butchers and greengrocers to history, they are moving into clothes, electrical goods, insurance and banking.

Now comes supermarket TV, adding yet more commercial "noise" to our lives. After trialling in-store TV for 10 months, Tesco plans to roll out the idea to 100 stores by June, and 300 by the end of the year. Last week it appointed poster contractor JC Decaux to sell advertising minutes on the channel.

Behind this activity lies a concept that could shake up the media landscape - retail media. It is based on the idea that supermarkets offer advertisers a captive audience at a time when it is especially receptive to sales messages.

This has already triggered the advent of supermarket media such as car-park posters, trolleys with panel ads and ads printed on the back of receipts.

Factor in shopper numbers and time spent in supermarkets, and the media maths behind Tesco TV starts to look compelling. With an average 13m visits a week, each comprising say 45 to 60 minutes on average, Tesco is effectively a mass medium.

Of course, petrol stations, post offices and the NHS have also tried to capitalise on captive audiences. They've failed because the viewing environment proved to be awful and they lacked the clout to attract advertisers. This time, when it comes to persuading suppliers to advertise on Tesco TV, only the bravest or daftest will refuse.

Mills (2004)

Scheduling TV ads

5.8 In addition to TARPs, which suggest where and when to schedule ads in order to reach an optimum number of target viewers an optimum number of times, the advertiser should consider the following.

(a) **Daytime audiences** are more responsive. Direct responses to TV ads are greatest between 12 noon – 2pm and 2pm – 4pm on weekdays.

(b) Audiences show greater recall of ads at the **beginning** of a long commercial break. The more ads they see, the lower the recall of each.

(c) Audiences tend to watch through commercial breaks in the **middle of TV programmes**, because they do not want to miss any of the programme. However, viewers are reluctant to take action in response to ads during the programme, so direct-response ads are more successful during **end breaks** (Most people respond within 15 minutes of the ad spot.)

(d) While most advertisers use 30-second ads, 90-second or even two minute ads can be more effective (as with long-copy press ads) especially for complex or expensive products.

(e) Very short (10 second) ads can also be effective, and offer much higher TARPs for the available budget, since you can get more exposures. However, the greater impact of longer commercials usually offsets the reduced TARPs which longer ads deliver.

(f) Repetition of ads increases TARPs, but is subject to the law of **diminishing returns**. It is essential for the message to sink in, but people easily become habitual and cease to notice or be motivated by the ad. One strategy is to have a **set of related ads** which can be rotated, reinforcing but varying the message.

Action Programme 4

All other things being equal, and subject to detailed research, at what time of day, or in what kind of programme, might you advertise the following products on TV?

- Shoe polish
- Home disinfectant
- Car repairs
- Chat/introduction lines

6 Other media

Outdoor media

6.1 **Poster advertising** is one of the oldest media for consumer goods advertising. Sites on walls, hoardings and bus shelters can be leased for a fee per calendar month. In addition, many vehicles (buses, trucks and taxis) now carry external advertising, and some are tailor-made to do so (advertising 'floats'). Trains and buses also offer internal advertising positions. Size and visibility of the sites are the main consideration.

Marketing at Work

Transit media in South Africa

It is predicted that turnover in the outdoor advertising industry could rise to R1-billion in five years.

Outdoor advertising currently claims 4.28% of the total adspend in SA annually, compared with adspend of 5% to 11% in developed countries.

The areas of transit media, including trains, taxis, buses and moving billboards on trailers, have a 16.34% share of the outdoor advertising expenditure.

As the economy develops and more people are absorbed into the workforce, so the numbers of commuters - the transit media audience – increase. ...

With 80% of the population dependant on public transport and much of the country's rural areas without electricity, transit and alternative media are taking advertising to a much broader demographic market. ...

SA is one of the first countries in the world to have developed transit media and the country is leading its growth.

Worldwide, the outdoor advertising industry is worth about R80-billion.

Bridge (2004)

For Polish speakers, another interesting site, showing examples of outdoor media in Poland is: www.mediadoran.pl.

Cinema

6.2 Cinema advertising takes advantage of high audio-visual impact and a captive audience but still requires a high quality and entertainment value.

Cinema advertising best suits 'lifestyle' products.

- **Branded consumer goods** with high style and profile, aimed mainly at young adults (such as jeans and alcohol)
- **Local services** in the area of the cinema (particularly restaurants)

New media

6.3 Technology has widened the range of advertising media to include the following.

(a) **Videos** including informational instructional videos and advertising accompanying entertainment videos

(b) **Teletext** (usually via sponsoring of relevant types of information which the target audience might access)

(c) **Enhanced CD and CD-ROM** (especially for selling merchandise related to the information or entertainment contained on the CD)

(d) **Websites**. Internet shopping and other transactions are on the increase. Websites with product/service information and related links vary in sophistication, but can provide an attractive **audio-visual and interactive** experience of promotional messages. In addition, they offer an opportunity for customers to access basic information which they might be reluctant to ask about over the phone.

(e) **Web advertising**, such as banner and pop-up ads, which contain a simple message designed to make users click on the link to the advertiser's website.

(f) **SMS advertising**, using mobile phone text messages.

(g) **Computer accessories** as advertising media: mouse pads, screen savers, mobile phone ring tones and so on.

7 Advertising on the Internet

7.1 The Internet has become a medium for carrying advertising in its own right. The same principles that we have already discussed in this chapter, centred around **matching medium to audience**, still apply. Companies need to be sure that the web provides the right environment and audience profile to meet marketing objectives.

Marketing at Work

Online advertisements are becoming ever more attention seeking. Animation, video and audio are moving the field beyond the normal banner advert. A company called *Eyeblaster.com* has facilitated the development of brash and noisy online advertising. The new formats are giving scope for greater creativity.

Newspapers, which invested heavily in putting their content online, are at the forefront of experimenting with the new formats to attract advertising revenue to their sites.

The use of interactive banner adverts is also increasing, adding value to the advertisement by providing services such as:

- Entering a destination to show the cheapest fare
- Filling in an e-mail address to receive further information

7.2 The most common form of web advertising occurs when the advertiser uses a range of sites to drive visitors to a corporate site.

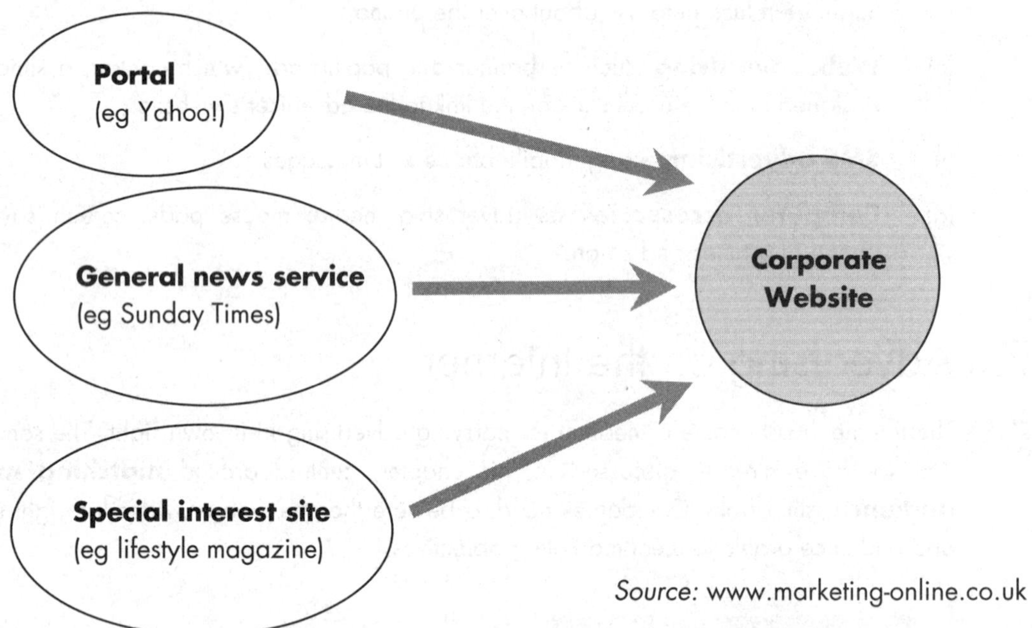

Source: www.marketing-online.co.uk

7.3 Companies are still learning what works with web advertising, and what does not. There are two basic types of promotion associated with the Internet.

(a) **Online promotion** uses communication via the Internet itself to raise awareness. This may take the form of links from other sites, targeted e-mail messages or banner advertisements.

(b) **Offline promotion** uses traditional media such as TV or newspaper advertising to promote a website address (URL).

Key Concept

A **banner advertisement** is "a typically rectangular graphic displayed on a web page for purposes of brand-building or driving traffic to a site. It is normally possible to perform a click through to access further information from another website. Banners may be static or animated". Banner adverts can be targeted at a particular audience.

Source: www.Marketing-online.co.uk

7.4 Here are some examples of banner advertisements.

OVER 60% OFF VIDEOS
buy now
The 6th Sense
£4.99
Life is Beautiful
£4.99
Chasing Amy
£4.99
Leon
£4.99
AND MANY MORE!
RED HOT SUMMER SALE
amazon.co.uk
and you're done.

Site Map - Yahoo! - News - My Yahoo! - Help

www.smile.co.uk
Click here

Thursday, August 22 2002 11:15AM - London Stock Exchange closes in 5 hours and 15 minutes.

Welcome Customise (Yahoo! ID required) - Sign In

Track your favourite stocks and more with Yahoo! Finance [Register/Sign In]

Yahoo! Finance symbol name London Get Quotes Symbol Lookup

Action Programme 5

Imagine that you are investigating the likely revenues from advertising on a website you are helping to set up. Why would you expect an organisation to want to pay for banner advertising on your web page?

Marketing at Work

In virtually every category, particularly high-consideration products and services, more and more customers are going online to perform critical tasks and meet their needs throughout the sales cycle. ...

Most online advertising is fundamentally flawed, and arguably getting worse. The most basic examples are the countless message-based banners bombarding customers across the Internet. The worst culprits are the pop-ups and unders that have proliferated in recent years. Let's not even mention span. What's the solution? People read magazines and watch TV. They use the Internet. Create something they can use.

Where do you start? Think about why your customers are going online. What can you provide that helps them to get things done? What would help meet their specific needs (emotional, functional and so on) and enable them to move forward in the sales cycle? Whatever it is, provide that information – or better yet utility – within the advertising itself. Make it so good your customers seek to interact with your advertising because they can get things done.

Once you've created advertising that your customers can actually use, make sure to deploy it where they actually need it on the Internet. Find those contextual spots, whether a search engine or a highly relevant media property, where customers want to pull information, content and functionality from your brand. More importantly, execute all of this in a manner that invites rather than invades.

(Johnson, 2004)

7.5 Banner advertising can generally be placed through a traditional agency. It is typically paid for according to the number of users who view the web page. Cost is calculated as **cost per thousand ad impressions**.

Other online advertising methods

7.5 These include:

(a) **Promotion in search engines and directories** (such as Yahoo). Your company may want to have its company website listed when a user types in a specific keyword, such as 'office equipment'. To achieve this, your website should be registered with each of the main search engines (Yahoo, MSN, Infoseek, Netscape, Excite, for example).

(b) **Links from other sites**. This involves making sure that your site is linked to as many related sites as possible.

(c) **Using e-mail** for advertising new products directly to customers.

8 Media scheduling

8.1 Having taken the decision on which media to use, they need to be scheduled so that they are used at the right time. We have already discussed most of the issues in media scheduling as we described each of the major media.

To summarise, an **efficient media schedule**

- Balances maximum **reach** and maximum **repeat exposure**
- To the most **specific target audience**
- At the lowest, or budgeted **cost per thousand**
- In accordance with specific **media objectives**

8.2 **Media software packages** have been compiled by media buyers and agencies, which contain detailed readership/audience breakdowns by demographic group of each programme on each channel and each supplement of each newspaper.

8.3 The mix of **reach and repetition** within time and budget parameters is infinitely variable. It may be concentrated over a short period of time or in peaks and troughs, or evenly spread over a long period. It may be spread over multiple media, to capture wide coverage, or a limited number of targeted media, to secure maximum repeat exposure.

8.4 With adequate research data, the schedule should be supported by an estimate of **reach and frequency**: the number and type of people who will have the opportunity to see each advertisement booked on the schedule, and how many times.

8.5 A comprehensive format for a media schedule might be as follows. If you were asked for a simple outline schedule, you might put together sections 1, 4 and 5 in our format. We have filled in as an example section 4.

Proposed Advertising Campaign

1 Media Rationale

Product/service:

Budget: £__________ (approx) — *[if known]*

Target Audience: — *[target demographic/ geographical groups]*

Timing of campaign: — *[period during which advertising will run]*

Objectives/ Special instructions: — *[direct response mechanisms, if any; support measures, such as manned response lines; target responses/results]*

Media selection: — *[Media selected, + reasons/criteria: circulation, targeting, timings available, costs]*

2 Audience Performance Estimate

[Based on research/data, if available]

Target audience:

Potential total numbers:

	Week 1 commencing: [date]	Week 2 commencing: [date]	Week 3 commencing: [date]	Total
Press				
% reach:	*[eg]* 57%	40%	65%	84%
Average frequency:	*[eg]* 1.4	1.2	1.1	2.4
TV				
% reach:				
Average frequency:				
Radio				
% reach:				
Average frequency:				

3 Television Placement

Station 1:

Week 1: Commencing [date] — Current programme

[Day] [Time slot] — [Programme scheduled]

Week 2: Commencing [date] — Current programme

[Day] [Time slot] — [Programme scheduled]

etc.

Station 2:

Week 1: Commencing [date] — Current programme

[Day] [Time slot] — [Programme scheduled]

etc.

4 Advertising Schedule

Media details and placement	Day	Week commencing: (month)				(month)				Total	@ rate	Cost
		(date)	(date)	(date)	(date)	(date)	(date)	(date)	(date)			
[Publication 1]												
[eg] 30 x 5cm –front half	Tue				1					150	15.00	2,250
+ 10% loading										%	10	225
[Publication 2]												
30 x 5cm – page 7	Thu		1				1			300	16.35	4,905
+ £4 right loading											4.00	1,200
[Radio Station 1]												
30 sec 30 x 30 sec												
Mon-Fri 8-9.30pm	Wk/c	1				1				2	1,500	3,000
[Radio Station 2]												
30 sec 15 x 30 sec												
Mon-Fri 8-9.30pm	Wk/c			1				1		2	1,000	2,000
[TV Station]												
30 sec 4-6pm	Sun			2	2		2			6	800	4,800
30 sec 7.30-8.30pm	Sun			1	1					2	1,400	2,800
30 sec 5.30-6.00pm	M-F					1				1	1,500	1,500

5 Summary of Costs

Press:		£
Radio:		£
Television -	Time:	£
	Monitors:	£
Total:		£

Exam Tip

You may be given basic circulation and rate card details for a number of newspapers (morning, evening, daily, weekly and free) and radio stations (new and established), plus creative estimates for artwork production, and asked to prepare an outline media schedule, including costs, to support a new service launch. You may also have to use the information on the availability of media opportunities and costs to appraise the viability of the launch in different regions.

Exam Tip

The examiner noted in his report to the December 2003 paper that 'prepare a media schedule' often crops up 'in some guise or other'. Be prepared. And be prepared to justify any schedule you propose, in terms of timing, reach, impact and so on of the media chosen.

In December 2003, you were asked to allocate a small budget of £2,000. A selection of media costings was given to help you. The examiner noted that students *assumed* they should use all the options given – thereby spreading the budget very thinly. The information given in a scenario is intended to guide you in making evaluations and choices: use it to 'weed out' unsuitable options, or to focus your time/budget on areas of maximum impact. Don't assume that every option presented to you in the scenario 'must be' a good one!

9 The printing process

How much do you need to know?

9.1 **Printing** is highly technical and involves a great many variables and decisions. Fortunately, **buying print related services** does not require a full and detailed grasp of all the process and machinery involved, nor even all the terminology.

- You must have a clear and specific idea of what you want to achieve and at what cost
- You should establish a good working relationship with a printer
- You should get a range of price quotations based on job specifications
- You need to formulate a clear and specific contract with the selected printer

9.2 In practice, you may be dealing with a marketing services agency which will handle the print management of a job for you. You may have a creative department in your own organisation, which will be able to supply you with the necessary technical specifications, and will already have embedded most of them in the artwork, film or discs which the printer will use.

9.3 If you are dealing direct with printers, you will often find yourself dealing with a sales representative, who may be little more technically expert than you are at the early stage of your print management career.

9.4 Printers are often delighted to educate their clients: it makes their job easier too.

(a) Most printers are happy to give **samples** of different weights and styles of paper. Some have comprehensive sample packs including different folds and finishes. You can also ask for a mock-up (using blank pages) of the format and size of booklet, catalogue or leaflet you are considering, so you can check total weight.

(b) Printers supply a **range of information** about their services and the machinery they use. Some have prepared simple guides to print processes and terminology.

(c) Most printers are happy to give a **guided tour** of their facilities.

9.5 In addition, there are manuals and short courses on print management, price guides (useful reference tool) and other sources of reference information.

Exam Tip

Much of this syllabus area would be difficult to assess via examination or case study without a large amount of data being provided: it is more likely to be part of a skills audit, as an area of competence. However, a case study may require you to be aware of:

(a) *The various relationships required by the production of printed matter and their communication/co-ordination requirements*

(b) *What information you would need to acquire in order to manage a print task*

(c) *What printed items are **available** as promotional tools*

(d) *Which you might **recommend** as generally cost-effective, given basic design parameters*

Action Programme 6

The Needle Works

You have realised that while direct marketing, using your customer database, is an efficient means of reaching the needlecraft market, you do not yet have a direct access to the less familiar knitting market. With the launch of the new knitting department imminent – on the 3rd September – you decide to look into the possibility of some local advertising. You gather the following information.

Local Newspapers	*Circulation*	Cost per column cm	
The Evening Gazette	90,000	£10.00	(£2 loading for front half)
The Morning News (Mon – Sat)	30,000	£ 4.50	(5% loading for right hand page)
The Community Weekly (free)	70,000	£ 5.00	(10% loading for position in weekly 'Events' section)

The *Evening Gazette* is the main paper for business and young people, sold extensively at commuter stations and on the streets after 5pm. The *Morning News* is the more traditional paper, mainly delivered to homes and sold in newsagents during the morning. The *Community Weekly* is distributed free to letterboxes on Wednesday mornings and contains local news and events.

Local Commercial Radio

'Home Sound'. Media pack shows catchment area 300,000 adults weekly: station penetration audited at 30 net ratings points. The station is mostly a talk and easy listening station. Ads sold as package of 20 x 15 second slots (5 peak, 15 off-peak) for £750. Off-peak hours are weekday mornings 10.00 – 12.00 and afternoons, 2.00 – 4.00pm and Sunday afternoons 12.00 – 4.00pm. 'Home Rock', is the sister station with a pop/rock music format. Penetration audited at 20 adult rating points, of which 80% are in the 18 – 24 age bracket. The ad rates and packages are the same as Home Sound.

Posters

Poster sites are available per calendar month at local bus stops (£150) on a hoarding outside the Post Office (£100) and in the underground station (£200).

You want to run a campaign for three weeks: weeks commencing Monday 15th, 22nd and 29th August (the launch is on Saturday 3rd September). You have an overall budget of £2,000 for the campaign.

Draft a proposed campaign schedule, with a budget of £3,000 over 2 weeks.

Chapter Roundup

- **Media selection** should be made in accordance with the organisation's **advertising objectives** on the following criteria
  - The size of the audience/circulation
  - The type of audience (in relation to the target audience)
  - The opportunity of the audience to use the medium
  - The effort required to use the media
  - The audience's familiarity with the medium
  - The selectivity/segmentation allotted by the medium
  - The suitability of the medium's technical characteristics for the message
  - The suitability of the medium's perceived function for the message
  - The cost-effectiveness of the medium
  - The medium's susceptibility to testing and measurement
- **Media research** is designed to provide data on circulated audience reach and media habits
- **Cost comparisons** are usually made on the basis of 'cost per thousand' (people reached, or impacts)
- The **advantages and disadvantages of the major media** can be found in the table following Paragraph 2.12
- **Media scheduling** requires a mix of:
  - reach
  - repeat exposure, or frequency, and
  - cost-effectiveness, in relation to
  - specific media objectives.

Quick Quiz

1. How can media be selective or targeted?
2. What does 'cost per thousand' not take into account as a measure of cost effectiveness?
3. What are the advantages and disadvantages of (a) cinema and (b) poster advertising?
4. What is 'pass on' readership, and why is it important?
5. Which are the most effective positions for press ads?
6. What advantages does radio have over TV for advertising?
7. What are TARPs, what do they tell the advertiser, and what *don't* they tell the advertiser?
8. How long should a TV ad be, and how often should it be repeated?
9. List three uses of websites and the Internet as an advertising medium.
10. What makes an efficient media schedule?

Now try Question 12 in the Question Bank

Action Programme Review

1 (suggestions only)

(a) Local radio (in car), bus stop, poster sites (driver visibility), local paper 'Auto' section.

(b) Local cinema (evening session, adult-appeal film), local paper 'Food' section, Good Food Guide (regional listing), local radio (classical music/news programmes?)

(c) UK Accountancy journals (various), Underground Station posters in financial districts, direct mail.

(d) Commercial TV (especially daytime for housewives, poster sites (shopper visibility), women's and household magazines. (Assuming mainly female buyer decision.)

(e) Trade (engineering journals, Research/home website of inventor.

2 (a) Opportunity and effort are good with radio: effortless background, portable etc. Familiarity may be a constraint where station newly launched: listeners may not want to switch from old favourites, may not be able to recall frequency.

(b) Daytime TV minimal effort and good familiarity with regular users, but limited opportunity if target audience includes workers/school-age commuters.

(c) Bus posters: minimal effort (depending on size, length of copy, sight lines: can be a strain to read bus posters), good familiarity, good opportunity because moving around (outside posters) but limited by bus users only (inside).

(d) Web pages: high effort (to search, wait, use hypertext queries etc, requires technological know-how) improving familiarity (biased towards young computer-literate), limited opportunity by virtue of technology, access and expertise required.

3 (a) 5cm ad x £4.00 = £20 per ad to reach 20,000 people = £1 per thousand

(b) £2,000 to reach 900,000 people = about £2.20 per thousand

(c) £700 to reach (30% x 210,000 =) 70,000 people = £10 per thousand (net)

The local newspaper is cheapest per thousand, but may not offer the coverage required by the advertiser: the magazine is not only high circulation and national, but the space offered is larger and in colour, for greater impact (if relevant). It is a trade magazine – which may (or may not) fit the target audience of the advertiser. The radio spots seem expensive per thousand but these are the net number of potential listeners: in effect, there will be repeat exposures over the package of 20 ads, so the figure for cumulative impacts may well be higher. (If only half of the 70,000 listeners heard the ad 3 times, and the rest once, for example, the impacts would be 140,000 and the cost per thousand £5.)

4 (a) Assuming mainly professional male buyers, next to business news, news or evening/weekend sports.

(b) Assuming mainly female buyers/decision makers, daytime (cost effective), home/lifestyle programmes, prime time soaps (eg for launch).

(c) Assuming car-owner buyers, not during commuting hours: driving/car programmes, motor sports, home/lifestyle (women buyers).

(d) Assuming single buyers, late-night television.

5 Two main reasons:

(a) They hope that the customer will click on the advert and be exposed to more detailed information.

(b) All visitors to the web page will see the advert, noting it either consciously or subconsciously.

6 PROPOSED ADVERTISING CAMPAIGN: KNITTING DEPT. LAUNCH

Media Rationale

Product/Service:	New knitting department (launch Sat 3 Sept)
Budget:	£2,000
Target Audience:	Women 30+ in local area Additional weighting to women 45+, knitters
Timing of Campaign:	3 weeks WK/C 15, 22, 29 August
Objectives/Special Instructions:	Advertising to generate: (a) personal enquiries re knitting products/services (address only: no telephone response) (b) attendance on launch day (target 500 customer visits)
Media Selection:	The *Community Weekly* (£1.43 per thousand) was selected as cheap space with relatively high audience relevance: older women tend to read community news, especially when delivered free. Wednesday a good day for Saturday event. *Evening Gazette* (£2.20 per thousand) higher circulation and lower c/p/t than *Morning News* (£3.00 per thousand), but the target audience favours morning papers plus smaller circulation encourages repeat exposure. *Radio* was selected as good value. *Home Rock* ruled out as inappropriate for target audience. *Home Sound:* 30% x 3000,000 = 100,000 *net* audience (£7.50 per thousand *net* + cumulative exposures: TARPs to be confirmed). *Posters:* convenient shopper reminder: target audience uses bus and post office, both local.

Advertising Schedule

Media details & placement		Day	W/C August			Total no	@ Rate	Cost
			15	22	29			
Community Weekly								
2 x 10cm	Semi-display – Events' section +10% load	Wed	1	1	1	60 %	£5.00 10	300 30
Morning News								
2 x 10cm	Semi-display – +5% load	Tues + Sat	2	2	2	120	£4.5 5	540 27
Home Sound								
15 sec	20 x 15 sec							
[Peak] Mon-Fri 8-10am		M-F	2	1	1	5	} *750*	*750*
[Off Peak] Mon-Sat 10am-12pm								
Poster site [one month]								
A1 – Bus stop A764		-	1			1	£150	150
A1 – Post Office Site B.3		-	1			1	£100	100
								£1,897

Answers to Quick Quiz

1 Selection of media is based on the best way of getting the message to the target audience. You need to know the strengths and weaknesses of the various media and match them with your audience profiles, resources and budget. A targeted audience is a selection already identified as being interested in your product. However, you may have to be more ingenious to reach the interested few than in appealing to a mass market.

2 The answer to Action Programme 3 gives full information. In summary you must consider coverage, target audience, and repeat exposures.

3 Cinema advantages: glamorous, high impact, captive audience, local. Cinema disadvantages: high cost, time specific, poor verification of response, limited number of people per exposure. Posters advantages: flexible sites, duration, low cost, exposure to shoppers and commuters. Posters disadvantages: difficulty of verification of response; weather, site specific and little audience selectivity.

4 Pass on readership is where a printed item (typically a magazine) is read by successive people (perhaps in a waiting room). It gives your advertisement a much longer shelf life and massively increases reach.

5 The covers, inside and out, because of the prestigious presentation. Also early in the publication, alongside popular editorials and on right hand pages, where they are more likely to catch the eye.

6 Radio is a cheaper medium, which often enjoys a captive audience (drivers/housewives employed in other tasks). Listener loyalty means that consumers are likely to hear an ad several times a week. Radio listeners do not have a fast forward control or flit to other stations during commercial breaks.

7 Target Audience Rating Points. See Paragraph 5.5.

8 It depends on your message. Ads of a minute and a half or longer can be valuable for complex product. 10 second ads can be similarly effective. Repeated exposure is good – up to a point, where the ad becomes habitual and hardly noticed.

9 Online advertising methods: promotion through search engines; banner advertising and using e-mail to target customers. Internet advertising can involve creation of your own website or using those of related organisations.

10 Refer to the list provided in Paragraph 8.1.

Promotional Activity 13

Chapter Topic List	
1	Setting the scene
2	Sales promotion
3	Trade promotion
4	Point of sale
5	PR and publicity
6	Collaborative programmes
7	Promotion on the Internet

Learning Outcomes

☑ Evaluate and select media and promotional activities appropriate to the organisation's objectives and status and to its marketing context

☑ Undertake basic marketing activities within an agreed plan and monitor and report on progress

Syllabus Reference

☑ Evaluate promotional activities and opportunities, including sales promotion, PR and collaborative programmes

Key Concepts Introduced

- Couponing
- Premiums
- Point of sale

1 Setting the scene

1.1 In Chapter 12, we looked at **above-the-line** promotional activity. In this chapter, we discuss the range of promotional activities which fall **'below-the-line'.** These are activities for which there is no cost of media space, and in which there is usually some form of negotiated incentive or augmented offer to the consumer. Again, you should be able to draw on your studies for *Marketing Fundamentals* and *Customer Communications* in this area.

1.2 Twenty years ago, **promotional incentives,** such as gift samples, coupons, prize draws, competitions, on-pack offers and collaborative programmes (get a free X cola when you buy a Y burger or rent a Z video), were considered as short-lived sales boosters. However, it has now been recognised that such campaigns can have long-term effects on consumer buying patterns and attitudes, and promotions marketing is a discipline in its own right, with agencies capturing a significant proportion of marketing budgets.

1.3 **PR or public relations** is now recognised to have significant advantages for carrying specialist messages to target audiences which are not sensitive to advertising, and for managing corporate communications and image in general.

1.4 On completion of this chapter, you should be able to:

- evaluate a range of promotional activities and opportunities
- appreciate various techniques and mechanisms of sales promotion
- understand the impact of point of sale material
- identify and exploit opportunities for free publicity and positive PR
- identify opportunities for collaborative promotional programmes

Exam Tip

It's worth noting that 'promotion' (in the sense of 'the promotion mix') is a wider concept (embracing advertising, direct marketing, personal selling and so on) than 'promotion' (in the sense of 'sales promotion'). If you get a question like 'How can the promotional mix be used to ...?' (as in June 2003), this refers to both above - and below-the-line methods (and ICT equivalents). If you get a question like 'How can you run joint promotions ...?' (as in June 2003 again) you may narrow your thinking to sales or trade promotions - but state this assumption clearly, if you're making it!

Meanwhile, don't neglect consumer and trade sales promotions as one of the tools in your mix!

2 Sales promotion

Planning sales promotions

2.1 The acronym 'COMPETE' may be used as a checklist for planning effective sales promotion competitions.

- **Co-sponsors** Plan any collaborations with retailers or other promoters
- **Objectives** Know what message the competition is intended to send and what results it is intended to produce
- **Mechanics** How will the competition be delivered, entered and judged? Plan the logistics of entry handling and prize distribution
- **Prizes** Decide the number and value of prizes to attract consumers and reinforce the product concept
- **Expenditure** Budget costs and time
- **Timing** Will the competition counteract seasonal laws or competitor promotions? How far away should the closing date be, before momentum is lost?
- **Evaluation** What criteria will be used to define the competition's success?

2.2 Different types of promotion are effective in achieving different objectives.

Purpose	Examples
■ Increase short-term sales volume	Free gifts or discount coupons with purchase Two-for-one offers
■ Encourage repeat/multiple purchase	Collectible coupons towards more substantial gifts Multiple entries in prize draws/competitions
■ Customer loyalty incentive/reward programmes	Coupons/vouchers for subsequent visits
■ Product launch, encourage new product trial or alternative brand trial (weaning away from competitors)	Money-off coupons Free samples and in-store trials Demonstrations of new products Free gifts with new products (eg magazines)
■ Convey and embed information	Competitions with questions based on product information
■ Convey a positive brand/corporate image	Purchase incentives linked to charitable donations, equipment for schools
■ Extend media coverage with 'free' space	Samples/give always supporting product reviews (press, radio) competitions: space to explain rules, prize (product)
■ Extend database	Coupon returns, competition entries, phone responses giving name/address details (plus high awareness)
■ Motivate supply chain	Consumer promos as 'push' technique to support retailer Gifts/prize draws/competitions to motivate sales force and/or retailers Discount/awards schemes
■ Motivate influencers (journalists, reviewers, style leaders)	Advance sampling/demonstration/showing of new/improved products

2.3 Note that all the above purposes are to do with **generating profitable sales**.

Action Programme 1

Visit your local supermarket, and spend some time identifying the various types of sales promotion you encounter.

This is a useful exercise 'on the ground' to enhance your everyday awareness of sales promotion techniques. Having begun such a programme of primary research, you will have a better understanding of relevant secondary sources: the analysis of promotional collaborations and campaigns in the marketing trade press and media sections of newspapers.

2.4 We will look at some of the main techniques in turn.

Bonus and discount offers

Coupons

Key Concept

Couponing is a fairly straightforward approach whereby the purchaser obtains a coupon - incorporated in the product packaging or labelling, or as an attached or separate printed item - which offers some incentive or bonus: a discount or free gift, say.

2.5 Couponing is a simple strategy for encouraging **repeat or volume purchases**, since they offer a benefit on the next purchase of the same item, or another specific item, or on a certain cumulative volume of purchases.

2.6 You should be familiar with promotions that require the consumer to send in a certain number of wrappers, labels, bar-codes, tokens or bottle caps/ring pulls. They are often used by soft-drink and confectionery marketers, particularly since free gifts for children tend to have a higher perceived value than their actual cost.

2.7 Coupons are also useful as one-off **incentives** supporting press advertising, overcoming inertia and attracting bargain hunters. Cinemas, museums and galleries, for example, often offer money off ticket prices via cut-out coupons in the press. Hairdressers, take-away food and video rental outlets similarly offer vouchers on products and services. You should be able to think of many other examples.

Premiums

Key Concept

Premiums are offers of a product or service free, or at a specially discounted price, usually for a limited time, in order to induce or trigger purchase of (usually another) product.

2.8 Premiums may be offered through coupons, or through product packaging or advertised 'v in' schemes or retailer administered promotion at point of sale.

2.9 Premiums are useful for **boosting sales of the 'parent' product** in the short-term, by motivating a purchase decision (free garlic bread with every special large pizza, say). They can also be used to get consumers to try the premium or give-away product itself. So, for example, you might get a sample jar of a newly-launched coffee blend when you buy a large jar of the market-leading blend.

2.10 Premiums are most effective when there is a natural **synergy** between the parent product and the give-away, and when the give-away has some perceived value, but not too much. A free pen with personal organiser, or honey 'twister' spoon with jar of honey, or drinking glass with premium spirits are examples of well-judged premium promotions.

Marketing at Work

Hoover

One of the most celebrated disasters in sales promotion was the 1992 joint Hoover/Your Leisure offer of two free flights (to Europe and the US) to any customer who spent a minimum of £100 on its products. Spot the mistake! Leonard Hadley, Chairman of Hoover's US parent company, Maytag, had to admit that the offer was like 'a bad accident ... you can't determine what was in the driver's mind'. The promotion attracted more than double the anticipated applications, leading to the dismissal of three senior managers and a £19 million provision to cover the costs. The promotion had not been insured against unforeseen demand. The bargain was just too good. And the second-hand vacuum cleaner market would take a long time to recover from the over-supply!

Bonus packs

2.11 **Bonus packs** provide extra product for the same price. They work on the same principle as premiums, but offer more of the same product (rather than another product) as the incentive. This is usually done via **product packaging**, in order to keep the process simple. It advertises itself by messages such as '10% extra' or '12 for the price of 10'. You will often see a dotted line or different coloration on the packaging to show the extent of the bonus.

2.12 Bonus packs can be particularly effective.

(a) To **lure consumers from competing brands** without discounting or altering your price. Bonuses are effectively a discount, without being a discount: people don't usually resent removal of the offer in the way that they would a return to higher prices.

(b) Competing brands are largely **undifferentiated**, so that consumers will buy whichever one offers value for money at the time.

Rebates

2.13 **Rebates**, or 'cash back' offers are a form of delayed bonus, and an alternative to up-front discounts.

Samples and demonstrations

Sampling

2.14 **Sampling** is a technique based on giving consumers an opportunity to try your product for free. This is a kind of hands-on advertising.

(a) **Motivates** people to try a new brand (curiosity and lack of cost or risk can overcome the inertia of habitual use and apathy)

(b) **Convinces** people of product claims and benefits that they may not have believed through advertising alone

(c) Is particularly effective in **launching** new and innovative products, the benefits of which may be hard to convey

(d) **Covers customers** of other brands which is important where market share is hotly contested

2.15 Sampling may be implemented

- At **retail** outlets
- As part of a **direct mail** or letterbox drop campaign
- As part of a **'home trial'** programme
- As part of an agency-negotiated **Mass Consumer Sampling** exercise

Demonstrations

2.16 **Demonstrations** work on the same principle as sampling for more **expensive and complex** products or services. Demonstrations showing how easy and versatile a food processor is to use, for example, attract interest and overcome potential sales objections. Demonstrations are effective in launching new products which are perceived as complex, difficult or risky to use - or the effects of which (in the hands of an expert) are particularly spectacular. ('Miracle' cleaning fluids and vacuum cleaners are often demonstrated on this basis, because no consumer is going to risk creating the kind of carpet stains the demonstrator can use.)

Competitions and games

2.17 Consumer competitions are now a major area of promotion. Competitions can be run using a variety of media incentives and an infinite variety of themes. Prizes offered can be an attractive incentive for a large number of consumers to try a product, make repeat purchases or send in mailing list details without involving huge outlay from the promoter. In addition, if consumers have been motivated to enter a competition, their general awareness of the product or organisation will be high, and competition 'losers' will be well primed for a direct-mail special offer of the product.

2.18 Competitions may be automatic entry (for example, prizes for the 'thousandth shopper' in a particular department store), or participative (where people have to send or ring in entries). Some of the many competition formats in regular use include the following.

(a) **Prize draws** where people send or ring in contact details (with or without answers to questions), and the first name (or correct answer) 'drawn' at random wins. This is a popular approach, because it requires little effort on the part of the organiser or entrant, for potentially high rewards. (Telephone competition lines often make a profit in their own right, via special premium-charge phone lines.)

(b) **Games** of skill or luck: for example, promotional scratch cards, bingo, puzzles, lotteries.

(c) **Participative contests**: for example, story-writing competitions, recipe competitions, photo competitions.

(d) **Informational competitions**. People may be asked to complete a quiz based on information to be researched (often used in travel and encyclopaedia/educational resource promotions) to whet the appetite. Alternatively, the questions may be based on product information supplied or to be researched by product inspection or trial. Questions such as 'in 25 words or less, complete the following sentence: 'I love Brand X because...' are often used because they provide useful feedback (and even advertising ideas).

Action Programme 2

Devise a creative competition concept to promote:

(a) candied fruit peel
(b) The Needle Works' store
(c) a range of new travel guidebooks
(d) a brand of household detergent

2.19 The number and value of **prizes** offered says a great deal about the organisation, although nobody expects charities to give away the same prizes as car manufacturers. The latter may give away a top of the range car or a foreign holiday to the top winner while charities may give away a small number of relatively low-value items (like food hampers). Promotional prizes (branded T-shirts or baseball caps) may be given away in their hundreds as a promotional tool. Think about the competitions you have seen, or even entered.

Gifts and merchandising

2.20 A wide variety of free gifts or purchasable merchandise can be used to promote products and brands, creating brand recognition and in many cases an extra 'medium' or space for advertising messages. Specialist agencies exist to source promotional gifts and merchandise for trade and consumer promotions. Some of the most popular include branded coasters, keyrings, mouse mats, computer screen savers on CD ROM, calendars, pens and pencils, baseball caps, T-shirts, beer mats, carrier bags, book marks ... you name it!

Action Programme 3

We dare you to come up with another 30 ideas for promotional merchandise! (There are at least that many already in use ...).

Events

2.21 A range of the kind of promotional events we discussed in Chapter 9 - launch parties, technical or discussion seminars, conferences, publicity stunts, entertainments, previews - are also included in sales promotion activities, since they are often opportunities not just to attract media interest and make contacts, but to showcase products. Just as an example, real estate developers often use informational seminars (which people pay to attend) on 'Wealth building through real estate investment' or 'What is negative gearing?' to demonstrate their expertise and generate client relationships. Record labels similarly host discos, and publishers readings, to showcase their products to willing audiences.

3 Trade promotion

3.1 We discussed some trade promotions in the chapter on developing supply chain relationships (Chapter 7). Bear in mind that not all promotions are aimed at consumers: some may be aimed at selling into ('push') or motivating retailers, distributors, sales force and trade/industry customers.

3.2 Trade promotions

(a) **Monetary incentives** such as increased trade discounts (increased margins on the product), allowances, extended credit or other favourable finance plans, extended warranty on products, performance bonuses for sales people

(b) **Joint advertising** and promotion, sharing advertising and other costs with the dealer or retailer

(c) **Point-of-sale support** from display materials, information, merchandising

(d) **Competitions and awards** for salespeople or dealers/distributors

(e) **Business gifts** linked to sales or purely relational (eg diaries, calendars, alcohol and other items traditionally given at Christmas)

(f) **Consumer promotions** promoted to retailers as aggressive 'pull policy'

(g) Gifts, competitions, events and information offered at **trade shows and exhibitions**

(h) **Corporate hospitality**: key trade partners invited to sporting and entertainment events

4 Point of sale

Key Concept

The **point of sale** (POS) is the place (usually in-store) where goods are bought and paid for. By extension 'point of sale' refers to promotional materials displayed in-store to stimulate purchase decisions.

4.1 Point of sale material

- **Product housing or display casing**, such as metal or plastic racks, carousels
- **Posters and showcards** (self-standing cardboard posters or images)
- **Mobiles** (ceiling-hung objects or display cards)
- **Shelf tags** and '**wobblers**' (attention grabbers attached to shelves)
- **Counter-standing leaflet dispensers** with promotional or informational handouts
- **Bookmarks, balloons, branded carrier bags**
- **Interactive kiosks**

4.2 Most point of sale material is **produced by manufacturers/suppliers** for use by retailers.

- **Attention-grabbing**
- **Easy to assemble** and used by retailers
- **Small enough** not to obstruct aisles or take up too much room
- **Compatible** with the retailer's own store design/display plans
- **Durable** enough for the period of the promotion

4.3 Offering POS material is a significant 'push' factor, indicting that the supplier is serious about highlighting its product and selling through to consumers.

5 PR and publicity

5.1 We have already introduced 'public relations' as a discipline, attitude and body of skills in Chapter 8, where we suggested that every employee of an organisation is practising public, or employee, relations as a representative of the organisation. Here, we will look briefly at some of the main PR activities that have not yet been discussed, and will suggest how PR activity can be monitored and evaluated.

Securing media coverage

5.2 Media coverage in editorial articles, product reviews and news items is free promotion, but it is only 'promotion' if the coverage is **positive**. Companies make news for all the wrong reasons, and despite the old saying that 'there's no such thing as bad publicity' - there probably is. When Perrier mineral water was found to contain tiny amounts of a toxic chemical after an accident in the bottling plant, there was an avalanche of headlines, of which the most memorable were 'Eau dear' and 'what a fiasceau'.

5.3 The advantages and disadvantages of coverage may be summarised as follows.

Advantages

- **Raise awareness** of your brand, message or image among a wider audience
- Generate **word-of-mouth** about your product
- **Get your message read**/listened to more carefully than advertising
- Have the effect of implied **endorsement or recommendation**
- **Support** advertising and sales promotion campaigns

Disadvantages

- You cannot **control** the content of editorial matter
- Journalists are interested in their own objectives (circulation and ratings)
- Mistakes and shortcomings are usually more newsworthy than successes

5.4 In order to have a chance of securing coverage you will have to do the following.

(a) **Build up a network of media contacts** (or use a PR or media relations agent). Cultivate contacts regularly, and make notes on each contact.

(b) **Send out media releases** alerting journalists to anything you can make newsworthy.

(c) **Send photographs**, or notify media of **photo calls** where possible. Print media are much hungrier for usable images (with suitable captions) than stories.

(d) **Add supporting incentives**. Magazines, local newspapers and radio stations are often happy to offer their readers special offers and competitions, which secure related explanation/description space.

(e) **Hold press conferences**, only in cases where something genuinely newsworthy can be revealed.

(f) **Offer products for trial and review,** if you are confident that they can stand up to scrutiny and possibly comparison with competitors.

(g) **Offer relevant spokesperson and 'experts'** for interview, comment or consultation on product-related areas. Offer technical articles to trade journals, for example, or publish informational booklets in order to gain a profile as an expert commentator or analyst.

5.5 Ensure that whoever undertakes media relations, and particularly live interviews, knows what they are doing!

(a) Know the angle, audience and style of the medium/publication/programme and journalist they will be talking to or writing for.

(b) Be on guard, however friendly, informal and 'off the record' the discussion may seem.

(c) Make the most of the opportunity to enhance the organisation's image of expertise or personability, and to get the message across.

Sponsorship

5.6 One way of gaining profile and publicity is **sponsorship**. Marketers may sponsor local groups or school teams, all the way up to national and international sporting and cultural events and organisations for a variety of purposes.

- Awareness creation in the audience of the sponsored event
- Media coverage generated by the sponsored event
- Opportunities for corporate hospitality at sponsored events
- Creation of a positive image among employees and the community

5.7 Sponsorship has offered marketing avenues for organisations which are restricted in their advertising, or wish to widen their awareness base among various target audiences. Examples include tobacco sponsorship of sporting events. There is wide corporate involvement in mass support sports such as football, while opera, concerts and orchestras tend to be sponsored by financial institutions and prestige marketing organisations.

5.8 When evaluating sponsorship opportunities, you need to be aware that there will be costs of supporting advertising and PR over and above the basic sponsorship costs. Advertising on team shirts, programmes and hoardings may or may not be included in the sponsorship package of benefits.

Marketing at Work

Vodafone and Manchester United

Vodafone currently has the largest share of the UK cellular market, and wants to retain this leadership through the development of new products and services. The mobile phone market in the UK has approached maturity in a very short space of time, particularly among young people. With fewer new customers available, the challenge is to provide added value to existing customers.

Vodafone's marketing objectives are as follows:

- Obtain new customers
- Keep the ones it already has
- Introduce new technologies and services
- Continue to develop the Vodafone brand

This latter objective in particular was furthered when it started a four year agreement in June 2000 to be the principal sponsor and telecommunications partner of Manchester United Football Club. The fact that Manchester United's matches are regularly televised in 139 countries should give the Vodafone name heightened exposure, especially in the Far East.

Marketing benefits for Vodafone cover three main areas:

(a) **Enhancing brand awareness and image**

Vodafone's logo will feature strongly in Manchester United's marketing material, as well as on the playing kit. Vodafone can use the Manchester United logo in promotions and advertising.

(b) **Extending the range of products and services**

Vodafone is offering a range of 'Reds' phones and accessories.

(c) **Adding value to services**

Fans can use the Vodafone manUmobile service to access news and information about the club and matches via their mobile phones.

Action Programme 4

What do you think are the benefits of the deal for Manchester United?

Other PR methodologies

5.9 A wide range of public relations (government relations, financial relations, public information vehicles) is available. The following are some of the more common examples, some of which we have touched on already.

- Media packs
- Informational literature: brochures, booklets, books
- Annual, financial, market research and other reports
- Newsletters and bulletins (internal and external)
- Video, audio or CD ROM packages

- Seminars, conferences, demonstrations
- Trade shows, exhibitions and fairs
- Product placement (use of the product identifiably in video, TV, cinema and novels)
- Tours, open days, factory/office visits
- Submissions, reports and lobbying of government
- Educational packs for schools/colleges
- Corporate entertainments and special events
- Staff conferences, communication programmes

Marketing at Work

'The Beverage Institute for Health and Wellness sounds, well, like a pretty decent sort of institute advancing, one assumes, knowledge about the relationship between what we drink and how we feel.

Which may be true. The fly in the ointment is that the Beverage Institute is in fact a body created last week by the Coca-Cola corporation.

In the light of mounting public concern about obesity, soft drinks companies like Coca-Cola are in the spotlight. It may be no coincidence that, of late, sales of Coca-Cola's most famous product, Coke, are in decline in its key home market.

The traditional response might have been to blast even more advertising dollars across the airwaves - now a more sophisticated response is required. Obesity and health are complex issues. Consumers are smarter, less trusting of big corporations and cynical about advertising.

On the other hand, shareholders in Coca-Cola might be justified in asking, if the pronouncements of the Beverage Institute don't promote sales of the fizzy stuff, what on earth are they funding it for? And if it does promote greater consumption of "beverages", how much does that serve rivals like Pepsi, Tropicana or Nestlé?

Either way, consumers should expect this kind of stealth marketing activity to increase as corporations look to gain public trust by positioning themselves as world citizens genuinely interested in pushing back the frontiers of knowledge and improving public health.

Mills (2004 (b))

Action Programme 5

Start collecting examples of

(a) editorial articles which quote representatives of named commercial organisations

(b) named or visibly identified brands (watches, cars, soft drinks) in movies and TV programmes

(c) lists acknowledging sponsors of the programmes of sporting and entertainment events, or in their names. Note their impact, memorability, frequency and credibility.

Evaluating the effectiveness of PR

5.10 The results of PR activity should be measured against defined purposes and objectives. The purposes of a given PR initiative may be one or more of the following.

(a) To **support and augment advertising** and sales promotion by securing credible product endorsement or review of products, and media coverage of launches, surveys, newsworthy events, competitions and special offers.

(b) To **reach specialist audiences** which are not sensitive to advertising, but appreciate information: for example, by educational programmes in schools, technical briefings in medical and scientific markets, marketing research to industry bodies or government.

(c) To **manage communications with stakeholders** on sensitive or controversial issues, and to minimise the damage caused to sales and corporate image by crises.

(d) To **influence specific strategic audiences** where threats or opportunities exist (for example, government lobbying).

(e) To **inform and motivate** the trade and **supply chain** about a new product or promotion.

(f) To **improve communication and morale** among employees.

(g) To **educate the community** or market about issues relevant to the product or service, raising consumer awareness of needs or problems which it answers.

5.11 Media coverage can be easily monitored using cuttings or media monitoring agencies, where this is a measure of effectiveness. However, where possible, the achievement of objectives should be the criterion: because PR is often perceived as 'free' and its results as invisible, it is too easy for costs to escalate without detailed justification.

Some useful measures include the following.

(a) Define the **key messages** that will fulfil the specific objectives of the programme, and use media monitoring, feedback, customer/audience research and communication audits.

- Reach the target audience
- Correctly convey the message, resulting in the desired attitudes and awareness.

(b) Monitor appropriate **performance measures** for the specific objectives, to assess whether PR programmes have any effect. Does employee turnover fall following the introduction of employee communications? Is awareness of product-related issues higher in consumer focus groups following a publicity campaign? Have sales recovered following a crisis management exercise? Expect to see some results.

5.12 However, it should be recognised that public relations can be a long-term process of education, attitude change, and relationship building. A realistic time-scale for return on investment should be established in the light of the organisation's strategic goals.

6 Collaborative programmes

6.1 One of the most popular ways in which sales promotions can augment the offer to the consumer is by exploiting synergistic relationships with other products or marketing organisations. (Remember, synergy is the effect whereby 2+2=5) There are various ways in which synergy can be obtained.

(a) One organisation may source **premiums**, **competition prizes** and **gifts** from other marketing organisations so that both benefit from the exposure and purchase incentives. Disney cartoon figures are often merchandised as special offers with kids' meals at McDonalds, for example - prestige cars, luggage and other brands are often used as competition prizes.

(b) Non-competing products in the same or related markets might **reinforce each other** (for example, promoting a stir-fry cookbook and a non-stick wok in a joint competition or premium offer). You get best use out of the one product by also purchasing the other, and if they can be purchased together (or are identified with each other), other brands may be ignored.

(c) Non-competing products with **different customer** bases can be jointly promoted to create cross-over between their respective audiences. Loyal customers of a video store may be persuaded to try the brand of cola or snack food offered free with rental. Loyal customers of that cola or snack food may be persuaded to use that video store because of the free offer.

(d) **Product placement** is a collaborative programme, because it allows the entertainment's producers to source costumes and props while the suppliers of product gain potential high-impact exposure. James Bond's choice of car and watch seldom go unnoticed.

(e) Non competing products or organisations can collaborate in informational or educational promotions to offer the consumer their **cumulative expertise or knowledge**, or one can offer **credibility** or expertise to another in exchange for exposure to its audience. Banks and youth magazines often give away promotional booklets of 'Exam tips' to students at revision time, 'in association with' exam experts such as study guide publishers.

(f) The costs of promotion and other collaborative programmes can be shared.

6.2 The issues involved in collaborative promotion can be complex. Creativity, ingenuity, wide networks and persuasive skills may be required to locate and put together synergistic partnerships that everyone will trust to bring mutual benefit. Introductions and negotiations are often carried out by promotional agencies, but you may approach or be approached by other organisations direct.

Exam Tip

The June 2003 exam explicitly asked you to write a letter proposing collaboration in promotion between two potential competitors. Bear in mind, though, that collaborative promotion may be a useful synergistic tool in the promotion mix: consider it as an option in any scenario.

6.3 As a co-ordinating exercise, collaborative programmes require the following.

(a) Detailed **negotiation** and agreement of objectives, responsibilities, schedules and costs

(b) Regular **communication** between promotional partners, agencies and suppliers of creative and other services required

(c) Provision of all **information, copy, photographs and samples** required for advertising, packaging and POS displays

(d) Rigorous **monitoring of progress** and checking of all details (especially those prepared by other parties) for correctness and conformity with agreed objectives

(e) **Monitoring** of the promotion, its **logistics** (competition entry handling) and **results**, especially if controlled by the other party

6.4 When considering the merits of a proposed collaborative programme you should think about the following.

- What is the potential **exposure** to our target audience?
- **What will they think** of this partnership?
- Will they **recognise** us within the collaboration?
- Is there any **threat** to our brand?
- Are our **marketing objectives** being met?

Marketing at Work

Increasingly, companies have been setting aside their differences: the new mantra is that 'two brand names are better than one' and that sharing databases, strategies and communication platforms is the most effective means of recruiting and retaining customers.

Philips, the electronics company, and Nike, the sportswear group, are finalisng plans for a wide-ranging joint advertising campaign. Legal & General, the financial services company, has joined forces with the electricity generator Powergen. The tie-up will give L&G access to the utility company's database of thousands of corporate customers, who will be offered special deals on financial products.

'It makes sense to join efforts when you have customers in common,' says Andre Manning, partnership marketing specialist for Philips. 'The Nike brand is huge in the US, an area where Philips could still improve and we in turn are a big name who will reflect well on their brand.'

The philosophy is simple, says Joe Craggs, a managing director in Mediator, a partnership marketing agency. 'In these economically straitened times, partnership marketing provides a cost-effective method of increasing both brand awareness and sales,' he says.

With only a finite number of consumers in any target market, why bombard them with different messages from different organisations when you can simplify the process and give them one focal point?

It is predicted that this style of marketing will take up an average of 23 per cent of companies' total marketing budget within the next four years.

Microsoft's partnering with NSPCC for its Full Stop child abuse campaign has gained the computer giant an ethical makeover – by getting its logo on advertisements and other promotional literature produced by the charity – that it could not have hoped to gain alone. In return, Microsoft's financial and technological support has raised about £14 million for its cause, the charity says.

However, if the association with a powerful brand can give a significant boost to sales, it can have the opposite effect if that brand is devalued in some way. Critics of partnership marketing point to the disastrous Hoover/Your Leisure travel venture in 1992.

If insufficient thought is given to the partnerships and the reasons behind them, they will bring little value to either the customer or the companies involved.

Abbey National's attempt at enhancing its Internet site with content from a variety of partners was not the roaring success it had hoped for and a review of the website earlier this year saw most of the third-party content ditched so that Abbey could focus its customers' minds on number one – itself.

Adapted from *The Times*, April 2002

Action Programme 6

The Needle Works

Following the success of your co-promotion with your supplier Threadlines, you decide that collaboration with related organisations can:

(a) widen the audience for your marketing message beyond your current customer base (without paying full advertising costs)

(b) reinforce The Needle Works' prestige and expert image among craft consumers.

Relations with the Craft Guilds have not yet improved, but you review your network contacts. See if you can come up with some ideas to discuss with one or more of those contacts for a collaborative promotion which will have benefit for the exposure and sales of both (or all) parties, and will also have PR potential for media coverage and wider interest (to save on advertising costs).

7 Promotion on the Internet

The Internet as a promotional tool

7.1 The Internet can be used for a broad range of promotional applications.

Advertising	■ Dedicated corporate websites, banner/button advertising, ranking on Internet search engines (to increase site exposure) ■ The forecast global penetration of the Internet over the next few years would give it a significantly larger audience than any of the television networks, print media outlets or other advertising vehicles ■ Studies show that brand awareness increases some 5% after using banner advertising
Direct marketing	■ E-mail messages sent to targeted mailing lists (rented, or developed by the marketing organisation itself) ■ 'Permission marketing' (targeting consumers who have opted to receive commercial mailings)

Direct response advertising	■ Immediate contact (information/transaction facilities) to follow up customer responses to TV/radio/print advertising
Sales promotion	■ On-line prize draws and competitions ■ On-line discounts (offset by lower transaction costs) ■ Downloadable or e-mailed discount vouchers
Customer loyalty programmes	■ Value-added benefits that enhance the Internet buying experience ■ User home page customisation ■ Virtual communities (chat rooms etc) ■ Free e-cards/SMS messages
Media/press relations	■ Online media/press kits ■ E-mailed media releases ■ 'About us' and 'contacts' pages ■ Technical briefings and articles on key issues
Pubic relations	■ 'About us' and 'FAQ' (frequently asked question) features ■ News bulletins (eg for crisis or issues management) ■ Publicity/information for sponsorships, exhibitions and events ■ Sponsorship of popular/ useful information sites
Relationship marketing	■ Customisation of Web pages and targeting of offers/promotions ■ E-mail follow-up contacts ■ **E-zines**: special interest newsletters published on the Web, or distributed by e-mail direct to subscribers and mailing lists
Grass roots marketing	■ Generating word of mouth promotion and recommendation among customers ■ Online chat or message board forums and 'introduce a friend' schemes/incentives ■ '**Viral marketing'** (so-called because it simulates the way a virus works!): giving visitors communication tools which they send to others, requiring them to visit the site: eg electronic postcards, greeting cards and links ('Send this page to a friend')
Direct distribution	■ Of products (through online shopping) and services (including access to information databases) ■ Products can be **ordered** via the Net ■ Some can also be **delivered** via the Net, by downloading direct to the purchaser's PC: examples include music, computer software, Clipart, product catalogues and instruction manuals
Partnership development	■ Strategic promotional collaborations with synergistic content-specific sites or 'portals' (search engines, Web directories or other high-traffic sites such as Yahoo! or MSN)
Customer service and **technical support**	■ E-mail contact ■ FAQs (frequently asked questions) ■ Access to databased information ■ Online messaging or voice interruption for interactive support

Market/customer research	■ Gathering information on customers and visitors for the purposes of market segmentation, personalisation/customisation of future contacts ■ Site monitoring ■ Online or e-mailed feedback questionnaires and surveys
Corporate identity	■ Website and e-mail messages must be designed to create a unified and coherent marketing message alongside all other marketing messages for **marketing synergy**

Marketing at Work

© 2004 Touchstone Pictures

Save 20%* when you spend $10, and get a FREE movie ticket courtesy of Ofoto!

Visit Ofoto today and save 20% on everything from prints and one-of-a-kind photocards to frames and photo albums. And get a movie ticket with any purchase while supplies last**.

Use this code when you order to get your ticket: ALAMO20

sign in

* Save 20% offer expires on 4/30/04. Does not apply to shipping costs, film processing, applicable sales tax, or Kodak Mobile Service Subscription. One coupon redemption per customer. Cannot be combined with other offers in one order. No substitutions, transfer rights or cash equivalents will be given.

** In order to receive MovieCash good for a free movie ticket, you must make a purchase at Ofoto using the coupon code ALAMO20 between 3/26/04 and 4/30/04. For those that qualify, MovieCash will be mailed out to eligible customers the week of 5/3/04 via USPS while supplies last. Cannot be combined with other offers. No substitutions, transfer rights or cash equivalent will be given.

(www.ofoto.com)

Action Programme 7

Smith and Chaffey (2001) suggest five benefits of promotion on the web. See if you can complete the table with some ideas of your own.

Benefit	How?
Sell – Grow sales	
Serve – Add value	
Speak – Get closer to customers	
Save – Save costs	
Sizzle – Extend the brand	

Chapter Roundup

- The purpose of **sales promotion** may be to increase short-term sales volume, encourage repeat purchase, encourage customer loyalty, encourage new product trial or brand trial, convey information, convey a positive PR image, extend media coverage, extend the database, motivate salespeople and distributors or attract and motivate purchase influencers.
- **Common promotional mechanisms** include coupons, premiums, bonus packs, rebates, samples, demonstrations, games and competitions, gifts, merchandising and events.
- **Trade promotions** may be used as 'push' techniques to sell products into distribution outlets.
- **Point of sale materials** may be supplied to retailers to support product displays and induce purchase decisions in-store.
- **PR methodologies** include media relations, press releases, photo calls, product submission for offers and reviews, press conferences and offering expert spokespersons, in order to secure 'free' media coverage.
- **Other methods** include sponsorship, events and a wide range of information programmes targeted at specific audiences: employees, government, public, financial media, trade and so on.
- **Collaborative promotional programmes** (often negotiated by promotional agencies) exploit the synergy available to non-competing, compatible products or organisations, by sourcing premiums, prizes and gifts, reinforcing marketing messages, sharing audiences, lending credibility and sharing costs.
- **Promotion on the Internet** may include
  - Web marketing
  - Banner advertising
  - E-mail targeting

Quick Quiz

1. Give examples of promotions designed (a) to encourage new product trial and (b) to enlarge the promoter's database.
2. What are premiums most useful for, and when are they most effective?
3. Why is sampling effective at converting customers of other brands?
4. Outline the 'COMPETE' formula for consumer competitions.
5. Give three examples of trade promotions.
6. What are the attributes of effective POS material?
7. What are the benefits and drawbacks of getting 'free' publicity?
8. What are the purposes of sponsorship?
9. Give four examples of collaborative promotions: one premium, one competition, one offering cross-over audiences and one based on expertise/prestige.
10. Describe some types of web promotion.

Now try Question 13 in the Question Bank

Action Programme Review

1. Some of the promotional tools you may have encountered are: on-pack coupons, discount vouchers, on-pack competitions and prize draws ('look out for the Special Packs/Bottles...'), in-store trials, tastings and demonstrations, free gifts and product samples (often with magazines), two for the price of one or free sample combo packaging, point of sale displays, vouchers and coupons with special offers printed on the back of your till receipt, special offers on selected products, prize draw entry forms, free recipe booklets for food products, store credit cards or loyalty schemes. You'll be amazed how much sales promotion is out there! (You might also like to consider whether or how far your buying behaviour is influenced by it...)
2. Just some suggestions.
   (a) A cake decorating competition, using candied peel, or a recipe competition using candied peel. Promoted on pack and by POS leaflets and ads: purchase required. Winning entries to be made and published in a range of promotional ideas/recipe cards. The winners to be given a gourmet weekend for two or cordon bleu cookery course; runners up to be given Jane Asher's Cake Decorating book.

   (b) The Needle Works might similarly promote (in-store) a tapestry design competition. The winning designs to be made up as Tapestry Kits (profits to be given to charity) and the tapestry to be stitched. Winning designer acknowledged in all publicity, plus royalty on design and prize (weekend in Normandy to see Bayeux Tapestry?).

   (c) Possibly a travel photo competition, or a less participative geography quiz, based on identifying photos from the new Guides (so entrants have to buy, borrow or at least inspect them). Prize: air miles or a camera or photography course: not too high price tag.

   (d) A simple prize draw, for which bottle 'crowners' (neck-hanging coupons) need to be sent in with contact details: purchase incentive. Widely advertised plus on-pack information. Prize: six months' use of household cleaning service or luxury holiday.

3 For example: balloons, towels, ashtrays, matchbooks, yo-yos, toy figures, directors' chairs, umbrellas, can coolers/holders, stickers, scarves, ties, badges, sports jackets, credit card holders, wallets, penknives, playing cards, footballs, rulers, notepads, sports bags, cigarette lighters, outdoor pub umbrellas, jewellery, seat covers, litter bins, glassware, mugs, torches. Keep going!

4 Manchester United receives significant revenue from Vodafone, and it benefits from the new services offered to fans.

5 You must develop 'radar' for this kind of thing.

6 Whatever ideas you came up with check them against the 'brief' you set yourself. We have developed the idea we floated in Action Programme 2. The Needle Works could run a collaborative tapestry design competition with a suitable partner: a national craft gallery or design council might see its PR potential (expressing the community's aspirations and identity) and would lend the promotion credibility - and a wide relevant mailing list, educational programme and other communication avenues. The Needle Works would gain exposure, and later revenue from merchandising (selling the design as a pattern, kits and so on): both parties could merchandise postcards or posters of the finished tapestry, and perhaps educational videos on 'The Making of the Tapestry'. There would be highly photogenic publicity opportunities as the winning designers were announced and given prizes, and on an on-going basis as the tapestry took shape and was finally presented to the public, and then toured round galleries and public institutions. Costs would have to be investigated and cost-sharing negotiated. In order to take full advantage of the spin-off sales potential, the Needle Works would probably need to have moved out of its local retail niche and into wider sales via mail order catalogue and perhaps Internet - but these initiatives should probably be on the agenda anyway.

7

Benefit	How?
Sell – Grow sales	Wider distribution Wider product range
Serve – Add value	Extra benefits from online transactions (eg discounts) Dialogue/feedback
Speak – Get closer to customers	Track customers, ask them questions, online interviews
Save – Save costs	Printing and postage reduced, for example
Sizzle – Extend the brand	Create brand awareness and involvement through interactive content

Answers to Quick Quiz

1 (a) money-off coupons, free samples, demonstrations.
(b) coupon returns, competition entries, phone responses

2 Premiums are the offer of a product or service free/discounted for a limited time. They are intended to encourage future purchase or to lure customers away from an undifferentiated brand.

3 Curiosity and lack of cost or risk can overcome the inertia of habitual use or apathy.

4 This is explained in Paragraph 2.1.

5 Monetary incentives, joint advertising, point-of-sale support. A full list is given in Paragraph 3.2.

6 You should have the five points listed in Paragraph 4.2.

7 Lack of control; conflicting interests between media/organisation; often negative publicity makes a juicier story.

8 Refer to the bullet points in Paragraph 5.6.

9 You should be vigilant for examples of your own. Some examples might be McDonalds with a give-away toy based on a Disney character (premium), a wok with a competition to win a related prize (perhaps a cookbook) (competition), a video rental outlet promoting snack food (cross-over) and an expensively produced technical manual on tyres, such as one produced by Dunlop Australia.

10 Refer to the table in Paragraph 7.1.

Mix Decisions 14

Chapter Topic List	
1	Setting the scene
2	Price
3	Place
4	Product
5	The extended marketing mix
6	ICT and the new marketing mix

Learning Outcomes

- ☑ Evaluate and select media and promotional activities appropriate to the organisation's objectives and status and to its marketing context
- ☑ Undertake basic marketing activities within an agreed plan and monitor and report on progress

Syllabus References

- ☑ Analyse the impact of pricing decisions, and role of price within the marketing mix
- ☑ Describe the current distribution channels for an organisation and evaluate new opportunities
- ☑ Describe how organisations monitor product trends
- ☑ Explain the importance of the extended marketing mix; how process, physical aspects and people affect customer choice
- ☑ Explain the importance of ICT in the new mix

Key Concepts Introduced

- Price
- Place
- Product
- Extended marketing mix

1 Setting the scene

1.1 So far in Part D of this Study Text - Co-ordinating the Marketing Mix - we have concentrated on one of the four Ps - promotion. The *Marketing in Practice* syllabus suggests a promotional bias, particularly since, at a practical level, much of the material on promotional activity may be new to you.

1.2 It may seem that we have therefore set ourselves (and you) a somewhat Herculean task in covering the other three Ps of the mix - plus its 'extensions' - all in one chapter. There is good news.

(a) You will be building substantially on the knowledge gained from *Marketing Fundamentals*.

(b) For this module, a practical co-ordinatory approach is required. We confine ourselves to the areas listed in the syllabus.

(c) These practical, co-ordinatory tasks largely involve the gathering, evaluation and presentation of information, which we covered in detail in Chapters 1-4 of this Text.

1.3 This chapter draws together material with which you should be familiar, and on completion you should be able to:

- Analyse current usage of the marketing mix
- Analyse the impact of pricing decisions and the role of price in the mix
- Analyse current distribution channels and new opportunities
- Monitor product trends
- Appreciate the importance of process, physicals and people in customer choice
- Appreciate the role of information and communication technology (ICT) in the marketing mix

2 Price

The role of price in the mix

Key Concept

Price can be defined as a measure of the value exchanged by the buyer for the value offered by the seller. It may be, for example, expressed as fees, fares, tuition or rent.

2.1 Price is important within the marketing mix.

(a) It influences profitability at the 'top line', by generating revenue, rather than at the 'bottom line' by striving to control costs (like place, product and promotion).

(b) It has an important role in differentiating products and organisations in a market. Pricing strategies are used to gain and maintain competitive advantage.

(c) It is part of the overall product offer, its perceived value to the buyer, and the image of the producer/seller. Price must therefore be consistent with the other elements of the marketing mix.

Marketing at Work

Customers like clear and concise messages that are easy to understand, so that they can make well-informed decisions. Confusing information may make them move to 'simpler' rivals.

Thomson, Britain's biggest tour operator, is to be investigated over misleading pricing after it launched a new way of selling package holidays in early 2002.

It proposes charging for 'optional' extras such as in-flight meals and hotel transfers. It has been calculated that these extras could cost a typical family of four up to £100 on top of the basic price. Comparisons with other operators could become more difficult. Other extras include guaranteeing families that they can sit together, reserving window or aisle seats, and increased baggage allowances.

Thomson says that it is merely responding to an increasing trend among travellers to plan their own holidays and use the low-cost airlines. This has been accelerated by the Internet. Customers can now 'personalise' their trips and only pay for what they want. But this lack of price clarity could lead to cynicism and rejection of the product.

2.2 In the absence of other information, customers tend to judge **quality** by price. A rise may be taken to indicate improvements, a reduction may signal reduced quality, for example through the use of inferior components or a poorer quality of raw material.

2.3 The ultimate objective of pricing is to produce the level of sales required to fulfil the organisation's marketing and financial objectives.

- **Maximising profits**, or the returns on assets or investments
- **Maintaining or increasing market share** or customer base
- **Market penetration**: getting a new product adopted and accepted quickly
- **Increasing short-term sales volume**

2.4 The **price sensitivity** of customers (that is, the extent to which price is an incentive or disincentive to purchase) should have been analysed prior to strategic price setting. Your tasks in regard to price might consist of monitoring this sensitivity: analysing the effect of price setting or changes on buying behaviour and sales (see Paragraph 2.8).

Price sensitivity

2.5 Research on price sensitivity of customers has shown the following.

(a) Customers have a good concept of a 'just price' - a feel for what is about the right price to pay for a commodity.

(b) Unless a regular purchase is involved, customers search for price information before buying, becoming price aware when wanting to buy but forgetting soon afterwards.

(c) Customers will buy at what they consider to be a bargain price without full regard for need and actual price.

(d) For consumer durables it is the down payment and instalment price rather than total price which is important to the buyer.

(e) In times of rising prices the price image tends to lag behind the current price, which indicates a resentment of the price increase.

2.6 Price sensitivity will vary amongst purchasers. Those (like trade buyers) who can pass on the cost of purchases will be least sensitive and will respond more to other elements of the marketing mix. For example, the business traveller will be more concerned about the level of service and quality of food in looking for an hotel than price. In contrast, a family on holiday are likely to be very price sensitive when choosing an overnight stay.

2.7 Price **perception** is important in the ways customers react to prices. For example, customers may react to a price increase by buying more.

- They expect further price increases to follow
- They assume the quality has increased
- The brand takes on a 'snob appeal' because of the high price

Monitoring the effect of pricing decisions

2.8 There are various quantitative and qualitative methods of measuring the factors discussed above.

(a) Quantity of products sold in comparable periods before and after the price change can be compared. Changes in quantity sold during a temporary promotional price offer can also be measured.

(b) The contribution to fixed cost and profit made by the product (sales revenue **minus** variable costs) can be compared at the old and new price.

(c) You could use a **market test** to estimate the effect on demand of a price change. This would involve a change of price in one region and a comparison of demand for the brand with past sales in that region and with sales in similar regions at the old prices. This is a high risk strategy.

(d) A **direct attitude survey** may be used to test buyers' reactions to price changes. **Pricing research** is notoriously difficult, especially if respondents try to appear rational to the interviewer or do not wish to offend him or her. Usually there is a lack of realism in such research.

Action Programme 1

Product X sold 1,300,000 units in the year 200X, at the price of 28p per unit. Variable cost per unit was 16p. In the year 200Y, the price of product X went up to 32p per unit and 1,100,000 units were sold at the same cost per unit. What is the effect of the price increase?

2.9 The reactions of **suppliers, distributors and competitors** will also need to be monitored.

(a) Suppliers may attempt to negotiate higher rates for their products or services if they perceive that the organisation has raised its prices.

(b) Distributors may deal with a range of suppliers, and are concerned with their own profits. If they feel product price rises are squeezing their profit margins, or cash flow, they may reconsider stock levels.

(c) Competitors' reactions to a price change are particularly important. Responsive price changes can be monitored through published price lists and advertising, suppliers and distributors and customers.

Other price-related issues

2.10 At a co-ordinating level, the marketing department will also have to give attention to the following.

(a) **Competitor pricing** will have to be monitored.

(b) Pricing decisions will have to be accurately and effectively **communicated to customers and consumers**, in all advertising and informational literature. Gathering, checking and cross-checking price data is one of the essential tasks in promotional co-ordination (especially for large-scale catalogues). The way prices are expressed may have an influence on purchase decisions, particularly in direct marketing. Prices must be easy to understand (how many customers will understand '£24.99 non net'?) and easy to calculate (how many customers will have a calculator to hand to add VAT or percentages for postage and packaging?).

(c) **Market research** may disclose pricing issues: customer perceptions or gaps in market segments related to prices. These should be input into pricing decisions.

(d) **Promotional proposals** may involve discounts, premiums and bonuses. These should be regarded as strategic pricing issues, since they represent an adjustment to the price positioning of the product.

Action Programme 2

What might (a) a price reduction and (b) a price rise suggest to buyers, and what would then help to *counteract* the expected incentive or deterrent effect on sales?

3 Place

Key Concept

'**Place**' as an element in the marketing mix is largely concerned with the selection of **distribution channels** to deliver the goods to the consumer, and with the **storage** and **physical distribution** of goods (**logistics**).

3.1 We have already discussed some elements of the marketing co-ordinator's role.

- Developing **business relationships** down the supply chain
- Promoting products to distributors by 'push' techniques or trade promotions
- Supporting distributors via 'pull' promotions to consumers

3.2 In addition, the marketing co-ordinator may have to monitor the effectiveness of current distribution channels and new opportunities.

Evaluating current distribution channels

3.3 Criteria which may be used to evaluate distribution channels and logistics

(a) **Effectiveness** in getting products to customers (ie sales) and in performing each of the distributive functions that leads to sales

(b) **Efficiency and economy** in terms of the costs of distribution

(c) **Level of service** offered to customers, supporting loyalty and repeat sales

(d) **Degree of control** achieved over the distribution channel, where desired for competitive advantage or integration of marketing effort up to the point of sale

(e) **Degree of co-operation or conflict** with the distributor (channel dynamics)

Exam Tip

A question in December 2002 asked you to draft a response to a retailer who has approached your firm with a view to join your retail network (basic relationship/PR/front-line skills) and to state what information you would need about the retailer and the market for your product in its country, before you made a decision to work with them (investigating distributor and investigating market opportunities). Another example of a question crossing over syllabus areas: stay flexible in your thinking!

Effectiveness

3.4 The measure of effectiveness will depend on specific objectives and criteria appropriate to the processes and channels used. **Sales** made through the distribution channel, however, are a key indicator

- Compared month-on-month or year-on-year to show growth or decline trends
- Compared for different channels, to show which are more effective than others

Efficiency

3.5 Cost of distribution is one of the key factors in selecting distribution channels. **Intermediaries** may reduce the costs of selling for the manufacturer by **bearing or sharing the costs** of stockholding, transportation and display. In addition, manufacturers may receive payment more quickly from intermediaries than by selling direct to the consumer.

3.6 Distribution costs should be monitored.

- Cost savings should be being obtained, compared to estimated costs of other channels
- Costs should be in line with negotiated and budgeted expenditure
- The channel should be cost-efficient

Level of service

3.7 **Customer service** is a key source of competitive benefit, and therefore a key objective of distribution systems.

- The availability of, and charges for, installation, repair and after-sales service
- Readiness to take back and quickly re-supply defective goods
- The preparation of orders delivered with correct contents and in good condition
- Lead time from placement of an order to delivery
- Choice and flexibility in product specifications, size of order accepted and ordering convenience
- The availability of product information and/or demonstration
- A customer service orientation in front line staff

Such factors are part of the offer to the customer, and responsibility for them should be clearly apportioned by negotiation between manufacturers and intermediaries, and monitored. If the manufacturer has a service policy of re-supplying faulty goods, the willingness of a retailer to mediate the return and exchange should be ascertained.

Degree of control

3.8 Manufacturers may wish to control or dominate a distribution channel.

(a) Ensuring that its policies with regard to pricing, promotion and sales service are carried out, and its marketing message is integrated all the way to the point of sale

(b) Maintaining closer contact with consumers and sources of marketing information

(c) Gaining competitive advantage by having exclusive distribution through major retailers or distributors

Degree of co-operation or conflict

3.9 As business relationships, channels are subject to conflicts of interest, culture, priorities and personalities. Attention will need to be given to channel management where negotiations and problem-solving take up an unacceptable amount of managerial time, or result in lost sales (for example, though lack of co-operation on promotions or point-of-sale display).

New opportunities in distribution

3.10 There are opportunities to be exploited in distribution.

(a) Offering EDI (**electronic data interchange**) enables a firm to cut lead times for orders. This can be a source of differentiation.

(b) Distribution has a 'branding effect'. Distribution can be a central and explicit part of a brand's identity, such as First Direct (Midland Bank's telephone banking subsidiary).

(c) Distribution might become 'essentially an information system'. Retailers (through using scanning technology) probably know more about customers than manufacturers.

3.11 Changes and new opportunities, from direct mail order marketing to Internet marketing to retail outlet refitting and re-sitting, should be evaluated. See Section 6 on the role of the Internet in the marketing mix.

Action Programme 3

The Needle Works

From your knowledge of The Needle Works so far, how effective is its present distribution strategy, and what new opportunities might profitably be exploited?

4 Product

Key Concept

A '**product**' is a **package of benefits**, although we tend to think of it as a 'thing' with 'features'.

4.1 The package of benefits includes:

(a) a **physical aspect**, which relates to the components, materials and specifications (colour, size etc.) of the product: for example, a size 12 pullover made of 100% pure wool in a natural colour

(b) a **functional aspect**, which is a statement of how a product performs and for what purpose it is likely to be bought: the wool pullover may give warmth and comfort

(c) **symbolic aspect**, which represents the qualities the product suggests to, or confers upon, the buyer: the '100% pure wool' label may represent quality, status or ecology (as a natural rather than synthetic product).

4.2 The overall package for the marketer includes:

- Product specifications and materials
- Product design or styling
- Product functions and benefits
- Product packaging
- The range of products in a 'line', and additions to or deletions from it

4.3 There are many strategic issues in product planning, positioning, branding and portfolio management. However, at the co-ordinatory level, you are most likely to be involved in the following.

(a) **Monitoring product performance** over time, through the product life cycle, and in relation to competitors.

(b) **Monitoring product trends**: new products entering the market, existing products becoming fashionable (or becoming fashionable again) and product modifications by competitors.

(c) **Co-ordinating product-related promotional activity:** launch marketing, market testing and consumer research, promotional packaging (special offers/competitions on pack).

Monitoring product performance

4.4 Product performance can be monitored and analysed using:

- Sales and profit/contribution figures
- Feedback from sales reps and retailers
- Customer research, (questionnaires, feedback forms, attitude surveys, perceptual mapping)
- Records of customer complaints, warranty claims
- Comparative competitor and market data
- Product life cycle (PLC) and Boston Consulting Group (BCG) Growth Share models, which show how sales, profitability and market share of a product can be expected to change over time

Marketing at Work

McDonald's fast food restaurants are slashing their burger menus across Europe to make way for a new range of healthier foods including chicken salads and chopped fruit.

Launched today in the UK, Salad Plus has been dubbed McDonald's 'most significant menu change' in its 30-year history.

The move follows the chain's decision last week to phase out 'super-size' fries and drinks in the US and is a major attempt to fight for the £445 million-a-year prepared salad market.

McDonald's, which has come under increasing pressure from anti-obesity campaigners who claim the company encourages an unhealthy lifestyle, will overhaul menus in 16 European countries by slashing its line-up of burgers for chicken salads, yoghurts and chopped fruits. The chain has already successfully introduced a premium salads range in the US.

Denis Hennequin, executive vice-present of McDonald's Europe, said the company was also working with nutritionists on a 'smart labelling' system which should be ready by the end of the year.

www.mad.co.uk: 9 March 2004

4.5 As we discussed in Part A of this Text, the quantitative data can tell you 'how' a product is doing, but not 'why': some qualitative data on consumer perceptions will need to be gathered to disguise potential threats and opportunities.

Monitoring product trends

4.6 This should form part of the environmental scanning discussed in Part A of this Text.

(a) To indicate opportunities for new products in order to anticipate or keep pace with consumer needs and wants, technological capability and/or competitor activity

(b) To indicate the need to modify existing products, positioning or promotion, for the same reasons.

We can talk about product trends because products alter in consumers' perceptions, competitive position and technological up-to-dateness with time.

4.7 The word 'trend' has also come to be used to describe 'fashions' and this is also a feature of product perception and buying patterns.

(a) **Technological development** can prompt buying (and supply) trends. As microchip technology gets cheaper and more sophisticated, for example, there has been increased miniaturisation of electronic products (from computers to calculators and watches), and trends toward more sophisticated and higher-quality audio-visual reproduction.

(b) **Social-cultural factors** can prompt fashions and fads, such as increased consumption of wine with meals in the UK (supported by exposure to Europe and an expanding world-wide range of choice) or a preference for 'green' and ethical products (free range eggs).

(c) **Economic and political factors** prompt trends based on disposable income, tax efficiency and attitudes towards financial responsibility. The market for small, fuel-economical cars, for example, is growing steadily at the expense of large and luxury models.

4.8 There is undoubtedly value in gathering environmental data in order to identify trends. However, there are limitations to the ability of apparent trends to 'predict' the future. Change is a complex phenomenon and it is possible to oversimplify the model underlying an apparent trend.

4.9 This is not to say that marketers should not use their 'antennae' for marketing opportunities! If you have an instinct that a certain product area or innovation is going to be The Next Big Thing - speak up! But be aware that this does not make for accurate R & D budgeting or sales forecasting. In real life - as in the *Marketing in Practice* assessment - you will usually need to justify any product recommendations you make.

Action Programme 4

The following is a *perceptual map* plotting consumer respondents' views on different brands of toilet tissue, asked whether they found it 'strong' or 'weak' to handle, and 'soft' or 'harsh' to the touch.

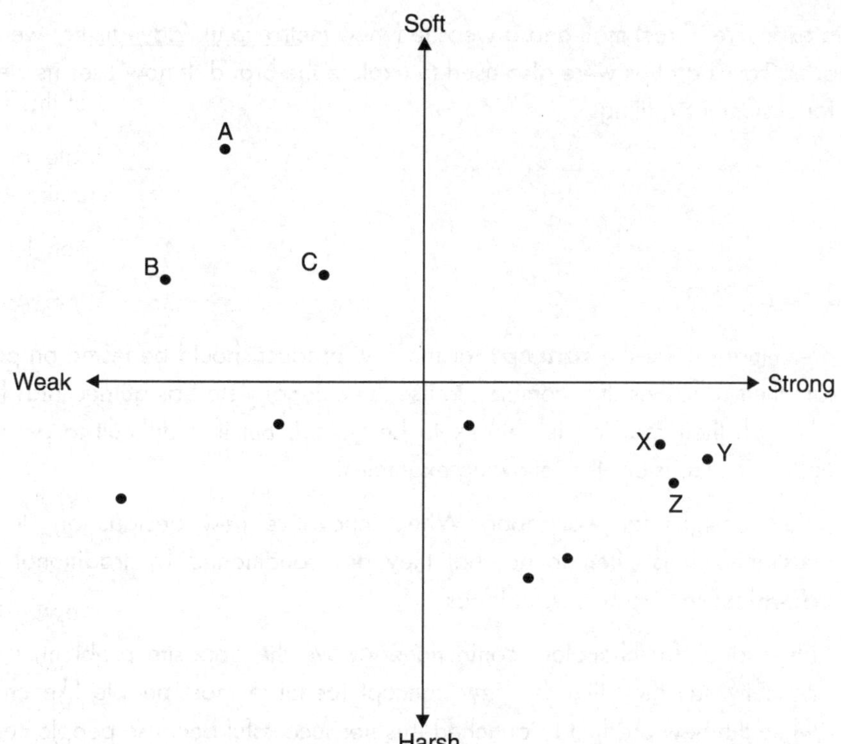

How would you report on the performance of Brand X, as its marketing co-ordinator?

4.10 Note that product trends are not just about new product opportunities. The energy and effort invested in adding new products and brands to the portfolio is seldom mirrored by the identification and weeding out of weak and declining, redundant and non-'fitting' products. Effective marketing co-ordination means directing resources to profitable activities: beware product proliferation or sentimental attachments to 'dead horses'.

Product-related launch and promotion activity

4.11 Bear in mind the following.

(a) A **'new' product** can be one that opens up an entirely new market, one that replaces an existing product, or one that broadens the market for an existing product.

(b) An **'old' product** can become 'new' if it is introduced to a new market, is packaged in a different way, or is promoted in a different way.

Marketing at Work

Marketing Metro

The *Metro* newspaper was launched in March 1999, aimed at the lucrative niche of 400,000 frequent London tube travellers who did not read a national newspaper. It is now the world's largest free newspaper.

Since its launch, it has taken over £40 million in advertising revenue. How was this success achieved?

Media exposure, direct mail and a website (www.metro.co.uk/advertising) were used to market the paper. Focus groups were also used to explore the brand. It now uses its website to collect data for customer profiling.

Product testing

4.12 At a preliminary stage the **concept** for the new product should be tested on potential customers to obtain their reactions. It is common to use the company staff as guinea pigs for a new product idea although their reaction is unlikely to be typical. But it is difficult to get sensible reactions from customers. Consider the following examples.

(a) New designs for wallpaper. When innovative new designs are tested on potential customers it is often found that they are conditioned by traditional designs and are **dismissive** of new design ideas.

(b) New ideas for chocolate confectionery have the opposite problem. Potential customers typically say they like the new concept (because most people like chocolate bars) but when the new product is launched it is not successful because people continue to buy **old favourites**.

4.13 A working **prototype of the product**, which can be tried by customers, can be used for **product testing**. This stage is also very useful for making preliminary explorations of production costs and practical problems. We need to have some idea of whether the product could be produced in sufficient quantities at the right price were it to be launched. The form the product test takes will depend very much on the type of product concerned. The best advice seems to be that to get realistic responses the test should replicate reality as clearly as possible.

(a) If the product is used in the home, a sample of respondents should be given the product to use at home.

(b) If the product is chosen from amongst competitors in a retail outlet (as with chocolate bars) then the product test needs to rate response against competitive products.

(c) If inherent product quality is an important attribute of the product then a 'blind' test could be used in which customers are not told who is producing the new product.

(d) An industrial product could be used for a trial period by a customer in a realistic setting.

5 The extended marketing mix

Key Concept

The 'added elements' of the **extended marketing mix** are:

- People
- Processes
- Physicals

Exam Tip

Questions have been set in December 2002, June 2003 and December 2003 along the lines of: 'How can the full (or extended) marketing mix be used to ...?' Aside from focusing on the purpose stated in your answer, you really need to take in the words 'full' and/or 'extended'! The examiner noted: 'This is the seven Ps . Candidates who thought this was about four, five or three Ps were obviously at a disadvantage!' Better candidates use the 7Ps as a framework, within which they make specific proposals: eg signage or uniforms (for Physical Evidence), staff training (for People), automated call answering (for Processes) and so on.

People

5.1 People are an important ingredient in the marketing mix and environment (as Part B of this Text should have indicated).

(a) The market itself consists of people, with different (or similar, within market segments) needs, values, attitudes and disposable income. Marketing involves attempting to understand people's needs and behaviour.

(b) Suppliers, distributors, business contacts and competitors are people: doing business involves building relationships.

(c) Marketers, salespeople and customer service personnel are people.

5.2 The importance of employees in the marketing mix is particularly important in **service marketing**, because of the **inseparability** of the service from the service provider: the 'creation' of the service and 'consumption' of the service generally happen at the same moment, at the interface between the server and the served. Front-line staff must be selected, trained and motivated with particular attention to customer care and public relations.

5.3 In the case of some services, the physical presence of people actually performing the service is a vital aspect of customer satisfaction: think of clerks in a bank, or personnel in catering establishments. The staff involved are performing or producing a service, selling the service and also liaising with the customer to promote the service, gather information and respond to customer needs.

5.4 Arguably, however, all members of the organisation are involved in 'marketing': all personnel should have the skills, motivation and attitudes to do their jobs to a professional standard as a 'quality workforce', and should be rewarded and valued accordingly. This means concrete policies and continuous development.

- Policies of selection
- Programmes of training
- Standard, consistent operational practices
- Standardised operational rules
- Effective motivational programmes
- Managerial appointments

- The attractiveness and appropriateness of the service offer
- Effective policies of staff reward and remuneration

Processes

5.5 Processes are the way in which marketing tasks are carried out. Efficient processes can become a marketing advantage in their own right. If an airline, for example, develops a sophisticated ticketing system, it can offer shorter waits at check-in or wider choice of flights through allied airlines. Efficient order processing not only increases customer satisfaction, but cuts down on the time it takes the organisation to complete a sale.

5.6 Issues to be considered include the following.

- Policies, particularly with regard to ethical dealings (a key issue for many consumers)
- Procedures, for efficiency and standardisation
- Automation/computerisation of processes
- Queuing and waiting times
- Information gathering, processing and communication times
- Capacity management, matching supply to demand in a timely and cost effective way
- Accessibility of facilities, premises, personnel and services

5.7 Such issues are particularly important in service marketing, because of the characteristic of '**heterogeneity**': because of the number of factors and different people, involved, it is difficult to standardise the service offered. The quality and precise specifications will vary with the circumstances and individuals.

(a) Establishing service standards and objectives, as far as possible

(b) Co-ordinating staffing levels to smooth out fluctuations in demand

(c) Managing customer contact points, to avoid unnecessary queuing and facilitate information-giving

5.8 Services are also innately **perishable**: a doctor's services may be put off, but not really 'kept until later' - still less an information request or seat on a bus. Services have a specific, often narrow, window of opportunity. This factor, too, creates a need for process planning for adequate staffing levels, without wasteful over-manning for efficient work flow.

Physicals

5.9 Physical elements include:

- Tangible evidence of purchase
- The corporate and purchase physical environment

5.10 Again, this is particularly important in service industries, because of:

- The **intangibility** or lack of physical substance involved in service
- The **lack of ownership** of services

These factors make it difficult for consumers to perceive, evaluate and compare the qualities of service provision, and may therefore dampen the incentive to consume.

5.11 Issues of intangibility and ownership can be tackled by making available a tangible symbol or representation of the service 'product' or ownership, and the benefits it confers. For example, tickets, programs and merchandise for entertainment, or certificates of attainment for educational services or customer loyalty, discount or credit cards are all 'cues' representing the service available and a history of past positive experiences.

5.12 Alternatively, the physical evidence may be incorporated into the design and specification of the service environment involving the building, location or atmosphere to achieve the following.

- Convey the nature of the service involved
- Transmit messages and information
- Imply aesthetic qualities, moral values or other aspects of a corporate image
- Reinforce an existing image
- Reassure
- Engender an emotional reaction in the customer

5.13 Such environmental factors include finishing, decor, colour scheme, noise levels, background music, smells and ambience.

Marketing at Work

'So-called 4S stores are retail outlets that deal in the sales, spare parts, services and surveys of particular brands of cars. The potential market is huge for incoming enterprises able to offer the best *services contracts* under this sector of the market.

Mazda's sales centre at Meilinguan in Shenzhen is one example. A clean and neat maintenance area, modern equipment and management, highly professional ambience, impressive service facilities, ample supply of spare parts and swift follow-up services make it a favourite location for car owners.

4S stores are also intensifying competition on the Chinese mainland. Consumer demand is diversifying and people are becoming more demanding with the products and services they pay for. The old dealership system can no longer meet market and consumer needs.

The emergence of 4S stores is apparently the answer to these needs. 4S stores seem to help cultivate consumers' faith in particular brands and increase their sales.

Mr Zhang, a traditional car dealer, admitted that his company's recent drop in sales was due to competition from 4S stores. It seems to suggest that conventional car dealers fail to provide the kind of personalised "quality service" that 4S stores have to offer.

Car sales have close profit margins and dealers mainly rely on after-sale service for their profits. After selling a car, they have to woo buyers into bringing it back for maintenance by offering a better service.

Lou (2004)

Action Programme 5

What physicals could be provided by:

(a) a provider of adventure sport activities?
(b) a provider of tourist information services?
(c) a provider of travel services?
(d) a TV rental provider?

6 ICT and the new marketing mix

6.1 Even with the advent of information and communication technology (ICT), the marketing mix still provides a sound framework for generating marketing strategy. According to Chaffey (2002) 'the Internet provides many new opportunities for the marketer to vary the marketing mix'.

6.2 The following are some examples of the use of ICT in the marketing mix.

Product

- www.Barbie.com has games online that involve styling the dolls. The most popular choices are fed through to new product development.
- Product information can be provided by analysing consumer queries. EasyJet has a detailed set of FAQ's, compiled from the hundreds of thousands of online questions it receives.
- Outline information may itself be the product, eg with online databases or access to information via mobile phones.

Price

- In theory, prices are more easily compared between many suppliers using the Internet.
- Offering differential pricing for products purchased over the Internet has become commonplace. EasyJet offered a £5 discount on flights booked online.

Place

- The Internet and mobile telephone technology has enabled worldwide and remote access to products and services.
- E-commerce and m-commerce empower customers to order, pay for and monitor the delivery of products themselves: a form of direct marketing, cutting out layers of the supply chain.

Promotion

- We looked in detail at the Internet as a promotional tool in Chapter 13.

Marketing at Work

The web division of Sainsbury's has launched a kitchen appliance shop which it claims is part of a strategy to move further into non-food online retail.

The new channel can be accessed through the Sainsbury's To You site and offers a database of 4,000 product lines.

'Supermarkets have changed, becoming more of a one-stop shop,' said online director Toby Anderson. 'We plan to turn Sainsbury's online store into more of a general retail business. The web division has elastic walls and we're able to provide a wider product range.'

Sainsbury's aims to offer lower prices than rival retailers, and promises to deliver goods in five to seven days.

'The range will only be available online so we'll have lower overheads and we're prepared to accept a lower profit margin,' said Anderson.

New Media Age, 5 March 2004

6.3 The **service** elements of the marketing mix are as important in the virtual world as they are in the physical world.

6.4 The **People** element of the marketing mix refers to the how an organisations' staff interact with customers and other stakeholders. Part of the consideration for the people element of the mix is the tactics by which their jobs can be automated.

- **Autoresponders**. These automatically generate a response when an e-mail is received.
- **E-mail notification**. Automatically generated to update customers on the status of their order.
- **Call-back facility**. Customers fill in their phone number on a form and specify a convenient time to be contacted.
- **Frequently Asked Questions** (FAQ).
- **On site search engines**. These help customers find what they're looking for quickly.

6.5 **Interactivity** is essential when considering ICT and the extended marketing mix.

Process	Speed of website access, via search engines Fast access to related links Stable website that does not break down Ease of navigation Tailor banner advertisements to customer needs
Physical evidence	Design and layout of the website Content and pictures easy to understand
People	Interactivity via personalised e-mail People using the site should be encouraged to leave their names and contact details.

6.6 In addition, physical evidence in the form of *printable* confirmations and vouchers may be important particularly for less accustomed users, who feel insecure with 'virtual' records of transactions.

Marketing at Work

The extended marketing mix adds a further three 'Ps' (people, process and physical evidence) to the standard marketing mix that are important elements of marketing services. Many products have a service element and it is this that helps differentiate them from their competitors. Mobile phone companies innovate to gain a period of competitive advantage.

New mobile phone products add complexity to an already confusing product market, making it difficult for consumers to evaluate alternatives. Therefore, **salespeople** are an essential source of information for consumers buying a mobile phone. Most consumers have some knowledge of how mobile phones work, but it is a product that is currently undergoing enormous technical development so the benefits need to be carefully explained.

The **process of purchase**, paying for calls and the potential cost of usage also needs to be easy to understand. Many consumers prefer a simpler system that they can easily understand, and therefore budget for, rather than a complex package that is difficult to evaluate even though it may be potentially cheaper. Some packages attempt to clarify exactly what the consumer will be paying for, and what the main benefits are, so they can readily take advantage of these.

Physical evidence includes all the paperwork that is issued to mobile phone users. In terms of monthly packages this might be a monthly bill. It is important that this is clear and concise so customers can readily identify the advantages that they signed up for.

(Adapted from CIM material)

Action Programme 6

How could a company use the Internet to:

■ Undertake market research?	
■ Generate sales leads?	
■ Offer after-sales support?	
■ Improve staff performance (and thereby customer satisfaction)?	

6.7 In summary, here are some ideas to consider: Figure 14.1.

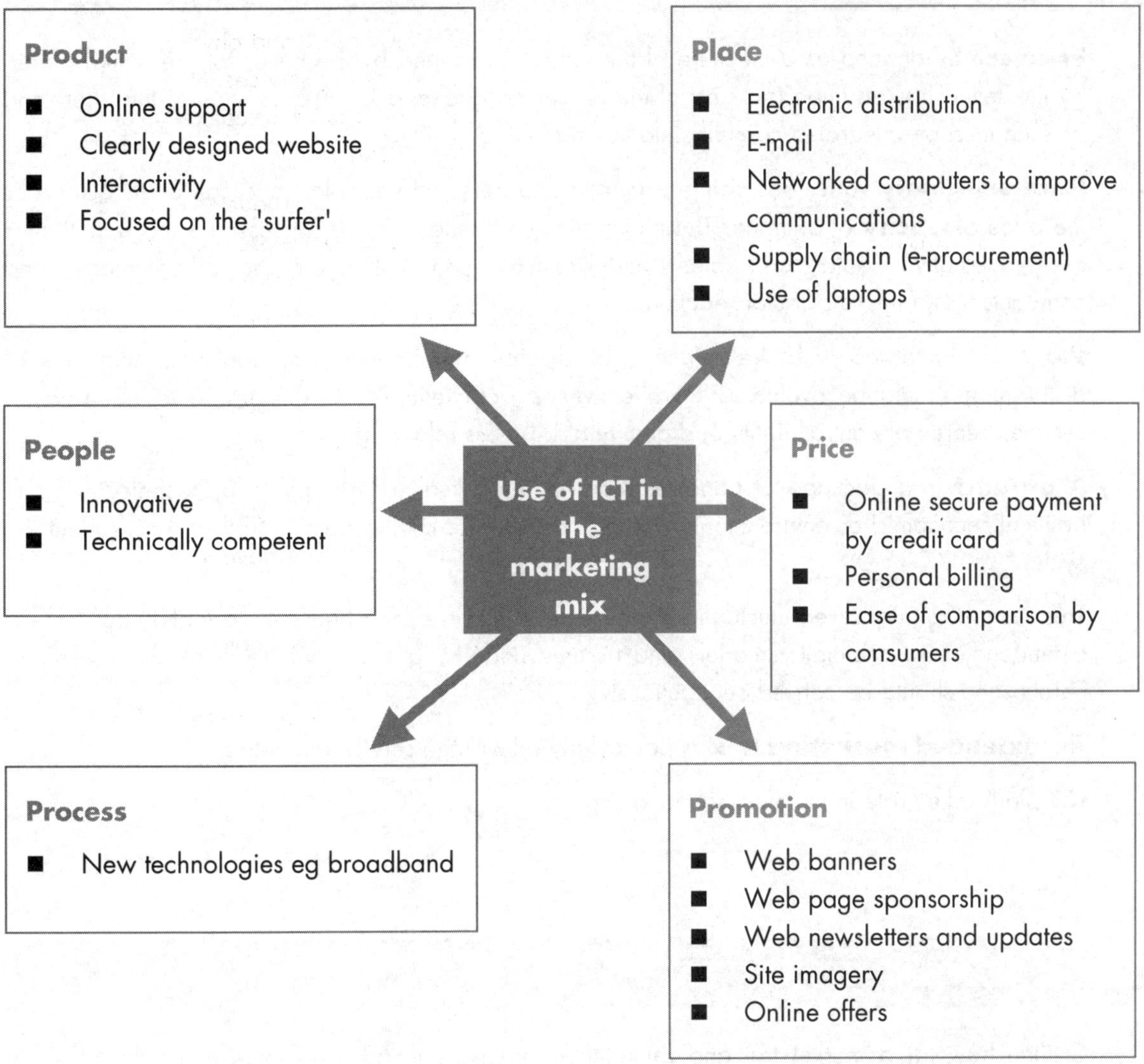

Figure 14.1: The cybermarketing mix

Exam Tip

There will invariably (December 2002, June 2003, December 2003) be a question such as: *'How can the firm use ICT to ...?'* Like all questions on this paper, you need to:

- Broaden your thinking – to include ICT applications in all 7Ps of the mix and all aspects of ICT (Internet, mobile phone, SMS, fax, digital TV/radio, database interrogation)
- Narrow your thinking – to answer the purpose set, in the context given.

As usual, a mnemonic may help to marshal your thoughts. (The examiner recommends Smith and Chaffy's Ss: 'Speak, Sell, Serve, Save, Sizzle' – if this doesn't ring a bell, see Action Programme 7 of Chapter 13.) However, it cannot substitute for contextualisation/application! Make practical, cost-effective, tactical proposals.

Chapter Roundup

- **Price** can be defined as a measure of the value exchanged by the buyer for the value offered by the seller. It is an important part of the perceived quality and differentiation of the offer, and as such must be integrated carefully into the marketing mix.
- **Price sensitivity** varies according to market and personal variables, and can be measured as the price **elasticity** of demand. The effect of price changes can be assessed using quantitative and qualitative data on sales performance, contribution, consumer attitudes and competitor/supplier/distributor reactions.
- **Place** is concerned with the selection of distribution channels and logistics. Channels of distribution should be evaluated for effectiveness, efficiency and economy, level of customer service, degree of controllability and quality of business relationship.
- A **product** is a package of benefits. Product trends may be prompted by technical, social, political, economic or environmental factors, as well as by the progression of the product life cycle.
- Trend analysis may reveal fluctuations over time and correlation between variables, but there is a tendency to over-simplify models and assume underlying trends where there may be none. Forecasting should be carried out cautiously.
- The **extended marketing mix** is particularly relevant to service marketing.
- **ICT** plays a key role in the modern marketing mix.

Quick Quiz

1 Outline how (a) a market test and (b) attitude surveys can be used to evaluate the effect of pricing decisions.

2 What measures of the effectiveness of a distribution channel might you consider?

3 What factors are prompting widespread changes in distribution methods?

4 How can product performance be monitored?

5 Give an example of product trends prompted by each of the PEST factors.

6 How can consumer response to a new product be pre-tested?

7 Explain the terms 'inseparability', 'intangibility' and 'perishability' as applied to service marketing.

8 What measures should be considered to manage (a) people, and (b) processes for consistent customer service?

9 Give examples of how ICT can be used in the marketing mix.

Now try Question 14 in the Question Bank

Action Programme Review

1 Quantity sold has gone down by 200,000 units, representing £64,000 of sales revenue. However, *contribution* by Product X is as follows.

Year 200X 1,300,000 x (0.28 - 0.16) = £156,000

Year 200Y 1,100,000 x (0.32 - 0.16) = £176,000

An increase of £20,000 in contribution

2 (a) A price reduction may mean: the item is about to be superseded by a later model; the item has some fault and is not selling well; the firm is in financial trouble and may not stay in business to supply future parts/service; the price may come down even further, so it will pay to wait; the quality has been reduced.

(b) A price increase may mean: the item is 'hot' and may be unobtainable unless bought soon; the item represents unusually good value; the seller is greedy and is charging what the traffic will bear.

3 The Needle Works' current distribution system relies entirely on its retail store. This functions well within its geographical area and market: it is the largest space of its kind used in craft retail, carries a wide range of stock, and is regarded as a kind of 'superstore' in the market. The premises are perceived as a 'quality' setting, and encourage customer re-visit. As far as we know, there are no problems involved in inventory, transportation or warehousing: The Needle Works controls all these stages of the distribution process.

However, there is a major shortcoming in the failure of the system to reach the wider geographical market for its products and services - which obviously exist, given the visitor/tourist sales. The Needle Works needs to consider

(a) mail order; direct selling through a catalogue of its products and services
(b) Internet promotion and/or selling.

With a warehouse of its own (the capacity of which would need to be evaluated) and an efficient EPOS system in place, attention would need to be given to postage/freight costs of sending products direct to consumers, plus the capacity and training of staff to handle the increased volume and information requirements of orders. The catalogue and website would need to be designed and produced, but the costs are likely to be minimal compared to increased orders. The Needle Works could retain control over its image for quality and personal service, and provide the specialist information it may not trust to intermediaries.

4 You would be fairly pleased that your brand was perceived as one of the strongest available. You would, however, worry slightly that people found it harsh to the touch: people who want a soft tissue, and are less worried about strength, are presumably buying Brands A, B or C. You would also be a bit concerned that people see little to choose between your Brand X and competing Brands Y and Z: it may come down to price on the supermarket shelves. However, you would be delighted to see that a great opportunity exists for a soft and strong toilet tissue: there is no competition there at the moment, and if people are buying Brand A for its softness, how much more eagerly they will buy Brand X if it were sold on 'softness - with strength'!

5 (a) A photo or video of the activity is a common one, or perhaps merchandise such as a T-shirt or baseball cap.

(b) A map or brochure, guide book or souvenir.

(c) An itinerary or ticket.

(d) A rental schedule, reminder card, customer card.

6

■ Undertake market research	■ Create an online focus group
■ Generate sales leads	■ Channel all website enquiries to the sales team
■ Offer after-sales support	■ Respond promptly to enquiries – set up a page featuring FAQs
■ Improve staff performance (and thereby customer satisfaction)	■ Set up online (via intranet) product information, to make sure all staff know about products and services

Answers to Quick Quiz

1 See (c) and (d) of Paragraph 2.8.

2 Effectiveness; efficiency and economy; level of service; degree of control; degree of co-operation or conflict.

3 Electronic data interchange; branding; information gathering (see Paragraph 3.10)

4 A full list is given in Paragraph 4.4.

5 Political: disposable income, tax. Environment: green sympathies, protection of the natural world. Social: fashions and must-haves, or ethical concerns. Technological: ease of production, range of possibilities.

6 Pre-testing should aim to replicate the real use of the product as much as possible with a prototype. Blind testing is an alternative.

7 Inseparability: the service cannot be separated from the service provider. Intangibility: lack of physical substance; Perishability: the opportunity for the service exists in time and if not used, is lost.

8 People: see the list of issues in Paragraph 5.4. Processes: a list of issues is given in Paragraph 5.6.

9 See Paragraphs 6.2, 6.5 and 6.7 for ideas.

Part E

Administering the marketing budget (and evaluating results)

15 Understanding Marketing Budgets

Chapter Topic List	
1	Setting the scene
2	Marketing budgets
3	Administration of the budget
4	Flexible budgets
5	Accuracy of budgets
6	Responsibility accounting
7	Computers and budgeting

Learning Outcomes

☑ Calculate and justify budgets for marketing mix decisions

☑ Apply planning techniques to a range of marketing tasks and activities

Syllabus References

☑ Demonstrate an ability to manipulate numbers in a marketing context

☑ Explain the process used for setting a budget

Key Concepts Introduced

- Marketing budget
- Principal budget factor
- Flexible budget
- Responsibility accounting

1 Setting the scene

Exam Tip

The senior examiner has said that he does not want this section of the syllabus to strike terror into the hearts of students and lecturers. You do need to have an appreciation of costs, how they are apportioned, and how cost effective are marketing activities. As such, basic manipulation of figures is essential. You may need to present a budget for a proposed promotional exercise.

1.1 Businesses must concentrate on their objectives if they are to be successful. Having established a long-term corporate plan, management should develop a co-ordinated short-term plan which will steer the business towards long-term goals. This is usually done using **budgeting**, a process which draws together the necessary actions and co-ordinates the activities of management, with a **master budget** as an end result. We will consider the process of budgeting in this chapter, with a focus on the marketing budget.

1.2 The organisation should gain from both the actual **preparation** and from the budget itself. Budgets are the concrete components of what is known as a **budgetary control system**. Such a system essentially ensures communication, co-ordination and control within an organisation and we will also be studying the control function of a budget.

1.3 We finish the chapter with a brief consideration of **flexible budgets** and the importance of budget accuracy. Both these concepts are strongly influenced by the fact that conditions change and budgets may have to change with them. A strong local campaign by a competitor, for example, may require you to change your priorities away from national advertising and match their local focus.

1.4 **Responsibility accounting** is the recognition that the marketing department is one of several units in an organisation, and that costs relevant to marketing activities will be traced to the managers concerned, who will be held responsible for them. No organisation can afford to squander its resources.

1.5 On completion of this chapter, you should be able to:

- understand how budgets are compiled and administered
- describe other sources of data for the budgeting process
- understand what is meant by the term 'flexible budget'
- understand the importance of budget accuracy and responsibility
- appreciate the role that computers play in the budget process

2 Marketing budgets

Key Concept

A **marketing budget** is a financial plan for a defined period of time which will include planned expenditure and revenues connected with marketing activities.

The purpose of budgetary control systems

2.1 **Communication**, **co-ordination** and **control** are general objectives of budgetary control systems. Specific objectives include the following.

(a) **To ensure the achievement of the organisation's objectives**

Objectives for the organisation as a whole, and for the marketing department as a unit within the organisation, are set. Quantified expressions of these objectives are then drawn up as targets to be achieved.

(b) **To compel planning**

This is probably the most important feature of a budgetary planning and control system. Planning forces management to look ahead, to set out detailed plans for achieving the targets for each department, operation and each manager and to anticipate problems.

(c) **To communicate ideas and plans**

A formal system is necessary to ensure that each person affected by the plans is aware of what he or she is supposed to be doing.

(d) **To co-ordinate activities**

The activities of different departments of the organisation need to be coordinated. This concept of co-ordination implies, for example, that the production budget should be based on sales expectations.

(e) **To provide a framework for responsibility accounting**

Budgetary planning and control systems require that managers are made responsible for the achievement of their budget targets. For the marketing manager, this is likely to mean that he or she must not overspend!

(f) **To establish a system of control**

Control over actual performance is provided by the comparisons of actual results against the budget. Departures from budget can then be investigated.

(g) **To motivate employees to improve their performance**

The interest and commitment of employees can be retained via a system of feedback of actual results, which lets them know how well or badly they are performing.

Marketing budgets

2.2 The overall marketing budget is made up of a number of **individual budgets** that relate to individual plans associated with **different marketing activities and functions**. If the marketer can estimate the benefits – financial and otherwise – that a particular investment will bring then the feasibility of going ahead with that plan can be assessed.

2.3 Following an activity, marketers should **evaluate** the plan and determine whether it should be repeated or not. Any promotional activity that is planned takes place in the future, and it is possible that hidden costs may emerge, or the situation change so that the plan is not implemented as expected. The evaluation process should investigate whether any increased costs could have been prevented, or whether the activity was not as **viable** as initial calculations identified.

Marketing at Work

'The marketing and advertising budget is the first to be raided when a company's business targets are not being met, finds a survey of 100 finance directors from large companies, commissioned by the Institute of Practitioners in Advertising and consultants KPMG.

Those questioned placed marketing and advertising top of the list for cuts when a company is under pressure, ahead of human resources, training, research and development and information technology.

The survey indicates that marketing expenditure has not increased in line with company turnover: 79 per cent of those questioned said turnover had increased, while only 30 per cent had increased marketing budgets. It also seems that 18 per cent did not know whether marketing expenditure in their companies had grown or not.

For those marketing directors who are getting fatter budgets, the days of automatic rises appear to be over. 'Zero base budgeting' - arguing from first principles each time - is now employed by half of all companies. Finance directors are also commonly involved in discussions about marketing and advertising each month.

The marketing plan

2.4 The marketing **plan** consists of several inter-related decisions.

(a) **Sales targets**: these must be set for each product and each sales division (with sub-targets also set for sales regions, sales areas and individual salesmen). Sales targets may be referred to as **sales quotas**.

(b) The **total marketing budget** must be set.

(c) Given an overall marketing budget, **resources must be allocated**.

- **Salaries** of salespeople
- **Above-the-line** expenditure (advertising)
- **Below-the-line** expenditure (sales promotion items, price reduction allowances)

(d) The overall sales target set by top management will incorporate sales price decisions, but there is likely to be an element of choice in the pricing decision. In other words, top management will decide on a 'rough pricing zone' and a specific price within this zone will be fixed later.

(e) Expenditure on marketing will also be allocated to **different products or services** within the organisation's range. Some products might justify additional marketing expenditure whereas others, nearing the end of their life cycle, may lose a part of their previous allocation.

The marketing budget

2.5 There are three types of budget planning for a marketing budget, depending on how the organisation is managed.

(a) **Top-down planning** involves the setting of goals for lower management by higher management.

(b) **Bottom-up planning** exists where employees set their own goals and submit them to higher management for approval.

(c) '**Goals down-plans up**' planning is a mixture of the two styles, whereby top management sets overall goals and employees lower in the organisation hierarchy then set plans for achieving those goals. This type of planning is well suited to the formulation of sales budgets.

Sales budgets

2.6 Budgeting for **sales revenue** and **selling costs** is plagued with uncertainty. The variables are so many and so difficult to estimate, even within a wide tolerance (largely because of competitive action and changing consumer habits and tastes), that both setting budgets and budgetary control on the marketing side are different from the more 'mechanical' approach which can be adopted with other budgets.

2.7 A sales and marketing budget is necessary for the following reasons.

(a) It is an element of the **overall strategic plan** of the business (the master budget) which brings together all the activities of the business.

(b) Where sales and other non-production costs are a large part of total costs, it is **financially prudent** to forecast, plan and control them.

(c) The uncertain nature of factors which influence selling makes the need for good forecasts and plans greater. If budgets are to be used for **control**, then where budget estimates are more uncertain, more budgetary control is necessary.

Expense budgets

2.8 Wilmshurst (1999) says that 'one of the problems often associated with advertising is that the costs are all too obvious but the gains not very clear'. He suggests that this difficulty can be minimised if **clearly quantified objectives** are set out. He gives the following examples.

1 **To produce direct sales of £100,000**, ie orders are to be received from people replying directly to the advertisement totalling this amount or more.

2 **To increase the number of people who have knowledge** of specific features of the product or the company from 15 per cent of the population to 25 per cent.

3 **To produce enquiries from genuinely interested potential customers** at a cost of not more than £9.50 per enquiry.

4 To achieve a situation where at least **60 per cent of our target audience can 'recall'** an advertisement up to two weeks after it has appeared.

2.9 **Value** objectives (such as 'increasing sales') will make it difficult to:

- Assess **whether the money was well spent** and the objective was achieved
- Produce properly and specifically **designed** advertising

2.10 Another crucial factor is 'how much do we have to spend?' This will have a fundamental influence on the type of advertising that can be carried out.

2.11 There are a number of ways of setting marketing budgets.

(a) **Percentage of sales**. Research has shown that in the UK, some marketing budgets are fixed by some rule-of-thumb, non-scientific methods, such as the following.

- A percentage of the previous year's sales
- A percentage of the budgeted annual sales
- A percentage of the previous year's profit

There is no reason, however, why marketing costs should relate directly to either total turnover or profits. Given that large amounts of expenditure may be incurred on advertising, these arbitrary guesswork systems reveal an alarming lack of proper financial control.

(b) **Competitive parity**, ie fixing marketing expenditure in relation to the expenditure incurred by competitors. (This is unsatisfactory because it presupposes that the competitor's decision must be a good one.)

(c) **The objective and task method**. The marketing task for the organisation is set and a budget is prepared which will help to ensure that this objective is achieved.

Exam Tip

Most papers require basic calculations for Part A, using numerical data given to add up costs, calculate profits and work out the cost/profit implications of changes in strategy. The examiner reminds candidates that numerical information can also be conveyed in words ('one hundred members') – and that 'per week', 'per month' or 'per year' make a great difference to calculations, depending on what is required. There is no substitute for practice in this area!

2.12 The example below shows a typical marketing cost budget. Notice that in this example only the selling and agency commission vary directly with the level of sales.

Marketing cost budget

	£
Salaries and wages of marketing staff	X
Advertising expenses	X
Travelling and distribution costs	X
Market research activities	X
Promotional activities	X
Selling and agency commission	X
	X

2.13 **Many cost items will be fixed**, although, as we can see from above, there will be some variable costs such as sales commission. We look at overheads in more detail in the next chapter. Some of the marketing budget will have to be prepared in conjunction with the sales budget since the level of sales anticipated will rely on marketing support. The balance of the budget may well be determined by the activity anticipated from new products which may be launched during the year, and which will need promotional support.

2.14 **Advertising** is an important feature of the marketing budget. The theory behind setting an advertising budget is the theory of **diminishing returns**, ie for every extra £1 of advertising spent, the company will earn an extra £x of profit. Further expenditure on advertising is justified until the marginal return £x diminishes until it is less than the amount spent in achieving it. Unfortunately, the marginal return from additional advertising cannot be measured easily in practice.

(a) Advertising is only **one aspect** of the overall marketing mix.

(b) Advertising has some **long-term effect**, which goes beyond the limits of a measurable accounting period.

(c) Where the advertising budget is fixed as a percentage of sales, **advertising costs tend to follow sales levels** and not vice versa.

2.15 Recommended practice for fixing advertising cost budgets would include the use of the following.

(a) **Empirical testing** (eg in a mail order business or in retail operations). It may be possible to measure the effect of advertising on sales by direct observation.

(b) **Mathematical models** using data about media and consumer characteristics, desired market share, and using records of past results. Regression analysis can be conducted to find out the likely cost of advertising (through several media) to achieve a given target.

2.16 As techniques for identifying market segments becomes more sophisticated (eg through the use of **marketing databases**) advertising will become less cost-efficient compared to other types of promotion, such as direct mail.

Control

2.17 Once the plan has been implemented, the task of marketing management is to control the use of resources. Aspects of control include the following.

- Comparison of actual sales against the budget
- Comparison of marketing costs against budgeted levels and actual sales
- Analysis of the profitability of individual products, and distribution outlets
- Strategic control, ie checking whether the company's objectives, products and resources are being directed towards the correct markets.

We will be looking at the evaluation of marketing decisions in Chapter 18.

2.18 The allocation of **direct selling costs** to products or type of outlet is fairly straightforward, but indirect costs must be allocated. This aspect of cost allocation should be carefully considered when deciding whether to eliminate an unprofitable expenditure from selling or distribution.

(a) The cost of distributing goods to a distant area may seem unprofitable but if, by not selling the goods in this area, there will be **unused production capacity**, the products which are produced and sold will have to bear a higher proportion of fixed costs.

(b) The allocation of fixed selling costs to products may make a product seem unprofitable, but the product may still be making a **contribution** to those fixed costs.

2.19 Eliminating unprofitable selling and distribution expenditure is sound commercial practice. If the removal of one part of selling costs relieves a company of a cost which is higher than the contribution to profit gained from it, then this part of selling activity can and should be eliminated. The unavoidable fixed costs of production as well as selling and distribution should be taken into account in any such decision.

Action Programme 1

Does your organisation operate a budgeting system? Talk to various managers to find out what functions budgets perform in your organisation.

3 Administration of the budget

3.1 Having seen why organisations prepare budgets, we will now turn our attention to the administrative procedures that ensure that the budget process works effectively.

Responsibility for the preparation of budgets

3.2 Managers responsible for preparing budgets should ideally be the managers (and their subordinates) who are responsible for carrying out the budget. For example, the marketing manager should draft the marketing expenditure budget and marketing overhead cost centre budget.

Budget committee

3.3 The co-ordination and administration of budgets is usually the responsibility of a budget committee (with the managing director as chairman). Every part of the organisation should be represented on the committee, so there should be a representative from sales, production and marketing. Functions of the budget committee include the following.

- **Co-ordination** of the preparation of budgets, which includes the issue of the budget manual
- Issuing of **timetables** for the preparation of functional budgets
- Allocation of **responsibilities** for the preparation of functional budgets
- Provision of **information** to assist in the preparation of budgets
- **Communication** of final budgets to the appropriate managers
- **Comparison** of actual results with budget and the investigation of variances

- **Continuous assessment** of the budgeting and planning process, in order to improve the planning and control function

Action Programme 2

The Needle Works

Discuss the role of a budget committee during the preparation phase of a new annual budget for The Needle Works.

The budget preparation timetable

3.4 Let us now look at the steps involved in the preparation of a budget for The Needle Works. The step-by-step approach described here is indicative of the steps followed by many organisations. The budget committee may meet several times before an organisation's budget is finally agreed.

Step 1 Communicating details of the budget policy and budget guidelines

The long-term plan is the starting point for the preparation of the annual budget. Managers of the Needle Works responsible for preparing the budget must be aware of the way it is affected by the long-term plan so that it becomes part of the process of meeting the organisation's objectives. For example, if the long-term plan calls for a more aggressive pricing policy, the budget must take this into account.

Step 2 Determining the factor that restricts output

Key Concept

The **principal budget factor** (or **key budget factor or limiting budget factor**) is the factor that limits an organisation's performance for a given period and is often the starting point in budget preparation.

In most organisations the principal budget factor is sales demand. The Needle Works will be restricted from making and selling more and more of its products, because there would eventually be no further demand at a price which would be acceptable to the company. The interface between sales and production is fundamental since the function of the sales and marketing department is to provide for the needs of the customer whilst maximising the benefit to the business. If sales are the principal budget factor then the production manager can only prepare his budget after the sales budget is complete. A company may also have limited distribution and selling resources, for example.

Management may not know what the limiting budget factor is until a draft budget has been attempted. The first draft budget will therefore usually begin with the preparation of a draft sales budget.

There are occasions when budgeting does not begin with the sales budget, because there is a shortage of a key resource which prevents the business from selling as much as it could. For example, there could be a shortage of skilled labour, of raw materials or of machine capacity. In these situations there is a **limiting budget factor**. Budgeting would start by looking at the problem of how to maximise profits within the resource constraints.

Step 3 Preparation of the sales budget

We have already established that, for many organisations, the principal budget factor is sales volume. The sales budget is therefore often the primary budget from which the majority of the other budgets are derived.

Before the sales budget can be prepared a **sales forecast** has to be made. Sales forecasting is complex and difficult and might involve the consideration of a number of factors for The Needle Works.

- Past sales patterns
- The economic environment
- Results of market research
- Anticipated advertising
- Pricing policies and discounts offered
- Competition
- Changing consumer taste

On the basis of the sales forecast of the organisation, a sales budget will be prepared. This may be subdivided, possible subdivisions being by product, by sales area or by management responsibility.

Step 4 Initial preparation of budgets for The Needle Works

Budget	Detail
Goods stock budget	Decides the planned increase or decrease in finished stock levels
Product sourcing budget	Stated in units of each product and is calculated as the sales budget in units plus the budgeted increase in finished goods stocks or minus the budgeted decrease in goods stocks
Budgets of resources for production and design	**Materials usage budget** is stated in quantities and perhaps cost for each type of material used. It should take into account budgeted losses in production **Labour budget or wages budget** will be expressed in hours for each staff grade and in terms of cost
Overhead cost budgets	**Production overheads** **Product sourcing overheads** **Design overheads** **Administration overheads** **Selling and distribution overheads**
Raw materials stock budget	Decides the planned increase or decrease of the level of stocks
Raw materials purchase budget	Can be prepared in quantities and value for each type of material purchased once the raw material usage requirements and the raw materials stock budget are known

Budget	Detail
Overhead absorption rate	Can be calculated once the production volumes are planned, and the overhead cost centre budgets prepared

Step 5 Negotiation of budgets with superiors

This process continues until the final budget is presented to the budget committee for approval.

Step 6 Co-ordination of budgets

Remember that it is unlikely that the execution of the above steps will be problem-free. The budgets must be reviewed in relation to one another. Such a **review may indicate that some budgets are out of balance with others and need modifying** so that they will be compatible.

Step 7 Final acceptance of the budget

When all the budgets are in harmony with one another they are summarised into a **master budget**.

Step 8 Budget review

The budgeting process does not stop once the budgets have been agreed. Actual results should be compared on a regular basis with the budgeted results. The frequency with which such comparisons are made depends very much on the organisation's circumstances and the sophistication of its control systems but it should occur at least monthly. Management should receive a report detailing the differences and should investigate the reasons for the differences. If the differences are within the control of management, corrective action should be taken to bring the reasons for the difference under control and to ensure that such inefficiencies do not occur in the future.

The differences may have occurred, however, because the budget was unrealistic to begin with or because the actual conditions did not reflect those anticipated (or could have possibly been anticipated). This would therefore invalidate the remainder of the budget.

The budget committee, who should meet periodically to evaluate the organisation's actual performance, may need to reappraise the organisation's future plans in the light of changes to anticipated conditions and to adjust the budget to take account of such changes.

The important point to note is that the budgeting process does not end for the current year once the budget period has begun: budgeting should be seen as a continuous and dynamic process.

4 Flexible budgets

4.1 The master budget prepared before the beginning of the budget period is known as the **fixed budget**. The term 'fixed' means the following.

(a) The budget is prepared on the basis of an **estimated volume** of production sales, but no plans are made for the event that **actual volumes** may differ from **budgeted volumes**.

(b) When actual volumes of production and sales during a period become known, a fixed budget is not adjusted to the new levels of activity.

4.2 A **flexible budget** is designed to change to relate to the actual volumes in a period. Flexible budgets may be used in one of two ways.

Key Concept

A **flexible budget**, by recognising different cost patterns, is designed to change as volume of output or sales changes.

(a) **At the planning stage**. For example, suppose that The Needle Works expects to sell 10,000 tapestry kits during the next year. A fixed budget would be prepared on the basis of these expected volumes. However, if the company thinks that sales might be as low as 8,000 units or as high as 12,000 units, it may prepare flexible budgets, at volumes of, say 8,000, 9,000, 11,000 and 12,000 units. This enables contingency plans to be drawn up.

(b) **Retrospectively**. At the end of each month or year, flexible budgets can be used to examine actual results achieved. Flexible budgets are an essential factor in **budgetary control**.

(i) Management needs to know how good or bad actual performance has been. There must be a yardstick against which actual performance can be measured.

(ii) Business is **dynamic**, and actual volumes of output cannot be expected to conform exactly to the fixed budget.

(iii) For useful control information, it is necessary to compare actual results **at the level of activity achieved** against the results that would have been expected at this level of activity, which are shown by the flexible budget.

Action Programme 3

Explain what is meant by the terms 'fixed budget' and 'flexible budget' and state the main objective of preparing flexible budgets.

Example: flexible budgets

4.3 Suppose that The Needle Works expects sales of kits during the next year to be 9,000 units. The following historical records of cost are available.

Units of sales	*Cost of sales*
9,800	£444,000
7,700	£381,000

Management is not certain that the estimate of sales is correct because they believe that competitors are planning promotional campaigns that may reduce The Needle Works' sales by as much as 1,000 units. On the other hand, there is every chance that the promotions may backfire and attract customers to The Needle Works, pushing sales up by 1,000 units. They have therefore asked you for flexible budgets to be prepared at sales levels of 8,000 and 10,000 units. The sales price per unit has been fixed at £50.

4.4 If we assume that within the range 8,000 to 10,000 units of sales, all costs are fixed or variable, the fixed and flexible budgets would be based on the estimate of fixed and variable costs.

		£
Total cost of 9,800 units	=	444,000
Total cost of 7,700 units	=	381,000
Variable cost of 2,100 units	=	63,000

The variable cost per unit is therefore (£63,000 ÷ 2,100) = £30

		£
Total cost of 9,800 units	=	444,000
Variable cost of 9,800 units (9,800 × £30)	=	294,400
Fixed costs	=	150,000

4.5 The fixed budgets and flexible budgets might now be prepared as follows.

	Flexible budget 8,000 units	*Master budget 9,000 units*	*Flexible budget 10,000 units*
	£	£	£
Sales (× £50)	400,000	450,000	500,000
Variable costs (× £30)	240,000	270,000	300,000
Contribution	160,000	180,000	200,000
Fixed costs	150,000	150,000	150,000
Profit	10,000	30,000	50,000

5 Accuracy of budgets

5.1 It is important that budgets should be as **accurate as possible**. Failure to present a sufficiently accurate budget would cause problems.

- Plans will be made on **false assumptions** of costs and profits
- Comparisons of actual results with the budget would give **meaningless information**

5.2 There are many practical difficulties in attempting to plan accurately, some of which cannot be overcome. Unnecessary inaccuracies, however, should be avoided. Seasonal variations should be carefully allowed for and individual cost items carefully budgeted.

Zero base budgeting

5.3 One way in which many organisations ensure that inefficiencies are not concealed by the practice of 'adding on a bit' is by introducing **zero-base budgeting**. This was very well defined by Morden (1986).

> 'Zero-base budgeting (ZBB) is a formalised system of budgeting for the activities of an enterprise *as if each activity were being performed for the first time,* ie from a zero base. Essentially, a number of alternative levels of provision for each activity are identified, costed and evaluated.

ZBB is based on the belief that management should be required to justify *existing* activities in exactly the same way as new proposals. Thus, established activities will have to be compared with alternative applications of resources.

Zero-based budgeting takes away the *implied right* of existing activities to receive a continued allocation of resources.'

5.4 Up to 50% of large companies now operate some form of ZBB and are particularly likely to require it of business areas where measures of effectiveness are not easy, as is often the case with advertising expenditure.

6 Responsibility accounting

6.1 In **budgetary control** managers are held responsible for investigating differences between budgeted and actual results, and are then expected to take corrective action or amend the plan. Such a process is part of what is known as **responsibility accounting**.

Key Concept

Responsibility accounting is the recognition of decentralised units throughout an organisation and the tracing of costs (and revenues, assets and liabilities where pertinent) to the individual managers responsible for them.

6.2 Responsibility accounting distinguishes between **controllable costs** and **uncontrollable** costs.

6.3 Brand managers will be responsible for a level of expenditure which is agreed as necessary to support the sales of a product. Part of the brand manager's bonus may include an element based on sales of the brand which his budget is intended to support, even though this will depend partly on external factors over which he will have very little control.

Responsibility centres

6.4 Responsibility accounting aims to provide reports so that every manager is made aware of all the items which are within his area of authority. There are three types of responsibility centre.

Cost centres

6.5 A **cost centre** is a location or function in respect of which costs may be ascertained and related to cost units for control purposes. A brand manager may be considered a cost centre if he has responsibility for all marketing support for that brand. As marketing manager for The Needle Works, you will have total responsibility for all marketing output as it is such a small department.

Profit centres

6.6 A **profit centre** is any division of an organisation to which both revenues and costs are assigned, so that the profitability of the sub-unit may be measured. These divisions will have their **own products** and their **own markets** and are hence self-contained businesses.

Investment centres

6.7 Where a divisional manager of a company is allowed some discretion about the amount of **investment undertaken** by the division, the profit earned must be related to the amount of capital invested.

7 Computers and budgeting

7.1 Budgeting used to be a dreaded task. You can imagine the complexity of the budgetary process which even small organisations have to undergo. Remember, also, that it is highly unlikely that the execution of the steps in the process will be problem free. Budgets will be out of balance with each other and will require modification so that they are compatible. The revision of one budget may well lead to the revision of all of the budgets. The manual preparation of a master budget and a cash budget in the real world would therefore be daunting to say the very least.

7.2 Computers, however, can take the hard work out of budgeting: a computerised system will have a number of basic advantages over a manual system.

7.3 Budgeting is usually computerised using either a computer program written specifically for the organisation or by a commercial spreadsheet package. Both methods of computerisation of the budgeting process will involve a mathematical model which represents the real world in terms of financial values. The model will consist of several, or many, interrelated variables, a variable being an item in the model which has a value. Once the planning model has been constructed, the same model can be used week by week, month after month, or year after year, simply by changing the values of the variables to produce new results.

7.4 A major advantage of budget models is the ability to evaluate different options and carry out **'what if' analysis.** By changing the value of certain variables (for example, increasing the annual pay award to the workforce) management are able to assess the effect of potential changes in their environment.

7.5 Computerised models can also incorporate actual results, period by period, and carry out the necessary calculations to **produce budgetary control reports**.

7.6 The use of a model also allows the budget for the remainder of the year to be adjusted once it is clear that the circumstances on which the budget was originally based have changed.

Spreadsheets

7.7 Most organisations do not have budgeting programs written for them but use **standard spreadsheet packages**. The idea behind a spreadsheet is that the model builder should construct a model in rows and columns format.

7.8 Advantages of using spreadsheet packages for budgeting are as follows.

(a) Spreadsheet packages have a facility to perform **'what if' calculations** at great speed. For example, the consequences throughout the organisation of sales growth per month of nil, 1/2%, 1%, 1 1/2% and so on can be calculated at the touch of a button.

(b) Preparing budgets may be complex. Budgets may need to go through several drafts. Spreadsheets aid this process in that one or two figures can be changed and then the **computer will automatically make all the computational changes to the other figures**.

(c) A spreadsheet model will **ensure that the preparation of the functional budgets and master budget is co-ordinated**. Data and information from the functional budgets will be automatically fed through to the master budget model, ensuring that the master budget is a true reflection of the subsidiary budgets.

Chapter Roundup

- A **budgetary control system** ensures communication, co-ordination and control within an organisation.
- A **marketing budget** is a statement for a defined period of time which includes planned income and expenditure connected with marketing activities.
- The **marketing plan** consists of several inter-related decisions – sales targets, salaries of sales people, above-the-line and below-the-line expenditure.
- **Data** for the budgeting process comes from both internal and external sources
- It is very important that budgets (especially the sales budget) should be **reasonable** , **realistic** and **accurate**. Seasonal variations, for example, should be recognised.
- A **flexible budget**, by recognising different patterns of costs and sales, is designed to change as volume of output or sales changes.
- **Zero-base budgeting** is a system of budgeting for the activities of an enterprise as if each activity were being performed for the first time.
- Budgeting nowadays is usually **computerised** by using either a computer program or a spreadsheet package.

Quick Quiz

1 What are the general objectives of a budgetary control system?

2 Describe some ways of setting marketing budgets.

3 What is the theory of diminishing returns?

4 What are the functions of a budget committee?

5 What is a flexible budget?

6 What is a cost centre?

7 What are the advantages of using spreadsheet packages for budgeting?

Now try Question 15 in the Question Bank

Action Programme Review

1 This is a useful exercise in helping you to understand the importance of budgets and to recognise that resources are limited and must be allocated carefully.

2 A budget committee usually comprises a chairman (possibly the managing director) and the heads of the various functional areas of the organisation. In The Needle Works the budget committee might consist of the General Manager, the head of administration and the various representatives of sales, production and marketing (you).

Functions of the budget committee include the following.

- Co-ordination of the preparation of budgets, which includes the issue of the budget manual
- Issuing of timetables for the preparation of budgets
- Allocation of responsibilities for the preparation of budgets
- Provision of information to assist in the preparation of budgets
- Reconciliation of divergent views
- Communication of final budgets to the appropriate managers
- Comparison of actual results with budget
- Continuous assessment of the budgeting and planning process

The preparation of a budget may take weeks or months, and the budget committee may meet several times before the master budget is finally agreed. Resource budgets and cost centre budgets prepared in draft may need to be amended many times over as a consequence of discussions between departments, changes in market conditions or reversals of decisions by management during the course of budget preparation.

3 Fixed budgets are based on estimated volumes of production and sales but do not include any provision for the event that actual volumes may differ from budget.

A flexible budget is designed to change so as to relate to actual volumes achieved. This has two advantages.

(a) At the planning stage, it may be helpful to know what the effects would be if the actual outcome differs from the prediction. This would enable contingency plans to be drawn up if necessary.

(b) At the end of each month or year, actual results may be compared with the flexible budget as a control procedure.

Answers to Quick Quiz

1 The key objectives are summarised in Paragraph 2.1.

2 Top-down planning; bottom-up planning; goals down-plans up.

3 Advertising expenditure generates corresponding marginal revenue only up to a certain point - after which the benefits of the outlay diminish.

4 A list of functions is given in Paragraph 3.3.

5 A flexible budget, by recognising different cost patterns, is designed to change as volume or output or sales changes.

6 A cost centre is a location or function in respect of which costs may be ascertained and related to cost units for control purposes.

7 By automating the process; a master budget can be automatically updated by linked departmental budgets, scenarios can be worked out through 'what if?' queries, formulae and macros can perform consequential calculations; a standard format is easy to design which is easy to interpret.

Justifying the Budget 16

Chapter Topic List	
1	Setting the scene
2	Overheads and contribution
3	The viability of marketing opportunities

Learning Outcomes

- ☑ Make recommendations based on information obtained from multiple sources
- ☑ Calculate and justify budgets for marketing mix decisions

Syllabus References

- ☑ Demonstrate an ability to manipulate numbers in a marketing context
- ☑ Apportion fixed and overhead costs
- ☑ Explain how organisations assess the viability of opportunities, marketing initiatives and projects
- ☑ Prepare, present and justify a budget as the basis for a decision on a marketing promotion
- ☑ Make recommendations on alternative courses of action

Key Concepts Introduced

- Overhead
- Production overhead
- Administration overhead
- Selling overhead
- Distribution overhead
- Contribution
- Relevant cost

1 Setting the scene

1.1 Marketing activities are generally undertaken with a view to increasing sales and (hopefully) profits – that is why most businesses are in business! How can marketing activities 'prove' themselves? A thorny problem – marketing budgets are often the most difficult to justify and the first to be cut – but in this chapter we look at some of the ways of assessing the viability of marketing opportunities by posing some key questions that should be asked of any significant marketing investment.

1.2 A company deploys its chosen marketing mix based, among other considerations, upon decisions of cost and budget constraints. No resources are infinite and each business has to make the best use it can of the resources available to it (money, time etc). The resulting mix may produce success or failure, leading to possible revisions of distribution channels or activities.

Marketing at Work

Philip Kotler, the world's leading marketing expert, who trained as an economist and mathematician, was advised by his publishers not to include rigorous mathematical models in his classic text *Marketing Management* because marketers were perceived as deeply uninterested in numbers.

Marketing Business, Nov 2001

2 Overheads and contribution

2.1 Let us emphasise again why marketers need to have accurate and timely information on costs. The CIM's definition of marketing helps us focus on this.

> 'Marketing is the management process responsible for identifying, anticipating and satisfying customer requirements **profitably**.'

2.2 It is a fundamental part of marketing that the activity is undertaken so that **revenue less costs equals a profit**. It is important in the context of budgeting that we know what the costs are in order to perform our jobs properly.

2.3 The basic principle of cost behaviour is that as the level of activity rises, costs will usually rise. It will cost The Needle Works more to have 20,000 promotional leaflets printed than it would cost for 10,000, for example.

What are overheads?

2.4 'What a stupid question' you may be thinking to yourself, but you would be surprised by the number of students who are not 100% certain about overheads and what they are.

Key Concept

An **overhead** is the cost incurred in the course of making a product, providing a service or running a department, but which cannot be traced directly and in full to the product, service or department.

2.5 **Overheads** are actually the total of the following.

- Indirect materials
- Indirect labour
- Indirect expenses

2.6 Before we go any further let us look at one common way of categorising overheads.

- Production overhead
- Administration overhead
- Selling overhead
- Distribution overhead

Key Concepts

- **Production overhead** includes all indirect material costs, indirect wages and indirect expenses incurred in the factory from receipt of the order until its completion.
- **Administration overhead** is all indirect material costs, wages and expenses incurred in the direction, control and administration of an undertaking.
- **Selling overhead** is all indirect materials costs, wages and expenses incurred in promoting sales and retaining customers.
- **Distribution overhead** is all indirect material costs, wages and expenses incurred in making the packed product ready for despatch and delivering it to the customer.

2.7 Examples of production overhead include the following.

(a) **Indirect materials** which cannot be traced in the finished product.

- Consumable stores, eg material used in negligible amounts

(b) **Indirect wages**, meaning all wages not charged directly to a product.

- Salaries and wages of non-productive personnel in the production department, eg foremen

(c) **Indirect expenses** (other than material and labour) not charged directly to production.

- Rent, rates and insurance of a factory
- Depreciation, fuel, power, repairs and maintenance of plant, machinery and factory buildings

2.8 Examples of **administration overhead** are as follows.

(a) **Depreciation** of office administration overhead, buildings and machinery.

(b) **Office salaries**, including salaries of administrative directors, secretaries and accountants.

(c) Rent, rates, insurance, lighting, cleaning and heating of general offices, telephone and postal charges, bank charges, legal charges, audit fees.

2.9 Examples of **selling overhead** are as follows.

(a) **Printing** and **stationery**, such as catalogues and price lists.

(b) **Salaries** and **commission** of salesmen, representatives and sales department staff.

(c) **Advertising** and **sales promotion**, market research.

(d) Rent, rates and insurance of sales offices and showrooms, bad debts and collection charges, cash discounts allowed, after-sales service.

2.10 Examples of **distribution overhead** are as follows.

(a) Cost of packing cases.

(b) Wages of packers, drivers and despatch clerks.

(c) Freight and insurance charges, rent, rates, insurance and depreciation of warehouses, depreciation and running expenses of delivery vehicles.

Contribution

2.11 The principles of analysing **contribution** are set out below.

Key Concept

The level of **contribution** made by a product or portfolio of products is defined as the total sales value less the variable costs associated with the units produced. The 'contribution' is the contribution made to profits and fixed costs.

(a) **Fixed costs (such as rent) are the same**, no matter what the volume of sales and production.

- **Revenue will increase** by the sales value of the item sold
- **Costs will increase** only by the variable cost per unit
- The increase in profit will equal the **sales value minus variable costs**, defined as the amount of **contribution** earned from the item

(b) If the volume of sales **falls** by one item, the profit will fall by the amount of contribution earned from the item.

2.12 This all has a major impact on the marketing manager because of its implications to both **pricing** and **decision making**, so we will look at two simple examples.

Example

2.13 The Needle Works is considering making another product, the 'silver standard' frame, which will have a variable production cost of £11 and a sales price of £30. It also expects to spend £3 per unit on marketing the product. Fixed costs for each month will be £65,000 (administration, sales and distribution).

What is the contribution to fixed costs and the profit for the month if sales are as follows?

- 4,000 frames
- 10,000 frames
- 15,000 frames

Answer

2.14 First, we identify the variable costs and deduct them from the sales value to derive the **contribution**. We then deduct the **fixed costs** to arrive at **profit**.

	4,000 frames	*10,000 frames*	*15,000 frames*
Sales revenue	120,000	300,000	450,000
Variable costs			
Production	44,000	110,000	165,000
Marketing	12,000	30,000	45,000
Contribution	64,000	160,000	240,000
Fixed costs	65,000	65,000	65,000
(Loss)/profit	(1,000)	95,000	175,000
(Loss)/profit per unit	£(0.25)	£9.50	£11.67
Contribution per unit	£16.00	£16.00	£16.00

2.15 The conclusions which may be drawn from this example are as follows.

(a) The **profit per unit** varies at **differing levels of sales**, because the average fixed overhead cost per unit changes with the volume of output and sales.

(b) The **contribution per unit is constant** at all levels of output and sales. Total contribution increases in direct proportion to the volume of sales.

(c) The most effective way of calculating the expected profit at any level of output and sales is as follows.

- Calculate the total contribution.
- Deduct fixed costs as a period charge in order to find the profit.

(d) In our example the expected profit from the sale of 17,000 frames would be calculated as follows.

	£
Total contribution (17,000 × £16)	272,000
Less fixed costs	65,000
Profit	207,000

2.16 You should be able to see the following.

- If total contribution exceeds fixed costs, a **profit** is made.
- If total contribution exactly equals fixed costs, the activity will **break even**.

- If total contribution is less than the fixed costs, there will be a **loss**.

2.17 Costing is very relevant to your studies and in practice.

(a) You may be faced with a situation where you must decide whether in the short term to produce one of two products.

(b) You may be the brand manager for a mature product which has not increased its sales volume for the several years. How would you assess the potential benefits for the company if you increased your promotional support and reduced the price? Look at the following example.

Example

2.18 The Needle Works' next door neighbour is Kestrel Cycles Ltd. It makes one type of mountain bike in addition to a range of conventional street cycles. Unfortunately their mountain bike sales have been languishing for the past three years, and management is considering the option of spending a one-off amount of £300,000 on extra advertising and dropping the unit selling price by £20 per bike to £150 for the coming year.

The bike has a variable product cost of £90 and current marketing costs of £5 per unit, which would continue to be spent. Sales for the coming year are expected to be 20,000 units with total fixed costs at last year's level of £250,000. The sales volume has been estimated by the marketing manager as a direct consequence of the increased advertising expenditure and reduced selling price. Sales last year were only 4,500 units.

2.19 Should management proceed? The analysis could be presented as follows.

	Last year	*Coming year*
	£	£
Sales revenue	765,000	3,000,000
Variable costs		
Production	405,000	1,800,000
Marketing	22,500	100,000
Contribution	337,500	1,100,000
Fixed costs	250,000	250,000
Extra marketing expenditure	-	300,000
Profit	87,500	550,000
Profit per unit	19.44	27.50
Contribution per unit	75.00	55.00

2.20 As can be seen from the analysis, contribution per unit has decreased by £20 because of the decreased selling price. Profit per unit has increased because the overall increased revenues have more than compensated for the increased advertising costs. On the face of it, management will want to go ahead, but they may wish to see more evidence of the achievability of the sales forecast. The fact that break-even level (where contribution equals fixed costs) is now $\frac{£550,000}{55.00} = 10,000$ units to be sold may give cause for concern, as this represents a sales increase of 122% on last year. If sales 'only' doubled in the coming year (respectable enough in itself), then the company would make a loss on its mountain bikes, calculated as (9,000 units x £55 contribution) – 550,000 = £(55,000) loss.

Action Programme 1

The Needle Works

The Needle Works budget committee has asked you to allocate the marketing budget for next year. Albert Smith has already decided that the company can afford to spend £70,000 (not including your salary) on marketing costs in the coming year: 'It is 2.7% of our budgeted sales of £2.6 million, which seems a reasonable proportion. Anyway, we cannot afford to spend more.'

You are not entirely happy with this 'all-you-can-afford' approach but recognise that Albert Smith's approach to marketing should become more sophisticated when you can prove the effectiveness of the marketing budget.

Based upon some costings you have undertaken, you decide upon the following activities for the coming year.

Activity	Months	Cost per month
Newspaper advertising	January - December	£750
Local radio	January - December	£1,000
Promotional coupons	February and August	£5,000
Garden party at old people's home	July	£2,000
Discount sale	January - February	£10,000
Knitting class party	April	£2,500
Posters and point of sale material	January - December	£500
Stand at London Craft Show	October	£4,500
Frames giveaway competition	March	£4,000

Present these numbers on the following grid for submission to the budget committee.

THE NEEDLE WORKS MARKETING BUDGET

ACTIVITY	Jan £	Feb £	Mar £	Apr £	May £	Jun £	**Half 1 Total £**	Jul £	Aug £	Sept £	Oct £	Nov £	Dec £	**Half 2 Total £**	**Year Total £**
Newspaper Advertising															
Local Radio															
Stand at London Craft Show															
Garden Party															
Class Party															
Promotional Coupons															
Discount Sale															
Posters, leaflets & point of sale material															
Frame giveaway Competition															
Total															

3 The viability of marketing opportunities

3.1 Marketing managers must remember that their decisions will have **financial implications**. It helps to be able to identify what the various types of decision facing a marketing manager might be.

(a) **Routine planning decisions**, for example budgeting - as we have been looking at in the most recent part of this text. Budgeting decisions commonly analyse costs and revenues. They are also often concerned with how to make the best use of scarce resources.

(b) **Short-run problem decisions**, typically, unforeseen 'one-off' special decisions of a non-recurring nature, where the costs and benefits are all obtained within a relatively short period. For example, what price should be quoted in the tender for a contract?

(c) **Longer-range decisions**, meaning decisions made once and reviewed infrequently, but which are intended to provide a continuing solution to a continuing or recurring problem. They include decisions about selling and distribution policies. For example, should goods be sold through middlemen or direct to customers? What type of customer should the sales force attempt to attract? What should the company's discount policies be? Should a new product or service be launched?

(d) **Control decisions**. For example, should disappointing performance be investigated, given that the benefits expected must exceed the costs of investigation and control?

3.2 **Pricing decisions** are sometimes put into a category of their own, but pricing decisions span most of the range of decision categories above: routine pricing decisions are made at periodic price reviews, 'one-off' short-run pricing decisions might be made for specific jobs or contracts or to dispose of surplus stocks, long-range decisions about price must be made for services, products or product ranges and some control decisions might have to be made about prices (for example, are excessive discounts being allowed?).

Relevant costs

3.3 The costs which should be used when assessing marketing opportunities are often referred to as **relevant costs**.

Key Concept

A **relevant cost** is a **future incremental cash flow arising as a direct consequence of a decision**. A decision is about the future; it cannot alter what has been done already.

3.4 Only costs which will **differ** under the available opportunities should be considered. Say you, as marketing manager of The Needle Works, have already contracted to pay £1,000 for some full-page advertisements in the local newspaper. It is the newspaper's policy that this booking is not refundable if cancelled. You now might be trying to decide whether to advertise on local radio instead. The £1,000 already contracted to is irrelevant to the decision, because it will be incurred whether you decide to advertise on radio or not.

Decisions in a marketing context

3.5 **Levels of marketing expenditure are often significant**, and any marketing strategy will have to be evaluated accordingly. However, according to Keith Ward: 'levels of marketing expenditure ... are often subjected to far less rigorous financial evaluations than smaller financial commitments on more tangible assets.'

3.6 Treating marketing expenditure as a **cost** is probably appropriate for reporting considerations, but for **decision-making** purposes, there is an argument for analysing it, and controlling it, as if it were an **investment**.

3.7 Ward highlights the dilemma: 'for many marketing-led businesses, their most valuable assets are their brands ... yet ... the easiest way ... to improve profitability is to reduce expenditure on marketing or on research and development.'

3.8 Part of the strategic marketing plan, should be some form of quantitative analysis of the proposed investment. For example, assume the marketing department of The Needle Works chooses to spend £50,000 on re-positioning a product.

- How can a link between future sales and the £50,000 expenditure be established?
- What would happen if the money was not spent? Would market share fall?
- Would an alternative use of £50,000 be more valuable?

3.9 The benefits from marketing expenditure might sometimes be much less easy to quantify than, say, the cost savings on new equipment. Markets are an environment, where customers and competitors cannot be controlled. **Instability and uncertainty** are inherent within them.

Exam Tip

The information on the marketing budget that we have presented so far is important, but it is equally important that you get used to dealing with numbers in the context of an examination question. Try the following exercise, which has been adapted from a question on the Specimen Paper when the Marketing in Practice module was first created.

EXAMPLE

Bettacars is a rapidly expanding car repair, servicing and spare parts company with 200 branches throughout the UK. It offers a full range of guaranteed repairs and services to all mainstream makes of car and light commercial vehicle. They keep fast moving lines in stock, but have negotiated deliveries from all suppliers which ensure prompt turnaround of business.

Turnover is anticipated to reach £200 million in 2005, comprising:

50% routine servicing and fitting of tyre exhausts etc

25% general repairs

25% spare parts

Helix employ 200 people at their head office and has a team of 18 area managers, while the average branch employs 12 people.

Project 24

Petrol stations, convenience stores and some major supermarkets are moving in the direction of 24-hour opening. One of Bettacars' competitors has trialled 24-hour opening in the London area. The operations director is keen not to be left behind. It is estimated that for an increase in wage costs of 5%, an extra 10% could be added to turnover. Two branches, both located in the West Midlands, are keen to be the first to offer this new service.

The branch trading accounts are shown below.

BRANCH TRADING ACCOUNTS 2003-2004

£'000s

Branch	Turnover	Purchases	Fixed Costs	Wages	Contribution
711	1,975	1,005	475	260	235
718	900	500	280	190	(70)

INTERNAL MEMO STRICTLY CONFIDENTIAL

To: J. Brown, Marketing
From: S. Smith, Operations
Date: 12/5/2004
Subject: **Project 24**

Further to our recent discussions, District 7 appears an excellent pilot for 24-hour opening. Two branches should be opened on a trial basis, these being 711 Shirley and 718 Wolverhampton, details of each branch are given below:

711 Shirley

- Situated on main arterial road from Birmingham
- Intense local competition (Halfords and Kwikfit)
- Large affluent commuter population
- Outlet revamped last year cost £200,000

718 Wolverhampton

- Located close to town centre on Ring Road
- Inner city site, has suffered from theft
- Due for refit January 2005

I look forward to the Marketing Department assisting these two Branches.

MEDIA COSTINGS

Newpapers

Wolverhampton	*Circulation*	*Cost per s.c.c.*
Evening Echo	90,000	£9.50
Weekly Tribune (free)	75,000	£4.75
Morning News	30,000	£4.00

Shirley		
Gazette (free)	80,000	£5.25
Evening Post	40,000	£3.25
Weekend News	25,000	£2.50

LOCAL RADIO

Wolf Radio (Wolverhampton) reaches 30% of its catchment of 230,000 adults each week. Package of 20 x 15 second slots (5 peak) costs £950.

Shirley Sound is a new radio station serving 100,000 homes set up three months ago. Costs for a 30 second slot is £50 peak, £20 off-peak (minimum 10 slots).

POSTERS

The Big Poster Co. have a range of sites from £100 p.c.m in close proximity to both branches.

CREATIVE ESTIMATES

DRFC have estimated £200 creative development plus £600 production for a 20 x 3 ad.

Advantage would charge £250 for an ad up to 25 x 4.

All local papers offer free artwork.

Use the above information to answer the following questions:

(a) One branch has to be put forward for an initial three-month trial. From the information given, which would you recommend and why?

(b) Prepare an outline media schedule for the trial period, showing costs.

(c) How would you propose supporting Project 24 over the next year, and what budget is required?

Suggested solution

(a) Branch 711 has been selected based on the following criteria.

(i) **Financial**

	711 Shirley	*Turnover up 10%*	*718 Wolverhampton*	*Turnover up 10%*
	£'000	£'000	£'000	£'000
Turnover	1,975	2,172.5	900	990
Purchases	1,005	1,105.5	500	550
Fixed costs	475	475	280	280
Wages (up 5%)	260	273	190	199.5
Contribution/(loss)	**235**	**319**	**(70)**	**(39.5)**

The above figures show that Shirley will make an additional contribution of £84,000 (£319,000 – £235,000), compared with losses recovered at Wolverhampton of £30,500.

(ii) **Other reasons**

(1) Shirley has recently had a refit

(2) The location appears to be superior, with a large affluent commuter population and no reports of theft (unlike Wolverhampton).

(3) Media costs are lower

(b) Before any media schedule can be devised, an appropriate **total promotional budget** needs to be set. On the limited amount of information available, the model we could use is **percentage of turnover**. A suggested figure is 6% of £1,975k, being £118,500, of which £17,850 will be used for the media launch.

(i) **Justification for the size of budget**

(1) The estimated increase in business could increase contribution

(2) Need to reach a wide audience quickly

(3) Need to increase revenue to help repay investment for site revamp

(4) This pilot is an important strategic move for the group, therefore every assistance must be given to ensure its success

Assumptions

With the lack of information certain assumptions need to be made.

(1) All newspapers are tabloid for cost purposes

(2) Gazette and Weekend News are weekly publications and the Evening Post is six evenings

(ii) **Schedule**

The **timing** of this pilot is crucial to its success. We have chosen a three-week teaser campaign across all media. This will be followed by a one-month explosion of coverage in the weeklies, and 25 × 4s on Friday in the evening paper, plus continuous peak slots on the radio. Finally, the campaign will settle down to a continuous drip in the print media and a small burst at the end on radio to reinforce the message.

Media	3 weeks Pre-Launch	Month 1	Month 2	Month 3	Cost
	£	£	£	£	£
Shirley Sound					
25 slots @ £50	1,250				
60 slots @ £50		3,000			
30 slots @ £50				1,500	
					5,750
Gazette					
25 × 4 @ £525	1,575	2,100	1,050	1,050	5,775
Weekend News					
25 × 4 @ £250	750	1,000	500	500	2,750
Evening Post					
25 × 4 @ £325	975	1,300	650	650	3,575
					17,850

Posters, PR and production costs will be allocated from the rest of the promotional budget.

(c) **Support for Project 24**

Given the turnover of the company is estimated to be around £200 million by 2005 and the introduction of 24-hour working is estimated to add another 10% to turnover to bring it to £220 million, the selection of a marketing budget is crucial to the project's success.

(i) **Affordable approach**: what is left after all the costs have been deducted from profit.

(ii) **Competitive parity**: using your competitors spend as a guideline.

(iii) **Percentage of sales**: applying a rough percentage between 5-10% (as we saw above)

(iv) **Objective and task approach**: the money to achieve the objectives set.

On our first launch we used a percentage of sales. If we felt that was successful, a figure of 5% is not unrealistic. This will give us a budget of £11 million (ie 5% of £220 million), of which a large proportion would be spent on advertising. This size budget will not become available straight away, as rollout will take time. A sensible figure for the support needed over a quarter to support the new project should be in the region of £1.5million.

Once the launch period is over, the 24-hour service can be incorporated in all aspects of future promotions.

Choice of recommendations

The size of the budget gives us the flexibility to use both **local** and **national** advertising. Research has shown that national advertising, reinforced by local advertising, gives far greater response.

The cost of any meaningful TV campaign would be too costly and take all of the budget. With the advent of national commercial radio stations, supplemented by local ones, listening figures have continued to climb steeply. This would be a far better use of the budget, coupled to national/local press, national/local specialist magazines and business directories. This will give the project the **synergy** and **coverage** it needs.

In today's increasingly 24-hour society, other options need to be considered. The **Internet** is one such place. A website could enable people to purchase spare parts online as well as offering a booking-in service, with a map to show all the national sites.

Chapter Roundup

- Marketing activities are generally undertaken with a view to increasing **sales** and **profits**. The problem comes when trying to evaluate the success of these activities.
- **Overheads** may be related to production, administration, selling or distribution
- The level of **contribution** made by a product is defined as the sales value minus the variable costs associated with the units produced. Contribution is what is 'left over' to pay for fixed costs of operation, such as rent.
- Marketing managers must remember that their decisions will have **financial implications**.

Quick Quiz

1 What is the CIM definition of marketing?

2 What is an overhead?

3 What is contribution?

4 Give an example of a fixed cost.

5 Why might the benefits from marketing expenditure be difficult to quantify?

Now try Question 16 in the Question Bank

Action Programme Review

1

THE NEEDLE WORKS MARKETING BUDGET

ACTIVITY	Jan £	Feb £	Mar £	Apr £	May £	Jun £	Half 1 Total £	Jul £	Aug £	Sept £	Oct £	Nov £	Dec £	Half 2 Total £	Year Total £
Newspaper Advertising	750	750	750	750	750	750	4500	750	750	750	750	750	750	4500	9000
Local Radio	1000	1000	1000	1000	1000	1000	6000	1000	1000	1000	1000	1000	1000	6000	12000
Stand at London Craft Show							-				4500			4500	4500
Garden Party							-	2000						2000	2000
Class Party				2500			2500							-	2500
Promotional Coupons		5000					5000		5000					5000	10000
Discount Sale	10000	10000					20000							-	20000
Posters, leaflets & point of sale material	500	500	500	500	500	500	3000	500	500	500	500	500	500	3000	6000
Frame giveaway Competition			4000				4000							-	4000
Total	**12250**	**17250**	**6250**	**4750**	**2250**	**2250**	**45000**	**4250**	**7250**	**2250**	**6750**	**2250**	**2250**	**25000**	**70000**

Answers to Quick Quiz

1 This should be ingrained! 'Marketing is the management process responsible for identifying, anticipating and satisfying customer requirements profitably' (CIM).

2 An overhead is a cost incurred in the course of making a product, providing a service or running a department which cannot be traced directly and in full to the product, service or department.

3 The contribution made to profit and fixed costs, which equates to total sales value less the variable costs associated with the units produced.

4 For example, a lithographic printer's make ready charge which is the same whether the print run is long or short.

5 Not all activities have a quantifiable benefit attached to them and they are performed in an uncertain and unstable environment. Because direct benefits cannot always be demonstrated, marketing budgets can be a tempting target for a short-term cost cutting exercise.

Evaluating Results

17

Chapter Topic List	
1	Setting the scene
2	The results of marketing mix decisions
3	Has the budget been well spent?

Learning Outcomes

- ☑ Gather information for, and evaluate marketing results against, financial and other criteria
- ☑ Undertake basic marketing activities within an agreed plan and monitor and report on progress

Syllabus References

- ☑ Demonstrate an ability to manipulate numbers in a marketing context
- ☑ Examine the correlation between marketing mix decisions and results
- ☑ Evaluate the cost effectiveness of a marketing budget, including a review of suppliers and activities

1 Setting the scene

1.1 We first looked at the marketing mix in Chapter 14. In this chapter we will examine the results that may arise from mix decisions and the actions that management may take to amend them if results are not as expected or hoped.

1.2 Having costed various activities, decided that they were worthwhile, and set them up in an approved budget for the forthcoming year, it is time for the evaluation process to start.

1.3 After all this, the company may be in a position to decide whether or not its budget was well spent. This is not a black and white analysis, as the decisions will vary from company to company. One company may desire a 50% cut in the level of customer complaints after spending £2million on a new call centre. Another may expect to see sales double as a result of a £100,000 promotional coupon campaign. The two companies are spending their marketing budget with very different aims in mind.

Exam Tip

Consider this advice from *Marketing Success* (May 2002).

'In order to make well-informed decisions about what to do, organisations need to learn lessons from the past. What worked well? Why did it work well? Can it be repeated?'

Evaluating marketing activities is not always something that many organisations do well. Even if it is done, the information may not be passed on or readily accessible for future planners.

Carry out some research in your own organisation, or one you know well. Find out:

- How exhibitions are evaluated – number of sales leads, customers contacted, new enquiries, publicity achieved.
- How the effectiveness of corporate hospitality is evaluated – response rate to invitations.
- How advertising results are measured – viewing rates, circulation figures, attitude surveys.
- How sales promotions are measured – increase in sales, coupons.

Do not forget the importance of qualitative evaluation, so look at how quantitative results are used. For example, the results from the exhibition may have been good, but were customers reporting that this was the last time they would attend because they were weary of exhibitions? Is this a lesson to be learnt? Success may not be repeatable next year.

Understanding why events and activities are successful is critical to whether they can be repeated. Measuring results and achievement of objectives is important, but evaluating why it happened is essential.

2 The results of marketing mix decisions

2.1 There are a number of benefits that a costing system can provide when evaluating mix results.

- The identification of profitable and unprofitable products and services
- Assistance in setting prices
- The provision of accurate stock valuations
- The analysis of changes in costs, volume and hence profit
- Assistance in planning, control and decision making (such as budgets and pricing)

2.2 You may still be wondering why, as a marketer, the costing aspects are relevant to you: after all, your main focus is the **customer**, and you might regard an inward looking concentration on costs and production processes as evidence of a **product-orientated attitude**.

2.3 Let us remember again that the essence of marketing is that **customer needs are satisfied profitably**. In the long run, profit is achieved because sales revenue from goods and services exceeds the costs.

2.4 Cost information is also important in **marketing mix decisions** because resources are always finite.

(a) **Price decisions**. A product's cost might be a constraint on the marketer's freedom to adjust the price element of the marketing mix. It is true that many supermarkets sell 'loss leader' products to entice their customers to buy higher-priced goods, but on the whole **cost is a constraint**.

(b) **Product decisions**. When deciding whether or not to launch a new product, marketers might discover that the market price is far below the cost of making a particular product or service. The marketer may then have to redesign or reposition the product to make it cheaper.

(c) **Place decisions**. Distribution expenses can affect overall profitability. Cost information can enable marketers to discover which distribution channels are the most effective use of resources.

(d) **Promotion decisions**. The marketer's budget often includes the costs of advertising, sales promotion and so on. Cost information can suggest which media might be best employed.

2.5 Every marketing mix strategy will lead to a certain level of profit.

Marketing at Work

The importance of marketers getting their heads round accounting information was emphasised in *Marketing Business*:

'from board representation through budget setting processes to effectiveness measurement, marketing and advertising come a poor second or third to other disciplines in finance directors' eyes ... Marketing directors simply must justify their activities in order to command the levels of expenditure they need.' The senior examiner has also commented: "we marketers must take on the accountants at their own game".'

3 Has the budget been well spent?

3.1 As we discussed in Section 1, the answer to this question will vary from company to company, depending upon factors such as the company objectives and how big or small the company is.

3.2 You put together a budget for The Needle Works in Action Programme 1, Chapter 16. The overall budget was £70,000 which you spread between a range of activities. What are some measures of success that you could look for from each activity?

3.3 Taking each activity in turn, we could suggest the following.

Activity	Spend	Objective
Newspaper advertising	£9,000	Increase customer traffic by 5%
Local radio	£12,000	
Stand at London Craft Show	£5,000	Meet new suppliers and out-of-town customers
Garden party	£2,000	Public relations
Class party	£2,500	
Promotional coupons	£10,000	Increase sales in those months by £20,000
Discount sale	£20,000	To get rid of old season stock and increase customer traffic
Posters and leaflets	£6,000	To decorate store and encourage awareness
Frames giveaway	£4,000	To encourage customer traffic and sales

3.4 As you can see, not all of the activities have a quantifiable benefit attached to them. The two parties are mainly aimed at public relations, while the newspaper and local radio advertising is aimed at increasing customer traffic by a stated amount. The success or otherwise of this advertising could be measured by comparing the levels of visitors before and after the campaigns (by examining the visitors' book, for example). The total cost of the advertising, £21,000, could be compared with incremental sales (sales pre- and post-campaign).

3.5 The redemption of promotional coupons may be so successful (and expensive!) that you decide not to do it again because the cost outweighed the additional sales gained. A printer may become so expensive that you decide to go somewhere else.

3.6 Each activity may or may not have a quantifiable effect and you may be constantly revising your portfolio of activities, but the overall benefit of marketing budgeting and planning is likely to lead to increased awareness by customers and suppliers which will translate into additional sales at some point. It may not be in the same week, or even the same year, but without marketing planning it is unlikely to happen at all.

Marketing at Work

Measuring the success of the strategy

Vodafone's sponsorship deal with Manchester United costs Vodafone £30 million over a four-year period. Vodafone clearly has to evaluate the effectiveness of this partnership in terms of its own marketing objectives. It does so in four ways:

- General awareness is measured through consumer research. For example, consumers may be asked questions such as 'Did you know that Vodafone sponsors Manchester United?'
- The impact of phones and accessories is measured by charting ongoing improvements in sales.
- The success of value added services such as manUmobile is monitored in terms of the number of people registered and usage of the services.
- Media evaluation – Vodafone monitors TV and press coverage to measure the exposure of the Vodafone brand resulting from the sponsorship.

Keeping check in this way enables Vodafone to assess whether or not it has made a wise strategic move in teaming up with Manchester United. Evidence strongly suggests that it has.

Chapter Roundup

- The essence of marketing is that **customer needs are satisfied profitably**.
- The decision as to whether or not the budget has been well spent will depend on individual **company objectives** for their marketing activities. Each activity may or may not have a quantifiable effect.
- Not all activities have a **quantifiable** benefit attached to them.
- Marketers are likely to be constantly **revising their portfolio** of activities to generate customer awareness.

Quick Quiz

1. Why is cost information generally important in marketing mix decisions?
2. What benefits does a proper costing system provide?
3. Give an example of how cost information can help with a 'place' decision.
4. What might be the marketing objective behind a retailer having a discount sale?
5. How could you measure the success of an advertising campaign?

Now try Question 17 in the Question Bank

Answers to Quick Quiz

1. This harkens back to the 'profitably' in the CIM definition of marketing.
2. Resources are always finite and a proper costing system enables better decisions as to their use.
3. Marketers can make decisions as to which distribution channels are the most cost effective.
4. To get rid of old season stock and increase customer traffic.
5. The Vodafone 'Marketing at Work' should give you plenty of ideas!

Exam Question Bank and suggested answers

1 Orientation

You are a marketing assistant for a small college of further education currently experiencing a declining number of students. You have been in your position for twelve months and you realise that the college is product orientated.

In an effort to communicate the concept of a marketing orientation you feel that you must write a report to the principal of the college detailing the following.

(a) The difference between product orientation and market orientation, citing examples of each

(b) The steps involved in establishing a marketing orientation approach

(c) The anticipated benefits to the college of introducing such a marketing approach

(15 marks)

2 Databases and market research

You are the new marketing manager for a local market gardener who supplies fruit and vegetables to retailers throughout the region, but uses an outdated card system for its database. Write a report to the Director outlining the benefits of electronic database marketing.

(20 marks)

3 In-house research

Your company has decided to bring all of its marketing research activity 'in house' because it is felt that to give knowledge of the company's products and plans to outside organisations is too risky in the commercial sense. Previously the company has used market research agencies to carry out 'ad hoc' marketing research as needed.

You have now been given the task of drawing up a list of the tasks that will have to be undertaken by the new marketing research department. **(20 marks)**

4 Report on company capabilities

For a number of years a small group of friends have pursued their interest in making hand-made Arts and Crafts style beds. The combination of their design and wood-turning has resulted in many requests for beds for friends. Others have encouraged them to go into business full-time, pointing out that a significant opportunity exists for custom-made beds. Produce a report which analyses the likely strengths and weaknesses of this new company's internal capabilities relative to this marketing opportunity. **(20 marks)**

5 Marketing teamwork

As the marketing manager for a wholesale market gardening company which is expanding into the retail side of the business, opening up two new garden centres in the region, you have to ensure that the key players involved in the expansion will work effectively together.

What steps should you take to ensure the team works effectively? **(20 marks)**

6 Non-verbal communication

(a) You are the marketing manager for a chain of hotels. You have been asked to write a short article for the company newsletter about the role of front line staff in marketing the company. In particular, you are asked to use the article to explain the importance of non-verbal communication in dealing effectively with customers. Use examples to illustrate the points you are making. **(12 marks)**

(b) Write a memo for circulation to all reception staff about the effective use of telephones. In particular, you should focus on the appropriate way to deal with incoming calls, the transfer of calls and message taking. **(8 marks)**

(20 marks)

7 Advertising agencies

(a) List briefly the process in selecting an advertising agency.

(b) What role does an advertising agency play in developing an advertising campaign?

(c) Outline a typical agency structure.

(15 marks)

8 Negotiations

You have been asked to write an article outlining the win/win strategy you could adopt when negotiating with another organisation. **(20 marks)**

9 Control, planning and evaluation

Little Fingers plc manufactures and retails a wide range of children's games and toys. Recently the following memorandum was circulated to all Little Fingers staff.

INTERNAL MEMORANDUM

To: All staff, all departments

From: The Managing Director

Each year this company spends 5% of turnover on marketing activities. Despite this high level of expenditure we have little feedback on their effectiveness. In order to encourage more monitoring and evaluation we will be offering a prize for the best suggestions for appropriate marketing control, planning and evaluation procedures in project management.

You decide to enter the competition. Prepare a report which explains different approaches to marketing, control, planning and evaluation. Provide details of how these approaches should be implemented. **(20 marks)**

10 International event management

You are the assistant marketing manager for an international engineering company with subsidiaries all over the world. They have just launched a new product and a sales conference has been arranged by the marketing manager. You have been asked to produce a checklist that takes into consideration all the factors that may be of interest and necessity for the international delegates who are attending the conference in the UK. **(20 marks)**

11 Venue appraisal

You are a marketing assistant for a medium-sized industrial company and the marketing manager has given you the task of compiling a checklist on "How to select a suitable venue" to be included in a hand-book he is compiling. **(20 marks)**

12 Media choice

You are the recently appointed marketing manager for a large car dealership with ten branches located throughout a promotional region. This region is served by a commercial television company and a separate independent radio company. There is one evening newspaper, and several weekly free newspapers. Your advertising spend is likely to be just over £1 million. Write a memorandum to your M.D. comparing the strengths and weaknesses of the different media available with specific reference to advertising new and used cars. **(20 marks)**

13 Magazine sales promotion

You are the promotions manager at a magazine publisher which produces a range of consumer specialist titles sold primarily via the news-stand. Produce an outline report for your marketing director, recommending and justifying how sales promotion techniques could be used to attract new readers and retain existing readers. **(20 marks)**

14 Price

(a) Explain why price is important within the marketing mix.

(b) What is meant by elasticity of demand?

(10 marks)

15 Market research for new product launch

You are a newly appointed as a marketing manager in a publishing company and have been given specific responsibility for a new product launch. Your organisation wants to introduce a new magazine aimed at the teenage female market as identified as part of last year's strategic review. In this respect you have been given a budget of £30,000 to conduct further market research prior to the launch. Explain how you would plan and conduct this research. You are required to give the specific stages in your research plan, explaining your chosen options.

(20 marks)

16 Flexible budgets

Forecast sales for a new product line have been estimated at 10,000 units per annum. Selling prices have been discussed at £100 per unit, £150 per unit and £200 per unit. Fixed costs associated with the product are budgeted at £50,000 per annum. Variable costs are budgeted at £10 per hour of direct labour and £40 per unit produced in material costs. It takes two hours of direct labour to assemble and pack the units for delivery. Each unit sold will incur delivery costs but these will be recouped from the customer in full and are forecast to make an additional contribution of £10 per unit sold.

(a) Prepare a budget for each price level that clearly shows sales, cost of sales, contribution and net profit.

(b) In addition flex the budget to show what would happen if the sales forecast is only 80 per cent accurate. **(20 marks)**

17 Budget building

You are the marketing manager with responsibility for sales, promotion and customer services. You have been asked to write a memorandum to the managing director that gives an indication of how you intend to prepare your next departmental budget. This should show budget headings, and an indication of how you intend to control expenditure. **(20 marks)**

1 Orientation

To: College Principal
From: A N Student
Date: June 2002
Subject: Market orientation

Contents

(a) The difference between product and market orientation

(b) The steps involved in establishing a marketing orientated approach

(c) The anticipated benefits to the college of introducing such an approach

(a) **Difference between product and market orientation**

The college will be **product orientated** if it displays the following characteristics.

(i) Courses designed and delivered without reference to market trends and customer needs

(ii) Limited use/adoption of MKIS systems

(iii) Short-term, reactive view to changes in the marketing environment

(iv) Lack of customer-focused systems and processes

(v) Organisation structure focused upon courses and not customer and market issues

The college will be **market orientated** if it displays the following characteristics.

(i) Course design and development clearly focused upon market trends and evolving customer needs

(ii) Flexible modes of course delivery and opening hours

(iii) Organisation structure and systems designed with a customer focus and not an internal organisation focus

(iv) Empowerment of staff to deliver excellent customer service

(v) Culture of change with limited bureaucracy

(b) **The steps to establish a marketing orientated approach**

(i) The philosophy that lies behind a marketing orientation must be embraced with a genuine belief and **commitment by the senior management** of the college.

(ii) The college will need substantially to upgrade its current student **information system** to provide more than just name, address and course records. Company and other key stakeholder information should also be accessible within the system.

(iii) The college **structure** will need to be revised if it is to achieve increased level of market and customer orientation. The structure should include **customer related** functions and roles and not those which just to satisfy internal organisation needs.

(iv) The college **culture** must be adapted to suit the more customer focused environment. The organisation and its employees will need to redefine current practice and functions, towards increased co-operation, autonomy and flexibility.

(v) Improved **internal communication** systems need to be designed to ensure all employees are kept informed of college activity and plans. Communication systems should facilitate **feedback**.

(vi) A programme of **customer care training** should be planned for all members of staff and targets agreed. This training should be provided on an ongoing basis.

(vii) An agreed system of **monitoring and control** should be implemented to ensure that any deviations or shortfalls from the desired standards can be actioned.

(c) **Benefits**

Several benefits will emerge as a result of the college changing from a product to marketing orientation. Some of these will not occur in the **short term** but will have a significant impact on the colleges performance and competitiveness **longer term**.

(i) The college will develop a sharper **competitive edge** clearly focused on the market and customers' needs.

(ii) Its perceived **image** in the local community will be changed from being seen as fairly staid to being more dynamic.

(iii) Increased **revenue** will be generated from courses positioned in growing markets.

(iv) The college will be seen to be more **responsive** to local education needs.

(v) Courses and programmes will be **tailored and targeted** and thus be seen as having more relevance.

(vi) **Recruitment** will become more effective through better targeting. As a direct result the college should retain more students to completion of programmes and continuing with further programmes.

(vii) **New course developments** can be developed in closer line with **market needs** and evaluated more effectively in terms of the colleges mission and goals.

Whilst this change from product to marketing orientation will involve significant commitment in terms of **time and resource**, the long-term benefits will be considerable.

2 Databases and market research

To: A. Director
From: A. Marketing Manager
Date: June 2002
Subject: Benefits of electronic database marketing

The objective of this report is to outline the contribution that a **marketing database** could make to the development and support of our business.

According to the **Institute of Direct Marketing** a marketing database is 'a collection of all available information of past, present and prospective customers, structured to achieve maximum usefulness'. The real value of a marketing database lies in its ability to be an invaluable aid in **decision making** and **communications strategy** development. The database can be used repeatedly, so reinforcing the point that it is four times more expensive to gain a new customer than it is to retain an existing one.

Database marketing is a customer-orientated approach to marketing, and its special power lies in the techniques used to harness the capabilities of computer and telecommunications technology. Building accurate and up-to-date profiles of existing customers would enable the company to increase its market share by:

(a) Increased customer retention by staying close to the target audience through better targeting and contact

(b) Better use of resources and cost reduction due to less duplication of information handling

(c) Better decision making through quality management information.

The database may be used to meet a variety of objectives with numerous advantages over traditional marketing methods.

- Focusing on prime prospects
- Evaluating new prospects
- Cross-selling related products
- Launching new products to potential prospects
- Identifying new distribution channels
- Building customer loyalty
- Converting occasional users to regular users
- Generating enquiries and follow-up sales
- Targeting niche markets

An effective database can provide the following **management information**.

(a) **Usage patterns** eg reasons for account closures/loyal repeat customers/seasonal or local purchase patterns/demographic purchase patterns and purchase patterns in response to promotional campaigns

(b) **Evaluation of marketing activities** eg response rates

(c) **Segmentation analysis** to ensure accurate targeting

(d) **Account analysis** eg value or product type

(e) Updated **market research information**

A database can only be as effective as the information which is input. This means that **accurate data is essential** and this will require investment of time and effort to ensure that both data capture and data entry are accurate. **Variables** which could be considered for inclusion are name, address, telephone number, gender, age occupation, services used, frequency of use, time of day of visit etc.

The **customer database** could be maintained through our new **EPOS system** in which all our purchasing data would be automatically updated, **transaction documents** such as order forms, invoices and customer account records, any customer care **feedback** questionnaires which are now distributed to all our customers and the new customers who visit our stalls at the shows and exhibitions we attend.

In conclusion, the development of a marketing database would take **time and money**. Consideration needs to be given as to whether we develop our own database or whether we purchase an **off-the-shelf package** and then set about tailoring it to our specific requirements. Overall, a marketing database has the potential to provide us with invaluable data regarding a wide range of marketing and consumer issues, as well as providing us with a tool for **competitive advantage**.

I look forward to discussing the contents of this report next week at our scheduled meeting.

3 In-house research

Marketing research can cover all of the marketing activities undertaken by an organisation. The **objective** of marketing research is to understand the **problems** and identify the level of **effectiveness** of this activity. Market research focuses upon the identification of **needs**, and market **opportunities** and **threats** facing an organisation.

The extent of the tasks that will have to be undertaken by the new marketing research department will be dependent upon the type of organisation and its current level and sophistication of research activity. Working on the assumption that the organisation invests substantially in marketing research, the following list of tasks would be paramount.

Market research

- Customer/consumer surveys (qualitative and quantitative)
- Market trends analysis
- Marketing environment analysis (SLEPT factors)
- Market share analysis
- Geodemographic analysis

Such data can be obtained from both primary and secondary sources. A decision would have to be made as to the level of sophistication required of such research and whether the in-house team has the appropriate skills.

Product research

- Brand perception/image studies
- Packaging and product design studies
- New product development research
- Test marketing
- Comparative studies between competitive products

Promotion research

- Promotion effectiveness (ie recall)
- Sales impact of promotional activity
- Corporate image
- Publicity generated
- Media research
- Sales force effectiveness

Distribution research

- Sales performance analysis
- Service delivery performance
- Costs/profitability studies
- Dealer satisfaction studies
- Location analysis
- The analysis of packaging for transportation and shelving
- Dealer advertising requirements

The **costs** of such a marketing research operation would have to be investigated. Additional investment would be required in **marketing information systems** and staffing levels. The required level of **expertise** may not be available in-house.

An estimation of the **time** and **resources** needed to effectively complete the range of marketing research indicated would need careful consideration.

4 Report on company capabilities

To: Bed Makers
From: A Consultant
Date: June 2002
Subject: **Strengths and weaknesses**

Introduction

This report reviews, in table format, the company's perceived strengths and weaknesses with regard to its internal capabilities for exploiting the opportunity for custom-made beds.

Strengths and weaknesses analysis

Area	Strengths	Weaknesses
Corporate management and organisation	Friends with a common interest Experience of working together Flexible, innovative responsive Willing to seek advice	No MD No formal structure No corporate objectives
Financial	None apparent	Need capital investment High risk borrowers Lack of expertise
Personnel	Enthusiastic/motivated Work well as a team	Assumed lack of investment and marketing experience No formal relationships
Production	Possess necessary skills Have necessary tools Make to order	No experience of higher volumes Might need new equipment
Marketing strategy	Niche marketing	No formal strategy Responsive rather than proactive No planning system No control systems
MkIS	Initiative	No formal MkIS No factual knowledge of market sizes and trends, buying motives etc.
Product	Custom built Good design High quality	None apparent
Price	Negotiable Potentially premium	No formal costings

Area	Strengths	Weaknesses
Promotion	Recommendation Exhibitions/Fairs Trade/Arts and Crafts Magazines	No promotional skills No promotional budget No agency
Place	Some existing space (production) Direct delivery	No showroom space? No office?

Conclusion

Although the proposed new company has a number of important strengths, there is an almost equal number of weaknesses.

Following Kotler's recommendations, the strengths and weaknesses should be scored and their degrees of importance assessed so as to facilitate **prioritisation**. For example, it seems clear that product design and craftsmanship skills would have both a high score and a high importance, and should therefore be ranked as a major strength. However, lack of finance, lack of marketing skills and lack of market knowledge would rank as major weaknesses. Worked through in this way, it would seem major weaknesses exceed major strengths. Issues arising are as follows.

(a) It is unlikely that sufficient **funding** could be attracted without a formal business plan (I would be pleased to assist in producing one).

(b) Should the new company **outsource** marketing/sales/distribution so as to exploit better its design/production skills?

(c) I propose a **management team** is elected from the group to further the group's interests.

5 Marketing teamwork

Marketing managers have to try to ensure that with the coming together of people from different disciplines a good **working relationship** is maintained to achieve objectives.

A good working relationship in this context means prompt and willing service, co-operation, co-ordination, communication and teamworking in which all parties achieve mutual respect, conflict resolution and opportunity for job satisfaction.

This is essential as team members rely on each other for **information** or input in order to fulfil objectives, for example interaction between **internal** and **external** promotion managers, interaction between managers of **different departments** in the company, and interaction between administration staff and management. General courtesy and respect at all times can be rewarded in times of crisis when favours may be needed (eg individuals being prepared to work an extra thirty minutes to ensure a deadline is met and objectives are achieved).

Objectives of team management

The overall objectives of the team should be agreed and clearly understood. The manager must obtain feedback to ensure that people not only think they understand the objectives, but really do so.

Team building

The team should go through the **group formation** process as quickly as possible. **Barriers** should be broken down, differences aired and the team move into its productive stage as quickly as possible. This is an on going process.

- Keep in contact
- Be dependable
- Work on shared values and interests
- Show willing
- Socialise but behave appropriately
- Avoid or mend conflict
- Show respect for other people's beliefs and values
- Maintain a net balance of benefit

Options

All options for achieving objectives should be examined. A common way of doing this is brainstorming. If everyone is encouraged to contribute you get the most out of all the members of the team.

Strategies and tactics

The team must then set out in detail how these objectives are to be achieved. The style that is adopted depends on your personality and the personality of those in the team, the work situation and relationship, the urgency of the decision, the importance of other people's commitment to the solution, the organisation and its culture.

Measurement

Methods of measuring progress should be agreed relating directly to the objectives.

Timescales and reviews

Timescales for the project and for review points should be set. The general progress of the team's activities need to be monitored.

Meetings

The usual way of monitoring progress is the team meeting. These act as a forum for discussion and joint decision making. They allow feedback on individual progress, support and ideas from other members. Grievances and problems can be aired and solved.

Control

The team must have a degree of flexibility and should be able to adapt activities as circumstances change.

In conclusion, many factors can affect the overall success of the group. The size will influence its ability to communicate. The relationships, personalities and experience of the members will also have an impact on the team's effectiveness. The objectives of the team and any time constraints will both influence the way in which members relate to each other. Generally a lot can depend on the encouragement and motivation the team members receive from the leader.

6 Non-verbal communication

(a) **Body language**

Body language shows people how we feel.

Consciously or not we will communicate with our movements and respond to the body language of others. If they smile we react - usually with another smile. We also observe the **behaviour** of others. If you have watched any docu-soaps such as 'Airline' you will doubtless have noted the body language of particular front line staff.

With such staff in mind it is easy to see a connection between front-line staff and **effective customer care**

Good initial eye contact demonstrates your interest in the client and allows staff to pick up on the client's mood - they may be relaxed, frustrated or demanding. One of the aspects of our job is to note this and make an appropriate **response** - body and words!

For example:

'Have you had a difficult journey?'

'I'm sorry to hear that'

'Would you like to .... '

However, one of the interesting things about our work is that every customer is an individual and needs **individual care**. Our training recognises this. For instance, we speak to old and young differently - we also use different body language. Sometimes it is appropriate to move closer to someone - frequently it is not! In this respect we need to be aware of **cultural differences**.

The subject has been studied by anthropologists such as Desmond Morris. He started with animals at London Zoo - but we are not that different. We have all developed postures and gestures, movements and personal habits to make a full range of **statements** about ourselves.

At work it is important that we ensure that these statements and personal body language are used skilfully, to add to the level of customer care which is reflected in all aspects of our work as a service-led industry.

(b) **MEMORANDUM**

To: All reception staff
From: Ava Lines, Marketing Manager
Date: June 2002
Subject: Effective use of telephones

In order to help ensure that we are maintaining the highest possible standards, I have drafted this memorandum to highlight three key areas in the **effective use of telephones**.

Your responses would as usual be most welcome. Remember our aim is to maintain our **competitive edge**.

(i) **Incoming calls**

Key points are as follows.

(1) **Interpersonal skills** and sensitivity to each caller

(2) **Identification** and greetings

- Audible, clear
- Use company **guidelines**

(3) Establish nature of call and name of caller

(ii) **Transfer of calls**

(1) Inform/agree with caller need to transfer

(2) Follow **correct procedure** - including explanation to caller of what you are doing

(3) **Maintain contact** until caller has been transferred

(iii) **Message taking**

(1) Use notepad

(2) Receive message

- Time
- Name of caller
- Intended recipient
- Outline of nature of call
- Response given to caller

(3) Check back important details with caller

(4) Reassure caller that message will be passed on

(5) Ensure that it is!

Remember, please let us know how you feel we might improve these procedures.

7 Advertising agencies

(a) **Selecting an agency**

Stage 1 - Research

Criteria for selection

(i) Advertising your company has admired
(ii) Recommendation
(iii) Use of professional associations and marketing journals to profile the ideal agency
(iv) Identify several agencies that may fit your requirements

Stage 2 - Fine screening

(i) Write to the agency for literature
(ii) Arrange a visit to the agency
(iii) Produce a simple checklist of the characteristics you are looking for in an agency
(vi) Take it with you on the visit, ticking where the agency meets your brief
(v) Reduce the agency list down to three

Stage 3 - Brief

(i) Prepare advertising brief which is presented to the agencies
(ii) Invite agencies to present credentials and outline proposals for campaign
(iii) Impose time limit for presentation of proposals

Stage 4 - Presentation

(i) Presentations to take place over no more than 2 days on your premises

(ii) Keep the decision team small

(iii) Each team member to score each agency

Stage 5 - Decision time

(i) Use your score sheet to guide your decision

(ii) The sheet isn't an exact science - so include instinct, based on the compatibility with your own team, how they view us

Finally, discuss the **contractual details** with the successful agency.

(b) If an organisation uses an advertising agency, the development of the advertising campaign is usually a joint effort, with the agency performing functions such as copywriting, artwork, technical production and the formulation of the media plan.

The use of an agency provides an organisation with highly skilled **specialists** who are generally more objective than the firm's employees and have more experience in advertising.

(c) While different types and sizes of agencies will have different structures, what is listed below serves as a guideline.

Account executive

This is a person who is dedicated to a particular group of clients or in some cases an individual client. They are responsible for **communications** such as attending meetings, writing reports and generally **liasing** between the client and the agency.

Planning department

These individuals are responsible for the **analysis and interpretation** of market research reports which they have commissioned.

Creative department

These are the 'ideas' people and deal with words and pictures.

Media department

This is where they plan what **media** are to be used and buy the space on radio, television, magazines etc.

Production department

This is the department which is actually responsible for making the advertisement. Often there is an element of **subcontracting** here, as studios, camera crew and actors may be required.

Traffic department

This deals with getting the artwork or film to the magazine or TV station. When the promotional campaign involves a number of media this process becomes complicated because accurate timing is crucial.

8 Negotiations

All our lives we have been involved with **negotiations**. As a child we negotiated what time we would come home from a party, or the amount of pocket money we would receive.

One of the most direct examples of **communications** with customers and suppliers involves negotiation. This can involve gaining a discount for a run of adverts through to complex negotiations of a contract.

The aim of negotiating is not necessarily to get the best position for your organisation at the expense of the other party, but to view it as an exchange which is mutually beneficial. This is desirable if the relationship is to flourish.

The matrix below outlines the possibilities during negotiations.

Seller \ Buyer	*Win*	*Lose*
Win	Both are winners	Buyer loses
Lose	Seller loses Buyer wins	Both parties lose

A basic win-win approach to negotiations is as follows.

(i) **Set the scene**. The participants should be relaxed and comfortable, possibly meeting beforehand to break the ice.

(ii) Agree the negotiating **procedure**. Then map out, in advance, what the needs and fears of both parties are.

(iii) Define your **desired outcome**, for example, 'If I can pay £500, it would be ideal, but I'd settle for £600. Above £700, it's just not worth my while.'. Start with the best case, leaving room to fall back. However keep sight of your goal.

The bidding must be realistic. A too high or low initial bid could offend the other party.

(iv) Look for mutual or trade-off benefits. For example, you could offer an early right hand page for a run of ads in exchange for pre-payment. Never agree a concession without securing a concession in return. Always offer something valuable to your customer, like the example above, that is cheap for you.

(v) Spell out the positive benefits to the other party and support them in saying 'yes' to your proposals by **making it as easy as possible**. Offer to supply **information** or help. Emphasise **areas of agreement** and common ground.

(vi) **Overcome negativity** by asking questions such as:

- 'What will make it work for you?'
- 'What would it take to make this possible?'

(vii) **Overcome side-tracks** by asking questions such as:

'How is this going to get us where we need/want to go?'

(viii) Be hard on the problem but soft on the person. **Work together** on problem solving (eg by using flip chart or paper to make shared notes).

(ix) Be **flexible**. A 'take it or leave it' approach breaks relationships. However, saying 'no' repeatedly to sales people is a good way of finding out just how far below the list price they are prepared to go! Make, and invite, reasonable counter offers.

(x) Be **culturally sensitive**. Some markets thrive on 'haggling'. Some cultures engage in a lot of movement up and down the bargaining scale (eg Asian and Middle Eastern), while others do their homework and fix their prices (eg German). In the former cultures, much emphasis is placed on building relationships and extending hospitality before getting down to terms.

(xi) **Take notes**, so the accuracy of everyone's recollection of what was proposed and agreed can be checked.

(xii) **Summarise and confirm** the details of your agreements to both parties by memo, letter, contract and acknowledge a mutually positive outcome. **Monitor** the agreement to ensure it is going to plan.

Experience, knowledge and expertise count in negotiation, but it is essential that the person negotiating is **well briefed** and thoroughly prepared. He or she needs to know the extent of their **authority** and the limits they can go to, as this is vitally important even in a win-win approach.

9 Control, planning and evaluation

To: E. Funne, Managing Director
From: A. Hopeful, Marketing Assistant
Date: June 2002
Subject: Suggestions for appropriate marketing control, planning and evaluation procedures in project management.

Introduction

It is recommended that the following steps need to be applied to ensure appropriate planning, control and evaluation in project management.

Budgeting control

(a) Estimate all **costs** involved in the event.

(b) Compare the estimated total cost with anticipated **returns**, **benefits** and **objectives**.

(c) Establish that the estimated cost is within the departmental expenditure **budget**.

(d) As the plan goes ahead, **monitor actual expenditure** against the budget and query any discrepancies.

(e) **Compare** actual total cost against actual returns.

Marketing objectives

Marketing objectives should show clearly where we want to be. Without knowing clearly where we want to be, we cannot possibly establish whether or not we are getting there. Objectives should be achievable, given market conditions and resources.

Project plan

(a) Break the project down into **manageable units of activity**, ensuring the correct sequencing of tasks for co-ordinated performance and achievement of the overall project objective.

A **network map** can be usefully applied when the sequence is not immediately obvious.

A **critical path** can be further developed from the network map to describe not only what should happen when but how long the whole project will take.

By using such a technique, the shortest possible timescale for a project can be identified, because the longest path determines the deadline. Once you have identified the estimated activity durations, you can start scheduling the earliest start date for each activity. The result is a detailed and effective schedule.

(b) Estimate the **resources** required; materials, money, time etc for each unit, as far as is practically possible, so that costs can be monitored and controlled.

Action plans and **timetables** are effective ways of reminding you of key times and dates and can help you **to allocate** time effectively. For long-term schedules charts are useful and can be referred to by all personnel involved in a project. The Gantt chart is particularly useful, not only in scheduling tasks but in evaluating planned work and actual progress.

Measuring and evaluating results

It is essential that tasks are **monitored** for deadlines, problems, and co-ordination. Tasks can get forgotten and the following procedure can help ensure objectives are reached.

- Check on progress of an operation
- Check completion when a deadline is reached
- Check payments when they fall due
- Retrieve files necessary for future meetings and correspondence

Evaluating marketing activity

(a) Performance can be measured against annual **targets** - sales, budgets, expenditure

(b) **Moving standards** allow performance measurement on an on-going **control** basis eg monthly sales targets.

(c) **Diagnostic standards** can be monitored to assess how the market is responding to any marketing activity eg through market research. Such **feedback** may include output against the marketing plan, comparing marketing activities to the previous year, measuring the accuracy of budgets and schedules etc.

In conclusion, in a fully marketing orientated company everyone is involved directly or indirectly in marketing and therefore in marketing evaluation. Discussion and comments should be encouraged both at meetings and through suggestion boxes to improve procedures. All staff should be asked for their opinions and those of others outside the company.

More specifically, formal marketing **evaluation and control** procedures should be the responsibility of the marketing director, implemented downwards through marketing, sales and retail personnel. Advertising, PR and marketing research agencies would also play a part in the evaluation process.

I would be pleased to clarify any of the above points if necessary.
A Hopeful

10 International event management

I will assume that the Marketing Manager will have produced a schedule and checklist for the conference venue itself, and that the international delegates will already be aware of the venue, date, time and the purpose of the event. They should also have information on speakers, schedule of meetings, and breaks.

The following criteria will be checked for the international delegates.

(a) Have the **English translators** been booked, and confirmed their attendance?

(b) Make it clear with the delegates that they are being invited to the conference as part of their employment with the company and they are not expected to pay for their hotel and travel expenses.

(c) Travel visas arranged if necessary and any letters of confirmation that delegates are travelling on company business.

(d) All travel itineraries have been dispatched and confirmed by the delegates.

(e) Transport booked for the airport collection and delivery of delegates to the hotel accommodation. Alternatively, if travelling independently, have they received detailed instructions for getting to their hotel and conference venue?

(f) Has the welcome meeting been arranged at the hotel with the interpreters confirming their attendance? Host personnel are trained and ready to hand for general assistance.

(g) Ensure the following:

  (i) All delegates are aware of the social events and outings (this encourages networking and can be a time when new ideas emerge for later discussion).

  (ii) Currency exchange/credit facilities are available at the hotel

  (iii) All international business and social customs are acknowledged, and religious and cultural requirements are known eg particular foods or consumption of alcohol.

11 Venue appraisal

Before an organisation books a space at an exhibition, the following points must be checked off to ensure suitability.

(a) **Organisers**

- Are they a reputable organisation?
- Do they belong to any association?

(b) **Venue**

- Is it a good venue?
- Has it the right status to be compatible with our goods and services?
- Is it in the right position to attract a good attendance?

- Does it have adequate space and size?
- Is it convenient to get to and easy for transporting exhibits to and from?
- Does it have adequate facilities?
- Does it comply with health and safety regulations for the anticipated numbers?
- If the venue is outdoors, has it suitable shelter if it rains?

(c) **Facilities**

- Are the guests suitably catered for, ie food, bar or accommodation near by?
- Have they the appropriate sound systems, presentation equipment, Internet facilities, along with other furniture like seating for staff and guests?
- Are the basic necessities like water, electricity and gas readily available?

(d) **Cost**

- Is the exhibition compatible with our marketing objectives?
- Does it fall within our budget?
- What returns do we expect after the event?
- What is the cost per square metre and could you negotiate depending on size?
- What are the estimated costs to design the stand, staff it, print sales literature and entertain customers?

(e) **Publicity/PR**

- How are the visitors to be attracted to the venue?
- Do they have a press office on site?
- What follow up publicity is going to take place?
- Are there any associated events like film/video shows in which we could take part?

(Please note. To ensure maximum coverage during the exhibition, early liaison with the exhibition press office is advised.)

(f) **Build-up and knock-down**

- Is there sufficient time to build the stand and take it down?

12 Media choice

Memorandum

To: Managing Director
From: Keith Reed
Date: June 2002
Subject: Advertising new and used cars
Strengths and weaknesses of different media.

As new marketing manager, I am summarising the strengths and weaknesses of different media to enable the most effective expenditure of our £1,000,000+ advertising budget.

Although our marketing objectives and strategy are not yet finalised, this memo gives you some preliminary thoughts on media selection. Operating in a highly competitive market means that we have to select our media mix carefully. This may mean some change from previous activities, but this is required if we are to maintain our excellent image and aggressive sales drive.

Medium	Strengths	Weaknesses
TV	High visual impact Wide coverage Low cost per thousand Ideal for launch of new models Allows demonstration Possible co-operative ad opportunity	Expensive production costs Expensive lump sum outlay Unsuitable for used cars Long lead time for booking Zapping away from commercial breaks using remote control
Medium	**Strengths**	**Weaknesses**
Radio	Drive time radio shows – right audience Mass medium – large audience at a single exposure Low cost per thousand Radio is portable Low production costs Used by car buyers	Office hours shows not right audience Sound only – pressure to retain message No shelf life Competition use it a lot
Papers (free and paid)	Targeted sections – motor section and special motoring features Good audience range Quick and responsive Possible links with local franchises Combine with leaflets Free auto papers available in supermarkets and petrol stations	Circulation doesn't mean readership Paid for newspapers expensive cost per thousand Free papers cheaper, but could lack quality in terms of content Free auto papers on stands not delivered to the home
Posters	Commuters and car drivers audience	Cannot get detailed information across
Direct mail	Low cost per order Good targeting tool since the database can track existing customers, lapsed customers and those about to buy a car	Low season

Conclusion

We should concentrate on regional evening papers and selected weeklies for both new and used cars at present. However, our TV region is becoming more flexible on rates for regional customers, and some of our competitors are moving onto radio as well as into the recent free auto papers.

Therefore, we really must look at the whole **database** facility with a view to examining a major re-investment in a hybrid **marketing system** which links sales staff, sales, complaints, customers buying patterns, and enquiries.

We can also control our media usage next year, as I will be instigating a media analysis which will reveal the media cost per enquiry and cost per order of every sale we achieve. This may well change our media selection in the future.

13 Magazine sales promotions

Report

To: Marketing Director
From: Promotions Manager
Date: June 2002
Subject: Sales promotions techniques

1 **Introduction and objectives**

1.1 Following our discussion last week I thought it might be useful for you to be aware of some of the ideas my department is considering regarding suitable **sales promotions** for our publications. The following provides a brief definition and an outline of suggested sales promotion techniques.

1.2 The **Institute of Sales Promotion (ISP)** defines sales promotion as 'a range of tactical marketing **techniques**, designed within a **strategic marketing framework**, to **add value** to a product or service, in order to achieve a specific sales and marketing **objective**'.

Sales promotions fall into three categories: those aimed at **trade, salesforce** and **consumers**. I will concentrate on those designed to stimulate consumers, although this strategy will have trade repercussions, because when magazine sales increase there will be a knock on effect for our advertisers.

1.3 The objectives of such a campaign would be to encourage **new customers** whilst reinforcing benefits to our **existing customers**. This is based on the Pareto principle whereby 80% of our business is derived from 20% of our customers. This strategy will also provide opportunities for **cross selling** across titles.

Promotional variations will depend on a number of factors: the **nature** of the publication and its readers, **frequency** of publication and **purchase cycle** (whether a publication is one that readers will be interested in for a period of time, such as a lifestyle magazine, or one that may be bought for a specific purpose, such as *What Mortgage?*).

Before selecting one or more of the techniques outlined below we need to determine our **objectives**, as different promotional methods may be more suitable than others. The key applications of promotional techniques are as follows.

- To add appeal to the **brand** and thus enhance its image
- To encourage trial or repeat **purchase**
- To defend the product from **competition**
- To encourage **customer loyalty**
- To increase **market penetration**

2 **Potential sales promotion techniques**

I have deliberately only selected a few of our titles for this exercise. These are: Gardening Today, Knitting for Your Family, You and Your Pet, and Ms.

2.1 **Free products**. These could include seeds or gardening gloves with our gardening magazines, knitting or sewing needles, samples of petfood, small paperbacks etc.

2.2 **Competitions**. These need to be linked to the publication's readership. Prizes could include tickets to exhibitions, a quantity of plants, wool, animal food for a year, a holiday etc. This strategy will also allow for the collection of data which may be used in a direct marketing campaign.

2.3 **Subscription offers**. Upon taking out an annual subscription, readers could be entitled to the following: a gardening video, a knitting book, reduced pet insurance, free cosmetics.

2.4 **Pricing**. Discounting would involve reducing the price on some or all of the titles in order to stimulate demand and increase circulation. There needs to be careful **analysis** of likely increases in circulation before this approach is adopted, along with a consideration of the impact on profitability.

2.5 **Coupons**. These could be offered in conjunction with campaigns being conducted by advertisers.

2.6 **Extra product**. A larger than normal issue for the same price. This could take the form of a supplement such as a guide to pruning, knitting patterns for Christmas, a health guide for your pet or a seasonal fashion supplement.

3 Conclusion

3.1 Sales promotions can be considered to be short term in the sense that they can boost sales and attract new customers, but they are highly valid techniques in this highly competitive market. The key to success with these promotions is to ensure **synergy** with the publication and the readership. Selection factors will include cost effectiveness balanced with high perceived value for our readers.

14 Price

(a) Price is important within the marketing mix because it influences **profitability** by generating **revenue**, unlike all the other elements in the mix that generate costs. Quite often, price is the only aspect a marketer can change quickly in response to **demand** or combat a **competitor**. So it has an important role as a **competitive tool**, helping to **differentiate** products and organisations. However, price must be **consistent** with other elements of the mix since it contributes to the overall image of the product.

In the absence of other information, customers tend to judge **quality** on price, and an organisation cannot hope to offer an exclusive quality product at a low price - the price must be consistent with the overall product offer.

The ultimate **objective** of pricing is to produce the **level of sales** required to fulfil the organisation's **marketing and financial objectives**.

(i) **Maximising profits**. This means maximising the returns on assets or investments.

(ii) Maintaining or increasing **market share** involves increasing or maintaining the **customer base**.

(iii) **Market penetration**. Getting a new product adopted and accepted quickly, in order to speed up the initial phase of the product's life cycle, by setting a low price to stimulate growth.

(iv) **Market skimming**. This involves setting a high initial price for a new product, if the new product to the consumer has a high value (Sony Play station, CD players etc). Once **economies of scale** come on line and **demand** increases, prices generally fall.

(v) Increasing short-term sales volume, by promotional **price cuts**, **discount** offers and **bonuses**.

Price setting is a complex process and needs to be carefully planned in conjunction with all the other elements of the marketing mix.

(b) **Elasticity of demand**

Elasticity of demand is the **responsiveness of demand** for a product to **changes in its price**.

(i) If **demand changes drastically** in response to a small change in price, then demand is said to be very **elastic**.

(ii) If **demand changes very little** or not at all in response to a small change in price, then demand is said to be **inelastic**.

Price elasticity is measured as:

$$\frac{\text{\% change in sales demand}}{\text{\% change in sales price}}$$

(1) When elasticity is greater than 1 (elastic), if the price is lowered, total sales revenue would rise because of the large increase in demand. If it is raised, total sales revenue would fall because of the large fall in demand.

(2) When elasticity is less than 1 (inelastic), if the price is lowered, total sales revenue would fall, because the increase in sales volume would be too small to compensate for the price reductions. If it is raised, total sales revenue would go up in spite of the drop in sales quantities.

Marketing management needs to be able to estimate the likely effects of price changes on total revenue and profits. Price elasticity of demand gives precision to the question of whether the firm's price is too high or too low.

15 Market research for new product launch

The following report outlines the market research plan to be conducted prior to the launch of our new magazine aimed at teenage females.

Research conducted last year revealed the UK female teenage market as a viable new market for our magazine publications. The secondary research carried out at this time has defined a **demographic** and **psychographic** profile of our target market.

The following plan has been developed for pre-launch into the market to define the most successful **product** characteristics, **pricing** and **advertising** support. As a wealth of secondary research has already been gathered, this plan will focus entirely on primary **sources of information**.

The stages of the research plan are as follows.

- Define the research objectives
- Ascertain the best methods for obtaining the information
- Collect the data

- Process the data
- Make recommendations
- Implement the recommendations

Research objectives

Research objectives must be devised to be specific, measurable, actionable, reasonable and timescaled (**SMART**). Suggested objectives for the research are as follows:

- To investigate attitudes to **magazine content and layout** styles amongst the target group, to discover the most appropriate product mix
- To investigate attitudes to **advertising message and content** amongst the target group to discover the most appropriate advertising mix.
- To quantify **media consumption** of the target group
- To investigate attitudes to **magazine pricing** amongst the target group.

Method for obtaining information

Focus groups

A group of six to ten respondents from the target group will be engaged in a group discussion with a moderator. The sessions will be recorded or videoed for later analysis. Props will be used, such as advertising visuals, magazine layouts etc.

Reasons for choice of method

(a) This method has been chosen because it is a cost effective way of gathering respondent data, leading to a larger number of respondents being involved within the budget.

(b) The recording of focus groups allows more in depth analysis of the discussion.

(c) There are potential legal and /or moral implications surrounding street recruitment of this target group.

Collect the data

The first issue to consider is that of sampling. Although we have defined demographic and psychographic profiles of the target group, it is recommended that we address geographic considerations for the sample. Previous research projects have used specific city locations in the North, Midlands and South East of the UK to mirror the UK population. It is suggested that this research uses the same locations.

Respondents will be recruited through snowballing techniques which could be achieved through schools and colleges within the target areas. We must also consider the legal and moral implications of respondent recruitment. We will need to gain parental permission and possibly parental accompaniment for the respondents.

Process the data

Discussions will be captured on video. Transcripts of discussions will be produced and qualitative analysis techniques applied to the results.

Recommendations

The results will be written into a report format and a presentation given to company directors and marketing management.

Resource/costs/timing issues

We do not have the in-house expertise to conduct a research project of this type. A research brief will be written and submitted to two external marketing research companies. Previous experience would suggest that the budget of £30,000 will finance recruitment, data collection, analysis and reporting of 15 focus groups. The likely timescale for this project is two months from the awarding of the contract.

16 Flexible budgets

(a)

Forecast sales (units)	10,000	10,000	10,000
	£	£	£
Selling price	100	150	200
Direct labour per unit	20	20	20
Direct materials per unit	40	40	40
Unit contribution	40	90	140
Delivery costs recovery	10	10	10
Total contribution	50	100	150

Budget at each price level

Forecast sales (units)	10,000	10,000	10,000
	£	£	£
Sales revenue	1,000,000	1,500,000	2,000,000
Cost of sales:			
Direct labour	200,000	200,000	200,000
Direct materials	400,000	400,000	400,000
Contribution	400,000	900,000	1,400,000
Delivery costs recovery	100,000	100,000	100,000
Total contribution	500,000	1,000,000	1,500,000
Fixed costs	50,000	50,000	50,000
Net profit	450,000	950,000	1,450,000

(b) Flexed to 80% budget at each price level

Forecast sales (units)	8,000	8,000	8,000
	£	£	£
Sales revenue	800,000	1,200,000	1,600,000
Cost of sales:			
Direct labour	160,000	160,000	160,000
Direct materials	320,000	320,000	320,000
Contribution	320,000	720,000	1,120,000
Delivery costs recovery	80,000	80,000	80,000
Total contribution	400,000	800,000	1,200,000
Fixed costs	50,000	50,000	50,000
Net profit	350,000	750,000	1,150,000

17 Budget building

To: Managing Director and members of the management team
From: Marketing Manager
Date: June 2002
Subject: Preparation of departmental budget

(a) **Information gathering**

Before the budget can be prepared, I intend to carry out an information-gathering exercise.

Internal information will be available from formal sources such as control and monitoring reports, and informal sources, such as discussions and meetings. The information may include the following:

- Marketing and sales information, eg revenue performance
- Production and operational information, eg production capacity
- Research and development information
- Personnel information, eg anticipated salary increases for departmental staff

External information will also be available from formal sources such as trade associations, and from informal sources such as discussions and meetings. The information may include:

- Market and competitors, eg level of competitor promotional activity
- Economic conditions, eg level of inflation
- Demographic trends and social factors

(b) **Budget profit and loss account**

Although the organisation will produce a **master budget** containing a profit and loss account, balance sheet and cash flow, the marketing department will be required to produce its own budgeted profit and loss account and cash flow details.

I propose to use the following **budget headings**.

- Revenue
- Promotional spend
- Advertising
- Gifts
- Donations
- Wages
- Light and heat
- Motor and travelling expenses
- Subsistence
- Postage, printing and stationery
- Telephone
- Subscriptions
- Publications
- Sundry expenses
- Sub-contracted work
- Apportionment of fixed overheads

Many of the above categories will be further analysed. For instance, advertising expenditure will be further subdivided into trade journal advertising, local newspaper advertising and so on.

(c) **Control of expenditure**

Using information obtained during the information-gathering exercise, **budget allocations** will be made against each of the budget headings above. These allocations will be broken down into **monthly periods**. For instance, if annual motor and travelling expenditure is expected to be £12,000, it may be sensible to set a budget of £1,000 for each month. Any **seasonal factors** which may cause fluctuations in the monthly budget will also be taken into account. (For example, if more travelling is likely to be done in a particular month, then the budget will be amended accordingly.)

At the end of each control period a **variance report** will be produced showing **differences between actual and estimated expenditure**. In this respect **flexed budgets** are vital, in order to take into account any changes in activities. I will give responsibility for some of the budget headings to members of my team and ask them to analyse and investigate variances.

A variance report is only one type of control information. Other reports which I should like to see on a monthly basis are as follows.

- Staff holiday and sickness
- New and discontinued product information
- Progress of promotional advertising campaigns
- Month-end stockholding, eg stationery, promotional literature
- Analysis of sub-contracted work
- Analysis of sundry expenses

Pilot paper and suggested answers

Certificate in Marketing

Marketing in Practice

5.26: Marketing in Practice

Time:

Date:

3 Hours Duration

This examination is in two sections.

PART A – Is compulsory and worth 40% of total marks.

PART B – Has **SIX** questions; select **THREE**. Each answer will be worth 20% of the total marks.

DO NOT repeat the question in your answer, but show clearly the number of the question attempted on the appropriate pages of the answer book.

Rough workings should be included in the answer book and ruled through after use.

Certificate in Marketing

5.23: Marketing in Practice – Specimen Paper

PART A

bizinfo/hungary.com

Following the collapse of Communism, the markets of Central and Eastern Europe have undergone massive change, and there is a great deal of inward investment by American, British and Multinational companies.

bizinfo/hungary.com was established three years ago by a former real estate salesman and an IT specialist. It serves as an English language portal (an Internet gateway) for a range of services needed by incoming investors, and provides comprehensive listings and information on property and land for commercial and residential use. There is also a subscription service for more detailed financial and business news, not just from Hungary, but also from the Czech and Slovak Republics and Romania.

Only six people are employed full-time by the company and the biggest expenditure is on advertising in order to ensure the maximum number of 'hits' on the web site. Advertising is placed not just in Hungary, but also in business publications in Western Europe, Asia Pacific and the USA.

The company has been successful and a similar operation is now planned for Turkey, which is looking towards European Union membership. The launch of bizinfo/turkey.com is only three months away and nothing has yet been done to publicise it in Istanbul. Looking further ahead, Estonia is also under consideration as it could serve not only the Baltic States but also Poland.

Your Role

You have just arrived in your exciting new job as the company's first Marketing Assistant, and have soon realised what a fast moving business environment this is. The Financial Controller is calling for reductions in expenditure, your relationship with the current advertising agency is unsettled, yet meanwhile, the company is about to expand rapidly. Also, bizinfo has little idea of who is actually visiting its web site, and there is an urgent need to gather information on site visitors via an electronic questionnaire.

Strictly Confidential

To: A. Jeffrey

In view of the planned expansion into two new countries, we need to carefully control our costs and **we need to make a 10% saving on all our expenditure including advertising.** This could possibly be achieved by moving away from our current Full Service Agency when its contract expires next month. We could then buy media and creative work from whoever offers the cheapest prices.

Attached are some figures obtained from our current agency and also quotes from a media buyer and a newly established creative agency.

Also, to help you understand how the business works I have enclosed a summary of costings and revenues from each of our three activities.

I trust this will be useful.

F. Varos
Financial Controller

Advertising Costs

Current Situation

bizinfo/hungary.com has an annual contract with Eurinter Advertising plc., who charges a monthly fee of $1,000 to cover account management and the production of visuals. Production costs for each of the four advertising campaigns in a typical year work out at an average of $3,000 each. The 10% average discount obtained on media expenditure means we spend $900,000 on media costs.

Alternatively...

Medialink Media Buying Company are confident of obtaining an average discount of 12% across the publications and media we currently use. Hotshots Creative charges $500 for visuals or roughs of proposed advertising and has quoted $5,000 for production of finished advertisements for a campaign.

The Company's Activities

bizinfo/hungary.com/businessportal

This service gives links to a full range of business services needed by incoming investors; translation services, legal services, investment advisors, software designers etc. etc. The service is free but advertising on banners and around the portal generates $350,000 per year.

bizinfo/hungary.com/property

This service is again free to site visitors but generates revenue from property developers and real estate agencies whose properties are featured on the web site. This has many search features to save the time of those looking to set up in Hungary or base their staff in the country. This generates $800,000 per year.

bizinfo/hungary.com/businessnews

This subscription-only service has 1,500 subscribers paying $10 per month for the latest financial and investment news.

The Company's Costs

An advertising sales manager, whose wage is $20,000 per year, manages the two free services, whilst a journalist is employed on the same wage to run the news service. Other costs, including wages, technical support and office rental amount to $180,000 per year. (This is divided between the three services.) There is also the cost of advertising as detailed earlier.

PART A

Question 1.

a. Will a move to separate buying of creative work and media give the required 10% saving on advertising costs over a twelve month period? (Show your calculations and state any assumptions you have made).

(15 marks)

b. What should be contained in a brief for an advertising agency? Provide a sample briefing document containing the information that is needed.

(15 marks)

c. What problems are likely to arise when dealing with a new supplier and how are these best avoided?

(10 marks)
(40 marks in total)

PART B – Answer THREE Questions Only

Question 2.

As part of a marketing audit being undertaken by bizinfo.com you have been asked to investigate the competition. As part of this process:

a. How will you identify competitors?

(7 marks)

b. What information do you need?

(6 marks)

c. How will you obtain and verify the information?

(7 marks)
(20 marks in total)

Question 3.

A launch event is planned for 100 guests from local businesses and the media in Istanbul.

a. What steps need be taken to ensure the smooth running of the event?

(10 marks)

b. Produce a Gantt chart showing tasks needing to be undertaken before and after the event takes place in three months' time.

(10 marks)
(20 marks in total)

Question 4.

How can all the elements of the promotional submix be used to promote bizinfo, a virtual company?

(20 marks)

Question 5.

Which is currently the most profitable of the company's three areas of business and how would this change if the savings were implemented? Justify your answer with appropriate calculations.

(20 marks)

Question 6.

a. Draft a letter to potential advertisers on your web site in Hungary, selling the company's offering.

(10 marks)

b. Suggest ways other than mailing by which businesses can be approached, highlighting the advantages and disadvantages of such methods.

(10 marks)
(20 marks in total)

Question 7.

What information does bizinfo need about the visitors to its web site, and how can this be used to further build the business?

(20 marks)

Guidelines for answering the BIZINFO' paper

Question 1.

(a) This is a very typical start to a Marketing in Practice paper, with a seemingly frightening calculation to perform. Look at the section of the case entitled 'advertising costs' and underline all the numerical information. This includes the words four, monthly and annual as these are also key to the calculations. The actual calculations are available on the CIM student website. A tip is to make assumptions – they give easy marks. For section (b) refer back to the section on agencies contained in Chapter 7 of this book, while in (c) a suitable list of criteria/potential problems is in the same chapter.

Question 2.

Refer to Chapter 4 for some ideas. Be careful of the marking scheme, ensuring you say enough, but not too much on each section.

Question 3.

Do not panic about this being in Istanbul! The basic criteria are the same the world over, just be careful you contextualise your answer. See Chapter 11 for a sound theoretical underpinning of venue selection.

Question 4.

The first issue here is to clarify what the 'promotional submix' is. Conventionally this is advertising, public relations, sales promotion and personal selling. You may also include sponsorship and conferences/exhibitions.

Question 5.

Unusually this question calls for calculations. Similar principles as question 1 apply.

Question 6.

Drafting letters is a favourite examiner topic. There are usually marks for layout, number of points made, and also tone/pitch. The second part of the question calls for a view on such methods as advertising, telemarketing, cold calling etc.

Question 7.

Information needs' is a another favourite. Look at past papers and model answers for tips.

1

(a) **To:** F. Varos Financial Controller
From: A Jeffrey Marketing Assistant
Date: June 11 2002
Subject: Savings on Advertising Costs

Thank you for all the information on the business activities and advertising costs. I have worked out the alternative costings for a 12 month period for a switch to a Creative and Media Buying House. The calculations are set out below:

Current situation	*Eurinter Advertising plc*	*Full Service Agency*
Media Spend $1,000,000	Discount Av. Disc 10%	Total cost $900,000
Account management/visuals $1,000 per month × 12		$12,000
Production costs for campaign $3,000 per campaign × 4		$12,000
		Total $924,000
Alternative	*Media Link/Hot Shot Creative*	*Agencies*
$1,000,000	Av. Disc 12%	$880,000
Visuals/roughs $500 per campaign × 4		$2,000
Production costs for campaign $5,000 per campaign × 4		$20,000
		Total $902,000

Overall difference over a 12 month period is $22,000 in favour of the two independents.

My assumptions were:

(i) We have an average of 4 campaigns a year.

(ii) The $500 for visuals/roughs relate to those for one campaign.

If these assumptions are correct, then the savings are going to be around $22,000. This is way short of the projected savings of 10% overall. ($924,000 × 10% = $92,400). My belief is that we need to maintain the current level of spending, because to spend less could jeopardise the launch in Turkey. However, I do realise the need to reduce costs to ensure the long term survival of the company.

In conclusion, I believe that we can reduce our costs by obtaining quotes from other relevant agencies (those who have expertise within our industry), or renegotiate with our existing one, who would not want to lose our business. It may not, however, give us the desired 10%.

I look forward to your comments via e-mail over the next few days.

Regards,

Andrew

(b) **To:** Nakita Lenin Chief Executive
From: A Jeffrey Marketing Assistant
Date: June 2002
Subject: Agency Brief

As our company is rapidly expanding, it is no longer feasible to give our current agency a verbal brief. We need to formalise the process, particularly as we may change our agency in the near future. In the long term, this will save us time as well as money. Enclosed is a shopping list of what should be contained in a brief to an advertising agency, along with the relevant briefing form.

Please could you get back to me as soon as possible with your comments.

Andrew Jeffrey

Marketing Assistant

Advertising Brief

Project name and description

We need to give each campaign a **meaningful** name. This will allow us to evaluate more easily each campaign with the range of media used in it.

Also as a guide, we should outline that the website is an English portal for a wide range of services for incoming investors that includes property and land information, financial and business news, as well as translation and legal services etc. This is essential for all new agencies.

Budget

The agency needs a budget to work to. In our case a tighter one is in place than in the previous year. We need to stress that it includes all additional costs like visuals and photographs.

Key deadlines

We need to set deadlines for presentation of **conceptual** themes for each campaign and discuss launch times. This may be with different agencies in the future. With a **Full Service Agency**, it will be with the various different departments.

Media placement

A media schedule will need to be devised, along with what media is being used at what cost. It should highlight copy dates as well, because posters and magazines require copy well in advance.

Company background

The agency require as much information as possible about the competition, marketing environment, our perceived strengths and weaknesses, market share, culture and so on. Anything that will assist the agency in getting to know the 'real' us and what we want to achieve through these campaigns, will be important.

Marketing/communications objectives

Once the agency know what our **marketing objectives** are, and how they cascade down into our **communications objectives,** they will have a very clear picture of what we are trying to achieve. From that, the communications message can be more tightly targeted.

Background to the brief

Essentially we need to explain the reason for the brief. Has it been brought about because of increased competition or expansion of the product/service? Things to discuss would include repeat campaigns (if successful), **abandonment** (if not), times of year to run and so on.

Product information

Here we need to offer any market research we have carried. We need to discuss where we are in the **product life cycle**, along with any literature about our company and that of our competitors.

Target audience

We need to offer as much information as we can about our target audience. In our case this will include any database information from our site, or **secondary** information about the types of people who use similar sites.

Finally, include anything that might further help the agency. For example, the websites we like and dislike and why, past advertising campaigns and those of competitors. The agency may come up with ideas that may make the site more interactive, because the selection of the 'right' agency is likely to be based on e-commerce knowledge.

CREATIVE BRIEF: ADVERTISING

AGENCY:
BRIEFING DATE:
COMPANY:
CONTACT NAME:
PROJECT NAME:
PROJECT DESCRIPTION:
BUDGET:
KEY DEADLINES:
MEDIA PLACEMENT:
COMPANY BACKGROUND:
MARKETING OBJECTIVES: COMMUNICATIONS OBJECTIVES:
BACKGROUND TO THE BRIEF:
PRODUCT INFORMATION:
TARGET AUDIENCE:

(c) Any company which is considering developing a new relationship with a new supplier (in this case an advertising agency and media buying company in an international context) needs to be aware of the following problems that can arise and how to overcome them.

Firstly, to set the scene, the *aim* of the advertising is to promote the existence of Bizinfo's service to existing and potential customers, via search engines, press room, events, links and banner advertising and, of course, traditional business publications.

(i) **Agency Competence**

The first thing that has to be considered is that e-commerce/business is not just a bolt-on service for this particular company. It is the core of its activities in a global market. The selection of the wrong agency could have disastrous consequences for the company. The agency should be selected on the basis of their **business competence** ie experience of the territory and the knowledge of customer needs. This means having empathy with Bizinfo/hungary.com's aims and objectives.

It is important that when first selecting an agency to work with you look at the type of work they are doing and consider several agencies before you make your decision. Ask them to present to you in order to see if the relationship can be built up successfully in the long term. This is essential as you need to be able to work together as a team. It is at this stage of selection that negotiation takes place. Commitments and compromises should be made which are acceptable to both parties. This provides a framework for reference if and when problems arise .

(ii) **Staff Turnover of Agency**

One very important factor that needs to be considered is the **staff turnover** of the agency. You do not want to establish a rapport with staff who leave at regular intervals.

(iii) **Agency Costs**

Try to avoid commission or media discounts as this can cause conflicts. Keep payment to the usual practise of fees for advice/creative work with design and production costs marked up by an agreed percentage.

(iv) **Agency Brief**

You need to provide a clear focused brief which provides guidance as to what you require when tasks are being carried out. At each stage of the brief the work should be checked and approved whilst the work is in progress. This process should be an established schedule in the brief that both parties have agreed on and regular team meetings should take place in which updates (information sharing) and problems can be discussed. Good communication is essential.

The basic procedure that needs to be followed is:

- Briefing
- Joint planning
- Negotiation of terms
- Sharing of information and resource
- Regular meetings, monitoring, checking and approval
- Feedback
- Payment

The underlying philosophy should be one of **a partnership** in which frequent and adequate **communication** is established at all times. And as mentioned earlier, with agreed objectives and controls, mutual respect should result in benefit to both parties.

2

(a) Firstly, check out the search engines, banner advertising, affiliated programmes, links, events and press room on the Internet itself. Then, of course, research the advertising being carried out in the traditional media publications such as trade magazines associated with international property and land/residential investment and financial, business and legal publications. This means identifying in particular the appropriate publications in Western Europe, the USA and the Asia Pacific because this is where the inward investors are resident. Similarly, look at the main property investment agencies (commercial and residential use) in the Hungarian, Czech and Slovak Republics, Romania and Estonia. Research all computer data-bases (available at many public libraries), annual reports, industry research and surveys, and the Yellow Pages. A more selective global approach needs to be taken with regard to the above focusing on the inward investors' perspectives and associated agencies.

(b) Create a file for each competitor listing any relevant information on their service offerings, market position etc.

- Summary of each competitor's products - It should include details about their location, quality, advertising, staff, distribution methods, promotional strategies, customer service, pricing, offerings and product innovations.
- Competitor's strengths and weaknesses. Identify how you will capitalise on their weaknesses (e.g. is there a gap in the market? Can you identify a new market niche?). Are you able to meet the challenges their strengths represent?
- Strength of the market - How is the market for bizinfo.com growing? Is the market growing for bizinfo's product service sufficiently so that there are plenty of customers for all market players? Or is the market so tight that you are selling primarily to your competitors' customers? (If so, do you have a strong competitive advantage?).

(c) By obtaining the above information bizinfo.com can make informed decisions about everything from marketing tactics to long term business strategies.

- Interview people connected with the competitors. This can be done by in-house employees or by an agency which specialises in competitor analysis, monitoring in general industry, economic and regulatory trends
- Personal visits - Observe how employees interact with customers. What do their premises look like? How are their products displayed? Pricing of the services offered.
- Talk to your customers! Learn what your customers are saying about your competitors and about you too!
- Analyse competitor's ads to gain information about their target audiences, market position, product features and benefits, prices etc.
- Attend speeches and presentations made by representatives of your competitors.
- Trade show displays - View your competitor's display with a critical eye and from a potential customer's point of view. What does their display 'say' about the

company? Observe which trade shows or industry events competitors attend which provides information on their marketing strategy and target market.

3

(a) Before the launch event takes place in Istanbul the following steps have to be taken:

Selection of Staff

- Employees are the key representatives of our company. We need to ensure that all the staff involved in the launch are fully trained and briefed for bizinfo/turkey.com website's main aims and objectives. Ensure the staff are sufficiently informed and confident to approach launch guests and build up relationships in order to 'pick up' on leads quickly and appropriately.
- Appropriate appearance is essential, wearing bizinfo's identification badge which is easily identified.
- Staff need to respond at appropriate times with bizinfo's publicity literature.

Venue

- Does the venue have the right ambience, space and size for this e-commerce launch?
- Is it easy to get to?
- Does it comply with health and safety regulations for the anticipated numbers?

Facilities

- Does it have sufficient Internet facilities to cater for 100 guests to interact on the systems during the launch? - absolutely essential!
- Can the venue provide all other technical needs e.g. sound systems, presentation equipment and appropriate seating for staff and guests?
- Separate and appropriate facilities for the media personnel attending the launch to contact and send their copy to their editor.

Costs

- Do we have sufficient funds to provide the appropriate launch that is in keeping with our corporate image?

Publicity/ PR

- How are visitors being attracted to the venue e.g. invitation, e-mail, banner advertising, Internet and business press releases
- Have follow-up calls to accepted invitations been carried out and all confirmations logged?
- Ensure the company literature is designed and printed in line with our corporate image.
- All media guests receive the appropriate 'media pack' upon entrance to the launch to assist with follow-up publicity.

(b)

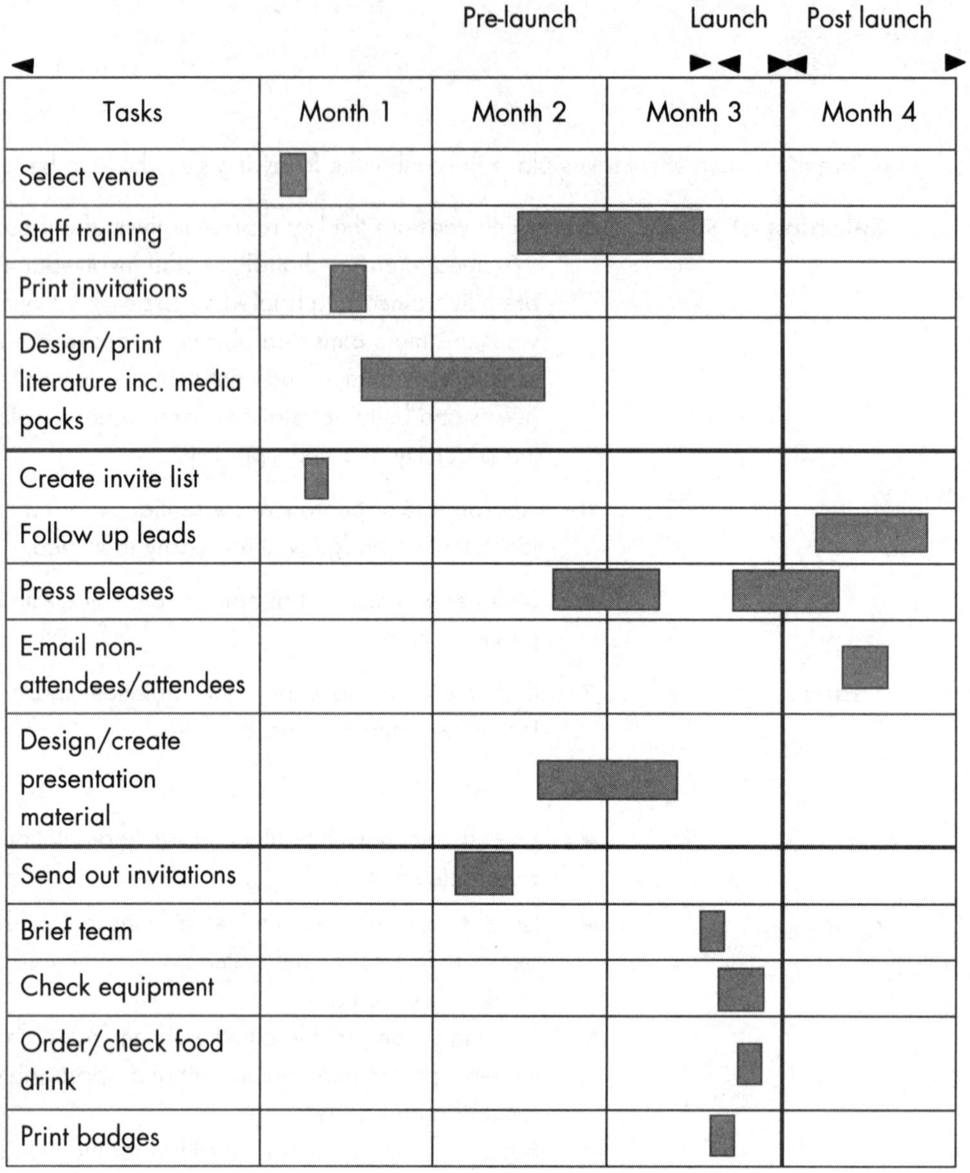

Pre-launch Launch Post launch

Tasks	Month 1	Month 2	Month 3	Month 4
Select venue				
Staff training				
Print invitations				
Design/print literature inc. media packs				
Create invite list				
Follow up leads				
Press releases				
E-mail non-attendees/attendees				
Design/create presentation material				
Send out invitations				
Brief team				
Check equipment				
Order/check food drink				
Print badges				

4

To: S Jones Advertising Manager
From: A Jeffrey
Date: May 31 2002
Subject: Promotion of Bizinfo

On my appointment as Marketing Assistant, one of my first tasks was to investigate all the available options to promote Bizinfo. Below is a list of **promotional** tool and activities we could engage in to ensure that we become more visible throughout the web. The tools I have chosen are those of the promotional submix, namely Advertising, Sales Promotion, Personal Selling, Public Relations and Direct Marketing. I have wherever possible looked at both online and offline techniques.

Advertising

Online

Banner advertising	We can place a banner advert on a search engine directory or another site. We could make it animated, static or both, and they could click through to our site. To reduce costs, a reciprocal arrangement on our site could be organised.
Search engines/directories	Alternatively we could simply buy space on a search engine or website, or be on a directory for users searching for key words such as 'Residential Properties in Eastern Europe'.
E-mails	Using our existing database we could e-mail existing and potential customers of our new services. We could also buy space on an e-mail newsletter.

Offline

Media	At present we advertise in a range of relevant business publications. As we are expanding, other forms of media like newspapers, TV could be used to promote our websites with a more focused approach by targeting our audience with the relevant web address ie bizinfo/hungary.com/businessnews
Stationery	We must ensure that our URL is on all our stationery (letterheads, business cards and so on).

Sales promotion

Online

Special offers	For new customers subscribing to our business news we could offer the first month free, or those who are advertising their properties for the first time will receive a free entry during their first month.
Public relations	Press releases can be emailed to interested groups, as well as using the many news sites on the web to promote our company.

Offline

Special offers	This could be interlinked with the above by direct mail to specifically targeted groups.
Public relations	Already we adopt a traditional approach – sending press releases to the appropriate trade press, newspapers and magazines. Other media like radio or specialist TV channels should also be considered as should sponsorship of the sites.

Personal selling

Offline	Face-to-face selling of our product offering still plays a vital role. The selling of space on the site along with persuading developers and real estate agencies to feature their properties generates over $1,000,000 for our company. As we refine our database, the information extracted can be used to target better prospects.

Direct marketing

Online	As well as using just e-mail as our direct marketing tool to build up a relationship with customers, we could utilise a call-back service online carried out by companies like RealCall. This allows our customers to state at what time a callback would be suitable for them. This could assist areas like legal and financial information where complex issues may need to be discussed.
Offline	Direct mail is only one of the methods of accessing our current and future customers and users of the site. Telemarketing of new and existing prospects allows us to up sell, cross sell or both. This is often in conjunction with a direct mail campaign. The results could also be used for a follow up from our sales manager.

In conclusion, an integrated approach is essential across all elements of the promotional mix, particularly online and offline where they must support each other. Each communication tool should be tied together, offering a unified and consistent message to our new and existing customers.

5

To: F Varos Financial Controller
From: A Jeffrey Marketing Assistant
Date: June 2002
Subject: Profitable areas of the company

From the set of information you supplied, I have been able to ascertain the most profitable areas of the business.

	Business portal	**Property**	**Businessnews**
Revenue	350,000	800,000	180,000
Less variable costs			
Ad production costs	(4,000)	(4,000)	(4,000)
Media costs	(300,000)	(300,000)	(300,000)
Contribution	46,000	496,000	(124,000)
Less fixed costs			
Ad manager	(10,000)	(10,000)	
Journalist			(20,000)
Other overheads	(60,000)	(60,000)	(60,000)
Ad fee	(4,000)	(4,000)	(4,000)
Profit/(loss)	(28,000)	422,000	(208,000)

As you can see from the figures the only profitable area of the business is the property service. I have worked out the 10% reduction of costs on all the expenditure.

	Businessportal	*Property*	*Businessnews*
	$	$	$
Revenue	350,000	800,000	180,000
Less variable costs			
Ad production costs	(3,600)	(3,600)	(3,600)
Media costs	(270,000)	(270,000)	(270,000)
Contribution	76,400	526,400	(93,600)
Less fixed costs			
Ad manager	(9,000)	(9,000)	
Journalist			(18,000)
Other overheads	(54,000)	(54,000)	(54,000)
Ad fee	(3,600)	(3,600)	(3,600)
Profit/(loss)	9,800	459,800	(169,200)

You can see by implementing a 10% reduction across all expenditure the business portal becomes profitable, while the businessnews still has a heavy loss attached to it. I hope this information will be of assistance to you.

6

(a) Dear Ms Jones,

I have great pleasure in enclosing the full range of services which are available on our website - bizinfo/hungary.com

Firstly, we can offer a full range of business services on our bizinfo/hungary.com businessportal such as legal services, investment advice, software design and a translation service. These are essential requirements when dealing with business transactions in Hungary.

This is augmented by up to the minute financial and investment news for subscribers, at only $10 on our site bizinfo/hungary.com/business news. You will never be out of touch with international business news.

Finally, you can advertise your property or development on bizinfo/hungary.com/property at a very reasonable cost, or utilise the facility to expand your existing product portfolio.

As you can see we offer a substantial range of services for both business-to-business and the consumer market.

We hope you can now log on with confidence to our website knowing we have the expertise you need.

(b) Here are some of the methods in which businesses can be approached highlighting the advantages and disadvantages of each chosen method:

	Advantages	**Disadvantages**
Outbound e-mailing- Using database	Targeted Personalised Cost effective Can be detailed Quantifiable	Unsolicited Generalised Easily ignored
Outbound telemarketing	Personalised Targeted Direct measurable response	Annoyance factor Not requested No demonstrable need Not cost effective Difficult to get hold of the decision maker
Banner advertising	Wide audience Cost effective Easy access	Not targeted Limited information Not personalised
Spamming *Bulk e-mailing of unsolicited mail*	Wide audience Cost effective	Unsolicited Not personalised Not targeted Easily ignored/deleted

7

The information bizinfo needs about the visitors to its website is as follows:

- Research the number of 'hits' on the website - You can see how long the user stayed on the website! (Use the tracking facility to measure responses/click through rates and conversion to follow-up actions.)
- You can then calculate what percentage you have of valid e-mail addresses i.e. those that have registered with bizinfo (entered a username and password to view)and given details on their product interests.
- Differentiate International user sessions.
- Calculate the number of hits and page views per day.
- Calculate the number of online sales.

There is software available that takes all the information contained in the server log file and summarises it using charts and tables. A good tool will provide all the different breakdowns of page impressions eg WebTrends, Microsoft Site Analysis, Hitbox, etc.

At a strategic level then differentiate between customers, potential customers, competitor interest and supplier links to bizinfo.com. Make your business objectives the starting point for your e-business operations and then Bizinfo needs to focus on improving its service to customers and potential customers.

- **Customers**

  Selling - Offer around the clock availability. The web allows you to get much closer to the customer than traditional methods do.

Use search engines, banner advertising, link rooms, events and the press room to advertise and increase the number of 'hits' to the site.

Assess Customer Satisfaction - Online surveys are one of the most cost-effective methods of determining visitor satisfaction. Great care needs to be taken to ensure respondents are representative of visitors as a whole. Virtual Surveys suggests that three key areas of questions should be gathered via online surveys:

- **Who is visiting the site**? Typical questions concern, Internet experience, access speed, demographics/segment and role in buying decision.
- **Why they are visiting?** How often do they visit? Which information/service did they use? Could they find it easily and what action was taken?
- **What is their overall opinion of the site/service?** Key areas of satisfaction? Specific likes/dislikes? What was missing?

From the above bizinfo.com can analyse customer information as suggested by Dave Chaffey *et al*, *Internet Marketing*, into the following:

- Customer acquisition/new leads generated by the web.
- The potential market, the served market and penetrated market.
- Sales generated directly and indirectly by the web site.
- Customer satisfaction and retention rates of clients who use the Internet compared with those who do not.
- Cross sales achieved through the Internet
- Impact of the internet on customer satisfaction, loyalty and brand.

By assessing the effects of such Internet marketing bizinfo.com need to consider how such information can then be implemented to further build the business. Patricia Seybold offers guidelines in her book *Customers.com* for such action as follows:

Aim	**Action**
Target the Right Customers	Concentrate on those customers that can be targeted by one-to-one marketing eg trail websites which are aimed principally at particular market segments, eg those who make buying decisions.
Streamline bizinfo's business process	Ensure that ordering, tracking and payment are all available on bizinfo.com's website.
Provide a total experience!	Ensure that bizinfo.com's service from selection, to after-sales is a total quality service which promotes loyalty.

Aim	Action
Extranet system	This would enable supply partners to access the company's internal systems in order that they can work more closely and more effectively with bizinfo.com. This will mean that different parts of bizinfo's network will have the same information about the customer thereby providing a consistent service. This will overcome problems that can occur when one aspect of the business does not have a complete background to the customer's requirements. This is absolutely essential in international investment.

Overall, the Internet provides an innovative means of communication and interraction between businesses and consumers. Perhaps bizinfo.com could in the future consider integrating their e-business with other channels such as interactive television and e-commerce over mobile phones in order to provide a 'seamless' experience when dealing with the company, providing a global service. This could be very reassuring but perhaps that is something for the future.

List of key concepts and index

Further Reading

Allen, C., Kania, D. & Yaeckel, B. (2001) *One to One Web Marketing* (2nd edition). New York: Wiley.

Belbin, M. (1993) *Team Roles at Work*. Oxford: Butterworth-Heinemann

Bride, S. (2004) 'Big, bold & heading for JSE', posted at www.btimes.co.za on 17 March

Chaffey, D. (2002) *E-Business and E-Commerce Management: Strategy, Implementation and Practice*. London: FT Management

Cornelius, H. & Faire, S. (1989) *Everyone Can Win*. Sydney: Simon & Schuster, Australia

Davies, R. (2002) 'Focus groups in Asia' posted at www.orientpacific.com/focusgroups, on 10/03/2004

Dibb, S., Simkin, LP, Pride, WM. & Ferell, OC. (2001) *Marketing Concepts and Strategies* . Houghton Mifflin

Dobler, DW., Burt, DN. & Lee, L. (1990) *Purchasing & Materials Management* (5th edition). New York: McGraw Hill

Drucker, P. (1955) *The Practice of Management*. London: Heinemann

French, J. & Raven, B. (1958) 'The bases of social power' in *Studies in Social Power* (ed Cartright). Ann Arbor, MI: Institute for Social Research

Gabay, JJ. (2002) *Cybermarketing* (*Successful Business in a Week*). London: Hodder & Stoughton

Gennard, J. & Judge, G. (2003) *Employee Relations* (3rd edition). London: CIPD

Gillen, T (1999) *Agreed! Improve your powers of influence*. London: CIPD.

Green, P (2002) 'Maximising Efficiency', *Marketing Business*, March

Hearne, J. (1987) *Advertising Management*. Melbourne: Nelson

Honey, P & Mumford, A. (1992) *A manual of learning styles* (3rd edition). Maidenhead: Peter Honey

Huczynski, A. & Buchanan, D. (2001) *Organisational Behaviour: An introductory text*. Harlow, Essex: FT Prentice Hall

Jay, R. (1998) *The Essential Marketing Sourcebook* (2nd edition). London: FT/Pitman

Johnson, N. (2004) 'How adverts let down online advertising' *New Media Age*. 4 March

Kaufeld, J. (1996) *Access 97 for Windows for Dummies*. Foster City, CA: IDG Books

Kotler, P (2002) *Marketing Management* (11th edition). US Imports & PHIPES

Kotler, P., Armstrong, G., Meggs, D., Bradbury, E. & Grech, J. (1999) *Marketing: an Introduction*. Sydney: Prentice Hall

Lou, M. (2004) 'Motor stores gear up to promise of sales in Shenzhen', *International Market News*, www.tdctrade.com/imn, 12 February

MacNamara, J. (1993) *The Australian Marketing and Promotion Handbook*. Melbourne: The Business Library

Mills, D. (2004) 'Tesco TV shows medium is the message', posted at www.telegraph.co.uk, 16 March

Mills, D. (2004 (b)) 'Coke calls in the men in white coats', posted at www.telegraph.co.uk, 16 March

Morden, AR. (1986) 'Zero based budgeting', *Management Accounting*, October

Murphy, D. (2000) 'Playing the buying game' *Marketing Business*, April

Niewierski, J. (2003) 'Picture Perfect', *DM* (Direct Mail) 1 (1)

Peppers, D. & Rogers, M. (1993) *The One-to-One Future: building business relationships one customer at a time*. Judy Piatkus

Postma, P. (1999) *The New Marketing Era*. New York: McGraw Hill

Quinn, P. (1988) *The Secrets of Successful Copywriting*. London: Heinemann

Smith, D. & Chaffey, PR. (2001) *eMarketing eXcellence*. Oxford: Butterworth-Heinemann

Solomon, CM. (2001) 'Managing Virtual Teams' *Workforce*, June

Taylor, JW. (1997) *Marketing Planning*. London: Prentice Hall.

Thomas, MJ (1986) *The Economist Pocket Guide to Marketing*. Oxford: Blackwell

Ting-Toomey, S., Gao, G., Trubisky, P., Yang, Z., Kih, H., Lin, SL. & Nishida, T. (1991) 'Culture, face maintenance and styles of handling interpersonal conflict', *International Journal of Conflict Management* (2)

Wilmshurst, J. (1999) *The Fundamentals of Advertising* (2nd edition). Oxford: Butterworth-Heinemann

See overleaf for information on other
BPP products and how to order

Mr/Mrs/Ms (Full name) ______

Daytime delivery address ______

Postcode ______

Daytime Tel ______ Date of exam (month/year) ______

	2004 Texts	2004 Kits	Passcards
PROFESSIONAL CERTIFICATE IN MARKETING			
1 Marketing Fundamentals	£19.95 ☐	£9.95 ☐	£6.95 ☐
2 Marketing Environment	£19.95 ☐	£9.95 ☐	£6.95 ☐
3 Customer Communications	£19.95 ☐	£9.95 ☐	£6.95 ☐
4 Marketing in Practice	£19.95 ☐	£9.95 ☐	£6.95 ☐
PROFESSIONAL DIPLOMA IN MARKETING			
5 Marketing Research and Information	£19.95 ☐	£9.95 ☐	£6.95 ☐
6 Marketing Planning	£19.95 ☐	£9.95 ☐	£6.95 ☐
7 Marketing Communications	£19.95 ☐	£9.95 ☐	£6.95 ☐
8 Marketing Management in Practice	£19.95 ☐	£9.95 ☐	£6.95 ☐
PROFESSIONAL POST-GRADUATE DIPLOMA IN MARKETING			
9 Analysis and Evaluation	£20.95 ☐	£9.95 ☐	£6.95 ☐
10 Strategic Marketing Decisions	£20.95 ☐	£9.95 ☐	£6.95 ☐
11 Managing Marketing Performance	£20.95 ☐	£9.95 ☐	£6.95 ☐
12 Strategic Marketing in Practice	£26.95 ☐	N/A	N/A

SUBTOTAL £ ______

CIM Order

To BPP Professional Education, Aldine Place, London W12 8AA

Tel: 020 8740 2211. Fax: 020 8740 1184

email: publishing@bpp.com

online: www.bpp.com

POSTAGE & PACKING

Study Texts and Kits

	First	Each extra	Online	
UK	£5.00	£2.00	£2.00	£
Europe**	£6.00	£4.00	£4.00	£
Rest of world	£20.00	£10.00	£10.00	£

Passcards

	First	Each extra	Online	
UK	£2.00	£1.00	£1.00	£
Europe**	£3.00	£2.00	£2.00	£
Rest of world	£8.00	£8.00	£8.00	£

Reduced postage rates apply if you **order online** at www.bpp.com

Grand Total (Cheques to *BPP Professional Education*) I enclose a cheque for (incl. Postage) £ ______

Or charge to Access/Visa/Switch

Card Number

Expiry date ______ Start Date ______

Issue Number (Switch Only) ______

Signature ______

We aim to deliver to all UK addresses inside 5 working days. A signature will be required. Orders to all EU addresses should be delivered within 6 working days.

All other orders to overseas addresses should be delivered within 8 working days.

** Europe includes the Republic of Ireland and the Channel Islands.

REVIEW FORM & FREE PRIZE DRAW

All original review forms from the entire BPP range, completed with genuine comments, will be entered into one of two draws on 31 January 2005 and 30 July 2005. The names on the first four forms picked out on each occasion will be sent a cheque for £50.

Name: ______________________ **Address:** ______________________

____

____

How have you used this Text?
(Tick one box only)

☐ Self study (book only)

☐ On a course: college ______________

☐ With BPP Home Study package

☐ Other ______________

Why did you decide to purchase this Text?
(Tick one box only)

☐ Have used companion Kit

☐ Have used BPP Texts in the past

☐ Recommendation by friend/colleague

☐ Recommendation by a lecturer at college

☐ Saw advertising in journals

☐ Saw website

☐ Other ______________

During the past six months do you recall seeing/receiving any of the following?
(Tick as many boxes as are relevant)

☐ Our advertisement in *Marketing Success*

☐ Our advertisement in *Marketing Business*

☐ Our brochure with a letter through the post

☐ Our brochure with *Marketing Business*

☐ Saw website

Which (if any) aspects of our advertising do you find useful?
(Tick as many boxes as are relevant)

☐ Prices and publication dates of new editions

☐ Information on product content

☐ Facility to order books off-the-page

☐ None of the above

Have you used the companion Practice & Revision Kit for this subject? ☐ Yes ☐ No

Your ratings, comments and suggestions would be appreciated on the following areas.

	Very useful	*Useful*	*Not useful*
Introductory section (How to use this text, study checklist, etc)	☐	☐	☐
Setting the Scene	☐	☐	☐
Syllabus coverage	☐	☐	☐
Action Programmes and Marketing at Work examples	☐	☐	☐
Chapter roundups	☐	☐	☐
Quick quizzes	☐	☐	☐
Illustrative questions	☐	☐	☐
Content of suggested answers	☐	☐	☐
Index	☐	☐	☐
Structure and presentation			

	Excellent	*Good*	*Adequate*	*Poor*
Overall opinion of this Text	☐	☐	☐	☐

Do you intend to continue using BPP Study Texts/Kits/Passcards? ☐ Yes ☐ No

Please note any further comments and suggestions/errors on the reverse of this page.

Please return to: Glenn Haldane, BPP Professional Education, FREEPOST, London, W12 8BR

REVIEW FORM & FREE PRIZE DRAW (continued)

Please note any further comments and suggestions/errors below.

FREE PRIZE DRAW RULES

1 Closing date for 31 January 2005 draw is 31 December 2004. Closing date for 31 July 2005 draw is 30 June 2005.

2 Restricted to entries with UK and Eire addresses only. BPP employees, their families and business associates are excluded.

3 No purchase necessary. Entry forms are available upon request from BPP Professional Education. No more than one entry per title, per person. Draw restricted to persons aged 16 and over.

4 Winners will be notified by post and receive their cheques not later than 6 weeks after the relevant draw date. List of winners will be supplied on request.

5 The decision of the promoter in all matters is final and binding. No correspondence will be entered into.